India: A Pocket Book of Data Series

India

A Pocket Book of Data Series

2010-11

EPW Research Foundation

ACADEMIC FOUNDATION
NEW DELHI

www.academicfoundation.com

First published in 2011
by

ACADEMIC FOUNDATION
4772-73 / 23 Bharat Ram Road, (23 Ansari Road),
Darya Ganj, New Delhi - 110 002 (India).
Tel : +91-11-23245001 / 02 / 03 / 04.
Fax : +91-11-23245005.
E-mail : books@academicfoundation.com
www. academicfoundation.com

in association with

EPW Research Foundation
(Unit of Sameeksha Trust)
E-mail: epwrf@vsnl.com

Cataloging in Publication Data--DK
Courtesy: D.K. Agencies (P) Ltd. <docinfo@dkagencies.com>

India : a pocket book of data series, 2010-11 / EPW Research Foundation.
p. cm.
ISBN 13: 9788171888573
ISBN 10: 8171888577

1. India--Economic conditions--1947- --Statistics. 2. India--Social conditions--1947- --Statistics. I. Economic and Political Weekly Research Foundation.

DDC 330.954 22

Design and typesetting : Italics India, New Delhi.
Printed and bound in India.

10 9 8 7 6 5 4 3 2 1

Contents

Horticulture and Allied Activities

Industry

Money & Banking

Regional Rural Banks

Capital Market

Corporate Statistics

Price Trends / Inflation

External Sector

II. Social Sector

Demography

Population

Vital Rates

Health & Family Welfare

Housing

Living Standard

Education

Law & Order

III. Infrastructure

Land Use Pattern

Mineral

Communication

Fuel & Energy

Road

Railway

Shipping

Aviation

IV. Profile of States

Population

Vital Rates

Education

Employment

Standard of Living

Agriculture

Factory Sector

V. International Comparisons

People

Environment

Economy

External Sector

Foreword

EPW Research Foundation (EPWRF), set up in January 1993, as a sister unit of Economic & Political Weekly under the Sameeksha Trust has been engaged in research on financial and macroeconomic issues in India. Over the years, the EPWRF has in particular been focussing upon systematic compilation and dissemination of current and long-term data series pertaining to several critical macro and sectoral dimensions of the Indian economy. These data sets are being disseminated along with underlying concepts and methods and procedure of data compilation. The foundation has so far either published or put on its website about 30 sets of long-term data series.

Building upon the strength and expertise on data base studies, EPWRF has decided to come out with a handy pocket book of data series on India with the objective of providing a ready reference for critical socioeconomic data series. The pocket book contains a comprehensive set of tables divided into five parts: I. Macroeconomy, II. Social Sector, III. Infrastructure, IV. Profile of States, and V. International Comparison. Attempt has been made to provide data at convenient intervals between 1950-51 to 2000-01 and on annual basis thereafter.

The data series have been mainly drawn from official sources meticulously compiled from scattered publications of various ministries and websites. For international comparison, data were sourced from the publications/ websites of multilateral institutions such as the International Monetary Fund, World Bank and Food and Agriculture Organization.

We sincerely believe that this maiden issue is a humble contribution with several value added features which would be found useful by academics, executives, students and researchers and public at large.

I record my wholehearted commendation to R. Krishnaswamy who worked on this publication with a single-minded devotion, ably supported by Rajesh Ambadaskar and Praveen S. Jadhav. I also acknowledge with thanks the meticulous copy editing done by Aarati Krishnan.

I acknowledge with grateful thanks suggestions received from Deepak Nayyar, Amit Bhaduri, Rammanohar Reddy and S.L. Shetty in improving the contents.

K. Kanagasabapathy

Director, EPW Research Foundation

I. MACRO ECONOMY

> National Income
> Agriculture
> Horticulture and Allied Activities
> Industry
> Money & Banking
> Regional Rural Banks
> Capital Market
> Corporate Statistics
> Price Trends / Inflation
> Government Finance - Centre
> Government Finance - State
> Government Finance - Centre and State
> External Sector

1 : Gross Domestic Product (GDP) at Factor Cost

	GDP (Rs. crore)	Growth (%)	Per Capita (Rs.)	GDP (Rs. crore)	Growth (%)	Per Capita (Rs.)
Series with Base Year 1999-2000	(At 1999-2000 Prices)			(At Current Prices)		
1950-51*	224,786		6,261	9,719		271
1960-61*	328,566	3.9	7,600	16,512	5.7	380
1970-71*	473,592	3.7	8,764	42,981	10.2	794
1980-81*	641,921	3.1	9,454	132,520	12.1	1,952
1990-91*	1,083,572	5.4	12,915	515,032	14.6	6,139
2000-01*	1,864,361	5.6	18,296	1,925,017	14.1	18,891
1999-00	1,786,526	6.4	17,847	1,786,526	10.5	17,847
2000-01	1,864,361	4.4	18,296	1,925,017	7.8	18,891
2001-02	1,972,606	5.8	18,967	2,097,726	9	20,170
2002-03	2,048,286	3.8	19,397	2,261,414	7.8	21,415
2003-04	2,222,758	8.5	20,735	2,538,170	12.2	23,677
2004-05	2,388,768	7.4	21,935	2,877,701	13.4	26,425
New Series with Base Year 2004-05	(At 2004-05 Prices)			(At Current Prices)		
2004-05	2,967,599		27,251	2,967,599		27,251
2005-06	3,249,130	9.5	29,377	3,402,316	14.6	30,762
2006-07	3,564,627	9.7	31,770	3,941,865	15.9	35,132
2007-08	3,893,457	9.2	34,213	4,540,987	15.2	39,903
2008-09QE	4,154,973	6.7	36,005	5,228,650	15.1	45,309
2009-10 AE	4,453,064	7.2	38,060	5,791,268	10.8	49,498

Note : * Growth for rows from 1950-51 to 2000-01 is CAGR (compounded annual growth rate) over the decade. Growth for subsequent periods is yearly growth rates.
AE : Advance Estimates.
QE : Quick Estimates.

Source : Central Statistical Organisation.

2 : Gross Domestic Product (GDP) at Market Prices

(Rs. crore)

	GDP (Rs. crore)	Growth (%)	Per Capita (Rs.)	GDP (Rs. crore)	Growth (%)	Per Capita (Rs.)
Series with Base Year 1999-2000	(At 1999-2000 Prices)			(At Current Prices)		
1950-51*	236,067		6,576	10,085		281
1960-61*	350,117	4.0	8,067	17,407	5.6	401
1970-71*	517,148	4.0	9,559	46,249	10.4	855
1980-81*	695,361	3.1	10,241	145,370	12.1	2,141
1990-91*	1,193,650	5.6	14,227	569,624	14.7	6,789
2000-01*	2,030,711	5.5	19,928	2,102,314	14.0	20,631
1999-00	1,952,036	7.4	19,501	1,952,036	11.5	19,501
2000-01	2,030,711	4.0	19,928	2,102,314	7.7	20,631
2001-02	2,136,655	5.2	20,545	2,278,952	8.4	21,913
2002-03	2,217,133	3.8	20,996	2,454,561	7.7	23,244
2003-04	2,402,727	8.4	22,413	2,754,620	12.2	25,696
2004-05	2,602,065	8.3	23,894	3,14,9407	14.3	28,920
New Series with Base Year 2004-05	(At 2004-05 Prices)			(At Current Prices)		
2004-05	3,239,224		29,745	3,239,224		29,745
2005-06	3,540,559	9.3	32,012	3,706,473	14.4	33,512
2006-07	3,874,632	9.4	34,533	4,283,979	15.6	38,182
2007-08	4,247,918	9.6	37,328	4,947,857	15.5	43,479
2008-09QE	4,465,360	5.1	38,695	5,574,449	12.7	48,305
2009-10AE	4,767,142	6.8	40,745	6,164,178	10.6	52,685

Note : * Growth for rows from 1950-51 to 2000-01 is CAGR (compounded annual growth rate) over the decade. Growth for subsequent yearly periods is annual growth rate.
AE : Advance Estimates
QE : Quick Estimates.

Source : Central Statistical Organisation.

3 : GDP by Economic Activity (Constant Prices)

	Agriculture, Forestry & Fishing		Industry		Services	
	Rs. crore	% to GDP	Rs. crore	% to GDP	Rs. crore	% to GDP
Series with 1999-2000 as Base Year						
1950-51*	123,884	55.3	33,796	15.1	66,417	29.6
1960-61*	166,954	50.8	61,620	18.8	99,992	30.4
1970-71*	209,843	44.3	104,661	22.1	159,088	33.6
1980-81*	243,421	37.9	154,340	24.0	244,159	38.0
1990-91*	339,893	31.4	280,882	25.9	462,797	42.7
2000-01*	445,403	23.9	480,961	25.8	937,937	50.3
2001-02	473,249	24.0	494,058	25.0	1,005,299	51.0
2002-03	438,966	21.4	528,926	25.8	1,080,394	52.7
2003-04	482,676	21.7	567,948	25.6	1,172,134	52.7
2004-05	482,910	20.2	626,663	26.2	1,279,195	53.5
New Series with 2004-05 as Base Year						
2004-05	560,308	18.9	830,016	28.0	1,577,275	53.1
2005-06	589,697	18.1	907,048	27.9	1,752,385	53.9
2006-07	611,409	17.2	1,022,653	28.7	1,930,565	54.2
2007-08	640,315	16.4	1,119,721	28.8	2,133,421	54.8
2008-09QE	650,461	15.7	1,163,028	28.0	2,341,484	56.4
2009-10AE	649,370	14.6	1,257,950	28.2	2,545,743	57.2

Note: * Growth for rows from 1950-51 to 2000-01 is CAGR (compounded annual growth rate) over the decade. Growth for subsequent yearly periods is annual growth rate.
Industry includes mining, manufacturing, construction and electricity. Services includes trade, hotels,transport & communication, financing and community, social and personal services.

Source: Central Statistical Organisation.

4 : GDP by Economic Activity

	GDP at Current Prices					
	Agriculture Forestry & Fishing		Industry		Services	
	Rs. crore	% to GDP	Rs. crore	% to GDP	Rs. crore	% to GDP
Series with 1999-2000 as Base Year						
1950-51	5,080	52.6	1,403	14.5	3,181	32.9
1960-61	7,090	42.9	3,242	19.6	6,214	37.6
1970-71	18,192	42.4	8,935	20.8	15,777	36.8
1980-81	47,312	35.7	32,716	24.7	52,491	39.6
1990-91	150,800	29.3	138,459	26.9	225,773	43.8
2000-01	449,565	23.4	504,137	26.2	971,315	50.5
2001-02	486,617	23.2	531,532	25.3	1,079,577	51.5
2002-03	472,060	20.9	598,474	26.5	1,190,881	52.7
2003-04	532,342	21.0	665,912	26.2	1,339,916	52.8
2004-05	552,422	19.2	811,078	28.2	1,514,201	52.6
New Series with 2004-05 as Base Year						
2004-05	560,308	18.9	830,016	28.0	1,577,275	53.1
2005-06	639,990	18.8	957,807	28.2	1,804,519	53.0
2006-07	714,254	18.1	1,141,207	29.0	2,086,404	52.9
2007-08	815,399	18.0	1,321,389	29.1	2,404,199	52.9
2008-09QE	898,378	17.2	1,484,956	28.4	2,845,316	54.4
2009-10AE	982,091	17.0	1,631,677	28.2	3,177,501	54.9

Note : Industry includes mining, manufacturing, construction and electricity. Services includes trade, hotels, transport & communication, financing and community, social and personal services.

Source : Central Statistical Organisation.

5 : Private Final Consumption Expenditure (PFCE) by Object

	PFCE (Rs. crore)	Growth (%)	Percentage Share in PFCE					
			Food	Clothing	Rent, Fuel and Transport	Medical Expenses	Education	Personal Care
			PFCE at Current Prices					
Series with 1999-2000 as Base Year								
1950-51*	9,643		61.0	3.4	25.9	1.1	0.6	2.8
1960-61*	16,312	5.6	51.3	4.6	29.7	1.5	0.9	2.7
1970-71*	39,493	9.4	55.9	4.8	23.5	1.8	1.0	2.5
1980-81*	120,094	12.0	52.2	6.1	21.6	2.9	1.3	2.8
1990-91*	392,142	12.6	47.7	5.7	25.0	2.0	1.6	2.7
2000-01*	1,345,583	14.3	41.3	5.3	26.9	4.8	2.0	2.9
2001-02	1,470,301	9.3	41.1	4.6	27.0	5.2	2.1	2.9
2002-03	1,552,618	5.6	38.8	4.6	28.1	5.2	2.2	2.9
2003-04	1,703,546	9.7	38.1	4.6	28.6	5.0	2.2	2.9
2004-05	1,848,110	8.5	36.4	4.5	29.3	5.4	2.3	2.9
New Series with 2004-05 as Base Year								
2004-05	1,926,858		33.5	5.6	32.6	5.0	2.1	
2005-06	2,158,349	12.0	33.1	5.9	32.2	4.9	2.1	
2006-07	2,477,209	14.8	31.5	6.5	31.9	4.7	2.0	
2007-08PE	2,825,356	14.1	31.0	5.8	31.1	4.5	2.0	
2008-09QE	3,226,826	14.2	29.2	5.5	31.7	4.4	2.1	

Note : PE : Provisional Estimates,
QE : Quick Estimates,
AE : Advance Estimates.
* Growth for rows from 1950-51 to 2000-01 is CAGR (compounded annual growth rate) over the decade.
Growth for subsequent yearly periods is annual growth rate.

Source : Central Statistical Organisation.

6 : Gross Domestic Saving (GDS) at Current Prices: Aggregate and by Type of Institution

	GDS (Rs. crore)	Rate (% to GDP)*	of which: Household Sector (Rs. crore)	Household Sector Rate	Private Sector (Rs. crore)	Private Sector Rate	Public Sector (Rs. crore)	Public Sector Rate
Series with 1999-2000 as Base Year								
1950-51	871	8.6	578	5.7	93	1.0	200	2.0
1960-61	1,952	11.2	1,136	6.5	281	1.6	535	3.1
1970-71	6,571	14.2	4,371	9.5	672	1.5	1,528	3.3
1980-81	26,881	18.5	18,724	12.9	2,339	1.6	5,818	4.0
1990-91	130,010	22.8	104,789	18.4	15,164	2.7	10,057	1.8
2000-01	499,033	23.7	454,853	21.6	81,062	3.9	(368,82)	-1.8
1999-00	484,257	24.8	412,516	21.1	87,234	4.5	(15,494)	-0.8
2000-01	499,033	23.7	454,853	21.6	81,062	3.9	(36,882)	-1.8
2001-02	534,885	23.5	504,165	22.1	76,906	3.4	(46,186)	-2.0
2002-03	647,970	26.4	569,134	22.2	94,772	3.9	(15,936)	-0.6
2003-04	820,685	29.8	664,064	24.1	127,100	4.6	29,521	1.1
2004-05	997,874	31.7	716,875	22.8	212,048	6.7	68,951	2.2
New Series with 2004-05 as Base Year								
2004-05	1044,280	32.2	755,445	23.3	212,812	6.6	76,023	2.3
2005-06	1226,044	33.1	858,705	23.2	277,493	7.5	89,845	2.4
2006-07	1474,788	34.4	980,195	22.9	342,130	8.0	152,463	3.6
2007-08	1801,469	36.4	1120,221	22.6	431,588	8.7	249,660	5.0
2008-09	1811,585	32.5	1261,332	22.6	470,256	8.4	79997.00	1.4

Note: * GDP at current market prices.
Negative values in brackets.

Source: Central Statistical Organisation.

7 : Gross Domestic Saving (GDS) : Share of Household Sector

	GDS (Rs. crore)	Household Sector Saving		of which: Financial Savings		Physical Assets	
		(Rs. crore)	(% to GDP)*	(Rs. crore)	Share in Household Savings (%)	(Rs. crore)	Share in Household Savings (%)
Series with 1999-2000 as Base Year							
1950-51	871	578	5.7	62	10.7	516	89.3
1960-61	1,952	1,136	6.5	456	40.1	680	59.9
1970-71	6,571	4,371	9.5	1,371	31.4	3,000	68.6
1980-81	26,881	18,724	12.9	8,640	46.1	10,114	54.0
1990-91	130,010	104,789	18.4	49,640	47.4	55,149	52.6
2000-01	499,033	454,853	21.6	215,219	47.3	239,634	52.7
1999-00	484,257	412,516	21.1	206,602	50.1	205,914	49.9
2000-01	499,033	454,853	21.6	215,219	47.3	239,634	52.7
2001-02	534,885	504,165	22.1	247,476	49.1	256,689	50.9
2002-03	647,970	569,134	22.2	253,255	44.5	315,879	55.5
2003-04	820,685	664,064	24.1	313,260	47.2	350,804	52.8
2004-05	997,874	716,875	22.8	317,547	44.3	399,328	55.7
New Series with 2004-05 as Base Year							
2004-05	1,044,280	755,445	23.3	317,901	42.1	437,544	57.9
2005-06	1,226,044	858,705	23.2	421,219	49.1	437,486	50.9
2006-07	1,474,788	980,195	22.9	469,051	47.9	511,144	52.1
2007-08	1,801,469	1,120,221	22.6	552,725	49.3	567,496	50.7
2008-09	1,811,585	1,261,332	22.6	581,428	46.1	679,904	53.9

Note : * GDP at current market prices. *Source* : Central Statistical Organisation.

8 : Gross Capital Formation (Unadjusted) at Current Prices

(Rs. crore)

	Total Capital Formation by Industry of Use	Rate (% to GDP)*	Agriculture	Rate (% to GDP)*	Manufacturing (Registered)	Rate (% to GDP)*	Infrastructure	Rate (% to GDP)*
Series with 1999-2000 as Base Year								
1950-51	1,037	10.3	178	1.8	215	2.1	203	2.0
			17.1		**20.7**		**19.5**	
1960-61	2,511	14.4	296	1.7	768	4.4	582	3.3
			11.8		**30.6**		**23.2**	
1970-71	7,211	15.6	1,109	2.4	1,810	3.9	1,771	3.8
			15.4		**25.1**		**24.6**	
1980-81	26,964	18.5	4,146	2.9	4,008	2.8	8,384	5.8
			15.4		**14.9**		**31.1**	
1990-91	137,598	24.2	14,596	2.6	30,295	5.3	39,550	6.9
			10.6		**22.0**		**28.7**	
2000-01	493,285	23.5	40,048	1.9	86,647	4.1	136,236	6.5
			8.1		**17.6**		**27.6**	
2001-02	536,854	23.6	52,009	2.3	87,453	3.8	139,774	6.1
			9.7		**16.3**		**26.0**	
2002-03	605,533	24.7	52,123	2.1	115,474	4.7	154,633	6.3
			8.6		**19.1**		**25.5**	
2003-04	713,648	25.9	51,570	1.9	145,058	5.3	179,177	6.5
			7.2		**20.3**		**25.1**	
2004-05	955,046	30.3	61,285	1.9	256,350	8.1	219,690	7.0
			6.4		**26.8**		**23.0**	

contd...

...contd...

	Total Capital Formation by Industry of Use	Rate (% to GDP)*	Agriculture	Rate (% to GDP)*	Manufacturing (Registered)	Rate (% to GDP)*	Infrastructure	Rate (% to GDP)*
New Series with 2004-05 as Base Year								
2004-05	1,010,923	31.2	71,758 **7.1**	2.2	223,203 **22.1**	6.9	231,316 **22.9**	7.1
2005-06	1,229,934	33.2	89,369 **7.3**	2.4	323,138 **26.3**	8.7	289,847 **23.6**	7.8
2006-07	1,492,352	34.8	104,489 **7.0**	2.4	396,781 **26.6**	9.3	358,358 **24.0**	8.4
2007-08	1,805,668	36.5	128,666 **7.1**	2.6	511,694 **28.3**	10.3	442,383 **24.5**	8.9
2008-09	1,912,522	34.3	175,314 **9.2**	3.1	451,192 **23.6**	8.1	474,430 **24.8**	8.5
2009-10	2,074,361	33.7						

Note : * GDP at current market prices.
Infrastructure investment is the summation of the investment in mining & quarrying, electricity, gas & water supply, construction and transport and equipment.
Figures in bold below each line are percentages to total GCF.

Source : Central Statistical Organisation.

9 : Net Capital Stock

(Rs. crore)

As of End-March	Net Capital Stock	Public Sector	Private Sector		Average Capital Output Ratio (ACOR)* Net Capital Stock to Output			Incremental Capital Output Ratio	
			Private Corporate Sector	Household Sector	Total	Public Sector	Private Sector	NDCF to Output**	NFCF to Output**
Series with 1999-2000 as Base Year									
Constant Prices									
1981	2,129,912	926,853	158,547	1,044,511	3.54	6.71	2.59	2.30	2.00
1991	3,364,499	1,567,343	1,797,157	1,396,383	3.33	5.82	2.42	3.73	3.09
2001	5,562,273	2,180,525	1,154,598	2,227,150	3.25	4.63	2.71	4.51	4.02
2002	5,842,615	2,247,335	1,209,672	2,385,607	3.23	4.51	2.74	2.84	3.01
2003	6,159,557	2,301,268	1,274,188	2,584,102	3.29	4.39	2.85	5.48	4.94
2004	6,525,010	2,363,654	1,373,722	2,787,634	3.20	4.35	2.77	2.62	2.25
2005	7,013,888	2,444,597	1,569,811	2,999,480	3.18	4.34	2.78	3.66	3.07
2006	7,632,389	2,557,941	1,856,559	3,217,688	3.14	4.30	2.76	3.27	2.69
2007	8,351,053	2,697,028	2,197,057	3,456,938	3.13	4.11	2.80	3.35	2.81
2008	9,206,589	2,888,247	2,592,359	3,725,984	3.16	4.09	2.86	3.92	3.23

contd...

...contd...

As of End-March	Net Capital Stock	Public Sector	Private Sector		Average Capital Output Ratio (ACOR)* Net Capital Stock to Output			Incremental Capital Output Ratio	
			Private Corporate Sector	Household Sector	Total	Public Sector	Private Sector	NDCF to Output**	NFCF to Output**
Series with 1999-2000 as Base Year Current Prices									
1981	392,849	166,975	42,650	183,224	3.06	5.85	2.27	0.87	0.75
1991	1,661,637	739,053	233,930	688,653	3.32	5.34	2.57	1.44	1.19
2001	5,792,328	2,247,493	1,218,422	2,326,414	3.21	4.54	2.70	2.62	2.34
2002	6,378,204	2,428,479	1,327,612	2,622,113	3.26	4.46	2.78	2.00	2.12
2003	6,886,689	2,566,647	1,413,590	2,906,452	3.30	4.33	2.88	2.61	2.36
2004	7,625,229	2,743,527	1,576,105	3,305,597	3.21	4.32	2.80	1.94	1.65
2005	8,885,251	3,055,665	1,923,944	3,905,644	3.24	4.33	2.85	2.35	1.95
2006	10,187,719	3,366,815	2,394,096	4,426,808	3.29	4.45	2.89	2.52	2.07
2007	11,732,465	3,729,645	2,992,639	5,010,180	3.28	4.41	2.92	2.46	2.06
2008	13,683,124	4,217,745	3,745,016	5,720,362	3.33	4.48	2.99	2.85	2.34

Note: ACOR data for each year pertains to fiscal year. For eg: 1981 refers to 1981-82 and so on.
It is worked out as average of beginning and year-end capital stock, as a ratio of the year's Net Domestic Product at Factor Cost.
* Based on increase in Net Domestic Product at Factor Cost.
NDCF: net domestic capital formation, NFCF: net fixed capital formation.

Source: Central Statistical Organisation.

10 : Increases in Financial Assets and Liabilities of Household Sector

Year	Increases in Financial Assets (Gross Savings) (Rs. crore)	Currency		Bank Deposits		LIC, PF, Pension & Claims on Govt.		Others including Trade Debt		Increases in Financial Liabilities (Rs. crore)	Net Savings (Rs. crore)
		(Rs. crore)	Share in %	(Rs. crore)	Share in %	(Rs. crore)	Share in %	(Rs. crore)	Share in %		
1970-71	2,110	355	16.8	754	35.7	802	38.0	199	9.4	591	1,519
1980-81	12,118	1,625	13.4	5,550	45.8	3,749	30.9	1,194	9.9	3,508	8,610
1990-91	58,908	6,251	10.6	18,777	31.9	24,637	41.8	9,243	15.7	9,267	49,641
2000-01	248,393	15,632	6.3	94,703	38.1	120,750	48.6	17,308	7.0	31,779	216,614
2001-02	296,582	28,156	9.5	112,936	38.1	139,784	47.1	15,706	5.3	51,727	244,855
2002-03	322,583	28,632	8.9	123,462	38.3	156,537	48.5	13,951	4.3	60,305	262,278
2003-04	377,387	42,675	11.3	141,967	37.6	188,564	50.0	4,181	1.1	69,982	307,405
2004-05	434,318	36,977	8.5	158,259	36.4	230,958	53.2	8,124	1.9	120,566	313,752
2005-06	597,867	53,071	8.9	274,864	46.0	233,289	39.0	36,643	6.1	183,424	414,443
2006-07	650,412	66,274	10.2	311,347	47.9	206,155	31.7	66,636	10.2	176,787	473,625
2007-08	715,994	81,278	11.4	360,993	50.4	171,493	24.0	102,230	14.3	173,135	542,859
2008-09	746,864	93,056	12.5	409,811	54.9	197,749	26.5	46,248	6.2	165,656	581,208

Source : Reserve Bank of India.

11 : All-India Area, Production and Yield : Foodgrains

Year	Area (million hectares)	Production (million tonnes)	Yield (kg/ hectare)	Per cent Area under Irrigation
1950-51	97.3	50.8	522	18.1
1960-61	115.6	82.0	710	19.1
1970-71	124.3	108.4	872	24.1
1980-81	126.7	129.6	1023	29.7
1990-91	127.8	176.4	1380	35.1
2000-01	121.0	196.8	1626	43.7
2001-02	122.8	212.9	1734	43.5
2002-03	122.8	174.8	1423	42.8
2003-04	123.5	213.2	1727	42.2
2004-05	120.1	198.4	1652	42.5
2005-06	121.6	208.6	1715	44.5
2006-07	123.7	217.3	1756	45.5
2007-08	124.1	230.8	1860	46.9
2008-09	123.2	234.5	1898	46.8
2009-10$	na	218.2	na	na

Note : $ Fourth advance estimates as on 21-07-2009.
Source : Ministry of Agriculture.

12 : All-India Area, Production and Yield : Rice

Year	Area (million hectares)	Production (million tonnes)	Yield (kg/ hectare)	Per cent Area under Irrigation
1950-51	30.8	20.6	668	31.7
1960-61	34.1	34.6	1013	36.8
1970-71	37.6	42.2	1123	38.4
1980-81	40.1	53.6	1336	40.7
1990-91	42.7	74.3	1740	45.5
2000-01	44.7	85.0	1901	54.4
2001-02	44.9	93.3	2079	54.4
2002-03	41.2	71.8	1744	50.2
2003-04*	42.6	88.5	2077	52.8
2004-05*	41.9	83.1	1984	55.2
2005-06*	43.7	91.8	2102	56.7
2006-07*	43.8	93.4	2131	57.8
2007-08*	43.9	96.7	2202	56.9
2008-09*	45.4	99.2	2186	na
2009-10$	na	89.1	na	na

Note : * Provisional data on area, yield and irrigation.
$ Fourth advance estimates.
Source : Ministry of Agriculture.

13 : All-India Area, Production and Yield : Wheat

Year	Area (million hectares)	Production (million tonnes)	Yield (kg/ hectare)	Per cent Area under Irrigation
1950-51	9.8	6.5	663	34.0
1960-61	12.9	11.0	851	32.7
1970-71	18.2	23.8	1307	54.3
1980-81	22.3	36.3	1630	70.0
1990-91	24.2	55.1	2281	81.1
2000-01	25.7	69.7	2708	88.4
2001-02	26.3	72.8	2762	88.6
2002-03	25.2	65.8	2610	88.0
2003-04*	26.6	72.2	2713	89.6
2004-05*	26.4	68.6	2602	89.9
2005-06*	26.5	69.4	2619	90.2
2006-07*	28.0	75.8	2708	90.7
2007-08*	28.0	78.6	2802	90.9
2008-09*	27.9	80.7	2891	na
2009-10$	na	80.7	na	na

Note : * Provisional area ,yield and irrigation.
$ Fourth advance estimates.

Source : Ministry of Agriculture.

14 : All-India Area, Production and Yield : Coarse Cereals

Year	Area (million hectares)	Production (million tonnes)	Yield (kg/ hectare)	Per cent Area under Irrigation
1950-51	37.7	15.4	408	7.9
1960-61	45.0	23.7	528	7.7
1970-71	46.0	30.6	665	8.3
1980-81	41.8	29.0	695	9.2
1990-91	36.3	32.7	900	9.0
2000-01	30.3	31.1	1027	12.5
2001-02	29.5	33.4	1131	11.3
2002-03	27.0	26.1	966	11.0
2003-04*	30.8	37.6	1221	6.6
2004-05*	29.0	33.5	1153	6.6
2005-06*	29.0	34.1	1172	13.0
2006-07*	28.7	33.9	1182	na
2007-08*	28.7	40.8	1418	na
2008-09*	na	40.0	na	na
2009-10$	na	33.8	na	na

Note : Coarse cereals includes *jowar*, *bajra*, maize, *ragi*, small millets and barley.
$ Fourth advance estimates.
* Provisional.

Source : Ministry of Agriculture.

15 : All-India Area, Production and Yield : Pulses

Year	Area (million hectares)	Production (million tonnes)	Yield (kg/ hectare)	Per cent Area under Irrigation
1950-51	19.1	8.4	441	9.4
1960-61	23.6	12.7	539	8.0
1970-71	22.6	11.8	524	8.8
1980-81	22.5	10.6	473	9.0
1990-91	24.7	14.3	578	10.5
2000-01	20.3	11.1	544	12.6
2001-02	22.0	13.4	607	13.4
2002-03	20.5	11.1	543	14.4
2003-04*	23.5	14.9	635	13.6
2004-05*	22.8	13.1	577	14.0
2005-06*	22.4	13.4	598	14.4
2006-07*	23.2	14.2	612	15.6
2007-08*	23.6	14.8	625	16.2
2008-09*	22.4	14.6	655	na
2009-10$	na	14.6	na	na

Note: Pulses includes gram, *arhar*, *urad* and *moong*.
$ Fourth advance estimates.
* Provisional.

Source: Ministry of Agriculture.

16 : All-India Area, Production and Yield : Oilseeds

Year	Area (million hectares)	Production (million tonnes)	Yield (kg/ hectare)	Per cent Area under Irrigation
1950-51	10.7	5.2	481	na
1960-61	13.8	7.0	507	3.3
1970-71	16.6	9.6	579	7.4
1980-81	17.6	9.4	532	14.5
1990-91	24.1	18.6	771	22.9
2000-01	22.8	18.4	810	22.4
2001-02	22.6	20.7	913	24.3
2002-03	21.5	14.8	691	22.7
2003-04*	23.7	25.2	1064	25.0
2004-05*	27.5	24.4	885	27.1
2005-06*	27.9	28.0	1004	28.0
2006-07*	26.5	24.3	916	28.8
2007-08*	26.7	29.8	1115	27.1
2008-09*	27.5	27.7	1007	na
2009-10$	na	24.9	na	na

Note: Oilseeds includes groundnut, rapeseed & mustard, castor seed, sesamum, nigerseed, linseed, safflower, sunflower and soyabean.
$ Fourth advance estimates.
* Provisional.

Source: Ministry of Agriculture.

17 : All-India Area, Production and Yield : Cotton

Year	Area (million hectares)	Production (million tonnes)	Yield (kg/ hectare)	Per cent Area under Irrigation
1950-51	5.9	3.0	88	8.2
1960-61	7.6	5.6	125	12.7
1970-71	7.6	4.8	106	17.3
1980-81	7.8	7.0	152	27.3
1990-91	7.4	9.8	225	32.9
2000-01	8.6	9.5	190	32.2
2001-02	9.1	10.0	186	33.8
2002-03	7.7	8.6	191	33.1
2003-04*	7.6	13.7	307	32.3
2004-05*	8.8	16.4	318	34.8
2005-06*	8.7	18.5	362	36.4
2006-07*	9.1	22.6	421	35.9
2007-08*	9.4	25.9	467	35.1
2008-09*	9.40	22.3	419	na
2009-10$	na	23.9	na	na

Note : * Provisional.
$ Fourth advance estimates.
Source : Ministry of Agriculture.

18 : All-India Area, Production and Yield : Sugarcane

Year	Area (million hectares)	Production (million tonnes)	Yield (kg/ hectare)	Per cent Area under Irrigation
1950-51	1.7	57.1	33	67.3
1960-61	2.4	110.0	46	69.3
1970-71	2.6	126.4	48	72.4
1980-81	2.7	154.2	58	81.3
1990-91	3.7	241.0	65	86.9
2000-01	4.3	296.0	69	92.2
2001-02	4.4	297.2	67	92.3
2002-03	4.5	287.4	64	91.3
2003-04*	3.9	233.9	59	92.3
2004-05*	3.7	237.1	65	92.4
2005-06*	4.2	281.2	67	93.2
2006-07*	5.2	355.5	69	93.4
2007-08*	5.1	348.2	69	93.4
2008-09*	4.4	285.0	65	na
2009-10$	na	277.8	na	na

Note : * Provisional.
$ Fourth advance estimates.
Source : Ministry of Agriculture.

19 : Availability of Cereals and Pulses

Year	Net Quantity Available* (million tonnes)		Per Capita Per Day (grams)		
	Cereals	Pulses	Cereals	Pulses	Foodgrains
1950-51	44.3	8.0	334.2	60.7	394.9
1960-61	64.6	11.1	399.7	69.0	468.7
1970-71	84.0	10.3	417.6	51.2	468.8
1980-81	104.8	9.4	417.3	37.5	454.8
1990-01	145.7	12.9	468.5	41.6	510.1
2000-01	145.6	11.3	386.2	30.0	416.2
2001-02	175.9	13.6	458.7	35.4	494.1
2002-03	159.3	11.3	408.5	29.1	437.6
2003-04	169.1	14.2	426.9	35.8	462.7
2004-05	157.3	12.7	390.9	31.5	422.4
2005-06	168.8	13.3	412.8	32.5	445.3
2006-07	169.0	14.7	407.4	35.5	442.8
2007-08	157.6	17.6	374.6	41.8	416.4

Note : Net availability of foodgrains is estimated to be gross production (-) seed, wastage and feed (-) exports (+) imports (+/-) change in stock.

Net availability is 82.5% of total production. The balance 12.5% is provided for feed & seed requirements, plus imports minus exports and net changes in stocks.

Net availability divided by population and by 365 days gives net availability in terms of grams per day.

Source : Directorate of Economics & Statistics, Department of Agriculture and Cooperation and *Economic Survey*.

20 : Availability, Procurement and Public Distribution of Foodgrains

Year	Availability	Procurement		Public Distribution	
	(million tonnes)	(million tonnes)	Share (%)	(million tonnes)	Share (%)
1950-51	52.4	3.8	7.3	8.0	15.3
1960-61	75.7	0.5	0.7	4.0	5.3
1970-71	94.3	8.9	9.4	7.8	8.3
1980-81	114.3	13.0	11.4	13.0	11.4
1990-01	158.6	19.6	12.4	20.8	13.1
2000-01	156.9	42.6	27.2	13.2	8.4
2001-02	189.5	40.3	21.3	18.2	9.6
2002-03	170.6	34.5	20.2	23.2	13.6
2003-04	183.3	41.1	22.4	28.3	15.4
2004-05	170.0	41.5	24.4	31.0	18.2
2005-06	181.9	37.0	20.3	31.8	17.5
2006-07	183.7	35.8	19.5	32.8	17.9
2007-08	183.5	54.2	29.5	34.7	18.9

Note : Figures for procurement and distribution are for respective calendar years.

Source : *Economic Survey*.

21 : Per Capita Availability of Important Articles of Consumption

Year	Edible Oils (net) Kg	Sugar (kg)	Cloth (metres)	Tea (gram)	Coffee (gram)
1955-56	2.5	5.0	na	362.0	67.0
1960-61	3.2	4.8	15.0	296.0	80.0
1970-71	3.5	7.4	15.6	401.0	65.0
1980-81	3.8	7.3	17.3	511.0	79.0
1990-01	5.5	12.7	24.1	612.0	59.0
2000-01	8.2	15.8	30.7	631.0	58.0
2001-02	8.8	16.0	32.0	650.0	67.0
2002-03	7.2	16.3	31.4	623.0	67.0
2003-04	9.5	16.1	31.0	662.0	70.0
2004-05	10.2	15.5	33.5	663.0	75.0
2005-06	10.6	16.3	36.1	687.0	80.0
2006-07	11.1	16.8	39.6	687.0	85.0
2007-08	11.4	17.8	41.9	na	na
2008-09	12.1	18.8	39.0	na	na

Note : Tea and coffee data upto 1971-72 refer to coffee season, thereafter to calendar years. Sugar data are based on November-October season.

Source : *Economic Survey.*

22 : Consumption of Fertilisers

Year	(Thousand Tonnes of Nutrients)			
	Nitrogenous	Phosphatic	Potassic	All
1950-51	59	7	0	66
1960-61	210	53	29	292
1970-71	1487	462	228	2177
1980-81	3678	1214	624	5516
1990-01	7997	3221	1328	12546
2000-01	10920	4215	1567	16702
2001-02	11310	4382	1667	17360
2002-03	10474	4019	1601	16094
2003-04	11076	4124	1598	16798
2004-05	11714	4624	2060	18398
2005-06	12723	5204	2413	20340
2006-07	13774	5543	2335	21652
2007-08	14419	5515	2636	22570
2008-09	15090	6506	3313	24909
2009-10	7486	4132	1607	13225

Note : Data for 2009-10 relates to *kharif* season only.

Source : *Economic Survey.*

23 : Agriculture Subsidies

(Rs. crore)

Year	Food	Fertiliser	Electricity	Irrigation	Others
1999-00	9434	13244	6033	11196	3118
2000-01	12060	13800	8919	13465	2733
2001-02	17499	12595	10410	13009	3234
2002-03	24176	11015	8521	12794	3173
2003-04	25181	11847	14544	10921	4132
2004-05	25798	15879	17852	12508	3598
2005-06	23077	18460	20301	14625	6504
2006-07	24014	26222			
2007-08	31328	32490			
2008-09	43751	76603			
2009-10	56002	52980			
2010-11	55578	49981			

Note : 1. Others include subsidies given to marginal farmers.

2. Electricity subsidy to electricity boards, separate estimates for agriculture are not available.

3. The rates for supply of water to farmers are kept low as a matter of policy, resulting in losses to the government irrigation system. The excess of operating costs over the gross revenue is treated as imputed irrigation subsidy.

Source : Ministry of Agriculture.

24 : Distribution of Operational Holdings : All-India

Category of Holdings	No. of Operational Holdings ('000 number)		Area Operated ('000 hectares)		Average Size of Operational Holdings (hectares)	
	1995-96	2000-01	1995-96	2000-01	1995-96	2000-01
Marginal	71179	75408	28121	29814	0.40	0.40
< 1 hectare (%)	**61.6**	**62.3**	**17.2**	**18.7**		
Small	21643	22695	30722	32139	1.42	1.42
1.0 to 2.0 hectares (%)	**18.7**	**19.2**	**18.8**	**20.2**		
Semi-medium	14261	14021	38953	38193	2.73	2.72
2.0 to 4.0 hectares (%)	**12.3**	**11.8**	**23.8**	**24**		
Medium	7092	6577	41398	38217	5.84	5.81
4.0 to 10.0 hectares (%)	**6.1**	**5.5**	**25.3**	**24**		
Large	1404	1230	24163	21072	17.21	17.12
>= 10 hectares (%)	**1.2**	**1**	**14.8**	**13.2**		
All Holdings	115580	119231	163357	159436	1.41	1.33

Note : Figures in bold refer to per cent of total area.

Source : Agricultural Census Division, Ministry of Agriculture, New Delhi.

25 : Indian Horticulture: Area, Production and Yield

	Area (in '000 ha)	Production (in '000 tonnes)	Productivity (tonne/ha)
1991-92	12770	96562	7.56
1992-93	12903	107399	8.32
1993-94	13033	114661	8.80
1994-95	13080	118394	9.05
1995-96	13723	125483	9.14
1996-97	14362	128482	8.95
1997-98	14754	128611	8.72
1998-99	15103	146200	9.68
1999-00	15247	149224	9.79
2000-01	15694	150197	9.57
2001-02	16592	145785	8.79
2002-03	16270	144380	8.87
2003-04	19449	157835	8.12
2004-05	18445	166938	9.05
2005-06	19327	185207	9.58
2006-07	19389	191813	9.89
2007-08	20207	211234	10.45
2008-09	20662	214716	10.39

Note : Horticulture includes fruits, vegetables, plantation crops, spices, flowers, nuts, honey, mushroom and aromatic & medicinal plants.

Source : Ministry of Agriculture.

26 : Production of Selected Horticultural Crops

(in '000 tonnes)

	Fruits	Vegetables	Flowers (loose)	Nuts	Plantation Crops	Spices
1991-92	28632	58532			7498	1900
1992-93	32955	63806	233		8347	2291
1993-94	37255	65787	261		8866	2515
1994-95	38603	67286	334		9767	2477
1995-96	41507	71594	366		9630	2410
1996-97	40458	75074	366		9730	2805
1997-98	43263	72683	386		9449	2801
1998-99	44042	87536	419		11063	3091
1999-00	45496	90831	509	111	9278	3023
2000-01	43138	93850	556	122	9458	3023
2001-02	43001	88622	535	114	9697	3765
2002-03	45203	84815	735	114	9697	3765
2003-04	45645	93165	580	121	13161	5113
2004-05	50867	101246	659	121	9835	4001
2005-06	58740	109050	694	134	11263	5108
2006-07	59563	114993	880	150	12007	3953
2007-08	65587	128449	868	177	11300	4357
2008-09	68466	129077	987	173	11336	4145

Note : Fruits include banana, mango, orange, *mosambi*, lime, grapes, guava, litchi, papaya, pineapple, apple, pomegranate, sapota etc.
Vegetables includes potato, onion, tomato, brinjal, cabbage, cauliflower, okra, peas, sweet potato, tapioca etc.
Spices includes black pepper, chillies, ginger, turmeric, garlic etc.

Source : Ministry of Agriculture.

27 : Production of Selected Fruits

(in '000 tonnes)

	Banana	Mango	Citrus Fruits	Others
1991-92	7790	8716	2822	9305
1992-93	10460	9223	2979	10293
1993-94	11901	10113	3912	11329
1994-95	13168	10993	3701	10741
1995-96	13095	10811	3798	13803
1996-97	12440	9981	4456	13581
1997-98	13340	10234	4311	15379
1998-99	15073	9782	4575	14613
1999-00	16814	10504	4651	13528
2000-01	14137	10057	4386	14558
2001-02	14210	10020	4789	13982
2002-03	13304	12733	5677	13488
2003-04	13857	11490	5787	14512
2004-05	16328	11830	5933	16776
2005-06	18702	12538	6326	21174
2006-07	20998	13734	7145	17686
2007-08	23823	13997	8015	19752
2008-09	26217	12750	8608	20891

Note: Citrus fruits include lime, *mosambi*, orange.
Others include grapes, guava, litchi, papaya, pineapple, pomegranate, sapota, apple etc.

Source: Ministry of Agriculture.

28 : Production of Selected Vegetables

(in '000 tonnes)

	Potato	Onion	Tomato	Brinjal	Others
1991-92	18195	4706	4243		31388
1992-93	18479	5705	4550		35073
1993-94	17392	4006	4934	4612	34842
1994-95	17401	4036	5261	6232	34355
1995-96	18843	4080	5442	6443	36786
1996-97	24216	4180	5788	6586	34305
1997-98	17652	3140	6184	7735	37972
1998-99	22495	5467	8272	7882	43421
1999-00	25000	4900	7427	8117	45387
2000-01	22243	4721	7242	7652	51992
2001-02	24456	5252	7462	8348	43104
2002-03	23161	4210	7617	8001	41826
2003-04	27926	6268	8126	8477	42369
2004-05	28788	7761	8825	8601	47272
2005-06	29094	9248	9362	9136	52210
2006-07	28600	10847	10055	9453	56038
2007-08	34658	13900	10303	9678	59910
2008-09	34391	13565	11149	10378	59594

Note: Others include cabbage, cauliflower, okra, peas, sweet potato, tapioca etc.

Source: Ministry of Agriculture.

29 : Production of Selected Livestock Products

	Milk (million tonnes)	Eggs (million numbers)	Fish ('000 tonnes)
1950-01	17.0	1832	752
1960-01	20.0	2881	1160
1970-01	22.0	6172	1756
1980-01	31.6	10060	2442
1990-01	53.9	21101	3836
2000-01	80.6	36632	5656
2001-02	84.4	38729	5956
2002-03	86.2	39823	6200
2003-04	88.1	40403	6399
2004-05	90.7	45201	6304
2005-06	97.1	46231	6572
2006-07	100.9	50653	6869
2007-08	104.8	53532	7127
2008-09	108.5	55638	7608

Source : Department of Animal Husbandry and Dairying.

30 : Production of Selected Plantation Crops

	Tea* (million kg)	Coffee ('000 tonnes)	Natural Rubber ('000 tonnes)
1950-51*	285		
1960-61	354		
1970-71	435		
1980-81	560		
1990-01	704	170	330
2000-01	847	301	630
2001-02	854	301	631
2002-03	846	275	649
2003-04	878	271	712
2004-05	907	276	750
2005-06	949	300	800
2006-07	973	300	900
2007-08	987	300	900
2008-09	973		865
2009-10			831

Note: * Calender year data for year ending December 1950 and so on.

Source : Tea, Coffee and Rubber Boards.

31 : Production of Selected Condiments and Spices

(in '000 tonnes)

	Black Pepper	Chillies	Dry Ginger	Turmeric
1990-01	48	719	154	342
2000-01	64	984	288	714
2001-02	62	1069	318	563
2002-03	64	897	na	574
2003-04	73	1235	302	565
2004-05	73	1186	359	718
2005-06	na	na	na	na
2006-07	69	1233	377	836
2007-08	47	1294	390	794
2008-09	47	1270	380	821

Source : Ministry of Agriculture.

32 : India's Position in World Fruit & Vegetable Production

	2008-09			
	World (million tonne)	India (million tonne)	Share in World Production (%)	Rank
Fruits	578.2	68.5	11.8	2
Banana	93.7	26.2	28.0	1
Mango	35.7	12.8	35.9	1
Papaya	10.0	3.6	36.0	1
Pineapple	19.2	1.3	6.8	6
Apple	69.6	2.0	2.9	7
Vegetables	966.3	129.1	13.4	2
Brinjal	34.6	10.4	30.1	2
Cabbage	71.3	6.9	9.7	2
Cauliflower	19.5	6.5	33.3	2
Okra	6.8	4.5	66.2	1
Onion	72.2	13.6	18.8	2
Potato	314.1	34.4	11.0	2
Tomato	130.5	11.1	8.5	3

Source : Ministry of Agriculture.

33 : Index of Industrial Production: (Base 1993-94=100) : Sector-wise and Use-Based Classification

Year	General Index	Industry: Sector-wise Indices			Use Based Classification of Industries Indices					
		Mining & Quarrying	Manufacturing	Electricity	Basic Industries	Capital Goods	Intermediate Goods Industries	Consumer Goods Industries	Consumer Durables Industries	Consumer Non-Durables
2000-01	162.5	130.3	167.9	154.4	148.5	166.2	177.4	165.2	227.6	150.8
2001-02	167.0	131.9	172.7	159.2	152.5	160.6	180.1	175.1	253.7	157.0
2002-03	176.6	139.6	183.1	164.3	159.9	177.4	187.1	187.5	237.8	175.9
2003-04	189.0	146.9	196.6	172.6	168.6	201.5	199.0	200.9	265.4	186.1
2004-05	204.8	153.4	214.6	181.5	177.9	229.6	211.1	224.4	303.5	206.2
2005-06	221.5	154.9	234.2	190.9	189.8	265.8	216.4	251.4	349.9	228.8
2006-07	247.1	163.2	263.5	204.7	209.3	314.2	242.4	276.8	382.0	252.6
2007-08	268.0	171.6	287.2	217.7	223.9	370.8	264.1	293.6	378.0	274.2
2008-09	275.4	176.0	295.1	223.7	229.7	397.9	259.0	307.5	395.0	287.3
2009-10	304.1	193.1	327.3	237.1	246.0	474.2	294.2	330.2	498.1	291.6

contd...

...contd...

Year	General Index	Industry: Sector-wise Indices			Use-Based Classification of Industries Indices					
		Mining & Quarrying	Manufacturing	Electricity	Basic Industries	Capital Goods	Intermediate Goods Industries	Consumer Goods Industries	Consumer Durables Industries	Consumer Non-Durables
Growth Rates (year-on-year)										(%)
2000-01	4.9	2.8	5.3	4	3.6	1.8	4.7	8	14.5	5.8
2001-02	2.8	1.2	2.9	3.1	2.7	(3.4)	1.5	6.0	11.5	4.1
2002-03	5.7	5.8	6.0	3.2	4.9	10.5	3.9	7.1	(6.3)	12.0
2003-04	7.0	5.2	7.4	5.1	5.4	13.6	6.4	7.1	11.6	5.8
2004-05	8.4	4.4	9.2	5.2	5.5	13.9	6.1	11.7	14.4	10.8
2005-06	8.2	1.0	9.1	5.2	6.7	15.8	2.5	12.0	15.3	11.0
2006-07	11.6	5.4	12.5	7.2	10.3	18.2	12.0	10.1	9.2	10.4
2007-08	8.5	5.1	9.0	6.4	7.0	18.0	9.0	6.1	(1.0)	8.6
2008-09	2.8	2.6	2.8	2.8	2.6	7.3	(1.9)	4.7	4.5	4.8
2009-10	10.4	9.7	10.9	6.0	7.1	19.2	13.6	7.4	26.1	1.5

Source : Central Statistical Organisation.

34 : Electronic Goods Production

(Rs. crore)

Year	Consumer Electronics	Industrial Electronics	Computers	Commercial Broadcasting & Equipments	Strategic Electronics	Components	Total Electronic Production	Software Production		Exports: Electronic Hardware
								for Exports	for Domestic	
1990-01	3000	1370	820	1710	635	1510	9045			
1998-99	9200	3300	2300	4400	1300	4750	25250			
1999-00	11200	3750	2500	4000	1450	5200	28100			
Growth (%)	21.7	13.6	8.7	-9.1	11.5	9.5	11.3			
2000-01	11950	4000	3400	4500	1750	5500	31100	28350	9400	4788
Growth (%)	6.7	6.7	36.0	12.5	20.7	5.8	10.7			
2001-02	12700	4500	3550	4500	1800	5700	32750	36500	10874	5800
Growth (%)	6.3	12.5	4.4	0.0	2.9	3.6	5.3	28.7	15.7	21.1
2002-03	13800	5550	4250	4800	2500	6600	37500	46100	13400	5600
Growth (%)	8.7	23.3	19.7	6.7	38.9	15.8	14.5	26.3	23.2	-3.4
2003-04	15200	6100	6800	5350	2750	7600	43800	58240	16250	7700
Growth (%)	10.1	9.9	60.0	11.5	10.0	15.2	16.8	26.3	21.3	37.5
2004-05	16800	8300	8800	4800	3000	8800	50500	80180	21740	8000
Growth (%)	10.5	36.1	29.4	-10.3	9.1	15.8	15.3	37.7	33.8	3.9

contd...

...contd...

Year	Consumer Electronics	Industrial Electronics	Computers	Commercial Broadcasting & Equipments	Strategic Electronics	Components	Total Electronic Production	Software Production		Exports: Electronic Hardware
								for Exports	for Domestic	
2005-06	18000.0	8800	10800	7000	3200	8800	56600	104100	29600	9625
Growth (%)	7.1	6.0	22.7	45.8	6.7	0.0	12.1	29.8	36.2	20.3
2006-07	20000	10400	12800	9500	4500	8800	66000	141000	37000	12500
Growth (%)	11.1	18.2	18.5	35.7	40.6	0.0	16.6	35.4	25.0	29.9
2007-08	22600	11910	15870	18700	5700	9630	84410	164400	47010	13200
Growth (%)	13.0	14.5	24.0	96.8	26.7	9.4	27.9	16.6	27.1	5.6
2008-09	25990	12740	13490	26000	6840	9630	94690	216300	57230	19000
Growth (%)	15.0	7.0	-15.0	39.0	20.0	0.0	12.2	31.6	21.7	43.9

Note: Growth per cent refers to year-on-year change in production.
Source : Department of Information Technology.

35 : Index of Industrial Production Growth : Sector-wise and Use-Based Classification

Period	Base	General Index	Industry: Sector-wise (Growth %)			Use Based Classification of Industries (Growth %)					
			Mining & Quarrying	Manufacturing	Electricity	Basic Industries	Capital Goods Industries	Intermediate Goods Industries	Consumer Goods Industries	Consumer Durables	Consumer Non-Durables
1956-60	1956=100	7.4	7.2	6.9	14.5	..	..	..	..	..	..
1961-70	1960=100	5.8	4.1	5.4	11.8	7.6	7.9	4.7	4.4	..	..
1971-80	1970=100	4.2	3.8	3.9	7.1	5.2	5.4	3.5	3.2	5.0	3.0
1981-90	1980-81=100	7.4	8.4	7.1	8.8	8.0	11.0	6.1	6.7	14.2	5.4
1991-00	1993-94=100	6.3	3.4	6.5	7.0	6.3	5.4	7.5	5.8	8.9	5.0
2000-10	1993-94=100	7.0	4.3	7.5	4.8	5.6	11.5	5.8	8.0	10.0	7.5

Note : Growth rate worked out by using calender year averages for the years 1956 to 1980 and fiscal year averages thereafter.
Source : Central Statistical Organisation.

36 : Principal Characteristics of Factories (All-India)

Year	Number of Factories	Fixed Capital (Rs. crore)	Number of Employees ('000)	Value of Output (Rs. crore)	Gross Value Added (Rs. crore)	Gross Capital Formation (Rs. crore)
1970-71	64565	8752	5216	13768	3753	
1980-81	96503	29900	7715	61084	13846	7920
Growth (%)*	5.1	15.1	5.0	18.4	16.6	
1990-91	110179	133648	8163	270564	61578	32559
Growth (%)*	1.4	14.9	0.6	16.1	15.3	14.7
2000-01	131268	399604	7918	926902	178350	61415
Growth (%)*	(0.2)	(0.6)	(2.8)	3.2	(5.4)	(5.0)
2001-02	128549	431960	7687	962457	183229	73873
Growth (%)	(2.1)	8.1	(2.9)	3.8	2.7	20.3
2002-03	127957	444759	7871	1130561	214376	63976
Growth (%)	(0.5)	3.0	2.4	17.5	17.0	(13.4)
2003-04	129074	473331	7803	1287401	247777	74188
Growth (%)	0.9	6.4	(0.9)	13.9	15.6	16.0
2004-05	136353	513069	8383	1672561	309620	110073
Growth (%)	5.6	8.4	7.4	29.9	25.0	48.4
2005-06	140160	606940	9039	1908355	364697	171567
Growth (%)	2.8	18.3	7.8	14.1	17.8	55.9

Note : Figures in brackets represents negative value.
*Values upto 2000-01 denote average annual growth rate for decade; thereafter, yearly rates.

Source : *Annual Survey of Industries* (Factory Sector).

37 : Performance of Micro, Small and Medium Enterprises (MSMEs)

	Number of MSMEs (in lakh)	Fixed Investment in (Rs. crore)	Production (Rs. crore)		Employment (number)	Export (Rs. crore)
1993-94 Prices						
1990-91	68	93555	78802	84728	158	9664
2000-01	101	146845	261297	184401	239	69797
2001-02	105	154349	282270	195613	249	71244
2001-02 Prices						
2002-03	110	162317	314850	306771	260	86013
Growth %	4.1	5.2	11.5	8.7	4.4	20.7
2003-04	114	170219	364547	336344	271	97644
Growth %	4.1	4.9	15.8	9.6	4.3	13.5
2004-05	119	178699	429796	372938	283	124417
Growth %	4.0	5.0	17.9	10.9	4.1	27.4
2005-06	123	188113	497842	418884	295	150242
Growth %	4.0	5.3	15.8	12.3	4.4	20.8
2006-07	261	500758	709398	..	595	182538
2007-08	273	558190	790759	..	626	202017
Growth %	4.5	11.5	11.5		5.3	10.7
2008-09	285	621753	880805	..	659	..
Growth %	4.5	11.4	11.4		5.3	

Note : Data upto 2005-06 refers to only small scale industries (SSI). Subsequent data refers to micro, small and medium industries.

Source : Ministry of Micro, Small and Medium Enterprises.

38 : Trends in Money Supply

(Rs. crore)

Year as at end March	Money Supply (M3)		Currency with the Public		Deposit Money		As Per cent of GDP		
	Rs. crore	Growth%	Rs. crore	Growth (%)	Rs. crore	Growth (%)	Money Supply	Currency	Deposit Money
1950-51*	2,352		1,405		946		23.3	13.9	9.4
1960-61*	3,964	5.4	2,098	4.1	1,865	7.0	22.8	12.1	10.7
1970-71*	11,020	10.8	4,371	7.6	6,649	13.6	23.8	9.5	14.4
1980-81*	55,774	17.6	13,426	11.9	42,348	20.3	38.4	9.2	29.1
1990-91*	265,828	16.9	53,048	14.7	212,780	17.5	46.7	9.3	37.4
2000-01*	1,313,220	17.3	209,550	14.7	1,103,671	17.9	62.5	10.0	52.5
2001-02	1,498,355	14.1	240,794	14.9	1,257,561	13.9	65.7	10.6	55.2
2002-03	1,717,960	14.7	271,581	12.8	1,446,378	15.0	70.0	11.1	58.9
2003-04	2,005,676	16.7	314,971	16.0	1,690,705	16.9	72.8	11.4	61.4
2004-05	2,245,677	12.0	356,314	13.1	1,889,363	11.8	69.3	11.0	58.3
2005-06	2,719,519	21.1	412,124	15.7	2,307,395	22.1	76.8	11.6	65.2
2006-07	3,310,068	21.7	482,854	17.2	2,827,213	22.5	85.4	12.5	73.0
2007-08	4,017,882	21.4	568,410	17.7	3,449,472	22.0	94.6	13.4	81.2
2008-09	4,777,069	18.9	666,276	17.2	4,110,793	19.2	107.0	14.9	92.1
2009-10	5,599,762	17.2	768,033	15.3	4,831,729	17.5	117.0	16.1	100.9

Note : * Growth rate for decades from 1950-51 to 2000-01 is the CAGR (compounded annual growth rate). Thereafter growth rates are annual. 2. Data from 2006-07 onwards is provisional.
3. Excluding the impact of merger on May 3, 2002, data on time deposits and broad money supply for the year 2002-03 works out to Rs. 12,14,708 crore and Rs. 16,88,289 crore, respectively.
4. Excluding the impact of conversion of a non-banking entity into a banking entity on October 11, 2004, data on time deposits and broad money for the year 2004-05 works out to Rs. 15,92,374 crore and Rs. 22,42,164 crore, respectively. 5. GDP upto 2004-05 is based on 1999-2000 series , thereafter it is based on the 2004-05 series all at current market prices.

Source : Reserve Bank of India.

39 : Sources of Changes in Money Supply

Year (as at end March)	Net Bank Credit to Government		Bank Credit to Commercial Sector		Net Foreign Exchange Assets of the Banking Sector		Net Non-Monetary Liabilities of Banking Sector	
	Rs. crore	Share in M3(%)	Rs. crore	Share in M3(%)	Rs. crore	Share in M3(%)	Rs. crore	Share in M3(%)
1950-51	808	34.4	588	25.0	860	36.6	145	6.2
1960-61	2,489	62.8	1,503	37.9	178	4.5	413	10.4
1970-71	5,455	49.5	6,522	59.2	551	5.0	1,892	17.2
1980-81	25,718	46.1	36,641	65.7	4,730	8.5	11,934	21.4
1990-91	140,193	52.7	171,769	64.6	10,581	4.0	58,336	21.9
2000-01	511,955	39.0	679,218	51.7	249,820	19.0	133,126	10.1
2001-02	589,565	39.3	759,647	50.7	311,035	20.8	168,258	11.2
2002-03	676,523	39.4	898,981	52.3	393,715	22.9	258,330	15.0
2003-04	742,904	37.0	1,016,151	50.7	526,586	26.3	287,261	14.3
2004-05	752,436	33.5	1,275,912	56.8	649,255	28.9	439,374	19.6
2005-06	759,416	27.9	1,688,681	62.1	726,194	26.7	462,429	17.0
2006-07	827,626	25.0	2,128,862	64.3	913,179	27.6	567,761	17.2
2007-08	899,518	22.4	2,578,990	64.2	1,295,131	32.2	764,980	19.0
2008-09	1,277,724	26.7	3,020,516	63.2	1,352,184	28.3	883,409	18.5
2009-10	1,668,258	29.9	3,483,253	62.4	1,275,039	22.9	857,902	15.4

Source : Reserve Bank of India.

40 : Structural Changes in Reserve Bank of India's Balance Sheet

(Rs. crore)

End-March	Total Assets/Liabilities	of Total Liabilities		of Total Assets		
		Currency with Public	Deposits (Govt. Bank)	Foreign Assets	GoI Securities	Loans & Advances
Outstandings						
1951	1612	1247	320	884	487	9
% to total	100.0	77.3	19.9	54.8	30.2	0.6
1961	2257	1985	264	136	1632	171
% to total	100.0	87.9	11.7	6.0	72.3	7.6
1971	5463	4212	553	350	3714	958
% to total	100.0	77.1	10.1	6.4	68.0	17.5
1981	20275	13733	6520	4320	11110	3504
% to total	100.0	67.7	32.2	21.3	54.8	17.3
1991	120691	53784	38542	4208	46924	18516
% to total	100.0	44.6	31.9	3.5	38.9	15.3
2001	386541	212851	89041	144013	110775	35442
% to total	100.0	55.1	23.0	37.3	28.7	9.2
2007	980097	495938	304124	836401	1046	6935
% to total	100.0	50.6	31.0	85.3	0.1	0.7
2008	1364028	581577	564844	1195828	1046	5250
% to total	100.0	42.6	41.4	87.7	0.1	0.4
2009	1479515	691099	387620	1231114	1046	23521
% to total	100.0	46.7	26.2	83.2	0.1	1.6

Source : Reserve Bank of India.

41 : Monetary Policy Measures at Some Selected Dates

Effective Date	Bank Rate (%)	CRR	SLR (%)	Repo Rate	Reserve Repo Rate
31-03-1951	3.5	5% of DL & 2% of TL	20		
31-03-1961	4	do	20		
31-03-1971	6	3	28		
31-03-1981	9	6	34		
31-03-1991	10	15	38.5		
04-07-1991	11	15	38.5		
09-10-1991	12	15	38.5		
16-04-1997	11	10	31.5		
19-03-1998	10.5	10.5	25		
03-04-1998	10	10.25	25		
29-04-1998	9	10	25		
02-03-1999	8	11	24		
02-04-2000	7	9	24		
22-07-2000	8	8	24		
17-02-2001	7.5	8.5	24		
02-03-2001	7	8.25	24		
23-10-2001	6.5	7.5	24	8.50	6.50
30-10-2002	6.25	5	24	8.00	5.50
30-04-2003	6.0	4.5	24	7.00	5.00
02-10-2004	6.0	5	24	6.00	4.50
23-12-2006	6.0	5.25	24	7.25	6.00
06-01-2007	6.0	5.5	24	7.25	6.00
17-2-2007	6.0	5.75	24	7.50	6.00
3-03-2007	6.0	6	24	7.50	6.00
14-04-2007	6.0	6.25	24	7.75	6.00
28-4-2007	6.0	6.5	24	7.75	6.00
04-08-2007	6.0	7	24	7.75	6.00
11-10-2007	6.0	7.5	24	7.75	6.00
26-04-2008	6.0	7.75	24	7.75	6.00
10-05-2008	6.0	8	24	7.75	6.00
24-05-2008	6.0	8.25	24	7.75	6.00
05-07-2008	6.0	8.5	24	8.50	6.00
19-07-2008	6.0	8.75	24	8.50	6.00
30-08-2008	6.0	9	24	9.00	6.00
11-10-2008	6.0	6.5	24	9.00	6.00
25-10-2008	6.0	6	24	8.00	6.00
17-01-2009	6.0	5	24	5.50	4.00
7-11-2009	6.00	5.00	25	4.75	3.25
24-04-2010	6.00	6.00	25	5.25	3.75
16-09-2010	6.00	6.00	25	6.00	5.00

Note : CRR: Cash reserve ratio; SLR: Statutory liquidity ratio; DL: Demand liabilities; TL: Time liabilities.

Source : Reserve Bank of India.

42 : Progress of Scheduled Commercial Banks at a Glance

	June/1969	June/1971	June/1981	March/1991	March/2001	March/2009
No. of Commercial Banks	89	85	187	276	300	170
1. Scheduled Commercial Banks	73	74	183	272	296	166
of which: Regional Rural Banks			102	196	196	86
2. Non-Scheduled Commercial Banks	16	11	4	4	5	4
Number of Offices in India	8,262	12,013	35,707	60,220	67,937	82,408
1. Rural	1,833	4,280	17,656	35,206	32,585	31,699
% Share	22	36	49	58	48	38
2. Semi-urban	3,342	4,040	8,474	11,344	14,843	19,082
3. Urban	1,584	1,949	5,454	8,046	11,193	16,614
4. Metropolitan	1,503	1,744	4,126	5,624	9,316	15,013
Population per Office (' 000)	64	46	19	14	15	14
No. of ATMs						43,651
Off-site						24,645
On Site						39,006
Per capita Deposit Rs.	88	113	587	2,368	9,770	34,372
Per capita Credit Rs.	68	86	385	1,434	5,228	24,945
Share of Priority Sector Advances to Non-food SC Bank Credit (%)	15.0	22.3	38.8	37.7	31	35.2
Credit-Deposit Ratio (%)	77.5	76.6	65.5	60.6	53.5	73.9
Investment Deposit Ratio (%)	29.3	29.1	35.1	37.7	37.1	35.7
Cash Deposit Ratio (%)	8.2	6.5	13.6	17.6	8.4	7.3

Note: ATM data pertains to 2008-09.

Source: Reserve Bank of India.

43 : Aggregate Deposits of Scheduled Commercial Banks

(Rs. crore)

Last Reporting Friday of March	Demand Deposits		Time Deposits		Aggregate Deposits		% of GDP
	Rs. crore	Growth (%)	Rs. crore	Growth (%)	Rs. crore	Growth (%)	
1950-51*	593		290		882		8.7
1960-61*	710	1.8	1,026	13.5	1,736	7.0	10.0
1970-71*	2,626	14.0	3,280	12.3	5,906	13.0	12.8
1980-81*	7,798	11.5	30,190	24.9	37,988	20.5	26.1
1990-91*	33,192	15.6	159,349	18.1	192,541	17.6	33.8
2000-01*	142,552	15.7	820,066	17.8	962,618	17.5	45.8
2001-02	153,048	7.4	950,312	15.9	1,103,360	14.6	48.4
2002-03	170,289	11.3	1,110,564	16.9	1,280,853	16.1	52.2
2003-04	225,022	32.1	1,279,394	15.2	1,504,416	17.5	54.6
2004-05	248,028	10.2	1,452,171	13.5	1,700,198	13.0	52.5
2005-06	364,640	47.0	1,744,409	20.1	2,109,049	24.0	59.6
2006-07	429,731	17.9	2,182,203	25.1	2,611,933	23.8	67.4
2007-08	524,310	22.0	2,672,630	22.5	3,196,939	22.4	75.3
2008-09	523,085	(0.2)	3,311,025	23.9	3,834,110	19.9	85.9
2009-10	639,137	22.2	3,847,436	16.2	4,486,574	17.0	94.1

Note : * Growth for decades from 1950-51 to 2000-01 based on CAGR, thereafter on annual growth.
Source : Reserve Bank of India.

44 : Investments by Scheduled Commercial Banks in SLR and Non-SLR Securities

(Rs. crore)

	SLR Securities			Non-SLR Securities							
	Investments in Government Securities	Investments in Other Approved Securities	Investment in SLR Securities	Commercial Paper	Shares of PSUs & Pvt. Corporate Sector	Bonds & Debentures	Mutual Funds	Financial Institutions	Investment in Non-SLR Securities	Total Investment	Investment Deposit Ratio (%)
1951-52	296		296							296	34
1960-61	559		559							559	32
1970-71	1,362	410	1,772							1,772	30
1980-81	9,219	3,967	13,186							13,186	35
1990-91	49,998	25,067	75,065							75,065	39
2000-01	340,035	30,125	370,160	8,049	5,690	62,105			75,844	446,004	46
2001-02	411,176	27,093	438,269	8,497	5,914	66,589			81,000	519,269	47
2002-03	523,417	24,129	547,546	4,041	9,230	81,284	6,455	31,066	132,076	679,622	53
2003-04	654,758	22,830	677,588	3,835	9,006	82,918	11,930	32,988	140,677	818,265	54
2004-05	718,982	20,172	739,154	3,944	12,219	85,913	12,744	31,557	146,377	885,531	52
2005-06	700,742	16,712	717,454	4,837	13,170	77,721	10,410	29,203	135,341	852,795	40
2006-07	776,058	15,458	791,516	9,038	18,428	74,660	11,761	26,568	140,455	931,971	36
2007-08	958,661	13,053	971,715	13,270	26,708	85,865	18,824	25,942	170,609	1,142,324	36
2008-09	1,155,786	10,624	1,166,410	20,001	28,236	89,660	37,035	32,585	207,517	1,373,927	36

Source : Reserve Bank of India.

45 : Credit by Scheduled Commercial Banks

Last Reporting Friday of March	Food Credit	Non-Food Credit		Total Scheduled Commercial Bank Credit			
	Rs. crore	Rs. crore	Growth (%)	Rs. crore	Growth (%)	% to GDP**	Credit-Deposit Ratio (%)
1950-51*				547		5.4	62
1960-61*	.	.		1,336	9.3	7.7	77
1970-71*	214	4,469		4,684	13	10	79
1980-81*	1,759	23,612	18	25,371	18	17	67
1990-91*	4,506	111,795	17	116,301	16	20	60
2000-01*	39,991	471,443	15	511,434	16	24	53
2001-02	53,978	535,745	14	589,723	15	26	53
2002-03	49,479	679,736	27	729,215	24	30	57
2003-04	35,961	804,824	18	840,785	15	31	56
2004-05	41,121	1,059,308	32	1,100,428	31	34	65
2005-06	40,691	1,466,386	38	1,507,077	37	43	71
2006-07	46,521	1,884,669	29	1,931,189	28	50	74
2007-08	44,399	2,317,515	23	2,361,914	22	56	74
2008-09	46,211	2,729,338	18	2,775,549	18	62	72
2009-10	48,489	3,191,909	17	3,240,399	17	68	72

Note: * Growth for decades from 1950-51 to 2000-01 based on CAGR, thereafter on annual growth; ** At current market prices.
Source: Reserve Bank of India.

46 : Sectoral Deployment of Non-Food Credit

Year-as at End March	Non-Food Gross Bank Credit (Rs. crore)	Share of Priority Sector in Non-Food Bank Credit of which: Total		Agriculture		Small Scale Industries		Medium & Large Industry	
		Rs. crore	% Share	Rs. crore	% Share	Rs. crore	% Share	Rs. crore	% Share
1979-80	19,135	6,730	35.2	2,767	14.5	2,635	13.8	8,269	43.2
1980-81	23,045	8,504	36.9	3,584	15.6	3,229	14.0	9,960	43.2
1990-91	113,513	42,915	37.8	16,750	14.8	17,181	15.1	44,508	39.2
2000-01	429,162	154,414	36.0	51,922	12.1	56,002	13.0	162,837	37.9
2001-02	482,749	175,259	36.3	60,761	12.6	57,199	11.8	172,324	35.7
2002-03	620,055	211,609	34.1	73,518	11.9	60,394	9.7	235,168	37.9
2003-04	728,422	263,834	36.2	90,541	12.4	65,855	9.0	247,210	33.9
2004-05	999,788	381,476	38.2	125,250	12.5	74,588	7.5	352,304	35.2
2005-06	1,404,840	510,738	36.4	173,972	12.4	91,212	6.5	459,232	32.7
2006-07	1,801,240	635,966	35.3	230,377	12.8	117,910	6.5	579,429	32.2
2007-08	2,202,890	747,380	33.9	275,342	12.5	194,842	8.8	672,033	30.5
2008-09	2,602,290	915,886	35.2	338,656	13.0	257,027	9.9	797,363	30.6

Source : Reserve Bank of India.

47 : Scheduled Commercial Banks' Direct Finance to Farmers (Short and Long Term)

As of End-June	Upto 2.5 Acres		2.5 Acres to 5 Acres		Above 5 Acres		Total	
	No. of ACs (in '000s)	Amount (Rs. crore)	No. of ACs (in '000s)	Amount (Rs. crore)	No. of ACs (in '000s)	Amount (Rs. crore)	No. of ACs (in '000s)	Amount (Rs. crore)
Disbursements								
1980-81	1587	252	693	168	790	594	3070	1014
(% to Total)	51.7	24.9	22.6	16.6	25.7	58.5	100.0	100.0
1990-91	1960	1181	1219	952	899	1782	4078	3915
(% to Total)	48.1	30.2	29.9	24.3	22.0	45.5	100.0	100.0
2000-01	2382	3740	1860	3642	1599	7135	5841	14516
(% to Total)	40.8	25.8	31.8	25.1	27.4	49.2	100.0	100.0
2001-02	2679	4352	1933	4371	2359	7578	6970	16300
(% to Total)	38.4	26.7	27.7	26.8	33.8	46.5	100.0	100.0
2002-03	2494	4834	1934	5578	1983	11445	6411	21857
(% to Total)	38.9	22.1	30.2	25.5	30.9	52.4	100.0	100.0
2003-04	3711	7953	2695	7340	2259	16592	8665	31885
(% to Total)	42.8	24.9	31.1	23.0	26.1	52.0	100.0	100.0
2004-05	4478	10833	3172	10550	2535	19735	10185	41119
(% to Total)	44.0	26.3	31.1	25.7	24.9	48.0	100.0	100.0
2005-06	5004	16823	3670	17619	3670	32682	12344	67124
(% to Total)	40.5	25.1	29.7	26.2	29.7	48.7	100.0	100.0
2006-07	5963	23246	4008	21588	4379	49335	14350	94169
(% to Total)	41.6	24.7	27.9	22.9	30.5	52.4	100.0	100.0

contd...

...contd...

As of End-June	Upto 2.5 Acres		2.5 Acres to 5 Acres		Above 5 Acres		Total	
	No. of ACs (in '000s)	Amount (Rs. crore)	No. of ACs (in '000s)	Amount (Rs. crore)	No of ACs (in '000s)	Amount (Rs. crore)	No. of ACs (in '000s)	Amount (Rs. crore)
Outstandings								
1980-81	3,017	477	1,645	396	1,931	1,454	6,593	2,326
(% to Total)	45.8	20.5	25.0	17.0	29.3	62.5	100.0	100.0
1990-91	6,137	2,895	4,346	2,870	3,563	6,624	14,045	12,389
(% to Total)	43.7	23.4	30.9	23.2	25.4	53.5	100.0	100.0
2000-01	4,600	7,215	3,689	7,308	3,555	16,963	11,844	31,486
(% to Total)	38.8	22.9	31.1	23.2	30.0	53.9	100.0	100.0
2001-02	4,902	8,759	3,961	9,686	3,394	19,083	12,257	37,529
(% to Total)	40.0	23.3	32.3	25.8	27.7	50.8	100.0	100.0
2002-03	4,749	9,813	4,092	11,316	3,835	23,831	12,676	44,961
(% to Total)	37.5	21.8	32.3	25.2	30.3	53.0	100.0	100.0
2003-04	6,086	14,805	4,806	13,974	4,377	28,786	15,268	57,565
(% to Total)	39.9	25.7	31.5	24.3	28.7	50.0	100.0	100.0
2004-05	7,299	20,499	5,874	20,759	5,274	37,218	18,447	78,476
(% to Total)	39.6	26.1	31.8	26.5	28.6	47.4	100.0	100.0
2005-06	8,239	29,719	6,677	29,255	6,321	52,769	21,237	111,743
(% to Total)	38.8	26.6	31.4	26.2	29.8	47.2	100.0	100.0
2006-07	9,954	37,336	7,548	37,815	6,985	64,810	24,487	139,961
(% to Total)	40.7	26.7	30.8	27.0	28.5	46.3	100.0	100.0

Note: Data for 1980-81 is as of end-March. *Source*: Reserve Bank of India.

48 : Deposits of Scheduled Commercial Banks : According to Population Group

Year	Rural		Semi-Urban		Urban		Metropolitan	
	No. of Accounts (in '000s)	Amount Outstanding (Rs. crore)	No. of Accounts (in '000s)	Amount Outstanding (Rs. crore)	No. of Accounts (in '000s)	Amount Outstanding (Rs. crore)	No. of Accounts (in '000s)	Amount Outstanding (Rs. crore)
1981	34,862	5,262	43,690	9,369	33,878	9,967	31,197	15,815
1991	108,876	31,010	98,084	41,439	80,889	49,140	67,342	78,979
2001	131,723	139,431	116,400	186,188	92,769	217,833	87,137	405,981
2002	133,000	159,423	117,394	214,990	94,622	255,478	94,975	493,501
2003	136,733	176,502	117,537	241,757	96,099	290,503	95,711	567,433
2004	138,760	195,082	120,651	268,217	99,571	330,296	98,176	717,679
2005	141,908	213,104	125,198	295,685	101,376	374,891	98,310	863,134
2006	139,570	226,061	121,664	302,213	106,172	430,813	117,692	1,132,087
2007	149,663	253,014	132,808	357,395	113,422	532,592	123,306	1,454,043
2008	168,034	303,423	148,361	430,280	128,021	657,699	137,241	1,858,544

Source : Reserve Bank of India.

49 : Distribution of Commercial Banks' Offices

(number)

As of End-June	Rural	Share in Total (%)	Semi-Urban	Urban	Metropolitan	Total
1969	1,833	22	3,342	1,584	1,503	8,262
1971	4,280	36	4,040	1,949	1,744	12,013
1981	17,656	49	8,471	5,454	4,126	35,707
1991	35,206	58	11,344	8,046	5,624	60,220
2001	32,562	49	14,597	10,293	8,467	65,919
2002	32,380	49	14,747	10,477	8,586	66,190
2003	32,303	49	14,859	10,693	8,680	66,535
2004	32,121	48	15,091	11,000	8,976	67,188
2005	32,082	47	15,403	11,500	9,370	68,355
2006	30,579	44	15,556	12,032	11,304	69,471
2007	30,551	43	16,361	12,970	11,957	71,839
2008	31,069	41	17,687	14,394	12,911	76,061
2009	31,682	40	18,878	15,430	13,732	79,722

Source : Reserve Bank of India.

50 : Statistics on Cheque Clearances

Year	All India		All RBI Centres*		Mumbai		Kolkata		New Delhi		Chennai	
	Number (in million)	Amount (Rs. crore)	Number (in million)	Amount (Rs. crore)	Number (in million)	Amount (Rs. crore)	Number (in million)	Amount (Rs. crore)	Number (in million)	Amount (Rs. crore)	Number (in million)	Amount (Rs. crore)
1970-71	151	46,332	112	36,960	37	13,344	13	6,924	7	2,628	8	2,136
1980-81	315	243,516	224	186,252	66	56,379	19	21,324	16	16,644	9	9,133
1990-91	764	2,287,353	352	1,839,460	125	1,182,587	33	104,051	55	239,979	36	176,123
2000-01	941	10,747,119	527	9,189,683	174	6,667,989	52	365,280	101	818,999	52	509,292
2001-02	902	12,575,254	538	10,947,391	168	8,217,816	52	373,131	108	990,315	52	500,872
2002-03	1,014	13,424,313	598	10,978,762	202	7,694,748	53	419,164	116	1,319,625	56	552,913
2003-04	1,023	11,595,960	624	9,178,751	216	5,511,293	47	465,308	111	1,354,677	60	612,158
2004-05	1,167	10,458,895	739	8,493,321	230	3,753,670	60	560,660	148	1,773,611	74	759,883
2005-06	1,287	11,329,134	794	8,194,977	239	3,342,829	64	658,640	160	1,697,583	81	655,278
2006-07	1,367	12,042,426	831	8,599,494	252	3,319,090	68	682,358	169	1,773,548	80	692,201
2007-08	1,461	13,396,066	878	9,451,748	265	3,685,407	73	778,304	178	1,800,975	85	778,854
2008-09	1,397	12,469,135	835	8,297,385	251	2,799,765	69	756,038	173	1,664,709	83	801,964
2009-10	1,380	10,409,942	813	6,522,135	248	1,939,327	68	658,229	162	1,299,000	79	631,101

Note: * RBI centres refer to all centres where RBI is the manager of cleaning houses.

Source : Reserve Bank of India.

51 : Number of Kisan Credit Cards Issued

(million)

As of End-March	Cooperative Banks	Regional Rural Banks	Commercial Banks	Total
1998-99	0.16	0.01	0.62	0.78
1999-00	3.59	0.17	1.37	5.13
2000-01	5.61	0.65	2.39	8.65
2001-02	5.44	0.83	3.07	9.34
2002-03	4.58	0.96	2.70	8.24
2003-04	4.88	1.27	3.09	9.25
2004-05	3.56	1.73	4.40	9.68
2005-06	2.60	1.25	4.16	8.01
2006-07	2.30	1.41	4.81	8.51
2007-08	2.09	1.77	4.60	8.46
2008-09	1.34	1.41	5.83	8.58
Total	36.20	11.50	37.00	84.60
% share	42.70	13.50	43.80	100.00

Source : Reserve Bank of India.

52 : Retail Portfolio of Scheduled Commercial Banks

(Rs. crore)

End-March	Retail Loans	% to Total Loans & Advances	*of which:*			
			Housing Loan	Consumer Durables	Credit Card	Auto Loans
2004	189,041	22	89,449	6,256	6,167	87,170
2005	266,610	24	134,276	3,810	8,405	35,043
2006	375,683	26	179,060	4,469	12,434	61,369
2007	487,860	26	224,481	7,296	18,317	82,562
2008	570,776	25	252,932	4,802	27,437	87,998
2009	593,815	21	263,235	5,431	29,941	83,915

Source : Reserve Bank of India.

53 : Non-Performing Assets of Scheduled Commercial Banks

End-March	Non-Performing Assets					
	Gross Amount (Rs. crore)	As % of Gross Advances	As % of Total Assets	Net Amount (Rs. crore)	As % of Net Advances	As % of Total Assets
1996-97	47,300	15.7	7.0	22,340	8.1	3.3
1997-98	50,815	14.4	6.4	23,761	7.3	3.0
1998-99	58,722	14.7	6.2	28,020	7.6	2.9
1999-00	60,408	12.7	5.5	30,073	6.8	2.7
2000-01	63,741	11.4	4.9	32,461	6.2	2.5
2001-02	70,861	10.4	4.6	35,554	5.5	2.3
2002-03	68,717	8.8	4.1	29,692	4.0	1.8
2003-04	64,812	7.2	3.3	24,396	2.8	1.2
2004-05	59,373	5.2	2.5	21,754	2.0	0.9
2005-06	51,097	3.3	1.8	18,543	1.2	0.7
2006-07	50,486	2.5	1.5	20,101	1.0	0.6
2007-08	56,435	2.3	1.3	24,734	1.0	0.6

Source : Reserve Bank of India.

54 : Value of Coins and Notes Issued : Denomination-wise

(Rs. crore)

Year	1950-51	1960-61	1970-71	1980-81	1990-91	2000-01	2009-10
Small Coins	76	71	137	243	685	1,300	1,455
Re. 1 Notes	1204	1942	219	207	335	307	-
Re. 1 Coins	130	142	43	141	616	1,393	2,964
Rs. 2 Coins	-	-	-	-	23	814	2,640
Rs. 5 Coins	-	-	-	-	-	1,544	3,880
Rs. 2 Notes	-	38	69	299	883	471	-
Rs. 5 Notes	-	203	310	634	1,810	1,016	-
Rs. 10 Notes	-	814	1,563	2,097	3,785	12,336	18,536
Rs. 20 Notes	-	-	-	1,090	2,952	1,012	4,681
Rs. 50 Notes	-	-	-	2,206	14,812	32,818	21,057
Rs. 100 Notes	-	865	2,210	7,406	24,570	108,141	138,364
Rs. 500 Notes	-	-	-	-	2,177	52,947	364,479
Rs. 1000 Notes	-	54	45	-	-	3,719	238,252

Source : Reserve Bank of India.

55 : Retail Electronic Payments

	ECS Credit	ECS Debit	EFT/NEFT	Credit Cards	Debit Cards	Total
Volume of Transactions (In '000)						
2003-04	20,300	7,900	819	100,179	37,757	166,955
2004-05	40,051	15,300	2,549	129,472	41,532	288,904
2005-06	44,216	35,958	3,067	156,086	45,686	285,013
2006-07	69,019	75,202	4,776	169,536	60,177	378,710
2007-08	78,365	127,120	13,315	228,203	88,306	535,309
2008-09	88,394	160,055	32,161	259,561	127,654	667,825
2009-10(Upto February)	91,042	134,815	58,061	213,660	154,584	652,162
Value of Transactions (Rs. crore)						
2003-04	10,228	2,254	17,125	17,663	4,874	52,143
2004-05	20,180	2,921	54,601	25,686	5,361	108,749
2005-06	32,324	12,986	61,288	33,886	5,897	146,381
2006-07	83,273	25,441	77,446	41,361	8,172	235,693
2007-08	782,222	48,937	140,326	57,984	12,521	1,041,990
2008-09	97,487	66,976	251,956	65,356	18,547	500,322
2009-10(Upto February)	108,191	63,228	365,610	56,129	24,000	617,158

Note : The substantial increase in ECS credit in 2007-08 is due to refund of the oversubscription amount of IPOs floated by companies using electronic mode as mandated by the stock exchange.
ECS: Electronic clearing system; EFI: Electronic fund transfer system; NEFT: National electronic funds transfer system.

Source : Reserve Bank of India.

56 : Business and Financial Indicators of Regional Rural Banks

	2000-01	2001-02	2002-03	2003-04	2004-05	2005-06	2006-07	2007-08	2008-09
No. of RRBs	196	196	196	196	196	133	96	90	86
Net Profit (Rs. crore)	601	608	519	769	748	617	596	1,328	1,830
Branch Productivity (Rs. crore)	3.8	4.4	5.0	5.7	6.6	7.7	9.1	10.7	12.4
Employee Productivity (Rs.crore)	0.8	0.9	1.0	1.2	1.4	1.6	1.9	2.3	2.7
Accumulated Loss as % to Assets	5.6	4.7	4.4	3.9	3.5	2.9	2.6	2.1	2.1
Salary as % to Assets	2.0	2.2	2.3	2.6	2.0	2.1	1.9	1.9	1.8
Financial Return (%)	9.4	10.6	9.6	8.9	8.2	7.7	7.7	8.1	8.2
Financial Cost (%)	6.0	6.8	6.1	5.4	4.6	4.1	4.1	4.4	4.5
Financial Margin (%)	3.4	3.8	3.5	3.5	3.6	3.6	3.6	3.7	3.7
Risk, Operational & Other Cost (%)	2.1	2.6	2.6	2.2	2.3	2.8	2.9	2.7	2.6
Net Margin (%)	1.2	1.2	0.9	1.3	1.3	0.8	0.7	1.0	1.1

Note :
1. The reduction in number of RRBs is due to amalgamation since September 2005.
2. Net profit is the difference between gross profit of profit making RRBs and losses made by loss making RRBs.
3. Branch productivity :Average level of business per branch in terms of total deposits and gross advances.
4. Employee productivity :Average level of business per employee in terms of total deposits and gross advances.
5. Financial return :Per cent of total income from both advances and investments against average working funds.
6. Financial cost : Per cent of total interest expended for deposits, borrowings etc., against average working funds.
7. Financial margin is the difference between financial returns and cost.
8. Net margin is the difference between financial margin and risk, operational & other costs (plus miscellaneous income).

Source : National Bank for Agriculture and Rural Development.

57 : Regional Rural Banks: Selected Indicators — Outstandings

(Rs. crore)

Year	Aggregate Deposits		Bank Credit		Investment		Credit-Deposit Ratio (%)	Investment-Deposit Ratio (%)
	Rs. crore	Growth (%)	Rs. crore	Growth (%)	Rs. crore	Growth (%)		
1980-81*	232		285		0		122.8	0.0
1990-91*	4560	34.7	3497	28.5	16		76.7	0.4
2000-01*	35995	22.9	15211	15.8	7489	84.9	42.3	20.8
2001-02	42494	18.1	18033	18.6	6871	(8.3)	42.4	16.2
2002-03	47644	12.1	21359	18.4	12008	74.8	44.8	25.2
2003-04	53390	12.1	25057	17.3	17532	46.0	46.9	32.8
2004-05	58286	9.2	31651	26.3	20213	15.3	54.3	34.7
2005-06	64195	10.1	36050	13.9	19050	(5.8)	56.2	29.7
2006-07	81620	27.1	48420	34.3	22424	17.7	59.3	27.5
2007-08	94412	15.7	57417	18.6	25387	13.2	60.8	26.9
2008-09	113828	20.6	64011	11.5	29414	15.9	56.2	25.8

Note : * Growth for decades from 1950-51 to 2000-01 is CAGR (compounded annual growth rate), growth from 2001-02 is annual growth rate.
Source : National Bank for Agriculture and Rural Development.

58 : Regional Rural Banks : Purpose-wise Outstanding Advances

(Rs. crore)

As of End-March	Total	Agriculture	Short Term	Long Term	Non-Agriculture	Rural Artisans	Other Industries	Retail Trade etc.	Others
1991	3,804	1,850	645	671	1,954		321*	1,143	490
2001	8,823	3,966	3,095	871	4,857	181	70	1,123	3,483
2002	18,629	8,405	4,883	3,522	10,224	671	226	2,984	6,343
2003	22,158	10,261	6,495	3,766	11,897	695	330	3,264	7,608
2004	26,114	11,722	7,664	4,058	14,393	715	433	3,607	9,638
2005	32,871	16,710	10,980	5,730	16,161	713	580	4,364	10,504
2006	39,712	21,509	13,877	7,632	18,204	748	757	3,452	13,246
2007	48,493	27,452	18,707	3,745	21,041	736	880	3,677	15,748
2008	58,984	33,216	22,748	10,468	25,768	671	1,227	4,531	19,339
2009	69,030	36,466	24,986	11,480	32,564	820	1,400	5,015	25,329

Note: * Separate data not available.
Source: National Bank for Agriculture and Rural Development.

59 : Capital Market Snapshot

As of End-March	Stock Exchanges (number)	Companies listed		Brokers Cash segment (number)	Registered FIIs (number)	Mutual Funds (number)	Market Capitalisation (% of GDP)	
		BSE (number)	NSE (number)				BSE	NSE
1991							13.9	
1992							43.0	
1993	21	2,861		5,200	18		21.7	
1994	22	3,585		6,413	158	12	36.2	
1995	22	4,702	135	6,711	308	22	36.5	
1996	22	5,603	422	8,476	367	27	38.2	
1997	22	5,832	550	8,867	439	37	36.6	30.4
1998	22	5,853	612	9,005	496	38	41.3	31.5
1999	23	5,849	648	9,069	450	41	35.4	28.0
2000	23	5,815	720	9,192	506	38	46.8	52.3
2001	23	5,869	785	9,782	527	39	27.2	31.3
2002	23	5,782	793	9,687	490	38	26.9	27.9
2003	23	5,650	818	9,519	502	38	23.3	21.9
2004	23	5,528	909	9,368	540	37	43.6	40.7
2005	22	4,731	970	9,128	685	39	52.4	48.9
2006	22	4,781	1069	9,335	882	38	81.5	75.9
2007	21	4,821	1228	9,443	996	40	82.8	78.6
2008	20	4,887	1381	9,487	1,319	40	103.8	98.2
2009	20	4,929	1432	9,628	1,626	44	55.4	52.0
2010	20	4,975	1470	9,772	1,713	47	98.9	96.4

Note : BSE: Bombay stock exchange; NSF: National stock exchange.
Source : Securities and Exchange Board of India.

60 : New Capital Issues By Indian Private Sector

Type of Issues	Total		Equity Shares		Preference Shares		Debentures	
	No.	Rs. crore	No.	Rs. crore	No.	Rs. crore	No.	Rs. crore
1970	113	66	64	38	41	13	8	15
1980	237	164	0	89	0	2	0	73
1981-82	438	598	357	305	5	3	73	290
1991-92	514	61,931	366	1,916	3	2	145	4,275
2001-02	19	5,692	6	860	0	0	13	4,832
2002-03	9	1,878	5	460	0	0	4	1,418
2003-04	38	3,722	35	2,471	0	0	3	1,261
2004-05	54	13,079	51	11,452	0	0	3	1,627
2005-06	131	21,154	128	20,899	1	10	2	245
2006-07	117	30,603	114	29,756	0	0	3	847
2007-08	115	63,638	111	56,848	1	5,481	3	1,309
2008-09	45	14,671	45	14,671	0	0	0	0
2009-10	68	25,479	67	25,299	0	0	1	180

Note : Data upto 1980 for calendar year and data from 1981-82 onwards for fiscal year.
Source : Reserve Bank of India.

61 : Resources Raised by Corporate Sector

(Rs. crore)

	Equity Issues	Debt Issues			Total Resources Mobilised	Share of Private Placements (%)		Share of Debt to Total Resources (%)
		Public & Right Issues	Private Placements	Total		Debt	Total Resource Mobilised	
1995-96	14,830	5,974	13,361	19,335	34,165	69.1	39.1	56.6
1996-97	7,853	6,286	15,066	21,352	29,205	70.6	51.6	73.1
1997-98	1,892	2,678	30,099	32,777	34,669	91.8	86.8	94.5
1998-99	935	4,652	49,679	54,331	55,266	91.4	89.9	98.3
1999-00	4,566	3,251	61,259	64,510	69,076	95.0	88.7	93.4
2000-01	3,368	2,740	67,836	70,576	73,944	96.1	91.7	95.4
2001-02	1,272	6,271	64,876	71,147	72,419	91.2	89.6	98.2
2002-03	1,457	2,613	66,948	69,561	71,018	96.2	94.3	97.9
2003-04	18,948	4,324	63,901	68,225	87,173	93.7	73.3	78.3
2004-05	24,388	3,867	83,405	87,272	111,660	95.6	74.7	78.2
2005-06	27,372	10	96,473	96,483	123,855	100.0	77.9	77.9
2006-07	32,907	605	145,866	146,471	179,378	99.6	81.3	81.7
2007-08	79,739	7,290	212,725	220,015	299,754	96.7	71.0	73.4
2008-09	14,272	1,948	202,745	204,693	218,965	99.0	92.6	93.5

Source : Securities and Exchange Board of India.

62 : Resource Mobilisation by Private Placements (Debt): By Borrower Categories

(Rs. crore)

	Private Sector		Public Sector		Total		Grand Total
	Financial Institutions	Non-Financial Institutions	Financial Institutions	Non-Financial Institutions	Financial Institutions	Non-Financial Institutions	
1995-96	2,136	1,934	4,552	4,739	6,688	6,673	13,361
1996-97	1,847	646	6,541	6,032	8,388	6,678	15,066
1997-98	4,324	4,879	9,660	11,237	13,984	16,116	30,100
1998-99	12,174	4,824	20,382	12,299	32,556	17,123	49,679
1999-00	10,875	8,528	17,981	23,874	28,856	32,402	61,258
2000-01	13,263	9,843	26,201	18,530	39,464	28,373	67,837
2001-02	16,019	12,601	17,358	18,898	33,377	31,499	64,876
2002-03	9,454	15,623	20,407	21,464	29,861	37,087	66,948
2003-04	12,551	6,209	26,461	18,679	39,012	24,888	63,900
2004-05	20,974	14,820	25,531	22,080	46,505	36,900	83,405
2005-06	26,463	14,727	39,165	16,119	65,628	30,846	96,474
2006-07	48,414	33,426	52,117	11,908	100,531	45,334	145,865
2007-08	88,291	41,386	56,186	26,863	144,477	68,249	212,726
2008-09	60,246	32,790	64,608	45,101	124,854	77,891	202,745

Source : Reserve Bank of India.

63 : Resources Mobilised from the Primary Market (Equities)

	Total		Category-Wise		Issuer Type		Pricing-Based		Sector-Wise	
	Number	Amount (Rs. crore)	Public (Rs. crore)	Rights (Rs. crore)	Listed (Rs. crore)	IPOs (Rs. crore)	At Par	At Premium	Private*	Public
1993-94	1,143	24,372	15,449	8,923	16,508	7,864	3,808	9,220	..	..
1994-95	1,692	27,633	21,045	6,588	11,061	16,572	5,529	12,441	26,270	1,362
1995-96	1,725	20,804	14,240	6,564	9,880	10,924	4,958	9,727	16,639	4,165
1996-97	884	14,285	11,565	2,719	8,326	5,959	3,441	4,412	10,249	4,035
1997-98	111	4,570	2,862	1,708	3,522	1,048	271	1,610	3,852	718
1998-99	58	5,586	5,019	568	5,182	404	197	660	5,516	70
1999-00	93	7,817	6,257	1,560	5,098	2,719	786	3,780	7,617	200
2000-01	151	6,107	5,378	729	3,385	2,722	818	2,408	5,893	215
2001-02	35	7,543	6,502	1,041	6,341	1,202	151	1,121	6,601	942
2002-03	26	4,071	3,639	431	3,032	1,039	143	1,314	1,897	2,173
2003-04	57	23,272	22,265	1,007	19,838	3,434	360	18,589	4,612	18,660
2004-05	60	28,256	24,640	3,616	14,507	13,749	420	23,968	17,162	11,094
2005-06	139	27,382	23,294	4,088	16,446	10,936	372	27,000	20,199	7,183
2006-07	124	33,508	2,997	3,711	5,004	28,504	12	32,889	31,728	1,779
2007-08	124	87,029	54,511	32,518	44,434	42,595	387	79,352	67,311	19,718
2008-09	47	16,220	3,582	12,637	12,637	2,082	96	14,176	16,220	0
2009-10	76	57,555	49,236	8,319	30,359	24,696	9	54,866	32,477	25,078

Note: * Joint sector issues, if any are clubbed with private sector issues. IPO: Initial public offers.

Source: Securities and Exchange Board of India.

64 : Resources Mobilised by Corporate through ADRs/GDRs and ECBs

(US $ mn)

	ADRs/GDRs	ECBs -Net
1992-93	240	(358)
1993-94	1,597	607
1994-95	2,080	1,030
1995-96	683	1,275
1996-97	1,366	2,848
1997-98	645	3,999
1998-99	270	4,362
1999-00	768	313
2000-01	831	3,732
2001-02	477	1,579
2002-03	600	(2,353)
2003-04	459	(1,856)
2004-05	613	5,194
2005-06	2,552	2,508
2006-07	3,776	16,103
2007-08	8,769	22,633
2008-09	1,162	8,158

Note : Negative numbers in brackets. ADR: American depository receipt; GDR: Global depository receipt; ECB: External commercial borrowing.

Source : Reserve Bank of India.

65 : Net Resources Mobilised By Mutual Funds

(Rs. crore)

Year	Unit Trust of India	Bank-Sponsored Mutual Funds	Financial Institution-Sponsored Mutual Funds	Private Sector Mutual Funds	Total
1970-71	18	-	-	-	18
1980-81	52	-	-	-	52
1990-91	4553	2,352	604	-	7,509
2000-01	322	249	1,273	9,292	11,136
2001-02	(7284)	863	406	16,134	10,119
2002-03	(9434)	1,033	861	12,122	4,582
2003-04	1050	4,526	787	41,510	47,873
2004-05	(2467)	706	(3,384)	7,933	2,788
2005-06	3424	5,365	2,112	41,581	52,482
2006-07	7326	3,033	4,226	79,477	94,063
2007-08	10678	7,786	2,178	163,356	183,998
2008-09	(4112)	4,489	5,954	(28,685)	(18,242)

Note : Negative numbers in brackets.

Source : Securities and Exchange Board of India.

66 : Working of Clearing Corporation of India Limited

	Outright		Repo		Forex		CBLO	
	Number of Trades	Volume (Rs. crore)	Number of Trades	Volume (Rs. crore)	Number of Trades	Volume (Rs. crore)	Number of Trades	Volume (Rs. crore)
2002-03*	191,843	1,076,147	11,672	468,229	100,232	136,102	159	852
2003-04	243,585	1,575,133	20,927	943,189	330,517	501,342	3,060	76,851
2004-05	160,682	1,134,222	24,364	1,557,907	466,327	899,782	29,351	976,790
2005-06	125,509	864,751	25,673	1,694,509	489,649	1,179,688	67,463	2,953,134
2006-07	137,100	1,021,536	29,008	2,556,501	606,808	1,776,981	85,881	4,732,271
2007-08	188,843	1,653,851	26,612	3,948,751	757,074	3,133,665	113,277	8,110,828
2008-09	245,964	2,160,233	24,280	4,094,286	837,520	2,758,904	118,941	8,824,784
2009-10	316,956	2,913,890	28,651	6,072,829	883,949	2,988,971	142,052	15,541,378

Note : * February 2002 to March 2003.
CCIL commenced operations from February 2002.
Forex transactions commenced from November 8, 2002. Under it cash and Tom settlement commenced from February 5, 2004. CBLO - Collateralised borrowing and lending obligation, commenced from January 20, 2003.

Source : Clearing Corporation of India.

67 : Trends in FII Investment in the Capital Market

Year	Gross Purchases (Rs. crore)	Gross Sales (Rs. crore)	Net Investment		Cumulative Net Investment ($ mn)
			Rs. crore	US $ mn.	
1992-93	17	4	13	4	4
1993-94	5,593	466	5,126	1,634	1,638
1994-95	7,631	2,835	4,796	1,528	3,167
1995-96	9,694	2,752	6,942	2,036	5,202
1996-97	15,554	6,979	8,574	2,432	7,634
1997-98	18,695	12,737	5,957	1,650	9,284
1998-99	16,115	17,699	(1,584)	(386)	8,898
1999-00	56,856	46,734	10,122	2,339	11,237
2000-01	74,051	64,116	9,935	2,159	13,396
2001-02	49,920	41,165	8,755	1,846	15,242
2002-03	47,061	44,373	2,688	562	15,804
2003-04	144,858	99,094	45,764	9,950	25,754
2004-05	216,951	171,071	45,880	10,352	36,293
2005-06	346,976	305,509	41,467	9,363	45,656
2006-07	520,506	489,665	30,841	6,821	52,477
2007-08	948,018	881,839	66,179	16,442	69,179
2008-09	614,579	660,389	(45,811)	(9,837)	59,081
2009-10	846,437	703,779	142,658	30,252	89,333

Note : FII - Foreign institutional investor.
Source : Securities and Exchange Board of India.

68 : Progress of Cash Segment in Bombay Stock Exchange

Year	No. of Companies Listed	No. of Trades (lakh)	Traded Quantity (lakh)	Turnover (Rs. crore)	Avg. Daily Turnover (Rs. crore)	Avg. Trade Size (Rs. crore)	Market Capitalisation (Rs. crore)
1992-93	2,861	126	35,031	45,696	238	3,632	188,146
2000-01	5,869	1,428	258,511	1,000,032	3,984	7,002	571,553
2001-02	5,782	1,277	182,196	307,292	1,244	24,060	612,224
2002-03	5,650	1,413	221,401	314,073	1,251	22,226	572,197
2003-04	5,528	2,028	390,441	503,053	1,981	24,806	1,201,206
2004-05	4,731	2,374	477,171	518,715	2,050	21,849	1,698,428
2005-06	4,781	2,640	664,455	816,074	3,251	30,911	3,022,190
2006-07	4,821	3,462	560,777	956,185	3,840	27,618	3,545,041
2007-08	4,887	5,303	986,010	1,578,857	6,290	29,771	5,138,014
2008-09	4,929	5,408	739,600	1,100,074	4,527	20,342	3,086,075
2009-10	4,975	6,056	1,136,513	1,378,809	5,651	22,768	6,165,619

Source : Bombay Stock Exchange.

69 : Progress of Cash Segment in National Stock Exchange

Year	No. of Companies Listed	No of Trades (lakh)	Traded Quantity (lakh)	Turnover (Rs. crore)	Avg. Daily Turnover (Rs. crore)	Avg. Trade Size (Rs. crore)	Market Capitalisation (Rs. crore)
1995-96	422	66	39,912	67,287	276	101,505	401,459
2000-01	785	1,676	329,536	1,339,510	5,337	86,980	657,847
2001-02	793	1,753	278,408	513,167	2,078	29,270	636,861
2002-03	818	2,398	364,065	617,989	2,462	25,776	537,133
2003-04	909	3,780	713,301	1,099,534	4,329	29,090	1,120,976
2004-05	970	4,508	797,685	1,140,072	4,471	25,283	1,585,585
2005-06	1,069	6,089	844,486	1,569,558	6,253	25,044	2,813,201
2006-07	1,228	7,847	855,456	1,945,287	7,812	24,790	3,367,350
2007-08	1,381	11,727	1,498,469	3,551,038	14,148	30,280	4,858,122
2008-09	1,432	13,650	1,426,355	2,752,023	11,325	20,161	2,896,194
2009-10	1,470	16,816	2,215,530	4,138,023	16,959	24,608	6,009,173

Source : National Stock Exchange.

70 : Aggregate Deposits of NBFCs

(Rs. crore)

Year (end-March)	NBFC		RNBC		Total Public Deposits
	No. of Reporting Companies	Public Deposits	No. of Reporting Companies	Public Deposits	
1998	1420	13,572	9	10,249	23,820
1999	1536	9,785	11	10,644	20,429
2000	996	8,338	9	11,004	19,342
2001	974	6,459	7	11,625	18,085
2002	905	5,933	5	12,889	18,822
2003	870	5,035	5	15,065	20,100
2004	774	4,317	3	15,327	19,644
2005	700	3,926	3	16,600	20,526
2006	432	2,447	3	20,175	22,622
2007	371	2,075	3	22,622	24,697
2008	335	2,037	2	22,358	24,395

Note : NBFC: Non-banking financial company.
RNBC : Residuary non-banking company.

Source : Reserve Bank of India.

71 : Derivative Segments at BSE and NSE

	Bombay Stock Exchange				National Stock Exchange			
			Open Interest at the End of Fiscal				Open Interest at the End of Fiscal	
	No. of Contracts	Turnover (Rs. crore)	No. of Contracts	Turnover (Rs. crore)	No. of Contracts	Turnover (Rs. crore)	No. of Contracts	Turnover (Rs. crore)
2001-02	105,527	1,922			4,196,873	101,925	93,917	2,150
2002-03	138,037	2,478	375	7	16,768,909	439,865	97,025	2,194
2003-04	382,258	12,452	35	1	56,886,776	2,130,649	235,792	7,188
2004-05	531,719	16,112	0	0	77,017,185	2,547,053	592,646	21,052
2005-06	203	9	408	13	157,619,271	4,824,250	1,028,003	38,469
2006-07	1,545,169	59,006	408	13	216,883,573	7,356,271	1,791,549	38,670
2007-08	7,453,371	242,309	3,175	74	425,013,200	13,090,478	2,282,671	48,900
2008-09	496,502	11,593	22	0	657,390,497	11,010,482	3,227,759	57,705
2009-10	9,026	234	-	-	679,293,922	17,663,665	3,489,790	97,978

Source : Securities and Exchange Board of India.

72 : Number of Joint Stock Companies and Paid-up Capital

As of March-31	Companies in Operation		Companies that Ceased Operation	
	Number	Paid-up Capital (Rs. crore)	Number	% to Operating Cos.
1951	28532	775	830	2.9
1961	26149	1819	2449	9.4
1971	30461	4423	472	1.5
1981	62714	15555	391	0.6
1991	224452	68111	173	0.1
2001	569100	341229	495	0.1
2002	589246	405753	760	0.1
2003	612155	457059	953	0.2
2004	641512	498791	498	0.1
2005	679649	654022	1777	0.3
2006	732169	619152	1380	0.2
2007	743678	649490	17818	2.4
2008	na	na	na	
2009	786774	na	32705	4.2

Note : Out of 7,86,744 companies, 1591 are government companies.
Source : Annual Report of Ministry of Company Affairs.

73 : Financial Assistance by All-India Finanical Institutions

(Rs. crore)

	Sanctions (Rs. crore)	Disbursements (Rs. crore)	Disbursement/ Sanctions (%)
1966-67	152	141	92.8
1970-71	254	160	62.9
1980-81	2927	1848	63.1
1990-91	19202	12810	66.7
2000-01	120548	75364	62.5
2001-02*	75089	58735	78.2
2002-03*	28311	26705	94.3
2003-04*	40759	30173	74.0
2004-05*	30404	21506	70.7
2005-06*	27665	21146	76.4
2006-07*	31259	38653	123.7
2007-08*	58693	46008	78.4
2008-09*	99967	88974	89.0

Note : * The adoption of the system of universal banking and the merger of institutions have produced kinks in the data series.
Source : Reserve Bank of India.

74 : Selected Performance Indicators of Corporate Sector (RBI Sample)

Ratios	Medium & Large Public Limited Companies				Public Limited Companies		
	1950-51	1960-61	1970-71	1980-81	1990-91	2000-01	2007-08
Number of Companies	750	1333	1501	1631	1802	2031	3114
Capital Structure Ratios (%)							
1. Net Fixed Assets to Total Net Assets	34.0	42.8	39.2	37.4	41.7	47.3	38.5
2. Net Worth to Total Net Assets	56.5	47.7	39.0	30.7	29.6	37.6	42.9
3. Debt to Equity	35.7	18.4	31.5	62.8	98.1	68.3	44.4
4. Debt to Equity (Adjusted)	na	na	na	na	116.6	72.4	46.2
5. Short-Term Bank Borrowings to Inventory	29.1	47.4	61.8	43.6	51.2	70.1	83.9
Liquidity Ratios (%)							
1. Current Ratio (Current assets to current liabilities)	na	1.3	1.2	1.2	1.3	1.2	1.3
2. Quick Ratio % (Quick assets to current liabilities)	na	na	na	na	48.8	48.4	53.9
3. Current Assets to Total Net Assets	na	na	na	na	53.9	43.5	48.1
4. Sundry Creditors to Current Assets	na	na	na	na	27.1	28.5	25.1
5. Sundry Creditors to Net Working Capital	na	na	na	na	115.3	178.4	114.1
Asset Utilisation Ratios (%)							
1. Sales to Total Net Assets	93.7	94.7	104.3	121.5	93.6	78	76.5
2. Sales to Gross Fixed Assets	na	na	na	na	139.3	110.8	135
3. Exports to Sales	na	na	na	na	6.2	13.6	19.4
4. Gross Value Added to Gross Fixed Assets	na	na	na	na	35	23.5	33.9

contd...

...contd...

	Medium & Large Public Limited Companies				Public Limited Companies		
	1950-51	1960-61	1970-71	1980-81	1990-91	2000-01	2007-08
Number of Companies	750	1333	1501	1631	1802	2031	3114
Turnover Ratios (%)							
1. Inventory to Sales	33.8	32.7	31.8	27.5	25.6	19.1	17.1
2. Sundry Debtors to Sales	na	na	13.5	12.3	16.4	16.1	15
3. Raw Material Consumed to Value of Production	na	51.8	50.2	51.3	49.8	53.7	54.5
4. Remuneration to Employees to Sales	na	na	na	na	9.9	7.3	7.1
Profitability Ratios (%)							
1. Gross Profit to Total Net Assets	9.0	10.0	10.6	12	10.8	7.4	11.4
2. Gross Profit to Sales	9.6	10.6	9.9	9.8	11.6	9.8	14.9
3. Profit after Tax to Net Worth	7.7	11.0	10.1	14.2	13.9	6.3	17.5
Profit Allocation Ratios (%)							
1. Tax Provision to Gross Profit					16.7	13.9	21.7
2. Tax Provision to Profit After Tax	39.5	38.6	45.9	43.8	30.6	30.4	24.8
3. Profit Retained to Profit after Tax	38.4	39.9	43.2	61.8	64.6	49.4	79.9
4. Dividend to Net Worth	4.7	6.6	5.7	5.4	4.9	3.2	3.5
5. Ordinary Dividend to Ordinary Paid-up Capital	na	12.0	10.6	12.7	18.4	13.4	30.6
6. Interest to Gross Profit	na	na	na	51.6	50.8	63.2	16.8
7. Profit Retained to Gross Profit	na	na	na	21.2	24.5	15.7	52.8

Note : na : Not available.
Number of companies indicates the number whose balance sheets have been included in this data and not the actual number of companies in existence.

Source : Reserve Bank of India.

75 : Financial Performance of Indian Corporate Sector

(Rs. crore)

	Medium & Large Public Limited Companies				Public Limited Companies		
	(1950-51)	(1960-61)	(1970-71)	(1980-81)	(1990-91)	(2000-01)	(2007-08)
Number of Companies	750	1333	1650	1651	1802	2031	3114
Sales	831	2390	6910	24544	89912	326464	1292146
Value of Production	na	2486	6910	24544	91837	328216	1316955
Operating Profits	74	218	518	1472	5124	11738	159745
Depreciation	24	96	291	732	3792	15923	45628
Gross Profits	79	255	735	2415	10407	31919	192064
Interest	6	37	218	943	5283	20181	32319
Profit Before Tax	64	218	533	1575	5697	14605	168648
Profit After Tax	39	134	310	885	3955	10159	126903
Profit Retained	15	53	165	547	2554	5021	101375
Profitability Ratios							
Operating Margin (%)	8.9	9.1	7.5	6.0	5.7	3.6	12.4
Gross Margin(%)	9.6	10.7	10.6	9.8	11.6	9.8	14.9
Net Margin(%)	4.6	5.6	4.5	3.6	4.4	3.1	9.8
Interest Cover (Times)	13.7	6.9	3.4	2.6	2.0	1.6	5.9

Note : The data given here is indicative only and not exhaustive, as the number of companies included in the study are limited;
Operating Margin is the per cent of operating profit to sales; Gross margin is the per cent of gross profit to sales; Net margin is the per cent of profit after tax to sales;
Interest cover measures the number of times gross profit can cover interest payments.

Source : Relevant issues of Reserve Bank of India Bulletin.

76 : Changing Trends in Cost Structure of Indian Corporate Sector

(Rs. crore)

	Medium & Large Public Limited Companies				Public Limited Companies		
	(1950-51)	(1960-61)	(1970-71)	(1980-81)	(1990-91)	(2000-01)	(2007-08)
Number of Companies	750	1333	1650	1651	1802	2031	3114
Sales	831	2390	6910	24544	89912	326464	1292146
Mfg. Expenses	557	1526	4426	16523	59855	219421	884048
% to Sales	*67.1*	*63.8*	*64.1*	*67.3*	*66.6*	*67.2*	*68.4*
Fuel and Power	na	na	273	1512	6775	22869	58339
% to Sales			*3.9*	*6.2*	*7.5*	*7.0*	*4.5*
Employee Costs	139	419	1042	3258	8897	23819	91956
% to Sales	*16.7*	*17.5*	*15.1*	*13.3*	*9.9*	*7.3*	*7.1*
Other Optg. Exp.	76	222	976	3352	26709	97979	398623
% to Sales	*9.1*	*9.3*	*14.1*	*13.7*	*29.7*	*30.0*	*30.8*
Depreciation	24	96	291	732	3792	15923	45628
% to Sales	*2.9*	*4.0*	*4.2*	*3.0*	*4.2*	*4.9*	*3.5*
Advertisement	na	na	na	82	589	3932	11398
% to Sales				*0.3*	*0.7*	*1.2*	*0.9*

Note : The data given here is indicative only and not exhaustive, as the number of companies included in the study are limited.
Source : Relevant issues of Reserve Bank of India Bulletin.

77 : Trend in Forex Transactions of Indian Corporate Sector

(Rs. crore)

Public Limited Companies	1982-83	1990-91	2000-01	2007-08
Number of Companies	1838	1802	2031	3114
Expenditure in Foreign Currencies	2382	8068	69025	389251
% to Total Expenditure	6.9	8.4	20.2	28.3
Imports	1980	7077	57469	316889
Imports/Sales ratio %	6.0	8.0	17.6	24.5
Raw Materials	1409	5587	47776	246233
% to Total Raw materials	8.1	12.2	27.1	34.3
Earnings in Foreign Currencies	1904	6434	57369	325169
% to Total Income	5.5	6.7	16.8	23.7
Exports	1601	5569	44281	250841
Exports/Sales%	4.8	6.3	13.6	19.4
Net Inflow(+)/Net Outflow(-)	-478	-1634	-11656	-64082

Note : The data given here is indicative only and not exhaustive, as the number of companies included in the study are limited.

Source : Reserve Bank of India.

78 : Decadal Inflationary Trends

	1. Wholesale Price Index		2. Consumer Price Index : Industrial Workers	
	Point-to-Point- March Growth	Based on Average Indices Growth	Point-to-Point- March Growth	Based on Average Indices Growth
Decadal Growth (Average Annual Increases)				
1951-60	1.7	1.7	5.0	2.3
1961-70	6.5	6.4	5.9	4.1
1971-80	9.7	9.0	8.0	7.2
1981-90	7.3	8.0	9.0	10.2
1991-00	8.6	8.1	9.4	9.5
2001-10	5.9	5.3	6.2	5.9

Note : Decadal growth is the average of annual growth rate.
Source : Office of the Economic Adviser and Labour Bureau.

79 : Inflation in India : Different Measures

Decades	Annual Averages of Inflation Rates			
	WPI (Average)	CPI-IW (Average)	GDP Deflator	PFCE Deflator
1950-51 to 1959-60	1.7	2.3	1.5	1.6
1960-61 to 1969-70	6.4	4.1	6.3	6.2
1970-71 to 1979-80	9.0	7.2	8.0	7.6
1980-81 to 1989-90	8.0	10.2	8.7	8.3
1990-91 to 1999-00	8.1	9.5	8.8	8.9
2000-01 to 2009-10	5.3	5.9	4.6	4.2

Note : PFCE: Private final consumption expenditure. WPI: Wholesale price Index; CIP-IW: Consumer price index (industrial workers); GDP: Gross domestic product.
Source : Office of the Economic Adviser and CSO.

80 : Annual Inflationary Trends

Year	1. Wholesale Price Index				2. Consumer Price Index - Industrial Workers			
	Point-to-Point- March		Based on Average Indices		Point-to-Point- March		Based on Average Indices	
	Index	Increase (%)	Index	Increase (%)	Index	Increase (%)	Index	Increase (%)
2000-01	159.1	7.1	155.7	7.2	445	2.5	444	3.7
2001-02	161.9	1.8	161.3	3.6	468	5.2	463	4.3
2002-03	171.6	6.0	166.8	3.4	487	4.1	482	4.1
2003-04	179.8	4.8	175.9	5.5	504	3.5	500	3.8
2004-05	189.4	5.3	187.3	6.5	113	3.7	520	3.9
2005-06	196.8	3.9	195.6	4.4	119	5.3	542	4.3
2006-07	209.8	6.6	206.2	5.4	127	6.7	579	6.8
2007-08	225.5	7.5	215.7	4.6	137	7.9	133	6.4
2008-09	228.2	1.2	233.9	8.4	148	8.0	145	9.0
2009-10	250.8	9.9	242.7	3.8	170	14.9	163	12.4

Note : With effect from October 17, 2009 the issue of weekly price indices on all commodities has been discontinued, instead monthly price indices are being disseminated. Hence, point-to-point values in all tables use data for March and not March 31.

Source : Office of the Economic Adviser and Labour Bureau.

81 : Changing Weights of Selected Commodities over years in Different Wholesale Price Indices

Base Year :	Aug 1939= 100	1952-53= 100	1961-62= 100	1970-71= 100	1981-82= 100	1993-94= 100
All Commodities	100.00	100.00	100.00	100.00	100.00	100.00
Primary Articles	51.72	54.04	38.78	41.67	32.30	22.03
Fuel, Power, Light & Lubricants	2.21	2.84	6.04	8.46	10.66	14.23
Manufacturing Products	46.07	39.03	55.18	49.87	57.04	63.75
Food Grains	20.77	23.48	14.78	12.92	7.92	5.01
Cereals	18.29	19.25	12.10	10.74	6.82	4.41
Rice	11.16	11.30	6.69	5.13	3.69	2.45
Wheat	3.72	5.34	3.22	3.42	2.25	1.38
Pulses	2.48	4.23	2.68	2.18	1.09	0.60
Gram	1.55	1.51	1.07	1.04	0.41	0.22
Arhar	0.93	na	0.66	0.52	0.27	0.13
Moong	na	na	0.21	0.26	0.20	0.11
Fruits & Vegetables	na	2.27	2.36	6.13	4.09	2.92
Potato	na	0.46	0.62	1.01	0.47	0.26
Onions	na	0.15	0.08	0.19	0.16	0.09
Banana	na	1.21	0.99	0.65	0.47	0.28
Milk & Milk Products	na	8.42	6.07	6.15	1.96	4.37
Milk	na	4.69	2.97	4.52	1.78	2.21
Condiments & Spices	na	2.17	1.20	1.09	0.95	0.66
Chillies	na	na	na	0.50	0.32	0.19
Tea	2.17	1.92	1.94	1.15	0.56	0.16
Sugar Group	6.82	4.79	6.49	7.24	4.06	3.93
Sugar	4.03	1.76	3.68	2.19	2.01	3.62
Gur	2.79	3.03	2.44	4.56	1.75	0.06
Edible Oils	2.72	4.69	5.37	3.72	2.45	2.76
Groundnut Oil	0.51	1.92	2.48	1.42	0.53	0.17
Rape Seed & Mustard Oil	1.19	1.31	1.03	0.67	0.28	0.49
Fibres	9.54	6.09	4.11	3.17	1.79	1.52
Raw Cotton	5.04	3.16	2.24	2.25	1.34	1.36
Oilseeds	5.40	6.01	5.26	4.20	3.86	2.67
Groundnut	2.16	2.74	2.52	1.82	1.82	1.03
Rapeseed & Mustard	0.90	1.04	0.90	0.82	1.75	0.58
Mineral Oils	2.21	1.44	3.02	4.91	6.67	6.99

Note : Weight of primary articles, fuel, power, light & lubricants and manufactured products for the years 1939, 1952-53 and 1961-62 are worked out by Economic and Political Weekly Research Foundation.

Source : Office of the Economic Adviser, (GoI).

82 : Annual Prices Increases as Measured by Wholesale Price Indices

Selected Agricultural Commodities and Mineral Oil

(Based on Fiscal Year Averages) (%)

Commodities	2000-01	2001-02	2002-03	2003-04	2004-05	2005-06	2006-07	2007-08	2008-09	2009-10
All Commodities	7.2	3.6	3.4	5.5	6.5	4.4	5.4	4.6	8.4	3.8
Foodgrain	(1.5)	(0.8)	1.1	1.1	0.7	5.4	10.2	4.6	8.6	11.9
Cereals	(2.7)	(1.7)	2.0	1.6	0.9	4.4	7.3	6.2	8.9	5.7
Rice	(2.2)	(0.3)	(0.6)	1.7	(0.4)	3.7	2.9	6.7	11.1	24.5
Wheat	1.1	(0.7)	0.2	3.2	1.5	4.0	13.1	4.2	6.2	39.6
Pulses	8.1	5.3	(4.5)	(2.2)	(1.2)	11.8	30.4	(4.4)	6.9	(20.8)
Gram	20.6	22.3	(12.1)	(4.8)	(3.8)	14.5	32.9	(4.2)	4.7	66.8
Arhar	(14.7)	(5.1)	10.4	9.7	3.8	(4.7)	6.6	14.0	10.2	84.0
Moong	3.5	10.0	1.2	(5.8)	(4.3)	17.0	38.2	(11.8)	7.3	(0.1)
Fruits & Vegetables	3.6	18.1	0.7	2.8	4.4	7.2	4.2	3.5	8.2	34.2
Potato	(9.9)	134.6	(4.3)	(41.4)	52.4	17.6	17.7	9.4	(16.1)	31.5
Onion	(18.9)	15.7	5.2	30.2	(19.3)	23.9	(5.2)	45.1	(0.2)	17.3
Banana	3.5	14.3	8.2	7.3	6.4	12.0	0.6	6.0	15.0	(3.0)
Milk	10.6	1.8	3.3	2.5	4.3	0.4	6.3	8.4	7.5	39.9
Condiments & Spices	(10.6)	(7.1)	3.1	5.7	(8.2)	(6.1)	29.2	5.0	11.7	73.5
Dry Chillies	(16.8)	(1.8)	1.6	15.9	(23.2)	(5.5)	61.7	0.6	21.7	(48.7)

contd...

...contd...

Selected Agricultural Commodities and Mineral Oil

Based on Fiscal Year Averages (%)

Commodities	2000-01	2001-02	2002-03	2003-04	2004-05	2005-06	2006-07	2007-08	2008-09	2009-10
Tea	(15.3)	(8.8)	0.5	(8.0)	20.9	(10.8)	18.8	(6.3)	43.4	17.2
Sugar Group	(1.8)	(4.6)	(7.9)	3.5	17.2	9.5	0.6	(13.7)	8.7	38.2
Sugar	3.8	(5.0)	(8.8)	0.7	19.1	10.7	0.5	(13.5)	12.4	76.2
Gur	(0.6)	6.7	(7.0)	(4.8)	41.7	11.3	(3.7)	(8.1)	20.4	(13.7)
Edible Oils	(15.4)	9.3	22.2	14.4	(0.9)	(6.6)	5.9	13.3	7.4	11.2
Groundnut Oil	(6.2)	5.2	22.7	8.8	(4.1)	(3.2)	12.8	22.1	(1.8)	(4.7)
Rapeseed & Mustard Oil	(20.0)	8.0	21.6	31.6	(8.7)	(9.8)	3.7	17.1	19.8	(100.0)
Fibres	8.1	(3.4)	(5.0)	23.6	(6.1)	(10.3)	4.1	14.9	21.3	0.3
Raw Cotton	6.8	(5.5)	(4.4)	27.1	(8.3)	(12.9)	5.1	17.4	23.6	15.7
Oilseeds	(3.1)	6.4	16.4	11.0	1.7	(7.6)	5.1	23.9	13.0	6.9
Groundnut	(0.1)	2.9	18.1	6.7	0.8	(5.5)	10.5	26.0	4.1	(2.7)
Rapeseed & Mustard	(14.9)	7.4	13.1	28.6	(6.5)	(4.4)	4.5	18.4	23.6	64.6
Mineral Oils	41.5	5.9	6.3	7.7	15.1	13.9	7.9	0.9	11.1	(44.3)

Note: Negative values in brackets.
Source: Office of the Economic Adviser.

83 : Average Annual Inflation as Measured by Wholesale Price Indices : Decadal Rates

Selected Agricultural Commodities and Mineral Oil (Based on Fiscal Year Average) (%)

Commodities	1950-51 1959-60	1960-61 1969-70	1970-71 1979-80	1980-81 1989-90	1990-91 1999-00	2000-01 2009-10
All Commodities	1.7	6.4	9.0	8.0	8.1	5.3
Foodgrain	0.8	8.0	7.2	8.8	10.9	4.1
Cereals	0.7	7.4	6.5	7.7	11.1	3.3
Rice	1.4	7.3	7.2	8.0	10.6	4.7
Wheat	0.0	7.9	6.3	7.0	11.7	7.2
Pulses	2.6	11.2	11.2	12.7	9.8	2.9
Gram	2.3	14.6	10.4	17.8	8.9	13.7
Arhar	4.5	9.6	13.8	10.5	12.8	11.4
Moong	3.1	8.6	13.8	10.4	10.1	5.5
Fruits & Vegetables	12.1	7.7	8.4	10.3	10.7	8.7
Potato	3.0	7.0	7.4	17.6	19.4	19.2
Onion	12.1	13.8	18.9	12.1	22.7	9.4
Banana	2.5	8.2	7.4	10.0	8.1	7.0
Milk	2.3	8.2	6.4	9.3	7.5	8.5
Condiments & Spices	2.5	13.9	5.9	14.3	17.3	9.6
Dry Chillies	5.7	20.4	7.8	28.5	23.7	0.5
Tea	5.7	1.4	10.7	8.7	7.6	5.2
Sugar Group	2.7	6.4	11.1	8.8	9.8	5.0
Sugar	2.0	5.7	6.5	7.7	7.4	9.6
Gur	3.0	11.5	13.7	9.7	9.4	4.2
Edible Oils	0.9	10.5	9.8	10.1	6.4	6.1
Groundnut Oil	2.0	12.0	9.9	10.3	7.6	5.9
Rapeseed & Mustard Oil	1.4	10.8	12.1	9.4	10.5	-4.4
Fibres	1.9	7.1	7.9	9.3	9.9	4.7
Raw Cotton	0.9	5.9	9.6	9.5	12.0	6.5
Oilseeds	2.3	10.1	9.6	9.4	7.8	7.4
Groundnut	3.5	10.2	9.5	10.1	8.2	6.1
Rapeseed & Mustard	1.1	9.7	11.4	9.0	9.9	13.4
Mineral Oils	2.4	4.6	13.9	9.0	10.8	6.6

Note: Decadal growth is average of annual growth rate.
Source: Office of the Economic Adviser.

84 : Annual Inflation as Measured by Wholesale Price Indices

Selected Agricultural Commodities and Mineral Oil

(Point-to-Point Basis : March over March) (%)

Commodities	2000-01	2001-02	2002-03	2003-04	2004-05	2005-06	2006-07	2007-08	2008-09	2009-10(RE)
All Commodities	6.4	1.8	6.0	4.8	5.3	3.9	6.6	7.5	1.2	9.9
Foodgrain	(3.1)	0.5	3.9	(1.1)	2.6	8.3	8.4	5.3	11.6	13.5
Cereals	(4.8)	1.0	4.5	(1.0)	3.3	5.6	7.4	6.5	11.7	10.7
Rice	(0.9)	(2.1)	4.2	(2.3)	3.5	1.9	5.8	8.3	16.7	8.0
Wheat	(4.6)	3.7	0.8	4.8	(0.7)	11.9	7.2	4.0	4.6	14.4
Pulses	9.2	(1.8)	(1.1)	(1.6)	(2.5)	28.7	15.3	(2.2)	10.8	31.4
Gram	24.4	6.4	(10.0)	(3.6)	(0.9)	25.3	18.0	5.8	(5.0)	(3.9)
Arhar	(13.8)	(4.7)	20.8	6.9	(7.5)	6.3	10.7	15.2	16.2	39.2
Moong	8.2	5.6	0.7	(10.7)	2.2	36.4	19.4	(16.8)	20.1	67.2
Fruits & Vegetables	7.4	13.3	(0.6)	(5.1)	13.5	(0.9)	15.3	6.2	2.0	7.8
Potato	40.1	78.8	(38.8)	(1.9)	40.4	37.2	(2.1)	18.9	(10.7)	(4.0)
Onion	37.0	(10.3)	4.9	53.3	(27.4)	(3.7)	87.1	(21.9)	71.6	(11.0)
Banana	6.6	11.5	13.0	5.8	9.2	1.0	4.4	14.8	4.1	10.3
Milk	0.9	3.7	2.1	7.0	(0.5)	2.0	7.6	9.1	7.4	17.6
Condiments & Spices	(13.3)	(0.3)	7.5	1.1	(12.8)	6.7	23.4	4.2	13.8	25.7
Dry Chillies	(8.4)	(1.6)	10.6	0.0	(24.4)	23.7	35.6	1.1	38.8	(3.6)

contd...

...contd...

Selected Agricultural Commodities and Mineral Oil

(Point-to-Point Basis : March over March) (%)

Commodities	2000-01	2001-02	2002-03	2003-04	2004-05	2005-06	2006-07	2007-08	2008-09	2009-10(RE)
Tea	14.1	(24.9)	23.2	(10.0)	13.5	(0.4)	8.0	7.2	25.3	0.1
Sugar Group	7.4	(17.1)	26.1	13.1	(20.2)	0.6	8.6	20.1	1.6	20.1
Sugar	7.9	(20.5)	33.9	13.3	(24.8)	0.2	12.8	21.5	1.9	17.5
Gur	1.1	7.7	27.8	1.9	(6.2)	(9.1)	29.9	22.4	(3.1)	9.8
Edible Oils	0.7	4.7	34.1	(5.2)	(7.2)	(7.6)	43.3	9.1	(3.8)	16.0
Groundnut Oil	(6.5)	8.9	22.7	17.0	(13.0)	0.2	16.6	32.0	(4.9)	4.0
Rapeseed & Mustard Oil	31.2	2.6	15.0	1.3	15.8	13.1	1.0	9.4	(8.6)	17.0
Fibres	(6.5)	(2.5)	(11.3)	16.1	18.4	6.2	(11.8)	(5.8)	22.5	46.2
Raw Cotton	(1.4)	(2.9)	(14.7)	17.0	20.5	6.8	(13.1)	(1.6)	22.7	48.8
Oilseeds	(1.7)	4.6	(8.3)	16.0	31.9	2.7	(3.6)	2.6	37.2	24.6
Groundnut	(6.9)	14.3	25.7	8.3	(7.7)	(3.5)	13.8	19.9	(8.9)	(1.6)
Rapeseed & Mustard	(12.5)	15.7	40.5	(10.4)	(4.9)	(2.5)	33.8	11.4	(12.7)	(5.0)
Mineral Oils	(2.2)	0.8	39.3	19.0	(16.5)	(5.4)	13.4	31.4	(3.0)	8.3

Note : RE: Revised Estimates; Negative values in brackets.
Source : Office of the Economic Adviser.

85 : Average Price of Gold and Silver : India and International

Year	Gold				Silver			
	Mumbai	London		Difference in Prices (Rs.)	Mumbai	New York		Difference in Prices (Rs.)
	Rs. per 10 gms	$ per Troy oz	In Re. Terms/10 gms		Rs. per kg	Cents per Troy oz	In Re. Terms/kg	
1950-51	97.3	..	..		159.4	..	..	..
1960-61	114.9	..	..	..	193.6	..	..	..
1970-71	185.0	36.8	89.4	95.5	536.1	170.8	415.0	121.1
1980-81	1522.4	584.9	1484.7	37.8	2617.6	1585.1	4020.3	-1402.7
1990-91	3451.5	374.7	2164.3	1287.3	6760.8	449.9	2579.2	4181.6
2000-01	4473.6	272.1	4007.8	465.8	7868.4	483.6	7098.2	773.7
2001-02	4579.1	277.7	4260.2	318.9	7447.2	437.3	6708.0	739.2
2002-03	5332.4	325.5	5062.1	270.3	7990.5	467.2	7271.8	718.7
2003-04	5719.0	377.7	5573.5	145.4	8721.9	541.6	7987.0	734.7
2004-05	6145.4	414.0	5976.1	169.2	10680.8	676.2	9761.8	919.0
2005-06	6900.6	476.6	6790.3	110.3	11828.8	801.2	11418.8	410.1
2006-07	9240.3	628.4	9137.8	102.5	19056.6	1247.7	18133.2	923.4
2007-08(RE)	9995.6	765.8	9897.1	98.5	19427.5	1449.0	18742.6	684.9
2008-09(BE)	12889.7	867.2	12876.7	13.1	21247.6	1375.0	20080.3	1167.2

Note: RE: Revised Estimates; BE: Budget Estimates.

Source : Reserve Bank of India.

86 : Receipt Budget of Centre

(Rs. crore)

Year	Revenue Receipts (Net)	Capital Receipts	Total Receipts	Growth (%)			Total Receipts as % of GDP
				Revenue	Capital	Total	
1950-51	406	106	512				5.1
1960-61*	877	1,156	2,033	8.0	27.0	14.8	11.7
1970-71*	3,293	2,046	5,339	14.1	5.9	10.1	11.5
1980-81*	12,373	7,918	20,291	14.2	14.5	14.3	14.0
1990-91*	54,954	38,997	93,951	16.1	17.3	16.6	16.5
2000-01*	192,605	134,184	326,789	13.4	13.2	13.3	15.5
2001-02	201,306	162,500	363,806	4.5	21.1	11.3	16.0
2002-03	230,834	180,531	411,365	14.7	11.1	13.1	16.8
2003-04	263,813	211,333	475,146	14.3	17.1	15.5	17.2
2004-05	305,991	200,391	506,382	16.0	-5.2	6.6	15.6
2005-06	347,077	179,549	526,626	13.4	-10.4	4.0	14.2
2006-07	434,387	144,482	578,869	25.2	-19.5	9.9	13.5
2007-08	541,864	197,978	739,842	24.7	37.0	27.8	15.0
2008-09	540,259	299,863	839,935	-0.3	51.5	13.5	15.1
2009-10(RE)	577,294	449,833	1,027,127	6.9	50.0	22.3	16.7
2010-11(BE)	682,212	426,537	1,108,749	18.2	-5.2	7.9	16.0

Note : RE: Revised Estimates
BE: Budget Estimates
* Decadal growth in CAGR %, annual growth from year 2001-02.
1. Data for 2009-10 from revised estimates and 2010-11 from budget estimates.
2. Tax revenue, direct tax and indirect tax are the net of state governments' share and amount assigned to National Calamity Contingency Fund (NCCF).
3. Capital Receipts and total receipts of 2007 include an amount of Rs. 34,309 crore which represents the Reserve Bank's surplus transferred to the Central government on account of transfer of its stake in SBI to the Central government.
4. The taxes and duties referred to in the Union list are now distributed in the same manner as laid down by the Constitution (Eightieth Amendment) Act, 2000 read along with the recommendations of the Twelfth Finance Commission.
5. GDP data upto 2004-05 pertains to 1993-94 series thereafter to the 2004-05 series.

Source : *Handbook of Statistics on the Indian Economy* (Reserve Bank of India, 2009); *Report on Currency and Finance 1970-71* and budget document (2010-11).

87 : Trends in Gross Tax Revenue of Centre

(Rs. crore)

Year		of which:				
	Gross Tax Revenue	Corporate Tax	Taxes on Income other than Corporation Tax	Union Excise Duties	Customs Duty	Service Tax
1950-51	405	41	133	157	68	0
(%)	100.0	10.1	32.8	38.8	16.8	0.0
1960-61	895	111	167	170	416	0
(%)	100.0	12.4	18.7	19.0	46.5	0.0
1970-71	3206	371	473	524	1759	0
(%)	100.0	11.6	14.8	16.3	54.9	0.0
1980-81	13179	1311	1506	3410	6500	0
(%)	100.0	9.9	11.4	25.9	49.3	0.0
1990-91	57577	5335	5371	20644	24514	0
(%)	100.0	9.3	9.3	35.9	42.6	0.0
2000-01	188605	35696	31764	47542	68526	2613
(%)	100.0	18.9	16.8	25.2	36.3	1.4
2001-02	187060	36609	32004	40268	72555	3302
(%)	100.0	19.6	17.1	21.5	38.8	1.8
2002-03	216266	46172	36866	44852	82310	4122
(%)	100.0	21.3	17.0	20.7	38.1	1.9
2003-04	254348	63562	41387	48629	90774	7891
(%)	100.0	25.0	16.3	19.1	35.7	3.1

contd...

...contd...

Year	Gross Tax Revenue	*of which:* Corporate Tax	Taxes on Income other than Corporation Tax	Union Excise Duties	Customs Duty	Service Tax
2004-05	304958	82680	49268	57611	99125	14200
(%)	100.0	27.1	16.2	18.9	32.5	4.7
2005-06	366151	101277	55985	65067	111226	23055
(%)	100.0	27.7	15.3	17.8	30.4	6.3
2006-07	473512	144318	75093	86327	117613	37598
(%)	100.0	30.5	15.9	18.2	24.8	7.9
2007-08	593147	192911	102644	104119	123611	51301
(%)	100.0	32.5	17.3	17.6	20.8	8.6
2008-09	605298	213395	106046	99879	108613	60941
(%)	100.0	35.3	17.5	16.5	17.9	10.1
2009-10RE	633095	255076	125021	84477	102000	58000
(%)	100.0	40.3	19.7	13.3	16.1	9.2
2010-11BE	746651	301331	120566	115000	132000	68000
(%)	100.0	40.4	16.1	15.4	17.7	9.1

Note: Lines below each year capture breakup of Gross Tax Revenue in %; BE: Budget Estimates RE : Revised Estimates.

Source: Budget Documents.

88 : Trends in Tax Revenue of Centre

Year	Gross Tax Revenue (Rs. crore)	Tax/ GDP (%)	States' Share (Rs. crore)	NCCF expenditure (Rs. crore)	Net Tax Revenues (Rs. crore)	Non-Tax Revenues (Rs. crore)	Revenue Receipts (Rs. crore)
1950-51	405	4.02	48		357	49	406
1960-61	895	5.14	179		730	147	877
1970-71	3,206	6.93	755		2,451	891	3293
1980-81	13,179	9.07	3,791		9,388	3,442	12,373
1990-91	57,577	10.11	14,598		43,042	11,976	54,954
2000-01	188,605	8.97	51,688		136,658	55,947	192,605
2001-02	187,060	8.21	52,842	686	133,532	67,774	201,306
2002-03	216,266	8.81	56,122	1,600	158,544	72,290	230,834
2003-04	254,348	9.23	65,766	1,600	186,982	76,831	263,813
2004-05	304,958	9.41	78,595	1,565	224,798	81,193	305,991
2005-06	366,151	9.88	94,385	2,825	268,941	76,813	347,077
2006-07	473,512	11.05	120,330	2,000	351,182	83,205	434,387
2007-08	593,147	11.99	151,800	1,800	439,547	102,317	541,864
2008-09	605,298	10.86	160,179	1,800	443,319	96,940	540,259
2009-10 RE	633,095	10.27	164,832	3,160	465,103	112,191	577,294
2010-11 BE	746,651	10.77	208,997	3,560	534,094	148,118	682,212

Note : RE: Revised Estimates; BE: Budget Estimates.
NCCF: National Calamity Contingency Fund. GDP data upto 2004-05 pertains to 1993-94 series thereafter to the 2004-05 series.

Source : *Handbook of Statistics on the Indian Economy* (Reserve Bank of India, 2009); *Report on Currency and Finance 1970-71* and Budget Document (2010-11).

89 : Trends in Non-Tax Revenue of Centre

(Rs. crore)

Year	Non-Tax Revenue	% to Gross Tax Revenue	% to GDP	Interest Receipt	Profit & Dividend	Others
1950-51	49	12.1	0.49	0	23	26
1960-61	147	16.8	0.84	15	53	9
1970-71	891	27.1	1.93	575	121	195
1980-81	3,442	27.8	2.37	1,795	292	1,355
1990-91	11,976	21.8	2.10	8,730	774	2,472
2000-01	55,947	29.0	2.66	33,895	9,553	9,763
2001-02	67,774	33.7	2.97	35,538	17,290	14,946
2002-03	72,290	31.3	2.95	37,622	21,230	13,438
2003-04	76,831	29.1	2.79	38,538	21,160	17,133
2004-05	81,193	26.5	2.51	32,387	22,939	25,867
2005-06	76,813	22.1	2.07	22,032	25,451	29,330
2006-07	83,205	19.2	1.94	22,524	29,309	31,372
2007-08	102,317	18.9	2.07	21,060	34,499	46,758
2008-09	96,940	17.9	1.74	20,717	38,607	37,616
2009-10 RE	112,191	19.4	1.82	19,212	51,983	40,996
2010-11 BE	148,118	21.7	2.14	19,252	51,309	77,557

Note : RE: Revised Estimates; BE: Budget Estimates. GDP data upto 2004-05 pertains to 1993-94 series thereafter to the 2004-05 series.
Source : Budget Documents.

90 : Capital Receipts of Centre

(Rs. crore)

Year	Market Borrowings (Net)	Small Savings PF, Special Deposit	Recovery of Loans	Disinvestment Receipts	External Loans (Net)	Other Capital Receipts	Total Capital Receipts	% of GDP
1950-51	30	60	10	nr	8		106	1.05
1960-61	181	344	126	nr	505		1156	6.64
1970-71	238	275	923	nr	332	278	2046	4.42
1980-81	2,679	1,997	2,096	nr	1,281	-135	7,918	5.45
1990-91	8,001	18,027	5,712	nr	3,181	4,076	38,997	6.85
2000-01	73,431	21,690	12,046	2,125	7,505	17,387	134,184	6.38
2001-02	87,724	20,998	16,403	3,646	5,601	28,128	162,500	7.13
2002-03	97,588	13,947	34,191	3,151	-11,934	43,588	180,531	7.35
2003-04	88,860	5,002	67,165	16,953	-13,488	46,841	211,333	7.67
2004-05	46,031	-440	62,043	4,424	14,753	73,580	200,391	6.19
2005-06	95,374	6,032	10,645	1,581	7,472	58,445	179,549	4.84
2006-07	110,446	5,178	5,893	534	8,472	13,959	144,482	3.37
2007-08	131,768	-7,405	5,100	38,795	9,315	20,405	197,978	4.00
2008-09	233,630	6,739	6,139	566	11,015	41,774	299,863	5.38
2009-10 RE	398,411	21,756	4,254	25,958	16,535	-17,081	449,833	7.30
2010-11 BE	345,010	20,256	5,129	40,000	22,464	-6,321	426,537	6.15

Note : RE: Revised Estimates; BE: Budget Estimates.
n r : not relevant. GDP data upto 2004-05 pertains to 1993-94 series thereafter to the 2004-05 series. PF - Provident fund.

Source : Budget Documents.

91 : Central Government Total Expenditure

(Rs. crore)

Year	Revenue Expenditure		Capital Expenditure		Total Expenditure		
	Rs. crore	% to GDP	Rs. crore	% to GDP	Rs. crore	Growth (%)	% to GDP
1950-51	346	3.4	184	1.8	530		5.3
1960-61*	826	4.7	1,029	5.9	1,855	13.3	10.7
1970-71*	3,130	6.8	2,494	5.4	5,624	11.7	12.2
1980-81*	14,410	9.9	8,358	5.7	22,768	15.0	15.7
1990-91*	73,516	12.9	31,782	5.6	105,298	16.5	18.5
2000-01*	277,839	13.2	47,753	2.3	325,592	12.0	15.5
2001-02	301,468	13.2	60,842	2.7	362,310	11.3	15.9
2002-03	338,713	13.8	74,535	3.0	413,248	14.1	16.8
2003-04	362,074	13.1	109,129	4.0	471,203	14.0	17.1
2004-05	384,329	11.9	113,923	3.5	498,252	5.7	15.4
2005-06	439,376	11.9	66,362	1.8	505,738	1.5	13.6
2006-07	514,609	12.0	68,778	1.6	583,387	15.4	13.6
2007-08	594,433	12.0	118,238	2.4	712,671	22.2	14.4
2008-09	793,798	14.2	90,158	1.6	883,956	24.0	15.9
2009-10(RE)	906,355	14.7	115,192	1.9	1,021,547	15.6	16.6
2010-11(BE)	958,724	13.9	150,025	2.2	1,108,749	8.5	16.1

Note : RE: Revised Estimates; BE: Budget Estimates.

* Growth from 1960-61 to 2000-01 refers to CAGR % over decade, thereafter annual growth. GDP data upto 2004-05 pertains to 1993-94 series thereafter to the 2004-05 series.

Source : Budget Documents.

92 : Selected Heads of Expenditure

Year	Centre's Expenditure (Rs. crore)	Defence		Interest Payments		Subsidies	
		Rs. crore	% to Total	Rs. crore	% to Total	Rs. crore	% to Total
1950-51	530	168	31.7	37	7.0		
1960-61	1855	281	15.1	77	4.2		
1970-71	5624	1206	21.4	606	10.8	94	1.7
1980-81	22768	3604	15.8	2604	11.4	2028	8.9
1990-91	105298	15426	14.6	21498	20.4	12158	11.5
2000-01	325592	49622	15.2	99314	30.5	26839	8.2
2001-02	362310	24266	6.7	107460	29.7	31210	8.6
2002-03	413248	55662	13.5	117804	28.5	43533	10.5
2003-04	471203	60066	12.7	124088	26.3	44323	9.4
2004-05	498252	75856	15.2	126934	25.5	45957	9.2
2005-06	505738	80549	15.9	132630	26.2	47522	9.4
2006-07	583387	85510	14.7	150272	25.8	57125	9.8
2007-08	712671	91681	12.9	171030	24.0	70926	10.0
2008-09	883956	114223	12.9	192204	21.7	129708	14.7
2009-10(RE)	1021547	136264	13.3	219500	21.5	131025	12.8
2010-11(BE)	1108749	147344	13.3	248664	22.4	116224	10.5

Note : RE: Revised Estimates; BE: Budget Estimates.
% to Total = per cent to total expenditure.

Source : Budget Documents.

93 : Major Deficit Indicators of Centre

(Rs. crore)

Year	Revenue Deficit		Fiscal Deficit		Primary Deficit		Net RBI Credit to Centre
		% to GDP		% to GDP		% to GDP	Annual Variations
1951-52	(126)	(1.2)		0.0		0.0	
1960-61	(50)	(0.3)		0.0		0.0	
1970-71	(163)	(0.4)	1,408	3.0	803	1.7	376.0
1980-81	2,037	1.4	8,299	5.7	5,695	3.9	3551.0
1990-91	18,561	3.3	44,632	7.8	23,134	4.1	14746.0
2000-01	85,234	4.1	118,816	5.7	19,502	0.9	6705.0
2001-02	100,162	4.4	140,955	6.2	33,495	1.5	(5150.0)
2002-03	107,879	4.4	145,072	5.9	27,268	1.1	(28399.0)
2003-04	98,262	3.6	123,273	4.5	(815)	(0.0)	(76065.0)
2004-05	78,338	2.4	125,794	3.9	(1,140)	(0.0)	(60177.0)
2005-06	92,300	2.5	146,435	4.0	13,805	0.4	28417.0
2006-07	80,222	1.9	142,573	3.3	(7,699)	(0.2)	(3024.0)
2007-08	52,569	1.1	126,912	2.6	(44,118)	(0.9)	(116772.0)
2008-09	253,539	4.5	336,991	6.0	144,788	2.6	174789.0
2009-10(RE)	329,061	5.3	414,040	6.7	194,540	3.2	158638.0
2010-11(BE)	276,512	4.0	381,409	5.5	132,745	1.9	

Note : RE: Revised Estimates; BE: Budget Estimates.
Numbers in brackets indicate negative values or a surplus in the deficit indicators. GDP data upto 2004-05 pertains to 1993-94 series thereafter to the 2004-05 series.

Source : Budget Documents.

94 : Financing Gross Fiscal Deficit (GFD)

(Rs. crore)

Year	GFD (Rs. crore)	Financing of GFD				
		External Finance (Rs. crore)	Internal Finance			
			Market Borrowings (Rs. crore)	% to GFD	Other Borrowings (Rs. crore)	Draw Down on Cash Balances Rs. crore
1980-81	8,299	1,281	2,679	32.3	1,862	2,477
1990-91	44,632	3,181	8,001	17.9	22,103	11,347
1991-92	36,325	5,421	7,510	20.7	16,539	6,855
1992-93	40,173	5,319	3,676	9.2	18,866	12,312
1993-94	60,257	5,074	28,928	48.0	15,295	10,960
1994-95	57,703	3,582	20,326	35.2	32,834	961
1995-96	60,243	318	34,001	56.4	16,117	9,807
1996-97	66,733	2,987	19,093	28.6	31,469	13,184
1997-98	88,937	1,091	32,499	36.5	56,257	(910)
1998-99	113,349	1,920	68,988	60.9	42,650	(209)
1999-00	104,716	1,180	62,076	59.3	40,597	864
2000-01	118,816	7,505	73,431	61.8	39,077	(1,197)
2001-02	140,955	5,601	90,812	64.4	46,038	(1,496)
2002-03	145,072	(11,934)	104,126	71.8	50,997	1,883

contd...

...*contd*... (Rs. crore)

Year	GFD (Rs. crore)	Financing of GFD				
		External Finance (Rs. crore)	Internal Finance			
			Market Borrowings (Rs. crore)	% to GFD	Other Borrowings (Rs. crore)	Draw Down on Cash Balances (Rs. crore)
2003-04	123,273	(13,488)	88,870	72.1	51,833	(3,942)
2004-05	125,794	14,753	50,940	40.5	68,231	(8,130)
2005-06	146,435	7,472	106,241	72.6	53,610	(20,888)
2006-07	142,573	8,472	114,801	80.5	14,782	4,518
2007-08	126,912	9,315	130,600	102.9	(39,597)	26,594
2008-09	336,991	11,015	233,630	69.3	39,751	52,596
2009-10 (RE)	414,040	16,535	398,411	96.2	4,675	(5,581)
2010-11 (BE)	381,409	22,464	345,010	90.5	13,935	

Note : 1) RE: Revised Estimates; BE: Budget Estimates.
2) Market borrowings include dated securities and 364-day treasury bills.
3) Other borrowings comprise small savings, state provident fund, special deposits, reserve funds, treasury bills excluding 364-day treasury bills, etc.
4) Market borrowings of 2004-05, 2005-06, 2006-07 and 2007-2008 exclude amounts raised under market stabilisation scheme.

Source : Budget Documents.

95 : Total Liabilities of Centre

(Rs. crore)

Year	Internal Liabilities		External Liabilities		Total Liabilities	
		% GDP		% GDP		% GDP
1950-51	2,833	28.1	32	0.3	2,865	28.4
1960-61	5,784	33.2	761	4.4	6,244	35.9
1970-71	13,379	28.9	6,485	14.0	19,864	43.0
1980-81	48,451	33.3	11,298	7.8	59,749	41.1
1990-91	283,033	49.7	31,525	5.5	314,558	55.2
1991-92	317,714	55.8	36,948	6.5	354,662	62.3
1992-93	359,655	54.9	42,269	6.5	401,924	61.4
1993-94	430,623	57.2	47,345	6.3	477,968	63.5
1994-95	487,682	56.3	50,929	5.9	538,611	62.2
1995-96	554,983	54.6	51,249	5.0	606,232	59.7
1996-97	621,437	52.1	54,239	4.6	675,676	56.7
1997-98	722,962	52.4	55,332	4.0	778,294	56.5
1998-99	834,552	54.6	57,254	3.7	891,806	58.4
1999-00	962,592	55.0	58,437	3.3	1,021,029	58.3
2000-01	1,102,596	56.5	65,945	3.4	1,168,541	59.9
2001-02	1,294,862	56.8	71,546	3.1	1,366,408	60.0
2002-03	1,499,589	61.1	59,612	2.4	1,559,201	63.5
2003-04	1,690,554	61.4	46,124	1.7	1,736,678	63.0
2004-05	1,933,544	59.7	60,877	1.9	1,994,421	61.6
2005-06	2,165,902	58.4	94,243	2.5	2,260,145	61.0
2006-07	2,435,880	56.9	102,716	2.4	2,538,596	59.3
2007-08	2,725,394	55.1	112,031	2.3	2,837,426	57.3
2008-09	3,036,132	54.5	123,046	2.2	3,159,178	56.7
2009-10(RE)	3,376,325	54.8	139,581	2.3	3,515,906	57.0
2010-11(BE)	3,782,553	54.8	162,045	2.3	3,944,598	57.1

Note : RE: Revised Estimates; BE: Budget Estimates.
GDP data upto 2004-05 pertains to 1993-94 series thereafter to the 2004-2005 series.

Source : Reserve Bank of India and Budget Documents.

96 : Components of Centre's Internal Liabilities

(Rs. crore)

Year	Internal Debt		Small Savings & PF		Other Liabilities	
		% to GDP		% to GDP		% to GDP
1950-51	2,022	20.0	337	3.3	474	4.7
1960-61	3,975	22.8	973	5.6	835	4.8
1970-71	7,663	16.6	3,050	6.6	2,666	5.8
1980-81	30,864	21.2	10,621	7.3	6,966	4.8
1990-91	154,004	27.0	61,771	10.8	67,258	11.8
1991-92	172,750	30.3	69,682	12.2	75,282	13.2
1992-93	199,100	30.4	77,005	11.8	83,550	12.8
1993-94	245,712	32.6	87,877	11.7	97,034	12.9
1994-95	266,467	30.8	106,435	12.3	114,780	13.3
1995-96	307,869	30.3	121,425	12.0	125,690	12.4
1996-97	344,476	28.9	138,955	11.7	138,007	11.6
1997-98	388,998	28.2	167,780	12.2	166,184	12.1
1998-99	459,696	30.1	206,458	13.5	168,397	11.0
1999-00	714,254	40.8	66,406	3.8	181,933	10.4
2000-01	803,698	41.2	96,343	4.9	202,555	10.4
2001-02	913,061	40.1	144,511	6.3	237,290	10.4
2002-03	1,020,689	41.6	226,400	9.2	252,500	10.3
2003-04	1,141,706	41.4	288,378	10.5	260,470	9.5
2004-05	1,275,971	39.4	390,477	12.1	267,096	8.2
2005-06	1,389,758	37.5	479,761	12.9	296,383	8.0
2006-07	1,544,975	36.1	539,450	12.6	351,455	8.2
2007-08	1,808,359	36.5	553,620	11.2	363,416	7.3
2008-09	2,028,549	36.4	556,723	10.0	454,065	8.1
2009-10(RE)	2,337,682	37.9	565,212	9.2	473,431	7.7
2010-11(BE)	2,736,754	39.6	574,805	(8.3)	470,995	6.8

Note : RE: Revised Estimates; BE: Budget Estimates.
Other liabilities include others and reserve fund and deposits.
PF - Provident fund.
GDP data upto 2004-05 pertains to 1993-94 series thereafter to the 2004-2005 series.

Source : Reserve Bank of India and Budget Documents.

97 : Receipts of State Governments

(Rs. crore)

Year	Total Revenue Receipts	Tax Receipts	Non-Tax Receipts	Total Capital Receipts	Total Receipts	% to GDP
1951-52	396	281	115	135	531	5.3
1960-61	1,012	625	387	580	1,592	9.1
1970-71	3,371	2,284	1,087	1,662	5,033	10.9
1980-81	16,294	10,405	5,888	5,473	21,767	15.0
1990-91	66,467	44,586	21,881	24,693	91,160	16.0
2000-01	232,509	164,314	68,195	109,705	342,214	16.3
2001-02	249,422	175,415	74,007	115,714	365,136	16.0
2002-03	273,674	193,474	80,200	140,866	414,539	16.9
2003-04	309,187	221,117	88,074	205,641	514,828	18.7
2004-05	363,512	260,577	102,935	200,148	563,660	17.4
2005-06	431,021	306,332	124,690	164,607	595,628	16.1
2006-07	530,556	372,841	157,714	142,802	673,358	15.7
2007-08	623,748	437,948	185,799	141,987	765,735	15.5
2008-09 RE	737,865	503,878	233,987	186,201	924,066	16.6
2009-10 BE	804,943	552,243	252,700	225,114	1,030,057	16.7

Note : 2008-09 numbers are revised estimates and 2009-10 budget estimates.
Source : Reserve Bank of India study on State Finances.

98 : Components of State Tax Receipts

(Rs. crore)

Year	Total Tax Receipts of States		of which:					
		% to GDP	Sales Tax	% Share of Total Tax Receipts	State Excise Duties	% Share of Total Tax Receipts	Transfer of Resources from Central Taxes	% Share of Total Tax Receipts
1951-52	281	2.6	54	19.2	49	17.4	53	18.9
1960-61	625	3.6	142	22.7	53	8.5	165	26.4
1970-71	2,284	4.9	755	33.1	194	8.5	756	33.1
1980-81	10,405	7.2	3,888	37.4	824	7.9	3,789	36.4
1990-91	44,586	7.8	17,667	39.6	4,795	10.8	14,242	31.9
2000-01	164,314	7.8	69,976	42.6	15,479	9.4	50,734	30.9
2001-02	175,415	7.7	73,181	41.7	16,504	9.4	52,215	29.8
2002-03	193,474	7.9	82,155	42.5	18,268	9.4	56,655	29.3
2003-04	221,117	8.0	93,172	42.1	18,928	8.6	67,080	30.3
2004-05	260,577	8.0	111,554	42.8	21,096	8.1	78,550	30.1
2005-06	306,332	8.3	128,769	42.0	25,036	8.2	94,024	30.7
2006-07	372,841	8.7	153,573	41.2	29,316	7.9	120,293	32.3
2007-08	437,948	8.9	173,422	39.6	34,127	7.8	151,402	34.6
2008-09 RE	503,878	9.0	202,610	40.2	39,167	7.8	173,473	34.4
2009-10 BE	552,243	9.0	225,009	40.7	45,961	8.3	185,720	33.6

Note: 2008-09 numbers are revised estimates and 2009-10 budget estimates.

Source: Reserve Bank of India study on State Finances.

99 : Details of Non-Tax Receipts of States

(Rs. crore)

Year	Non-Tax Receipts	% to Total Receipts	Interest Receipts	% Share to Non-Tax Receipts	Grants from the Centre	% Share to Non-Tax Receipts
1951-52	115	1.1	27	0.3	38	0.4
1960-61	387	2.2	78	0.5	140	0.8
1970-71	1,087	2.4	183	0.4	566	1.2
1980-81	5,888	4.1	824	0.6	2,623	1.8
1990-91	21,881	3.8	2,403	0.4	12,643	2.2
2000-01	68,195	3.2	10,961	0.5	37,289	1.8
2001-02	74,007	3.2	8,415	0.4	42,602	1.9
2002-03	80,200	3.3	8,761	0.4	45,170	1.8
2003-04	88,074	3.2	7,748	0.3	50,836	1.8
2004-05	102,935	3.2	8,648	0.3	56,322	1.7
2005-06	124,690	3.4	9,380	0.3	76,750	2.1
2006-07	157,714	3.7	11,825	0.3	94,451	2.2
2007-08	185,799	3.8	12,637	0.3	108,622	2.2
2008-09 RE	233,987	4.2	16,572	0.3	154,373	2.8
2009-10 BE	252,700	4.1	13,010	0.2	168,683	2.7

Note : 2008-09 numbers are revised estimates and 2009-10 budget estimates.
Source : Reserve Bank of India study on State Finances.

100 : States' Expenditure Pattern

(Rs. crore)

Year	Total Expenditure	% to GDP	*of which:* Interest	% to Total Expenditure	Pension etc.	% to Total Expenditure
1970-71	5,174	11.2	398	7.7	165	3.2
1980-81	22,664	15.6	1,225	5.4	375	1.7
1990-91	91,088	16.0	8,655	9.5	3,593	3.9
2000-01	339,835	16.2	50,985	15.0	28,483	8.4
2001-02	368,680	16.2	61,596	16.7	32,754	8.9
2002-03	410,249	16.7	69,027	16.8	36,563	8.9
2003-04	514,302	18.7	80,396	15.6	39,110	7.6
2004-05	553,428	17.1	86,421	15.6	44,747	8.1
2005-06	561,682	15.2	84,024	15.0	48,401	8.6
2006-07	657,280	15.3	93,164	14.2	52,646	8.0
2007-08	752,324	15.2	99,831	13.3	56,098	7.5
2008-09 RE	940,423	16.9	106,220	11.3	66,938	7.1
2009-10 BE	1,055,778	17.1	116,427	11.0	87,220	8.3

Note : 2008-09 numbers are revised estimates and 2009-10 budget estimates.

Source : *Handbook of Statistics on Indian Economy*, Reserve Bank of India; *State Finances : A study of budgets of 2009-10.*

101 : Deficit Indicators of State Governments

(Rs. crore)

Year	Fiscal Deficit	% to GDP	Revenue Deficit	% to GDP	Primary Deficit	% to GDP	Net RBI Credit
1970-71	901	1.9	19	0.0	503	1.1	-
1980-81	3,713	2.6	(1,486)	(1.0)	2,488	1.7	487
1990-91	18,151	3.2	5,309	0.9	10,132	1.8	420
2000-01	82,412	3.9	55,316	2.6	36,937	1.8	(1,092)
2001-02	89,298	3.9	60,398	2.7	32,665	1.4	3,451
2002-03	95,255	3.9	57,179	2.3	30,399	1.2	(3,100)
2003-04	117,494	4.3	63,407	2.3	40,235	1.5	293
2004-05	100,743	3.1	39,158	1.2	21,353	0.7	(2,705)
2005-06	86,054	2.3	7,013	0.2	6,060	0.2	2,425
2006-07	78,219	1.8	(24,857)	(0.6)	(15,672)	(0.4)	640
2007-08	75,455	1.5	(42,943)	(0.9)	(24,376)	(0.5)	1,140
2008-09 RE	146,349	2.6	(10,701)	(0.2)	40,128	0.7	602
2009-10 BE	199,510	3.2	32,295	0.5	83,083	1.3	na

Note : 2008-09 numbers are revised estimates and 2009-10 budget estimates.

Source : *Handbook of Statistics on Indian Economy*, Reserve Bank of India; *State Finances : A study of budgets of 2009-10.*

102 : Liabilities of State Governments

(Rs. crore)

Year (End-March)	Total Internal Debt	% to GDP	Market Loans	Loans & Advances:Centre	Provident Funds etc.	Reserve Funds	Deposits and Advances	Continency Funds	Total Liabilities	% to GDP
1980-81	4,443	3.1	2,988	16,980	2,536	449	2,338	37	26,783	18.4
1990-91	19,274	3.4	15,652	73,521	16,861	4,734	12,769	995	128,155	22.5
1991-92	23,270	3.6	19,008	82,979	19,790	5,519	14,502	969	147,030	22.5
1992-93	26,853	3.6	22,480	91,626	23,515	6,698	18,911	762	168,365	22.4
1993-94	30,933	3.6	26,119	101,122	27,972	8,180	19,009	658	187,992	21.7
1994-95	35,875	3.5	31,200	115,238	32,894	9,013	22,963	489	217,100	21.4
1995-96	43,895	3.7	37,088	129,264	38,216	10,577	26,654	929	250,889	21.1
1996-97	51,338	3.7	43,602	146,168	44,095	12,350	31,436	511	288,103	20.9
1997-98	59,289	3.9	50,847	168,656	50,843	14,498	36,609	921	333,897	21.9
1998-99	77,190	4.4	61,477	199,007	63,256	17,320	42,357	445	403,364	23.0
1999-00	126,346	6.5	75,427	230,331	80,523	19,769	52,193	1,533	515,877	26.4
2000-01	181,623	8.6	86,767	238,655	93,629	22,868	59,328	714	594,148	28.3
2001-02	249,069	10.9	104,027	249,551	103,815	27,389	64,325	1,042	690,747	30.3
2002-03	333,753	13.6	133,066	249,179	113,678	32,188	65,036	314	786,430	32.0
2003-04	476,772	17.3	208,901	192,981	132,043	42,217	69,116	246	913,376	33.2
2004-05	595,064	18.4	243,362	160,045	145,936	52,311	75,290	527	1,029,174	31.8
2005-06	698,773	18.9	260,506	157,004	160,955	63,120	86,691	1,322	1,167,866	31.5
2006-07	760,224	17.7	268,033	147,526	171,325	70,754	99,487	1,503	1,250,819	29.2
2007-08	835,792	16.9	328,679	150,615	183,471	61,130	104,513	1,523	1,337,044	27.0
2008-09 RE	924,052	16.6	389,614	157,299	196,473	62,333	109,325	1,688	1,451,169	26.0

Note: 2008-09 numbers are revised estimates and 2009-10 budget estimates.

Source: *Handbook of Statistics on Indian Economy*, Reserve Bank of India.

103 : Deficit Indicators of Centre and States

(Rs. crore)

Year	Revenue Deficit		Gross fiscal Deficit		Primary Deficit	
		% to GDP		% to GDP		% to GDP
1980-81	551	0.4	10,780	7.4	7818	5.4
1990-91	23,871	4.2	53,580	9.4	28585	5.0
1995-96	37,932	3.2	77,671	6.5	18598	1.6
1996-97	48,768	3.5	87,244	6.3	17156	1.2
1997-98	62,782	4.1	110,743	7.3	32466	2.1
1998-99	110,618	6.3	157,053	9.0	63956	3.7
1999-00	121,393	6.2	184,826	9.5	74375	3.8
2000-01	138,803	6.6	199,852	9.5	75035	3.6
2001-02	159,350	7.0	226,425	9.9	84039	3.7
2002-03	162,990	6.6	234,987	9.6	75927	3.1
2003-04	159,408	5.8	234,501	8.5	56928	2.1
2004-05	114,761	3.5	234,721	7.2	42409	1.3
2005-06	99,312	2.7	239,560	6.5	35583	1.0
2006-07	55,366	1.3	230,432	5.4	(399)	(0.0)
2007-08RE	40,959	0.8	247,831	5.0	(15905)	(0.3)
2008-09BE	26,758	0.5	244,460	4.4	(43017)	(0.8)

Note : Numbers in brackets represent negative values and indicate a surplus. Numbers for 2007-08 are revised estimates and for 2008-09 budget estimates.

Source : Reserve Bank of India.

104 : Combined Receipts and Disbursements of Centre and States

Year	Aggregate Receipts		Aggregate Disbursements	
	Rs. crore	% to GDP	Rs. crore	% to GDP
1980-81	34,505	23.7	37,879	26.1
1990-91	152,245	26.7	163,520	28.7
1995-96	296,629	24.9	303,582	25.5
1996-97	323,322	23.5	343,548	24.9
1997-98	388,316	25.4	385,302	25.2
1998-99	460,634	26.3	463,945	26.5
1999-00	536,446	27.5	540,423	27.7
2000-01	599,141	28.5	595,595	28.3
2001-02	651,039	28.6	652,967	28.7
2002-03	707,634	28.8	704,904	28.7
2003-04	799,162	29.0	796,383	28.9
2004-05	888,345	27.4	869,757	26.9
2005-06	1,014,689	27.4	959,855	25.9
2006-07	1,125,252	26.3	1,109,174	25.9
2007-08RE	1,331,711	26.9	1,355,830	27.4
2008-09BE	1,488,330	26.7	1,485,535	26.6

Note : 1. Numbers for 2007-08 are revised estimates and for 2008-09 budget estimates.
2.Capital receipts, capital disbursement, aggregate receipts and aggregate disbursements include discharge of internal debt.
3.Tax revenues from 2000-01 to 2008-09 exclude the amounts transferred to National Calamity Contingency Fund (NCCF).

Source : Reserve Bank of India.

105 : Trends in Revenue Receipts of Centre and States

(Rs. crore)

Year	Total Tax Revenue	% to GDP	Gross Revenue of Centre	% to GDP	States' Own Tax Revenue	% to GDP
1950-51	627	6.2	405	4.0	222	2.2
1960-61	1,350	7.8	895	5.1	455	2.6
1970-71	4,752	10.3	3,206	6.9	1,546	3.3
1980-81	19,844	13.7	13,179	9.1	6,665	4.6
1990-91	87,722	15.4	57,577	10.1	30,145	5.3
2000-01	305,322	13.4	188,605	8.3	116,717	5.1
2001-02	314,535	12.8	187,060	7.6	127,475	5.2
2002-03	356,277	12.9	215,905	7.8	140,372	5.1
2003-04	414,084	12.8	254,348	7.9	159,736	4.9
2004-05	494,370	13.3	304,957	8.2	189,413	5.1
2005-06	587,688	13.7	366,151	8.5	221,537	5.2
2006-07	736,708	14.9	473,513	9.6	263,195	5.3
2007-08RE	891,303	16.0	585,410	10.5	305,893	5.5
2008-09BE	1,039,040	18.6	687,715	12.3	351,325	6.3

Note : Numbers for 2007-08 are revised estimates and for 2008-09 budget estimates.

Source : *Indian Public Finance Statistics.*

106 : Combined Liabilities of Centre and States

(Rs. crore)

Year	Total Liabilities of the Centre	% to GDP	Total Liabilities of the States	% to GDP	Combined Liabilities of the Centre & States	% to GDP
1980-81	59,749	41.1	26,783	18.4	69,552	47.8
1990-91	314,558	55.2	128,155	22.5	368,824	64.7
1991-92	354,662	54.2	147,030	22.5	418,428	63.9
1992-93	401,924	53.4	168,365	22.4	479,035	63.7
1993-94	477,968	55.2	187,992	21.7	564,806	65.2
1994-95	538,611	53.0	217,100	21.4	640,796	63.1
1995-96	606,232	50.9	250,889	21.1	728,208	61.1
1996-97	675,676	49.0	288,103	20.9	818,206	59.3
1997-98	778,294	51.0	333,897	21.9	944,228	61.8
1998-99	891,806	50.9	403,364	23.0	1,096,659	62.6
1999-00	1,021,029	52.3	515,877	26.4	1,300,088	66.6
2000-01	1,168,541	55.6	594,148	28.3	1,484,106	70.6
2001-02	1,366,408	60.0	690,747	30.3	1,733,033	76.0
2002-03	1,559,201	63.5	786,430	32.0	1,970,807	80.3
2003-04	1,736,678	63.0	913,376	33.2	2,241,950	81.4
2004-05	1,994,421	61.6	1,029,174	31.8	2,562,016	79.1
2005-06	2,260,145	61.0	1,167,866	31.5	2,879,705	77.7
2006-07	2,538,596	59.3	1,250,819	29.2	3,190,698	74.5
2007-08RE	2,897,038	58.6	1,337,044	27.0	3,627,260	73.3
2008-09BE	3,062,913	54.9	1,451,169	26.0	3,891,740	69.8

Note : 1. Numbers for 2007-08 are revised estimates and for 2008-09 budget estimates. Inter-governmental transfers have been netted. Hence the sub-totals do not add up to the combined total.
Source : Reserve Bank of India.

107 : Distribution of Total Expenditure

(Rs. crore)

Year	Total Expenditure*	of which:									
		Interest Payments		Defence		Pension		Education		Health	
			% to Total		% to Total		% to Total		% to Total		% to Total
1990-91	143,196	25,006	17.5	15,426	10.8	5,184	3.6	17,378	12.1	7,496	5.2
1999-00	495,617	110,051	22.2	47,071	9.5	37,018	7.5	63,174	12.7	25,365	5.1
2000-01	534,944	122,792	23.0	49,622	9.3	38,819	7.3	63,756	11.9	27,187	5.1
2001-02	590,451	140,890	23.9	54,266	9.2	40,321	6.8	67,881	11.5	28,440	4.8
2002-03	640,169	154,399	24.1	55,662	8.7	43,038	6.7	71,117	11.1	29,420	4.6
2003-04	729,843	176,373	24.2	60,066	8.2	45,227	6.2	76,160	10.4	32,919	4.5
2004-05	799,197	192,367	24.1	75,856	9.5	55,437	6.9	85,717	10.7	37,702	4.7
2005-06	909,474	206,390	22.7	80,549	8.9	60,871	6.7	98,184	10.8	45,486	5.0
2006-07	1,064,457	233,020	21.9	85,510	8.0	69,069	6.5	117,312	11.0	53,058	5.0
2007-08(RE)	1,307,246	266,244	20.4	92,500	7.1	80,315	6.1	138,763	10.6	67,281	5.1
2008-09(BE)	1,438,670	289,957	20.2	105,600	7.3	87,927	6.1	164,261	11.4	75,627	5.3

Note : RE: Revised Estimates; BE: Budget Estimates.

* Total expenditure excludes loans and balances, self-balancing items and transfer to funds. Health includes medical & public health, water supply & sanitation and family welfare.

Source : *Indian Public Finance Statistics* (2008-09), Ministry of Finance.

108 : Small Savings

(Rs. crore)

Year	Outstandings	% to GDP	Net Receipts	% to GDP	Gross Receipts	% to GDP
1950-51	336	1.2	34	0.3	101	1.0
1960-61	982	4.5	105	0.6	239	1.4
1970-71	2,222	4.8	192	0.4	783	1.7
1980-81	8,244	5.7	1,266	0.9	3,119	2.1
1990-91	50,279	8.8	5,950	1.0	17,669	3.1
1991-92	58,595	8.9	8,316	1.3	17,238	2.6
1992-93	60,948	8.1	2,353	0.3	17,735	2.4
1993-94	67,696	7.8	6,748	0.8	24,077	2.8
1994-95	83,337	8.2	15,641	1.5	34,667	3.4
1995-96	93,728	7.9	10,391	0.9	32,748	2.7
1996-97	106,111	7.7	12,383	0.9	33,612	2.4
1997-98	126,755	8.3	20,644	1.4	46,935	3.1
1998-99	155,296	8.9	28,541	1.6	55,820	3.2
1999-00	187,510	9.6	32,214	1.7	69,695	3.6
2000-01	225,087	10.7	37,577	1.8	79,311	3.8
2001-02	262,856	11.5	37,769	1.7	81,753	3.6
2002-03	313,793	12.8	50,937	2.1	105,602	4.3
2003-04	375,737	13.6	61,944	2.2	135,970	4.9
2004-05	457,732	14.1	81,995	2.5	158,519	4.9
2005-06	527,629	14.2	69,897	1.9	173,283	4.7
2006-07	564,372	13.2	36,743	0.9	154,836	3.6
2007-08	509,411	10.3	(54,961)	(1.1)	123,652	2.5
2008-09	544,340	9.8	34,929	0.6	143,668	2.6
2009-10*	569,226	9.2	24,886	0.4	149,178	2.4

Note : * Upto December 2009.

Source : *Handbook of Statistics on Indian Economy.*

109 : Foreign Trade

(US$ million)

Year	Exports	Growth (%)	Imports	Growth (%)	Trade Balance	RBI BoP Data		
						Export	Import	Balance
1950-51	1,016		1,292		(276)	1,355	1,366	(11)
1960-61*	1,346	3.6	2,353	6.1	(1,007)	1,326	2,324	(998)
1970-71*	2,031	3.5	2,162	0.8	(131)	1,876	2,416	(540)
1980-81*	8,485	15.8	15,867	20.1	(7,382)	8,429	16,284	(7855)
1990-91*	18,145	8.0	24,073	7.2	(5,927)	18,477	27,915	(9438)
2000-01*	44,560	8.6	50,537	9.6	(5,976)	45,452	57,912	(12460)
2000-01	44,560	21.0	50,537	1.7		45,452	57,912	(12460)
2001-02	43,827	(1.6)	51,413	1.7	(7,587)	44,703	56,277	(11574)
2002-03	52,719	20.3	61,412	19.4	(8,693)	53,774	64,464	(10690)
2003-04	63,843	21.1	78,149	27.3	(14,307)	66,285	80,003	(13718)
2004-05	83,536	30.8	111,517	42.7	(27,982)	85,206	118,908	(33702)
2005-06	103,091	23.4	149,166	33.8	(46,075)	105,152	157,056	(51904)
2006-07	126,414	22.6	185,735	24.5	(59,321)	128,888	190,670	(61782)
2007-08	163,132	29.0	251,654	35.5	(88,522)	166,162	257,629	(91467)
2008-09	185,295	13.6	303,696	20.7	(118401)	189,001	307,651	(118650)
2009-10	176,574	(4.7)	278,681	(8.2)	(102106)	182,163	299,491	(117328)

Note: * Growth for decades from 1950-51 to 2000-01 is CAGR (compounded annual growth rate), that from 2000-01 onwards is the annual growth rate.

Source: Directorate General of Commercial Intelligence and Statistics (DGCI&S), Calcutta; Reserve Bank of India for balance of payment data.

110 : Imports of Some Selected Commodities

($ million)

	1960-61	1970-71	1980-81	1990-91	2000-01	2008-09	2009-10
Total Imports	2,353	2,162	15,869	24,075	50,536	303,696	286,823
Pulses	—	—	—	268	109	1,289	2,047
% of Total				1.1	0.2	0.4	0.7
Edible Oils	8	31	857	182	1,334	3,398	5,601
% of Total	0.3	1.4	5.4	0.8	2.6	1.1	2.0
Raw Materials and Intermediates							
Petroleum Oil & Lubricants	145	180	6656	6028	15,650	93,667	87,121
% of Total	6.2	8.3	41.9	25.0	31.0	30.8	30.4
Fertilisers	27	113	1034	984	664	13,693	6,602
% of Total	1.1	5.2	6.5	4.1	1.3	4.5	2.3
Medicinal & Pharmaceuticals	21	32	107	261	377	1,890	2,103
% of Total	0.9	1.5	0.7	1.1	0.7	0.6	0.7
Iron & Steel	258	194	1078	1178	781	9,521	8,258
% of Total	11.0	9.0	6.8	4.9	1.5	3.1	2.9
Pearl,Precious & Semi-Precious Stones	2	33	527	2083	4,838	16,804	16,330
% of Total	0.1	1.5	3.3	8.7	9.6	5.5	5.7
Gold & Silver					4,638	22,430	29,132
% of Total					9.2	7.4	10.2
Capital Goods*	747	534	2416	6495	8,941	70,214	61,701
% of Total	31.7	24.7	15.2	27.0	17.7	23.1	21.5

Note : * Capital goods include manufacture of metals, machine tools, machinery, electronic goods, computer goods, transport equipment and project goods.

Source : *Economic Survey*, *Handbook of Statistics on Indian Economy* and Dept. of Commerce.

111 : Exports of Some Selected Commodities

($ million)

	1960-61	1970-71	1980-81	1990-91	2000-01	2008-09	2009-10
Total Exports	1,346	2,041	8,486	18,143	44,560	185,295	178,662
Tea & Yerba Mate	260	196	538	596	433	585	623
% of Total	11.0	9.1	3.4	2.5	0.9	0.2	0.2
Tobacco	34	43	178	147	191	751	916
% of Total	1.4	2.0	1.1	0.6	0.4	0.2	0.3
Sugar & Molasses	60	39	50	21	112	1057	27
% of Total	2.5	1.8	0.3	0.1	0.2	0.3	0.0
Iron ore	36	155	384	585	358	4769	6030
% of Total	1.5	7.2	2.4	2.4	0.7	1.6	2.1
Textile	153	192	1,179	3,807	10,694	19,324	19,124
% of Total	6.5	8.9	7.4	15.8	21.2	6.4	6.7
Gems & Jewellery	2	59	782	2,924	7,384	28,411	29,000
% of Total	0.1	2.7	4.9	12.1	14.6	9.4	10.1
Chemicals & Products	15	39	284	1,176	5,002	24,066	24,377
% of Total	0.6	1.8	1.8	4.9	9.9	7.9	8.5
Machinery **	46	261	1,045	2,158	6,976	47,654	38,352
% of Total	2.0	12.1	6.6	9.0	13.8	15.7	13.4
Mineral Fuel & Lubricants	15	17	35	528	1,931	27547**	28131**
% of Total	0.6	0.8	0.2	2.2	3.8	9.1	9.8

Note : ** Machinery includes machinery and machine tools, iron and steel and other engineering items and also electronic and computer goods.* Data mainly pertains to petroleum products.

Source : *Economic Survey, Handbook of Statistics on Indian Economy* and Dept. of Commerce.

112 : Index Numbers and Terms of Foreign Trade

Year	Unit Value Index		Quantum Index		Terms of Trade		
	Exports	Imports	Exports	Imports	Gross	Net	Income
Base: 1978-79 =100							
1970-71	45	35	59	67	114	128	75
1980-81	109	134	108	138	128	81	87
1990-91	293	268	194	238	123	109	212
2000-01	624	487	571	698	122	128	732
2001-02	618	493	593	733	124	125	743
2002-03	620	546	722	802	111	114	820
2003-04	672	545	765	970	127	123	943
2004-05	732	663	899	1,113	124	110	993
2005-06	798	592	1,005	1,649	164	135	1,355
2006-07	863	608	1,164	2,047	176	142	1,652
2007-08	939	575	1,227	2,603	212	163	2,004

contd...

...contd...

Year	Unit Value Index		Quantum Index		Terms of Trade		
	Exports	Imports	Exports	Imports	Gross	Net	Income
Base: 1999-2000 =100							
2000-01	102	109	125	99	79	94	118
2001-02	103	112	126	103	82	92	116
2002-03	106	128	150	109	73	83	125
2003-04	114	132	161	128	80	86	138
2004-05	131	157	179	150	84	83	149
2005-06	139	179	206	174	84	78	161
2006-07	158	206	227	191	84	77	175
2007-08	166	210	245	218	89	79	194
2008-09	194	239	267	262	98	81	216

Note : The Index number of foreign trade of a country indicates the temporal fluctuations in export/import in terms of volume and unit price. It may be defined as a meaure of average change in a group of related variables between two different situations.

1. Gross terms of trade is the ratio of overall import quantum index to similar export index.
2. Net terms of trade (NTT) is the ratio of overall export unit value index to similar import index.
3. Income terms of trade = (NTT X QIE)/100. QIE - Quantum Index-Export.

Source : *Economic Survey, Handbook of Statistics on Indian Economy.*

113 : India's Share in World Exports of Principal Commodities

	World Exports (US$ billion)			India's Share (% of World Exports)		
	1900	2000	2006	1900	2000	2006
Meat & Preparations	34.1	44.7	79	0.2	0.7	0.9
Fish etc. & Preparations	32.8	50.9	79	1.6	2.7	2.2
Rice	4	6.4	11.1	6.4	10.2	14
Vegetables & Fruits	50.2	68.4	127.3	0.8	1.3	1.3
Sugar, Honey,etc.	14.2	13.9	30	0.1	0.9	2.6
Coffee & Substitute	8.7	11.6	18.1	1.7	2.3	2.4
Tea & Yerba Mate	2.7	3.1	4.8	22.1	14	9.1
Spices	1.4	2.5	3.6	7.7	10.3	13.1
Animal Feed	15.6	20.3	32.9	2.2	2.3	3.8
Tobacco & Manufactures	17.9	21.6	26.5	0.8	0.7	1
Oilseeds & Oleaginous Fruit	10.5	14.4	24.3	0.8	1.7	1.7
Iron Ore & Concentrates	7.7	9.2	32.8	7.6	3.9	11.9
Organic Chemicals	70.7	134.1	274.6	0.3	1.1	2
Medicine & Pharmaceuticals	37.8	107.5	75.4	1.2	1.2	0.9

contd...

...*contd*...

	World Exports (US$ billion)			India's Share (% of World Exports)		
	1900	2000	2006	1900	2000	2006
Leather & Products	13.2	24.4	27.6	6.3	3.3	3.1
Textiles	105.1	167.5	228.6	2.1	3.6	3.9
Pearls, Precious Stones	27.6	54.1	91.3	9.9	12	11.9
Iron & Steel	106.3	146.1	369.7	0.3	1	1.9
Metal Manufacturers	66.1	125.3	253.1	0.5	0.9	1.2
Machinery	775.2	2461.8	3203.9	0.1	0.1	0.3
Road Vehicles	96.3	157.7	320.3	2.3	3.5	2.9
Apparel	94.6	201.4	320.3	2.3	3.5	2.9
Total Exports	3303.6	6254.5	11887.5	0.5	0.7	1.1

Source : United Nations : *International Trade Statistics Year Book, 2006.*

114 : Direction of Trade from India

(US$ million)

Year	1990-91		2000-01		2008-09	
	Export	Import	Export	Import	Export	Import
OECD Countries	10,249	13,773	23,474	20,158	68,277	92,750
EU	4,988	7,067	10,411	10,510	38,953	41,653
Belgium	702	1,515	1,471	2,870	4,415	5,441
France	427	727	1,020	641	2,995	4,588
Germany	1,421	1,936	1,908	1,760	6,344	11,694
Italy	558	608	1,309	724	3,776	4,308
Netherlands	359	442	880	438	6,280	1,876
UK	1,186	1,613	2,299	3,168	6,595	5,792
Canada	156	312	657	397	1,358	2,451
USA	2,673	2,923	9,305	3,015	20,818	18,163
Australia	179	816	406	1,063	1,426	8,423
Japan	1,694	1,808	1,795	1,842	3,001	7,607
Switzerland	224	268	438	3,160	766	11,447
OPEC	1,020	3,924	4,850	2,689	38,806	95,027
Indonesia	109	81	400	910	2,517	6,674
Iran	79	567	227	211	2,510	12,134
Kuwait	41	202	199	113	788	9,303

contd...

...contd...

(US$ million)

Year	1990-91		2000-01		2008-09	
	Export	Import	Export	Import	Export	Import
Saudi Arabia	233	1,616	823	621	4,988	19,493
UAE	439	1,059	2,598	659	23,921	20,605
Developing Countries	3,099	4,490	13,013	11,156	68,621	95,774
Asia	2,610	3,372	10,038	8,460	51,388	77,581
SAARC	*533*	*131*	*1,929*	*466*	8,438	*1,791*
Bangladesh	305	17	935	80	2,461	308
Nepal	48	45	141	255	1,556	488
Pakistan	41	47	187	64	1,418	362
Sri Lanka	131	21	640	45	2,370	350
People's Republic of China	18	31	831	1,502	9,276	31,334
Hong Kong	597	166	2,641	852	6,662	6,411
South Korea	183	366	451	894	3,991	8,591
Malaysia	151	555	608	1,177	3,431	7,021
Singapore	379	796	877	1,464	8,207	7,432
Thailand	247	65	530	338	1,978	2,656
Africa	394	573	1,956	1,996	11,561	12,501
Latin America	95	546	1,018	701	5,672	5,692
Total	18,145	24,073	44,560	50,537	182,631	291,475

Source : Ministry of Finance and Reserve Bank of India.

115 : India's Direction of Trade (% Share)

(US$ million)

Year	1990-91		2000-01		2008-09	
	Export	Import	Export	Import	Export	Import
OECD Countries	56.5	57.2	52.7	39.9	37.4	31.8
EU	27.5	29.4	23.4	20.8	21.3	14.3
Belgium	3.9	6.3	3.3	5.7	2.4	1.9
France	2.4	3.0	2.3	1.3	1.6	1.6
Germany	7.8	8.0	4.3	3.5	3.5	4.0
Italy	3.1	2.5	2.9	1.4	2.1	1.5
Netherlands	2.0	1.8	2.0	0.9	3.4	0.6
UK	6.5	6.7	5.2	6.3	3.6	2.0
Canada	0.9	1.3	1.5	0.8	0.7	0.8
USA	14.7	12.1	20.9	6.0	11.4	6.2
Australia	1.0	3.4	0.9	2.1	0.8	2.9
Japan	9.3	7.5	4.0	3.6	1.6	2.6
Switzerland	1.2	1.1	1.0	6.3	0.4	3.9
OPEC	5.6	16.3	10.9	5.3	21.2	32.6
Indonesia	0.6	0.3	0.9	1.8	1.4	2.3
Iran	0.4	2.4	0.5	0.4	1.4	4.2
Kuwait	0.2	0.8	0.4	0.2	0.4	3.2
Saudi Arabia	1.3	6.7	1.8	1.2	2.7	6.7

contd...

...contd...

(US$ million)

Year	1990-91		2000-01		2008-09	
	Export	Import	Export	Import	Export	Import
UAE	2.4	4.4	5.8	1.3	13.1	7.1
Developing Countries	17.1	18.7	29.2	22.1	37.6	32.9
Asia	14.4	14.0	22.5	16.7	28.1	26.6
SAARC	2.9	0.5	4.3	0.9	4.6	0.6
Bangladesh	1.7	0.1	2.1	0.2	1.3	0.1
Nepal	0.3	0.2	0.3	0.5	0.9	0.2
Pakistan	0.2	0.2	0.4	0.1	0.8	0.1
Sri Lanka	0.7	0.1	1.4	0.1	1.3	0.1
People's Republic of China	0.1	0.1	1.9	3.0	5.1	10.8
Hong Kong	3.3	0.7	5.9	1.7	3.6	2.2
South Korea	1.0	1.5	1.0	1.8	2.2	2.9
Malaysia	0.8	2.3	1.4	2.3	1.9	2.4
Singapore	2.1	3.3	2.0	2.9	4.5	2.5
Thailand	1.4	0.3	1.2	0.7	1.1	0.9
Africa	2.2	2.4	4.4	3.9	6.3	4.3
Latin America	0.5	2.3	2.3	1.4	3.1	2.0
Total	100.0	100.0	100.0	100.0	100.0	100.0

Source : Ministry of Finance and Reserve Bank of India.

116 : Exchange Rate for the Rupee

Year-End	(Rs. per Unit of Foreign Currency) SDR	US Dollar	Pound Sterling	Deutsche Mark/Euro	Japanese Yen	US $ (Annual Average)
1970-71	7.50	7.50	18.13	2.07	2.10	7.56
1980-81	10.06	8.19	18.38	3.90	3.90	7.91
1990-91	26.41	19.64	34.05	11.43	13.90	17.94
1991-92	35.51	31.23	53.69	18.35	23.28	24.47
1992-93	43.65	31.24	46.62	19.29	26.99	30.65
1993-94	44.31	31.37	46.52	18.76	35.52	31.37
1994-95	49.16	31.50	50.57	22.36	35.28	31.40
1995-96	50.16	34.35	52.43	23.30	32.30	33.45
1996-97	49.80	35.92	58.69	21.39	28.95	35.50
1997-98	52.77	39.50	66.16	21.34	29.78	37.16
1998-99	57.61	42.43	68.61	23.29	35.32	42.07
1999-00	58.75	43.61	69.51	41.80	41.48	43.33
2000-01	58.80	46.64	66.58	41.01	37.43	45.68
2001-02	60.84	48.80	69.59	42.64	36.81	47.69
2002-03	65.26	47.51	74.92	51.49	39.89	48.40
2003-04	64.24	43.45	79.68	53.17	41.67	45.95
2004-05	66.10	43.76	82.11	56.59	40.81	44.93
2005-06	64.26	44.61	77.80	54.19	38.02	44.27
2006-07	65.83	43.60	85.59	58.15	37.03	45.28
2007-08	65.73	39.99	79.51	63.10	40.07	40.24
2008-09	76.17	50.95	72.86	67.47	51.89	45.92

Note : 1. Exchange rate for Yen is expressed in Rs. per 100 Yen.
2. Data from 1970-71 to 1991-92 are based on official exchange rate and for later years based on FEDAI rate.
3. Euro replaced Deutsche Mark with effect from 1-1-1999.

Source : *Handbook of Statistics on Indian Economy.*

117: India's Share in World Merchandise Trade

	Imports		Exports	
	World (US$ billion)	India (%)	World (US$ billion)	India (%)
1948	62	2.3	59	2.2
1953	85	1.4	84	1.3
1963	164	1.5	157	1.0
1973	595	0.5	579	0.5
1983	1,882	0.7	1,838	0.5
1993	3,787	0.6	3,676	0.6
2003	7,692	0.9	7,377	0.8
2008	16,222	1.9	15,993	1.1

Source : Ministry of Commerce and Trade and International Monetary Fund.

118 : Indices of Real Efffective Exchange Rate (REER) and Nominal Effective Exchange Rate (NEER)

Year	36-Currency Export & Trade-Based Weights (Base 1993-94=100)(Financial Year Average)							
	Export-Based Weights				Trade-Based Weights			
	REER	Change (+/-)*	NEER	Change (+/-)*	REER	Change (+/-)*	NEER	Change (+/-)*
1993-94	100.00		100.00		100.00		100.00	
1994-95	104.88	4.9	98.18	(1.8)	104.32	4.3	98.91	(1.1)
1995-96	100.10	(4.6)	90.94	(7.4)	98.19	(5.9)	91.54	(7.5)
1996-97	98.95	(1.1)	89.03	(2.1)	96.83	(1.4)	89.27	(2.5)
1997-98	103.07	4.2	91.97	3.3	100.77	4.1	92.04	3.1
1998-99	94.34	(8.5)	90.34	(1.8)	93.04	(7.7)	89.05	(3.2)
1999-00	95.28	1.0	90.42	0.1	95.99	3.2	91.02	2.2
2000-01	98.67	3.6	90.12	(0.3)	100.09	4.3	92.12	1.2
2001-02	98.59	(0.1)	89.08	(1.2)	100.86	0.8	91.58	(0.6)
2002-03	95.99	(2.6)	87.01	(2.3)	98.18	(2.7)	89.12	(2.7)
2003-04	99.07	3.2	87.89	1.0	99.56	1.4	87.14	(2.2)
2004-05	98.30	(0.8)	88.41	0.6	100.09	0.5	87.31	0.2
2005-06	100.54	2.3	91.17	3.1	102.35	2.3	89.85	2.9
2006-07	97.42	(3.1)	87.46	(4.1)	98.48	(3.8)	85.89	(4.4)
2007-08	104.12	6.9	95.30	9.0	104.81	6.4	93.91	9.3
2008-09	94.12	(9.6)	84.67	(11.2)	94.32	(10.0)	84.66	(9.8)
2009-10	92.03	(2.2)	81.87	(3.3)	94.23	(0.1)	84.68	0.0

Note : Change(+/-)* indicates appreciation (+)/depreciation (-) of the rupee over the year.
1. Data in brackets indicate negative value i.e., depreciation of the rupee over the year.
2. Data for 2009-10 are provisional.
3. The 36-country indices are revised as 36-currency indices respectively.

Source : *Handbook of Statistics on Indian Economy.*

119 : Balance of Payments

(US$ million)

	1990-91	2000-01	2007-08	2008-09	2009-10
Current Account	(9,680)	(2,666)	(15737)	(28728)	(38411)
Export f.o.b	18,477	45,452	166,162	189,001	182,163
Import c.i.f	27,915	57,912	257,629	307,651	299,491
Trade Balance	(9,438)	(12,460)	(91,467)	(118,650)	(117,328)
Invisibles					
Receipt	7,464	32,267	148,875	163,534	161,246
Payment	7,706	22,473	73,144	73,612	82,329
Net	(242)	9,794	75,731	89,923	78,917
Capital Account	7,056	8,840	106,585	7,246	53,597
Foreign Investment (net)	103	5,862	43,326	3,467	52,105
In India (Net)	103	5,862	61,998	21,139	64,078
Direct (Net)	97	3,272	34,728	34,992	31,682
Portfolio (Net)	6	2,590	27,270	(13,853)	32,396
Abroad	-	(759)	(18672)	(17672)	(11973)

contd...

...contd...

(US$ million)

	1990-91	2000-01	2007-08	2008-09	2009-10
Loans (Net)	5,533	5,264	40,653	8,669	12,217
External Assistance (Net)	2,204	410	2,114	2,637	2,044
Commercial Borrowings (Net)	2,254	4,303	22,609	7,941	2,521
Short Term to India (Net)	1,075	551	15,930	(1909)	7,652
Banking Capital (Net)	682	(1,961)	11,759	(3,245)	2,084
Commercial Banks (Net)	904	(1,882)	12,112	(2774)	1,927
of which NRI deposits (Net)	1,537	2,316	179	4,290	2,922
Others (Net)	(222)	(79)	(353)	(471)	157
Rupee Debt Service (Net)	(1,193)	(617)	(122)	(100)	(97)
Other Capital (Net)	1,931	292	10,969	(1,545)	(12732)
Errors & Omissions	132	(305)	1,316	1,402	(1745)
Overall Balance	(2,492)	5,869	92,164	(20,080)	13,441
Monetary Movements	2,492	(5,869)	(92,164)	20,080	(13441)
IMF	1,214	(26)	-	-	-
Foreign Exchange Reserves (Increase - /Decrease +)	1,278	(5,842)	(92,164)	20,080	(13441*)

Note : *' includes SDR allocation of US $ million 5160. f.o.b. - Free on board; c.i.f. - Cost, insurance and frieght.

Source : Reserve Bank of India.

120 : Selected Balance of Payment Indicators

(%)

	Per cent to Gross Domestic Product at Current Market Prices							
	Current Net Account	Capital Net Account	Merchandise Trade			Invisibles		
			Export	Import	Merchandise (Total)	Receipts	Payments	Net
1950-51	0.4	(0.0)	6.4	6.4	12.9	1.4	1.0	0.4
1960-61	(2.3)	2.0	3.6	6.4	10.0	1.5	1.0	0.5
1970-71	(1.0)	1.1	3.1	3.9	7.0	1.1	1.2	(0.1)
1980-81	(1.5)	1.0	4.6	8.9	13.4	3.9	1.2	2.7
1990-91	(3.0)	2.2	5.8	8.8	14.6	2.4	2.4	(0.1)
1991-92	(0.3)	1.5	6.9	7.9	14.7	3.6	2.9	0.7
1992-93	(1.7)	1.6	7.3	9.6	16.8	3.6	3.0	0.6
1993-94	(0.4)	3.2	8.2	9.7	17.9	4.1	3.1	1.0
1994-95	(1.0)	2.6	8.3	11.1	19.4	4.8	3.1	1.8
1995-96	(2.5)	1.2	9.1	3.4	12.5	5.0	3.4	1.5
1996-97	(1.2)	3.1	8.8	12.6	21.4	5.5	2.9	2.6
1997-98	(1.4)	2.4	8.7	12.5	21.2	5.6	3.2	2.4

contd...

...contd...

(%)

	Per cent to Gross Domestic Product at Current Market Prices							
	Current Net Account	Capital Net Account	Merchandise Trade			Invisibles		
			Export	Import	Merchandise (Total)	Receipts	Payments	Net
1998-99	(1.0)	2.0	8.2	11.4	19.7	6.2	4.0	2.2
1999-00	(1.0)	2.3	8.3	12.3	20.6	6.7	3.8	2.9
2000-01	(0.6)	1.9	9.8	12.9	22.6	7.6	5.2	2.3
2001-02	0.7	1.8	9.4	12.1	21.5	7.7	4.9	2.8
2002-03	1.2	2.1	10.4	12.9	23.3	8.5	5.3	3.2
2003-04	2.3	2.8	11.0	13.3	24.4	8.9	4.3	4.6
2004-05	(0.4)	3.9	11.8	16.5	28.3	9.6	5.3	4.3
2005-06	(1.2)	3.0	12.6	18.8	31.3	10.7	5.7	5.0
2006-07	(1.0)	4.8	13.6	20.1	33.7	12.1	6.6	5.5
2007-08	(1.3)	8.6	13.5	20.9	34.4	12.1	5.9	6.1
2008-09	(-2.4)	0.5	15.4	25.1	40.5	13.4	6.1	7.3
2009-10	(2.9)	4.1	14.0	23.0	37.0	12.4	6.3	6.1

Source : *Economic Survey*.

121 : Foreign Exchange Reserves

(US$ million)

End -March	SDRs	Gold	Foreign Currency Assets	Reserve Tranche Position	Total	Import Cover (No. of Months)
1950-51	.	247	1,914	.	2,161	20
1960-61	.	247	390	.	637	3
1970-71	148	243	584	.	975	5
1980-81	603	370	5,850	.	6,823	5
1990-91	102	3,496	2,236	.	5,834	3
1991-92	90	3,499	5,631	.	9,220	6
1992-93	18	3,380	6,434	.	9,832	5
1993-94	108	4,078	15,068	.	19,254	10
1994-95	7	4,370	20,809	.	25,186	11
1995-96	82	4,561	17,044	.	21,687	7
1996-97	2	4,054	22,367	.	26,423	8
1997-98	1	3,391	25,975	.	29,367	8
1998-99	8	2,960	29,522	.	32,490	9
1999-00	4	2,974	35,058	.	38,036	9
2000-01	2	2,725	39,554	.	42,281	10
2001-02	10	3,047	51,049	.	54,106	13
2002-03	4	3,534	71,890	672	76,100	15
2003-04	2	4,198	107,448	1,311	112,959	17
2004-05	5	4,500	135,571	1,438	141,514	15
2005-06	3	5,755	145,108	756	151,622	12
2006-07	2	6,784	191,924	469	199,179	13
2007-08	18	10,039	299,230	436	309,723	15
2008-09	1	9,577	241,426	981	251,985	11

Source : Handbook of Statistics on Indian Economy.

122 : Trend in Invisibles

(US$ million)

	Receipts	Growth	Payments	Growth	Net
1950-51	293		203		90
1960-61	548	7.0	375	6.9	173
1970-71	663	3.1	712	6.8	-49
1980-81	7183	49.1	2118	11.9	5065
1990-91	7464	0.6	7706	14.3	-242
2000-01	32267	16.2	22473	12.0	9794
2000-01	32267	6.4	22473	30.9	9794
2001-02	36737	13.9	21763	-3.2	14974
2002-03	41925	14.1	24890	14.4	17035
2003-04	53508	27.6	25707	3.3	27801
2004-05	69533	29.9	38301	49.0	31232
2005-06	89687	29.0	47685	24.5	42002
2006-07	114558	27.7	62341	30.7	52217
2007-08	148875	30.0	73144	17.3	75731
2008-09	163534	9.8	73612	0.6	89922
2009-10	161246	(-1.4)	82329	11.8	78917

Note : 1 :Growth between 1950-51 and 1960-01 and so on upto 2000-01 is CAGR (compounded annual growth rate) and from 2001-02 it is annual growth rate.

Source : Rerserve Bank of India.

123 : NRI Deposit Outstandings Under Various Schemes

(US$ million)

Year (End-March)	NR(E)RA	FCNR Accounts	Others	Total
1991	3,618	10,103	265	13,986
1992	3,025	9,792	744	13,561
1993	2,740	10,617	1,668	15,025
1994	3,523	10,408	2,300	16,231
1995	4,556	10,114	2,490	17,160
1996	3,916	9,975	3,544	17,435
1997	4,983	9,802	5,604	20,389
1998	5,637	8,468	6,262	20,367
1999	6,045	7,835	6,618	20,498
2000	6,758	8,172	6,754	21,684
2001	7,147	9,076	6,849	23,072
2002	8,449	9,673	7,052	25,174
2003	14,923	10,199	3,407	28,529
2004	20,559	10,961	1,746	33,266
2005	21,291	11,452	232	32,975
2006	22,070	13,064	1,148	36,282
2007	24,495	15,129	1,616	41,240
2008	26,716	14,168	2,788	43,672
2009	23,570	13,211	4,773	41,554
2010	26,251	14,258	7,381	47,890

Note : NR(E)RA : Non-resident (external) rupee accounts.
FCNR A/c includes both foreign currency non-resident accounts and banks.
Others includes foreign currency non-resident(banks), foreign currency (bank & other) deposits, foreign currency (ordinary) non-repartiable deposits and non-resident ordinary rupee accounts.

Source : *Handbook of Statistics on Indian Economy.*

124 : Invisibles by Categories of Transaction (Net)

(US$ million)

Year/Item	Non-Factor Services	Investment Income	Compensation to Employees	Private Transfers	Official Transfers	Invisibles
1950-51	59	(50)	.	73	4	86
1960-61	120	(101)	.	59	95	173
1970-71	11	(338)	.	116	162	(49)
1980-81	1,297	325	.	2,693	750	5,065
1990-91	980	(3,752)	.	2,069	461	(242)
1991-92	1,207	(3,829)	.	3,783	459	1,620
1992-93	1,129	(3,423)	.	3,852	363	1,921
1993-94	534	(3,270)	.	5,264	369	2,897
1994-95	602	(3,431)	.	8,093	416	5,680
1995-96	(200)	(3,205)	.	8,507	345	5,447
1996-97	726	(3,307)	.	12,367	410	10,196
1997-98	1,319	(3,459)	(61)	11,830	379	10,008
1998-99	2,165	(3,569)	25	10,280	307	9,208
1999-00	4,064	(3,695)	136	12,256	382	13,143

contd...

...contd...

(US$ million)

Year/Item	Non-Factor Services	Investment Income	Compensation to Employees	Private Transfers	Official Transfers	Invisibles
2000-01	1,692	(4,664)	(340)	12,854	252	9,794
2001-02	3,324	(3,844)	(362)	15,398	458	14,974
2002-03	3,643	(3,544)	98	16,387	451	17,035
2003-04	10,144	(3,757)	(748)	21,608	554	27,801
2004-05	15,426	(4,095)	(884)	20,525	260	31,232
2005-06	23,170	(5262)	(593)	24,493	194	42,002
2006-07	29,469	(6762)	(569)	29,825	254	52,217
2007-08	38,853	(4433)	(635)	41,706	239	75,731
2008-09	49,631	(4023)	(484)	44,567	232	89,923
2009-10	34,205	(6613)	(791)	52,055	59	78,917

Note : G.n.i.e : Government not included elsewhere.
Source : Reserve Bank of India.

125 : Non-Factor Services by Components (Net)

(US$ million)

Year/Item	Non-Factor Services	Travel	Transport	Insurance	Gnie	Misc.
1950-51	59	(25)	44	11	6	23
1960-61	120	7	42	4	63	4
1970-71	11	25	40	-	9	(63)
1980-81	1,297	1,107	7	21	51	111
1990-91	980	1,064	(110)	23	(158)	161
1991-92	1,207	1,512	(349)	(18)	(103)	165
1992-93	1,129	1,713	(503)	12	(25)	(68)
1993-94	534	1,725	(332)	(72)	(123)	(664)
1994-95	602	1,547	(167)	(29)	(155)	(594)
1995-96	(200)	1,544	(158)	36	(205)	(1,417)
1996-97	726	2,020	(441)	64	(106)	(811)
1997-98	1,319	1,477	(686)	57	116	355
1998-99	2,165	1,250	(755)	112	272	1,286
1999-00	4,064	897	(703)	109	312	3,449

contd...

...contd...

(US$ million)

Year/Item	Non-Factor Services	Travel	Transport	Insurance	Gnie	Misc.
2000-01	1,692	693	(1,512)	47	332	2,132
2001-02	3,324	123	(1,306)	8	235	4,264
2002-03	3,643	(29)	(736)	19	65	4,324
2003-04	10,144	1,435	879	56	28	7,746
2004-05	15,426	1,417	144	148	(10)	13,727
2005-06	23,170	1,215	(2,012)	(54)	(215)	24,236
2006-07	29,469	2,439	(94)	553	(150)	26,721
2007-08	38,853	2,091	(1,500)	595	(45)	37,712
2008-09	49,631	1,469	(1,534)	289	(404)	49,812
2009-10	34,205	2,517	(787)	314	(86)	32,245

Note : Non-factor services includes travel, transport, insurance; gnie - government not else where classified; and miscellaneous.
Source : Reserve Bank of India.

126 : Portfolio Investments

	In Rs. crore	Annual Change (%)	In US$ million	Annual Change (%)
1990-91	11		6	
1991-92	10	(9.1)	4	(33.3)
1992-93	748	7380.0	244	6000.0
1993-94	11,188	1395.7	3,567	1361.9
1994-95	12,007	7.3	3,824	7.2
1995-96	9,192	(23.4)	2,748	(28.1)
1996-97	11,758	27.9	3,312	20.5
1997-98	6,794	(42.2)	1,828	(44.8)
1998-99	(257)	(103.8)	(61)	(103.3)
1999-00	13,112	(5201.9)	3,026	(5060.7)
2000-01	12,609	(3.8)	2,760	(8.8)
2001-02	9,639	(23.6)	2,021	(26.8)
2002-03	4,738	(50.8)	979	(51.6)
2003-04	52,279	1003.4	11,377	1062.1
2004-05	41,854	(19.9)	9,315	(18.1)
2005-06	55,307	32.1	12,492	34.1
2006-07	31,713	(42.7)	7,003	(43.9)
2007-08	109,741	246.0	27,271	289.4
2008-09	(63,618)	(158.0)	(13,855)	(150.8)
2009-10	na		32,375	(333.7)

Note : na : not available.
Source : Handbook of Statistics on Indian Economy, Reserve Bank of India.

127 : Foreign Direct Investment Inflows (Incl: Advance)

	In Rs. crore	Annual Change (%)	In US$ million	Annual Change (%)
1990-91	174		97	
1991-92	316	81.6	129	33.0
1992-93	965	205.4	315	144.2
1993-94	1,838	90.5	586	86.0
1994-95	4,126	124.5	1,314	124.2
1995-96	7,172	73.8	2,144	63.2
1996-97	10,015	39.6	2,821	31.6
1997-98	13,220	32.0	3,557	26.1
1998-99	10,358	(21.6)	2,462	(30.8)
1999-00	9,338	(9.8)	2,155	(12.5)
2000-01	18,406	97.1	4,029	87.0
2001-02	29,235	58.8	6,130	52.1
2002-03	24,367	(16.7)	5,035	(17.9)
2003-04	19,860	(18.5)	4,322	(14.2)
2004-05	27,188	36.9	6,051	40.0
2005-06	39,674	45.9	8,961	48.1
2006-07	103,367	160.5	22,826	154.7
2007-08	138,276	33.8	34,835	52.6
2008-09	161,481	16.8	35,180	1.0
2009-10	na		34,167	(2.9)

Note : na : not available.
Source : Handbook of Statistics on Indian Economy, Reserve Bank of India.

128 : Inflow (+) and Outflow (-) Under Various NRI Deposit Schemes

(US$ million)

Year (End-March)	NR(E)RA	FCNR Accounts	Others	Total
1991-92	324	(311)	564	577
1992-93	255	825	1,083	2,163
1993-94	777	(242)	636	1,171
1994-95	1,049	(270)	207	986
1995-96	(208)	(127)	1,283	948
1996-97	1,244	(176)	2,237	3,305
1997-98	1,197	(1,299)	1,255	1,153
1998-99	799	(632)	793	960
1999-00	885	337	318	1,540
2000-01	860	904	553	2,317
2001-02	1,626	594	508	2,728
2002-03	6,195	526	(3,745)	2,976
2003-04	4,695	762	(1,816)	3,641
2004-05	84	492	(1,538)	(962)
2005-06	1,177	1,612	930	3,719
2006-07	1,830	2,065	426	4,321
2007-08	109	(960)	1,030	179
2008-09	2,508	(957)	2,738	4,289

Note : All figures are inclusive of accrued interest and valuation factor
NR(E)RA : Non-resident (external) rupee accounts
FCNR includes both foreign currency non-resident accounts and banks.
Others includes foreign currency non-resident(banks), foreign currency (bank & other) deposits, foreign currency (ordinary) non-repartiable deposits and non-resident ordinary rupee accounts

Source : Handbook of Statistics on Indian Economy. Reserve Bank of India.

129 : Tourism Statistics

	Number of Tourist Arrivals (in million)			Foreign Exchange Earnings in (US$ billion)		
	World	India	% Share	World	India	% Share
1980	284.8	0.80	0.3	102.4	1.40	1.4
1990	463.6	1.71	0.4	265.1	1.51	0.6
2000	701.9	2.65	0.4	475.8	3.46	0.7
2001	696.5	2.54	0.4	457.9	3.20	0.7
2002	692.3	2.38	0.3	472.5	3.10	0.7
2003	681.7	2.73	0.4	605.7	4.46	0.7
2004	777.5	3.46	0.4	743.0	6.17	0.8
2005	736.1	3.92	0.5	787.3	7.49	1.0
2006		4.45			8.63	
2007		5.08			10.73	
2008		5.37			11.75	

Source : Ministry of Tourism (website).

130 : India's External Debt

(US$ million)

	1991	2001	2007	2008	2009	2010
Multilateral Debt	20900	31105	35337	39490	39538	42733
Bilateral Debt	14168	15975	16065	19708	20613	22596
IMF	2623	0	1029	1120	1018	6041
Trade Credit	4301	5923	7165	10358	14490	16878
Commercial Borrowings	10209	24408	41443	62334	62413	70986
NRI & FC(BO) Deposits	10209	16568	41240	43672	41554	48092
Rupee Debt	12847	3719	1951	2017	1527	1657
Long-Term Debt	75257	97698	144230	178669	181153	208983
Short-Term Debt	8544	3628	28130	45738	43362	52471
% to Gross Debt	10.2	3.6	16.4	20.4	19.3	20.1
% to Foreign Exchange Reseves	146.5	8.6	14.1	14.8	17.2	18.8
Gross Debt	83801	101326	172360	224407	224515	261454
% to GDP	28.7	22.5	18.2	18.1	20.5	18.9
Concessional Debt to Total Debt	45.9	35.4	23.0	19.8	18.7	16.8
Debt Service Ratio	35.3	16.6	4.7	4.8	4.6	5.5
Ratio of Foreign Exchange Reserve to Total Debt	7.0	41.7	115.6	138.0	112.2	106.7

Source : Ministry of Finance and Reserve Bank of India.

131 : External Commercial Borrowings

(US$ million)

	Approvals	Gross Disbursements	Amortisation	Interest	Total Servicing	ECB Outstandings
1990-91	1903	4252	2004	1410	3414	10209
1991-92	2127	3133	1677	1153	2830	11715
1992-93	2200	1167	1525	1182	2707	11643
1993-94	2585	2913	1978	1254	3232	12363
1994-95	4469	4152	2812	1478	4290	12991
1995-96	6286	4252	3868	1380	5248	13873
1996-97	8581	7571	4605	1354	5959	14335
1997-98	8712	7371	3550	1384	4934	16986
1998-99	5200	7226	3477	1593	5070	20975
1999-00	3398	3187	4147	1653	5800	19943
2000-01	2837	9621	5378	1695	7073	24408
2001-02	2653	2684	4107	1456	5563	23320
2002-03	4235	3505	5019	1167	6186	22472
2003-04	6671	8225	8045	2119	10164	22007
2004-05	11490	9084	3571	959	4530	26405
2005-06	17175	14343	11584	3165	14749	26452
2006-07	25353	20257	3814	2517	6331	41443
2007-08	28900	28784	6119	3652	9771	62337
2008-09	17200	13377	6439	3962	10401	62508

Source : Ministry of Finance and Reserve Bank of India.

132 : India's Debt Service Payments

(US$ million)

	1990-91	2000-01	2005-06	2006-07	2007-08	2008-09
External Assistance	2315	3444	2652	2942	3241	3381
Repayment	1187	2338	1945	1960	2099	2372
Interest	1128	1106	707	982	1142	1009
ECBs	3414	7073	14839	6331	9771	10401
Repayment	2004	5378	11824	3814	6119	6439
Interest	1410	1695	3015	2517	3652	3962
IMF	778	26				
Repayment	644	26				
Interest	134					
NRI Deposit						
Interest	1282	1661	1497	1969	1813	1547
Rupee Debt Service						
Repayment	1193	617	572	162	121	101
Total Debt Service	8982	12821	19560	11404	14946	15430
Repayment	5028	8359	14341	5936	8339	8912
Interest	3954	4462	5219	5468	6607	6518
Current Receipts #	25479	77467	194170	242811	314014	337095
Debt Service Ratio	35.3	16.6	10.1	4.7	4.8	4.6

Note : Debt service ratio is defined as total repayment of principal and interest on debt as a ratio of current receipts.
current receipts minus official transfers.

Source : Ministry of Finance and Reserve Bank of India.

II. SOCIAL SECTOR

- Demography
  - Population
  - Vital Rates
- Health & Family Welfare
- Housing
- Living Standard
- Education
- Law & Order
- Trade Union
- Mass Media
- Insurance
- Employment

133 : Growth of Population : All India

Census Year	Population (in million)	Growth Over Decade	
		Total (%)	CAGR (%)
1901	238.40		
1911	252.09	5.7	0.56
1921	251.32	-0.3	-0.03
1931	278.98	11.0	1.05
1941	318.66	14.2	1.34
1951	361.09	13.3	1.26
1961	439.23	21.6	1.98
1971	548.16	24.8	2.24
1981	683.33	24.7	2.23
1991	846.42	23.9	2.16
2001	1028.74	21.5	1.97

Note :
1. CAGR or compounded annual growth rate.
2. Reference period of various Census is March 1 except for 1971 where it was April 1.
3. 1981 numbers for Assam and 1991 for J&K based on interpolation as Census could not be held in those states.
4. 2001 population data include estimated figures for Kachchh and Morvi, Malia-Miyana and Wankaner *talukas* of Rajkot district, Jodiya *taluk* for Gujarat and entire Kinnaur district of Himachal Pradesh where Census could not be conducted due to natural calamities.

Source : Office of the Registrar General of India, Ministry of Home Affairs (Census documents).

134 : Rural-Urban Distribution of Population : All India

Census Year	Rural			Urban		
	(in million)	CAGR (%)	% Share	(in million)	CAGR (%)	% Share
1901	212.54		89.2	25.85		10.8
1911	226.15	0.62	89.7	25.94	0.03	10.3
1921	223.24	-0.13	88.8	28.09	0.79	11.2
1931	245.52	0.96	88.0	33.46	1.76	12.0
1941	274.51	1.12	86.1	44.15	2.81	13.9
1951	298.64	0.85	82.7	62.44	3.53	17.3
1961	360.30	1.90	82.0	78.94	2.37	18.0
1971	439.05	2.00	80.1	109.11	3.29	19.9
1981	523.87	1.78	76.7	159.46	3.87	23.3
1991	628.86	1.84	74.3	217.56	3.16	25.7
2001	742.62	1.68	72.2	286.12	2.78	27.8

Source : Office of the Registrar General of India, Ministry of Home Affairs (Census documents). For Notes see Table 133.

135 : Density of Population

	1961	1971	1981	1991	2001
Density	142	177	216	267	328
CAGR (%)	1.96	2.23	2.01	2.14	1.99

Note : Density is the number of people per square kilometre of area.
CAGR: compunded annual growth rate worked out on density numbers.
Notes and source : see Table 133.

136 : Gender Composition of Population : All India

Census	Male		Female		
Year	(in million)	CAGR (%)	(in million)	CAGR (%)	Sex-Ratio
1901	120.89		117.51		972
1911	128.36	0.60	123.73	0.52	964
1921	128.55	0.01	122.77	-0.08	955
1931	143.07	1.08	135.91	1.02	950
1941	163.84	1.36	154.82	1.31	945
1951	185.55	1.25	175.54	1.26	946
1961	226.29	2.00	212.94	1.95	941
1971	284.05	2.30	264.11	2.18	930
1981	353.37	2.21	329.96	2.25	934
1991	439.36	2.20	407.06	2.12	927
2001	532.22	1.94	496.51	2.01	933

Note : Sex-ratio is defined as number of women per thousand men.
Source : Office of the Registrar General of India, Ministry of Home Affairs (Census documents). For notes, see Table 133.

137 : Age-Wise Composition of Population : All India

(population in million)

Census	Age-Distribution (All India)					of which:	
Year	All Ages	0-14	15-19	20-34	35-59	60+	80+
1951	356.80	133.62	35.88	86.80	80.31	13.05	na
%		**37.4**	**10.1**	**24.3**	**22.5**	**3.7**	
1961	438.94	180.08	35.88	104.76	93.33	24.71	2.50
%		**41.0**	**8.2**	**23.9**	**21.3**	**5.6**	**0.6**
1971	548.16	230.34	47.47	120.11	117.43	32.70	3.2
%		**42.0**	**8.7**	**21.9**	**21.4**	**6.0**	**0.6**
1981	665.29	263.11	64.14	150.44	144.10	43.17	4.127
%		**39.5**	**9.6**	**22.6**	**21.7**	**6.5**	**0.6**
1991	838.57	312.37	79.04	202.12	183.68	56.68	6.375
%		**37.2**	**9.4**	**24.1**	**21.9**	**6.8**	**0.8**
2001	1028.61	363.64	100.22	247.46	237.96	76.62	8.039
%		**35.4**	**9.7**	**24.1**	**23.1**	**7.4**	**0.8**

Note : na: not available
Figures in **bold** after each year are proportion to total .
Total includes age not stated and thus individual % number will not add up to 100
Notes and source ; As in Table 133.

138 : Age Distribution of Population : All India — By Gender

(in million)

Age-Group	Male			Female			Sex-Ratio		
	1981	1991	2001	1981	1991	2001	1981	1991	2001
Child	42.2	52.4	57.1	41.3	50.0	53.3	978	955	934
(0-4)	**12.3**	**12.0**	**10.7**	**12.8**	**12.4**	**10.7**			
Children	135.8	161.7	189.5	127.3	150.6	174.1	938	931	919
(0-14)	**39.5**	**37.2**	**35.6**	**39.6**	**37.3**	**35.1**			
Youth	110.4	144.2	179.2	104.2	136.9	168.5	944	950	940
(15-34)	**32.1**	**33.1**	**33.7**	**32.4**	**34.0**	**33.9**			
Women of Fertile Age	163.7	216.3	271.5	153.3	200.7	252.7	937	928	931
(15-49)	**47.6**	**49.7**	**51.0**	**47.7**	**49.7**	**50.9**			
Worker	186.1	244.1	304.9	172.9	225.4	283.5	929	923	930
(15-59)	**54.1**	**56.1**	**57.3**	**53.8**	**55.9**	**57.1**			
Senior Citizen	22.0	29.4	37.8	21.1	27.3	38.9	960	930	1029
(60+)	**6.4**	**6.7**	**7.1**	**6.6**	**6.8**	**7.8**			
Septuagenarian	7.8	11.0	14.7	7.6	10.1	14.6	974	922	992
(70+)	**2.3**	**2.5**	**2.8**	**2.4**	**2.5**	**2.9**			
All Ages	343.9	435.2	532.2	321.4	403.4	496.5	934	927	933

Note : Figures in bold below each year are percentages to total.
Notes and Source ; As in Table 133.

139 : Population by Religion : All India

Census	1951	1961	1971	1981	1991	2001
All	356.8	438.9	548.2	665.3	838.6	1028.6
Hindus	303.6	366.4	453.4	549.7	687.6	827.6
% to Total	85.1	83.5	82.7	82.6	82.0	80.5
Muslims	35.4	46.9	61.4	75.6	101.6	138.2
% to Total	9.9	10.7	11.2	11.4	12.1	13.4
Christians	8.4	10.7	14.3	16.2	19.6	24.1
% to Total	2.4	2.4	2.6	2.4	2.3	2.3
Sikhs	6.2	7.8	10.4	13.1	16.3	19.2
% to Total	1.7	1.8	1.9	2.0	1.9	1.9
Jain	1.6	2.0	2.6	3.2	3.4	4.2
% to Total	0.4	0.5	0.5	0.5	0.4	0.4
Budhists	0.2	3.2	3.8	4.7	6.4	8.0
% to Total	0.1	0.7	0.7	0.7	0.8	0.8

Note : Total includes others and those who have not disclosed information.
Notes and Sources : As in Table 133.

140 : Distribution of Rural Population by Size of Village

(%)

Size of Village in Terms of Population	1961	1971	1981	1991	2001
< 200	3.8	2.7	1.8	1.7	1.2
200-499	12.6	9.9	7.5	7.8	5.9
500-999	18.3	16.5	14.2	16.8	14.2
1000-1999	19.8	19.9	19.3	25.7	24.7
2000-4999	17.2	18.7	20.1	29.8	32.2
5000-9999	5.1	5.9	6.9	11.2	13.2
=>10000	2.8	4.1	4.6	7.0	8.5
Rural Population in mn	360.3	439.05	523.87	628.86	742.62
% to Total	82.0	80.1	76.7	74.3	72.2
Total Population in mn	439.23	548.16	683.33	846.42	1028.74

Note : Individual figures will not add upto total rural population as village population is not exhaustive.
Notes and Sources : As in Table 133.

141 : Share of Scheduled Caste and Scheduled Tribe Population

	1961	1971	1981	1991	2001
All Population (million)	439.2	548.2	683.3	846.4	1028.7
SCs (% to total population)	14.7	14.6	15.8	16.5	16.2
STs (% to total population)	6.9	6.9	7.8	8.1	8.2

Source : As in Table 133.

142 : Urbanisation by Class of Towns

Class & Size of Towns in Terms of Population	1961	1971	1981	1991	2001
	Number of Towns				
Class 1	106	150	226	322	441
=> 1 lakh	**4.0**	**4.9**	**5.7**	**7.0**	**8.5**
Class II	138	214	325	421	496
50000-99999	**5.2**	**7.0**	**8.2**	**9.1**	**9.6**
Class III	508	643	883	1161	1388
20000-49999	**19.2**	**21.1**	**22.4**	**25.2**	**26.9**
Class IV	811	962	1247	1451	1561
10000-19999	**30.6**	**31.5**	**31.6**	**31.4**	**30.2**
Class V	827	797	920	971	1041
5000-9999	**31.2**	**26.1**	**23.3**	**21.0**	**20.2**
Class VI	257	288	348	289	234
<5000	**9.7**	**9.4**	**8.8**	**6.3**	**4.5**
All Classes	2647	3054	3949	4615	5161
	100.0	**100.0**	**100.0**	**100.0**	**100.0**
	Population (in million)				
Class 1	35.0	53.2	83.0	122.3	178.2
=> 1 lakh	**44.8**	**49.4**	**52.6**	**56.7**	**62.3**
Class II	9.5	14.4	22.0	28.8	34.5
50000-99999	**12.1**	**13.4**	**14.0**	**13.3**	**12.1**
Class III	15.5	19.7	26.9	35.3	42.1
20000-49999	**19.8**	**18.3**	**17.1**	**16.4**	**14.7**
Class IV	11.2	13.6	17.7	21.1	22.6
10000-19999	**14.3**	**12.6**	**11.2**	**9.8**	**7.9**
Class V	6.2	6.0	6.9	7.4	7.9
5000-9999	**7.9**	**5.6**	**4.4**	**3.4**	**2.8**
Class VI	0.8	0.9	1.1	0.9	0.8
<5000	**1.0**	**0.8**	**0.7**	**0.4**	**0.3**
All Classes	78.2	107.8	157.7	215.8	286.1
	100.0	**100.0**	**100.0**	**100.0**	**100.0**

Note : Figures in bold below each class are percentages to total (as on 21.3.2005).
Source : As in Table 133.

143 : Literacy Rate by Gender/Area

(%)

	1951	1961	1971	1981	1991	2001
All	18.3	28.3	34.5	43.6	52.2	64.8
Rural	12.1	19.1	23.7	36.1	44.7	60.0
Urban	34.6	47.0	52.4	67.3	73.1	81.0
Male	27.2	40.4	46.0	56.4	64.1	75.3
Female	8.9	15.3	22.0	29.8	39.3	53.7
Male-Female Gap	18.3	25.1	24.0	26.6	24.8	21.6

Note : Literacy rate: literate population as proportion of those aged 7 years and above. Male-female gap expressed in percenatge points.
Notes and source : see Table 133.

144 : Crude Birth and Death Rates

(per '000 population)

	Crude Birth Rate (CBR)			Crude Death Rate (CDR)		
Year	Total	Rural	Urban	Total	Rural	Urban
1951	41.7	na	na	22.8	na	na
1961	41.2	na	na	19.0	na	na
1971	36.9	38.9	30.1	14.9	16.4	9.7
1981	33.9	35.6	27.0	12.5	13.7	7.8
1991	29.5	30.9	34.3	9.8	10.6	7.1
2001	25.4	27.1	20.3	8.4	9.1	6.3
2002	25.0	26.6	20.0	8.1	8.7	6.1
2003	24.8	26.4	19.8	8.0	8.7	6.0
2004	24.1	25.9	19.0	7.5	8.2	5.8
2005	23.8	25.6	19.1	7.6	8.1	6.0
2006	23.5	25.2	18.8	7.5	8.1	6.0
2007	23.1	24.7	18.6	7.6	8.0	6.0
2008	22.8	24.4	18.5	7.4	8.0	5.9

Note: na : not available.
Crude birth rate is the number of live births during the year divided by mid-year population. Crude death rate is the number of deaths during the year divided by mid-year population. The difference between the two is the natural growth rate.

Source: Sample Registration System (SRS) reports and early bulletins, Office of the Registrar General, India.

145 : Infant Mortality Rate and Neonatal Mortality Rate

	Infant Mortality Rate (IMR)			Neonatal Mortality Rate (NMR)		
Year	Total	Rural	Urban	Total	Rural	Urban
1961	52	na	na	na	na	na
1971	129	138	82	75	81	45
1981	110	119	62	70	76	39
1991	80	87	53	51	55	32
2001	66	72	42	40	44	25
2002	63	69	40	na	na	na
2003	60	66	38	37	41	22
2004	58	64	40	37	41	24
2005	58	64	40	37	41	23
2006	57	62	39	na	na	na
2007	55	61	37	na	na	na
2008	53	58	36	na	na	na

Note: na: not available
Infant mortality rate is the number of infant deaths during the year related to the number of live births multiplied by thousand. Neo-natal mortality rate is the ratio of deaths of infants aged less than 29 days during the year, to the number of live births multiplied by thousand.

Source: Sample Registration System (SRS) reports and early bulletins, Office of the Registrar General, India.

146 : Total Fertility Rate and General Fertility Rate

Year	Total Fertility Rate (TFR)			General Fertility Rate (GFR)		
	Total	Rural	Urban	Total	Rural	Urban
1971	5.2	5.4	4.1	161.1	168.7	130.1
1981	4.5	4.8	3.3	140.9	149.4	107.2
1991	3.6	3.9	2.7	119.2	127.2	93.3
2000	3.2	3.5	3.3	102.8	112.7	76.5
2001	3.1	3.4	2.3	99.5	108.6	74.4
2002	3.0	3.3	2.2	97.1	106.0	72.5
2003	3.0	3.3	2.1	95.3	103.5	71.9
2004	2.9	3.3	2.1	98.6	109.7	72.0
2005	2.9	3.2	2.1	95.8	106.2	70.9
2006	2.8	3.1	2.0	93.3	103.4	69.1
2007	2.7	3.0	2.0	89.5	98.6	67.3
2008	2.6	2.9	2.0	88.0	96.9	66.5

Note: Total Fertility Rate is defined as the average number of children that would be born to a woman if she experiences the current fertility pattern throughout her reproductive span (15-49 years).
General Fertility Rate is defined as numbered of live births per thousand women in the reproductive age group (15-49 years) in a given year.

Source : Sample Registration System (SRS) reports and Previous Bulletins, Office of the Registrar General, India.

147 : Expectation of Life at Birth in Years

Year	Male	Female	All	Rural	Urban
1941-1951	32.4	31.7	32.1	na	na
1951-1961	41.9	40.6	41.3	na	na
1961-1971	46.4	44.7	45.6	na	na
1971-1975	50.5	49.0	49.7	48.0	58.9
1976-1980	52.5	52.1	52.3	50.6	60.1
1981-1985	55.4	55.7	55.4	53.7	63.4
1985-1990	57.7	58.1	57.7	56.1	63.8
1991-1995	59.7	58.6	60.3	58.9	65.9
1996-2000	61.0	62.7	61.9	60.7	67.3
2001-2005	62.3	63.9	63.6	na	na
2002-2006	62.6	64.2	63.4	na	na

Note : na : not available
Expectation of life at birth is the average number of years expected to be lived at the time of birth if current mortality trends were to continue.
Data from 1941-1951 to 1961-1971 are based on census actuarial reports.
Data from 1970-1975 onwards are based on SRS estimates. Data from 1991-1995 excludes J&K.

Source : Sample Registration System (SRS) reports and Early Bulletins, Office of the Registrar General, India.

148 : Health Infrastructure

As on 1st Jan	No. of Doctors (in thousands)	Medical Persons per Lakh People				Medical Infrastructure	
		Doctors	Nurses	Health Visitors	Auxiliary Nurses	No. of Hospitals (in thousands)	No. of Beds (per lakh of population)
1951	61.8	17	10	0.2	5	8	33
1961	83.7	19	18	0.4	10	7	53
1971	151.1	28	14	0.8	14	7	65
1981	268.7	39	21	1.4	10	10	84
1991	393.6	47	41	2	18	11	95
2001	555.6	54	79	3.5	42	4	41
2002	607.1	58	na	na	na	na	41
2003	625.4	59	80	3.8	48	5	36
2004	644.0	59	81	4.7	47	7	44
2005	660.9	61	83	4.7	48	6	43
2006	na	61	na	na	na	7	42
2007	682.6	61	129*	na	na	8	44
2008	696.7	61	127*	na	na	10	42

Note: * : includes both general nurses and auxiliary nurse mid-wifes.
From 2000 community health centres have been excluded from the numbers of hospitals and beds.

Source: Director General of Health Services.

149 : Combined Health Expenditure (Central and State Governments)

	Rs. crore	% GDP	Per capita (Rs.)
1986-87	4566	1.5	59.2
1990-91	7309	1.3	87.1
1995-96	14135	1.2	152.3
2000-01	27960	1.3	274.4
2001-02	28578	1.3	274.8
2002-03	30184	1.2	285.8
2003-04	33504	1.2	312.5
2004-05	37535	1.2	344.7
2005-06	45428	1.2	410.7
2006-07	52126	1.2	464.6
2007-08	60869	1.2	534.9
2008-09 (RE)	76489	1.4	662.8
2009-10 (BE)	89314	1.4	763.4

Note: RE: Revised Estimates; BE: Budget Estimates.
From 2004-05, per cent to GDP worked out by using GDP figures as per 2004-05 series.
Amount are at current prices.

Source : Government of India, Economic Survey.

150 : Percentage of Couples Protected Under Family Planning Methods

	Eligible Couples (in million)	% of Couples Protected by		
		Sterilisation	Intra-Uterine Devices	All Methods*
1965-66	1525.8	1.6	1.7	3.1
1970-71	94.5	8.0	1.4	11.5
1980-81	116.0	20.1	1.1	24.4
1990-91	145.1	30.3	7.0	49.6
2000-01	176.6	28.4	7.4	50.3
2004-05	185.2	28.2	6.8	46.6
2005-06	188.0	27.9	6.7	46.7
2006-07	190.7	27.6	6.5	46.2
2007-08	193.5	27.5	6.4	46.5

Note: * Including other methods such as pill, condom etc., and also traditional methods.

Source : Ministry of Health and Family Welfare.

151 : Deficit in Housing

Census Year	Number of Households (in million)			Number of Occupied Residential Houses (in million)			Deficit in Housing Stock (in million)		
	Rural	Urban	Total	Rural	Urban	Total	Rural	Urban	Total
1951	53.6	12.3	65.9	54.1	10.3	64.4	-0.5	2.0	1.5
1961	68.9	15.6	84.5	65.1	13.8	78.9	3.8	1.8	5.6
1971	79.6	20.9	100.4	72.7	18.0	90.8	6.9	2.9	9.6
1981	90.9	28.9	119.8	86.1(a)	27.6	113.7	4.8	1.3	6.1
1991(b)	111.6	40.4	152.0	107.9	39.1	147.0	3.7	1.3	5.0
2001	137.7©	55.8	193.6	135.1	52.1	187.2	2.6	3.7	6.4

Note : A household is a group of persons who commonly live together and would take their meals from a common kitchen unless the exigencies of work prevented any of them from doing so. There may be a household of blood relatives, or unrelated persons or a mix of both. Unrelated person households include boarding houses, messes, hotels, rescue home, jails, asylums and are included in the number.

Deficit has been worked out on the assumption that each household requires a house and the difference between number of households and occupied residential houses indicates the apparent gap in housing.

a: excludes Assam, b: excludes J&K, c: excludes Mao Maram, Paomata, Purul and Senapati districts of Manipur.

Source : Office of the Registrar General, India (National Sample Survey Organisation survey).

152 : Per cent Distribution of Households by Type of Housing Structure

Year	Rural			Urban		
	Pucca	Semi-*Pucca*	*Kutcha*	*Pucca*	Semi-*Pucca*	*Kutcha*
1986-87	17.2	33.1	49.6	57.2	25.7	17.0
1987-88	19.5	31.9	48.6	57.9	24.3	17.8
1988-89	27.1	33.5	59.3	71.1	18.0	10.9
1992	26.7	35.3	37.8	67.3	22.5	10.2
1993-94	29.2	38.1	32.7	70.7	19.5	9.9
1994-95	29.6	37.9	32.4	70.4	20.0	9.5
2000-01	38.4	31.6	30.0	75.2	19.4	7.4
2003	43.9	34.9	21.1	81.7	13.4	4.8
2004	48.2	32.8	17.2	85.5	10.2	3.5
2005-06	50.0	31.0	19.0	86.0	10.0	4.0
2006-07	49.0	29.0	22.0	85.0	11.0	4.0

Source : National Sample Survey Organisation, NSSO surveys.

153 : Distribution of Households by Size of Dwellings

Year		No Exclusive Room	One Room	Two Rooms	Three Rooms	More than 3 Rooms
		(Per cent of Total)				
1981	Total	0.7	44.7	28.6	12.2	13.8
	Rural	0.7	44.4	28.9	12.2	13.8
	Urban	0.5	45.8	27.9	12.2	13.6
1991	Total	0.0	40.5	30.6	13.9	15.1
	Rural	0.0	40.8	30.7	13.5	15.0
	Urban	0.0	39.6	30.4	14.8	15.2
2001	Total	3.1	38.5	30.0	14.4	14.1
	Rural	3.4	39.8	30.2	13.3	13.4
	Urban	2.3	35.1	29.5	17.1	15.9

Source : Census documents.

154 : Per capita Net Availability of Foodgrains

(per day in grams)

Mid Year	Foodgrains	Cereals	Pulses
1951	394.9	334.2	60.7
1961	468.7	399.7	69.0
1971	468.8	417.6	51.2
1981	454.8	417.3	37.5
1991	510.1	468.5	41.6
2001	416.2	386.2	30.0
2002	494.1	458.1	35.4
2003	437.6	408.5	29.1
2004	462.7	426.9	35.8
2005	422.4	390.9	31.5
2006	445.3	412.8	32.5
2007	442.8	407.4	35.5
2008	436.0	374.6	41.6

Source : *Economic Survey.*

155 : Population Below Poverty Line, Poverty Ratio and Poverty Line

	BPL Population (in million)			Poverty Ratio (%)		
	Rural	Urban	Combined	Rural	Urban	Combined
1973-74	261.3	60.0	321.3	56.4	49.0	54.9
1977-78	264.2	64.6	328.9	53.1	45.2	51.3
1983	252.0	70.9	322.9	45.7	40.8	44.5
1987-88	231.9	75.2	307.1	39.1	38.2	38.9
1993-94	244.0	76.3	320.3	37.3	32.4	36.0
1999-00	193.2	67.0	260.3	27.1	23.6	26.1
2004-05	220.9	80.8	301.7	28.3	25.7	27.5

Note: Based on poverty lines defined in terms of per capita total consumer expenditure (PCTE) at 1973-74 prices and adjusted over time and across states for change in prices. The estimates were anchored on the per capita calorie norms of 2400 for rural and 2100 for urban persons per day.

Source: Planning Commission.

As Per Professor Suresh Tendulakar Committee Report 2009

	Head Count Ratio of BPL		
	Rural	Urban	All-India
1993-94	50.1	31.8	45.3
2004-05	41.8	25.7	37.2

The Committee has proposed that the poverty line basket should take into account all items of consumption (except transport and conveyance) for constructing of price indices to derive the updated poverty line. Separate allowance for private expenditure on transport and conveyance has been made in the recommended poverty line.

156 : Private Final Consumption Expenditure (At Current Prices)

	PFCE (Rs. crore)	PFCE (per capita Rs.)	*of which:* Food (Rs.)	Clothing (Rs.)	Rent (Rs.)	Medicine (Rs.)	Education (Rs.)
1999-2000 = Series							
1950-51	9643	268.6	163.8	9.2	55.0	3.1	1.6
1960-61	16312	375.9	192.9	17.5	90.6	5.5	3.3
1970-71	39493	730.0	408.2	35.1	127.4	13.2	7.6
1980-81	120094	1768.7	924.6	107.5	234.5	50.6	22.9
1990-91	392142	4673.9	2231.0	268.0	517.6	113.8	75.2
2000-01	1345583	13204.9	5593.8	568.6	974.2	538.0	233.4
2001-02	1470301	14137.5	5342.7	681.9	1060.0	622.9	258.5
2002-03	1552618	14702.8	5727.1	641.4	1150.5	724.7	286.2
2003-04	1703547	15891.3	5614.6	669.5	1228.3	756.9	317.3
2004-05	1848490	16974.2	5961.2	713.0	1301.9	789.7	351.5
2004-05 = Series							
2004-05	1926858	17693.8	5931.0	994.0	1541.1	877.5	374.0
2005-06	2158349	19514.9	6467.8	1144.7	1673.2	951.6	404.3
2006-07	2477209	22078.5	6953.9	1435.2	1857.8	1033.0	437.6
2007-08	2815675	24742.3	7690.6	1448.3	2143.2	1121.7	507.6
2008-09	3218198	27887.3	8159.9	1543.2	2586.2	1218.2	586.4
2009-10	3571999	30529.9					

Source : CSO National Account Statistics.

157 : Number of Recognised Schools

As on Sept.-30	Boards of Education (Nos.)	Schools for General Education				Technical Education Schools*		
		Pre-Primary/ Nursery	Primary/ Basic	Middle/ Sr.Basic/ Upper Primary	Secondary/ Sr. Secondary/ Higher Secondary/Jr. Colleges	Vocational/ Professional Schools	Special Education Schools	Other Schools
1951	7	303	209671	13596	7416	1857	83	53212
1961	13	1909	330399	49663	17329	4431	144	66654
1971	37	4174	408378	90621	37051	2337	305	103815
1981	49	10697	494503	118555	51573	2562	399	na
1991	42	15877	560935	151456	79796	1277	398	na
2001	35	37288	638738	206269	126047	na	na	na
2002	39	60840	664041	219626	133492	na	na	na
2003	39	64712	651382	245274	137207	4647	1173	..
2004	39	63167	712239	262286	145962	4877	1105	..
2005	41	63596	767520	274731	152049	5114	1171	..
2006	41	67157	772568	288493	159667	na	na	na
2007	na	na	784852	305584	169568	na	na	na

Note : na: not available

* Vocational and professional schools include institutions imparting instructions in diploma/certificate courses at school level in agriculture/forestry/medicine/nursing/mid-wifery/teachers training/industry (arts and crafts), music and fine arts.

Special education schools includes institutions imparting instructions in diploma/certificate courses at school level, handicapped and reformatory/certified.

Other schools includes oriental studies, social adult education and other institutions imparting instructions in diploma and certificate courses at school level.

Source : Department of Education, Ministry of Human Resources Development (website).

158 : Number of Institutions for Higher Education

(numbers)

As on Sept.-30	University/ Deemed University/ Institution of National Importance	Degree Colleges									
		Arts, Science, Commerce	Oriental Learning Colleges	Agriculture Colleges	Law Colleges	Medical Colleges	Veterinary Science Colleges	Teachers' Training Colleges	Enginee-ring Colleges	Other Colleges	Total Degree Colleges
1951	29	542	na	20	19	49	10	53	33	100	826
1961	45	1122	na	39	38	151	18	478	78	234	2158
1971	82	2912	na	84	91	243	22	1338	738	1582	7010
1981	110	4100	na	72	154	496	21	1294	1011	2045	9193
1991	184	4877	723	79	241	441	37	506	289	153	7346
2001	254	8640	826	102	335	1069	50	694	678	412	12806
2002	2720	10517	828	103	368	1255	51	785	1077	453	15437
2003	304	10753	847	122	370	1393	44	904	1172	601	16206
2004	304	10796	850	137	401	1639	44	1026	1227	622	16742
2005	490	11698	na	na	na	2053	na	1669	1562	na	18482

Note : na : not available.
Deemed university includes institutes established under state legislature act.
Medical colleges includes *ayurveda*, dental, pharmacy, nursing and physiotherapy.
Veterinary colleges includes fisheries, animal science and dairy etc.
Other colleges includes library science, physical education, yoga, music, fine arts, social science, journalism and mass communication.

Source : Central Statistical Organisation publications.

159 : Number of Teachers and Pupil-Teacher Ratio

Year	Number of Teachers (in '000)									Pupil-Teacher Ratio (%)		
	Primary			Upper Primary			Sec/Sr.Sec/Intermediate					
	Total	Male	Female	Total	Male	Female	Total	Male	Female	Primary (I-V)	Middle (VI-VIII)	Secondary (IX-XI)
1950-51	538	456	82	86	73	13	127	107	20	24	20	21
1960-61	742	615	127	345	262	83	296	234	62	36	31	25
1970-71	1057	832	225	638	463	175	629	474	155	39	32	25
1980-81	1363	1021	342	851	598	253	926	669	257	38	33	27
1990-91	1616	1143	473	1073	717	356	1336	919	417	43	38	32
2000-01	1896	1221	675	1326	820	506	1761	1184	577	43	38	32
2001-02	1928	1213	715	1468	921	547	1777	1157	620	43	34	34
2002-03	1913	1167	746	1581	936	645	2033	1221	812	42	34	33
2003-04	2097	1260	837	1592	944	648	2024	1250	774	45	35	33
2004-05	2161	1319	842	1589	992	597	2083	1282	801	46	35	33
2005-06	2184	1326	858	1671	998	673	2154	1333	821	46	34	33

Source : Department of Education, Ministry of Human Resources Development (website).

160 : Enrolment by Stages of School Education (All Students) and Gross Enrolment Ratio (GER)

(in million)

Year	Primary (I-V) Age 6-11 Years				Middle/Upper Primary (VI-VIII) Age 11-14 Years				Sec/Sr.Sec/Inter/Pre-Degree (IX-XII) Age 14-18 Years			
	Enrolment	GER (%)			Enrolment	GER (%)			Enrolment	GER (%)		
	Total (in million)	Total	Male	Female	Total (in million)	Total	Male	Female	Total (in million)	Total	Male	Female
1970-71	19.2	43.1	60.6	24.8	3.1	12.7	20.6	4.6	1.5	na	na	na
1970-71	35.0	62.4	82.6	41.4	6.7	22.5	33.2	11.3	3.4	10.6	16.7	4.1
1970-71	57.0	78.6	95.5	60.5	13.3	33.4	46.5	20.8	7.6	19.0	26.8	10.2
1980-81	73.8	80.5	95.8	64.1	20.7	41.9	54.3	28.6	11.0	17.3	23.1	11.1
1990-91	97.4	100.1	113.9	85.5	34.0	76.6	47.0	62.1	19.1	19.3	33.9	10.3
2000-01	113.8	95.7	104.9	85.9	42.8	58.6	49.9	58.6	27.6	30.1	24.6	35
2001-02	113.9	96.3	105.3	86.9	44.8	60.2	67.8	52.1	30.5	33.3	38.2	27.7
2002-03	122.4	95.3	97.5	93.1	46.9	61.0	65.3	56.2	33.2	37.5	41.3	33.2
2003-04	128.3	98.2	100.8	95.7	48.7	62.4	66.9	57.7	35.0	38.9	42.9	34.3
2004-05	130.8	107.8	110.7	104.7	51.2	69.9	74.3	65.1	37.1	39.9	44.3	35.1
2005-06	132.1	109.4	112.2	105.8	52.2	71.0	75.2	66.4	38.4	39.4	44.6	35.8
2006-07	na	111.4	114.6	108.0	na	73.8	77.6	69.6	na	40.4	44.6	35.8

Note : na : not available

Gross enrolment ratio (GER) - percentage of number of pupils enrolled in different age-groups to total population in the appropriate ages.

Source : Department of Education, Ministry of Human Resources Development (website).

161 : Dropout Ratio

(In percentages)

Year	(I-V Classes)			(I-VIII Classes)			(I-X Classes)		
	Boys	Girls	Total	Boys	Girls	Total	Boys	Girls	Total
1960-61	61.7	70.9	64.9	75.0	85.0	78.3	na	na	na
1970-71	64.5	70.9	67.0	74.6	83.4	77.9	na	na	na
1980-81	56.2	62.5	58.7	68.0	79.4	72.7	79.8	86.6	82.5
1990-91	40.1	46.0	42.6	59.1	65.1	60.9	67.5	77.0	71.3
2000-01	39.7	41.9	40.7	50.3	57.0	53.7	66.4	71.5	68.6
2001-02	38.4	39.9	39.0	52.9	56.9	54.6	64.2	68.6	66.0
2002-03	35.9	33.7	34.9	52.3	53.5	52.8	60.7	65.0	62.6
2003-04	33.7	28.6	31.5	51.9	52.9	52.3	61.0	64.9	62.7
2004-05	31.8	25.4	29.0	50.5	51.3	50.8	60.4	63.9	61.9
2005-06	48.7	21.8	25.7	48.7	49.0	48.8	60.1	63.6	61.6
2006-07	46.5	26.6	25.6	46.5	45.3	45.9	58.6	61.5	59.9

Note : Total dropouts during a course as percentage of intake in the first year of the course (stage) has been taken.
Dropout rate is the per cent of pupils who dropped out from a given grade/cycle/level of education in a given school year. It does not includes repeaters.

Source : Ministry of Human Resource Development.

162 : Percentage Distribution of Population by Education Level in India

Year	1971		1981		1991		2001	
	Female	Male	Female	Male	Female	Male	Female	Male
Illiterate	81.3	60.6	75.2	53.1	67.8	47.3	54.9	36.8
Literate without Education	6.8	12.2	8.6	14.4	8.9	12.5	14.6	17.4
Primary	7.1	13.7	8.1	13.6	10.1	14.4	12.7	15.7
Middle	3.0	7.5	4.2	8.4	6.6	11.2	6.9	10.5
Matric/ Secondary	1.5	4.9	2.3	5.9	3.6	7.6	5.7	9.6
Higher Secondary/ Intermediate Pre-University	na	na	0.8	2.2	1.4	3.2	2.7	4.6
Diploma Non-technical	-	0.10	-	-	0.06	0.10	0.03	0.05
Technical	-	0.10	0.10	0.30	0.11	0.40	0.15	0.55
Graduate/ Above	0.30	0.91	0.70	2.10	1.44	3.40	2.44	4.80

Note : na: not available.

Source : Ministry of Human Resource Development.

163 : Percentage Distribution of Literate Population by Age

Age-Group		5-9 Years	10-14 Years	15-19 Years	20-24 Years	25-34 Years	35 Years	All
1961	Persons	19.8	42.3	38.4	33.6	28.5	22.2	24.0
	Female	14.4	28.4	23.8	18.2	13.9	7.7	13.0
	Male	25.0	54.4	52.0	49.8	42.5	35.3	34.5
1971	Persons	23.1	49.6	51.3	44.7	34.8	25.2	29.5
	Female	18.9	38.2	37.7	28.7	19.3	10.7	18.7
	Male	27.2	59.8	63.3	60.7	50.1	38.0	39.5
1981	Persons	30.2	56.4	55.4	52.0	45.1	30.3	36.2
	Female	25.6	44.8	43.3	37.1	28.9	14.5	24.8
	Male	34.7	66.8	66.1	66.6	60.7	44.7	46.9
1991	Persons	56.9	68.8	65.8	57.8	50.8	38.1	52.2
	Female	51.0	59.7	54.9	43.8	36.6	22.0	39.3
	Male	62.6	77.0	75.3	71.6	64.7	52.6	64.1
2001	Persons	71.0	81.7	79.3	73.2	64.5	50.0	64.8
	Female	67.9	77.0	72.7	62.5	52.0	34.0	53.7
	Male	74.1	86.0	85.0	83.3	77.1	65.0	75.3

Note : Figures for 1961, 1971, 1981 calculated using total population in the denominator. For 1991 and 2001, only population aged 7 years and above is used in denominator. First age-group 7-9 for 2001 alone.

Source : Census documents.

164 : Educational Composition of Population by Number of Years of Schooling in India

Age Group		No Education or < 3 Years		3-6 Years		7-11 Years		12-14 Years		15+ Years		Total
		Number	Share	Number	Share	Number	Share	Number	Share	Number	Share	Number
1971	Persons	386.8	70.6	110.5	20.2	33.0	6.0	14.6	2.7	3.3	0.6	548.2
	Female	214.7	81.3	36.9	14.0	9.0	3.4	2.8	1.1	0.7	0.3	264.1
1981	Persons	435.0	63.7	154.5	22.6	56.7	8.3	29.1	4.3	8.0	1.2	683.3
	Female	247.9	75.1	55.4	16.8	17.6	5.3	7.1	2.2	2.0	0.6	330.0
1991	Persons	489.6	57.8	189.8	22.4	123.7	14.6	20.3	2.4	23.0	2.7	846.4
	Female	278.1	68.3	75.4	18.5	41.3	10.1	5.9	1.4	6.3	1.5	407.0
2001	Persons	469.5	45.7	284.7	27.7	198.3	19.3	40.5	3.9	34.1	3.3	1027.1
	Female	273.1	55.4	123.3	25.0	72.3	14.7	13.0	2.6	11.4	2.3	493.1

Note : In 1991, the estimated population of J&K was added. Revised figures for 1991 arrived at by assessing population by level of education available from social and cultural tables, census of India 1991 and estimates of J&K.

Estimates of 2001 were prepared by taking total population figures by broad level of education (illiterate and literate) available from provisional totals, census of India 2001. Then literate was distributed in different level of education by applying NSSO's proportion for 2000-01. For number of years of schooling, the appropriate grouping levels of education was done.

Source : As published in *Manpower Profile : India Year Book 2004.*

165 : Gross Enrolment Ratio in Higher Education (%)

	Total	Male	Female
2001-02	8.1	9.3	6.7
2002-03	9.0	10.3	7.5
2003-04	9.2	10.6	7.7
2004-05	10.0	11.6	8.2
2005-06	11.6	13.5	9.4

Note: Gross Enrolment Ratio is percentage of number of pupils enrolled in different age-groups to total population in the appropriate ages.

Source : Ministry of Human Resource Development.

166 : Public Expenditure on Education

	Expenditure		
	Rs. in billion	% to Public Expenditure	% to GDP
1951-52	0.6	7.9	0.6
1961-62	2.6	11.7	1.4
1971-72	10.1	9.5	2.0
1981-82	43.0	10.3	2.5
1991-92	223.9	13.1	3.4
2001-02	798.7	12.9	3.5
2002-03	855.1	12.6	3.5
2003-04	890.8	12.0	3.2
2004-05	966.9	12.1	3.1
2005-06	1132.3	12.7	3.2
2006-07	1373.8	13.3	3.2
2007-08	1614.2	13.3	2.9
2008-09	1865.0	13.6	3.0

Note : Public expenditure pertains to both Centre and states.

Source : Department of Secondry Education.

167 : Enrolment according to Faculty and Stages in Education

(in '000)

Year	General Education				Professional Courses							
	Arts	Science	Commerce	Total	Agriculture	Engineering	Medicine	Education	Veterinary	Law	Others	Total
1990-91	2200	950	950	4100	42	258	153	89	11	229	42	824
1995-96	3160	1230	1120	5510	41	387	188	101	12	261	71	1061
2000-01	3880	1670	1500	7050	50	577	263	109	14	267	74	1354
2001-02	4080	1840	1600	7520	54	641	273	123	14	271	75	1451
2002-03	4160	1830	1660	7650	55	692	301	133	15	298	81	1575
2003-04	4490	2040	1790	8320	59	717	313	146	15	304	84	1638
2004-05	4730	2140	1890	8760	62	755	330	154	16	320	88	1725

Source : As published in *Manpower Profile : India Year Book 2004.*

168 : Stock of Scientific Personnel

(in '000)

Beginning of the Year	Engineering		Medical Graduates/ Licentiates Dental	Agricultural Graduates + PG	Veterinary Graduates	Science Graduates + PG	Total
	Degree	Diploma					
1950	21.6	31.5	51.0	7.9	1.5	76.0	189.5
1960	62.2	75.0	75.6	23.9	na	213.3	455.5
1970	185.4	244.4	124.8	60.7	na	559.2	1189.5
1980	221.4	329.4	167.6	96.5	na	967.8	1782.7
1991	546.7	873.9	310.3	168.4	34.4	2912.3	4846.0
2001	1024.4	1531.7	415.9	238.6	46.7	4830.9	8088.2
2002	1078.3	1606.7	na	na	na	na	na
2003	1180.0	1720.0	na	na	na	na	na

Note : na : not available
Source : As published in *Manpower Profile : India Year Book 2004.*

169 : Police Strength and Cognizable Crime

As of End-Dec.	Police Strength			Cognizable Crimes in '000s				Disposal of Cognizable Crime Ratio of			
	Strength of Police (in '000s)	No. of Police (per 100 sq km)	No. of Police (per lakh population)	Crime	Crime (per lakh population	Murder (in '000)	Theft (in '000)	Cases on Trial & Carry Forward	Cases Disposed	Cases Pending	Pending to those on Trial (%)
1951	..	..	..	612	170	10	252	..	..	..	..
1961	..	..	..	625	144	11	233	..	..	..	..
1971	707	22	131	953	176	16	335	943	369	574	60.9
1981	898	27	132	1386	204	23	422	2112	627	1485	70.3
1991	1153	35	137	1678	200	39	363	3965	786	3179	80.2
2001	1308	41	128	1769	174	36	253	6221	1103	5118	82.3
2002	1309	41	126	1780	171	35	247	6465	1152	5313	82.2
2003	1312	41	124	1716	163	33	245	6578	1126	5452	82.9
2004	1337	42	125	1832	171	34	273	6769	1135	5634	83.2
2005	1343	42	129	1823	167	33	273	6992	1169	5823	83.3
2006	1406	42	127	1878	170	32	274	7192	1193	5999	83.4
2007	1696	42	149	1990	175	32	285	..	..	..	..

Source : National Crime Records Bureau, Ministry of Home Affairs.

170 : Prison Statistics

	Number of Jails		Capacity (in '000)		Inmates (in '000)		Occupancy Rate (%)	
	2001	2007	2001	2007	2001	2007	2001	2007
Central Jail	98	113	103.8	123.1	130.1	166.0	125.3	134.9
District Jail	266	309	76.4	103.9	122.2	157.7	159.8	151.9
Sub-Jail	671	769	34.5	37.5	52.2	42.3	151.1	112.6
Women Jail	13	16	2.0	3.0	2.1	2.8	103.8	91.1
BORSTAL School	12	10	2.3	1.6	1.2	0.7	54.7	46.0
Open Jail	25	28	4.3	3.1	1.6	2.3	36.8	76.3
Special Jail	25	25	4.9	4.6	3.6	4.0	73.6	86.9
Others	9	6	1.4	0.5	0.7	0.5	47.2	98.1
Total	1119	1276	229.7	277.3	313.6	376.4	136.5	135.7

Note : BORSTAL School is the school to reform criminal youths.
Source : National Crime Records Bureau, Ministry of Home Affairs.

171 : Juvenile Delinquency Statistics

End-Dec.	Number of Cases		Deliquents Apprehended				Crime (per lakh of Population)
	IPC (in '000)	SLL (in '000)	IPC (in '000)	SLL (in '000)	Total (in '000)	Girls (in '000)	
1968	213.9	na	na	na	na	na	na
1971	268.5	142.7	36.4	67.0	103.4	5.4	4.9
1981	614.7	108.2	82.3	108.2	190.6	8.7	5.6
1991	12.6	22.1	15.9	13.7	29.6	6.4	1.5
2001	16.5	8.3	23.6	10.0	33.6	2.3	1.6
2002	18.6	9.0	25.0	10.8	35.8	2.2	1.8
2003	17.8	7.9	24.7	8.6	33.3	2.3	1.7
2004	19.2	5.8	24.7	6.2	30.9	2.1	1.8
2005	18.9	6.7	25.4	7.3	32.7	2.1	3.0
2006	21.1	5.2	26.9	5.2	32.1	1.8	2.9
2007	22.9	4.2			34.5	1.9	3.0
2008	24.5	3.2	31	3.5	34.5	1.7	3.0

Note : Before 1988 juvenile was defined as boys and girls below 21 years. Since 1988 juvenile boys were defined as boys below 16 years and girls, below 18 years. As per the revised definition of Juvenile Justice Act 2000, boys in the age group 16-18 years are also included in the defintion. IPC: Indian penal code; SLL: Special & Local laws.

Source : National Crime Records Bureau, Ministry of Home Affairs.

172 : Incidence of Suicides by Gender

(in '000)

	Number of Suicides				Important Causes		
	Male	Female	All	Rate	Illness	Dowry	Poverty
1961	22.6	16.2	38.8	8.9	..	..	..
1971	26.3	17.3	43.7	8.1	8.0	..	1.8
1981	23.9	16.4	40.2	5.9	5.7	..	1.2
1991	46.3	32.1	78.4	9.2	..	..	..
2001	69.3	41.1	110.4	10.6	24.1	2.4	2.5
2002	70.2	40.6	110.9	10.5	26.0	2.4	2.4
2003	72.7	41.0	113.7	10.6	24.9	2.4	2.7
2004	72.9	41.0	113.9	10.5	25.5	2.6	3.4
2005	72.9	41.0	113.9	10.5	25.1	2.4	2.5
2006	75.7	42.4	118.1	10.5	26.6	2.3	2.6
2007	79.6	43.3	122.9	10.8	21.3	3.1	2.8
2008	80.5	44.5	125.0	10.8	27.4	3.0	3

Note : Rate is defined as incidence of suicides per one lakh population.
Source : *Accidental Death and Suicides in India*, National Crime Record Bureau.

173 : Profile of Suicide Victims : Number of Suicides by Gender

(in '000)

	Total Suicides					
	Male	Female	Total	*of which:* Housewives	Students	Farmers/ Agri-culturists
1996	51206	37035	88241	19490	5244	13729
% to Total	58.0	42.0	100.0	22.1	5.9	15.6
2000	66032	42561	108593	22205	5352	16603
% to Total	60.8	39.2	100.0	20.4	4.9	15.3
2001	66314	42192	108506	21659	5474	16415
% to Total	61.1	38.9	100.0	20.0	5.0	15.1
2002	69332	41085	110417	22730	5355	17971
% to Total	62.8	37.2	100.0	20.6	4.8	16.3
2003	70221	40630	110851	23301	6089	17164
% to Total	63.3	36.7	100.0	21.0	5.5	15.5
2004	72651	41046	113697	23170	5610	18241
% to Total	63.9	36.1	100.0	20.4	4.9	16.0
2005	72916	40998	113914	24141	5138	17131
% to Total	64.0	36.0	100.0	21.2	4.5	15.0
2006	75702	42410	118112	25063	5857	17060
% to Total	64.1	35.9	100.0	21.2	5.0	14.4
2007	79595	43342	122937	24162	6248	16632
% to Total	64.7	35.3	100.0	19.7	5.1	13.5
2008	80544	44473	125017	24367	6060	16196
% to Total	64.4	35.6	100.0	19.5	4.8	13.0

Source : National Crime Records Bureau, Ministry of Home Affairs.

174: Number of Trade Unions and Membership

End-Dec.	All Union			Workers Union			Employees Union		
	Regd. Trade Unions (number)	Unions Submitting Returns (number)	Member-ship (number in '000)	Regd. Trade Unions (number)	Unions Submitting Returns (number)	Member-ship (number in '000)	Regd. Trade Union (number)	Union Submitting Return (number)	Member-ship (number in '000)
1952	4623	2556	1996						
1961	11312	6813	4013						
1971	22484	9029	5470	22121	8909	5431	363	120	39
1981	37539	6682	5397	36930	6590	5377	609	92	20
1991	53535	8418	6100	52773	8351	6094	762	67	6
2001	41984	6531	5874	41568	6513	5871	416	18	3
2002	38092	7812	6974	37903	7734	6924	189	78	50
2003	46215	7258	6277	42207	7229	6272	419	29	5
2004	30391	5242	3396	30009	5217	3391	382	25	5

Note : Data collected from annual returns submitted under Indian Trade Union Act, 1936.
Data for years from 1952 and 1961 pertain to March 31 of that year.

Source : Ministry of Labour and Employment.

175 : Industrial Disputes

Calandar Year	Number			Workers Involved (in million)			Man-Days Lost (in '000)		
	Strike	Lockout	Total	Strike	Lockout	Total	Strike	Lockout	Total
1951	..	..	1071	..	..	0.7	..	..	3819
1961	1240	117	1357	0.4	0.1	0.5	2969	1950	4919
1971	2478	274	2752	1.5	0.1	1.6	11803	4743	16546
1981	2245	344	2569	1.3	0.3	1.6	21208	15375	36583
1991	1278	532	1810	0.9	0.5	1.3	12428	14000	26428
2001	372	302	674	0.5	0.2	0.7	5563	18204	23767
2002	295	284	579	0.9	0.2	1.1	9665	16921	26586
2003	255	297	552	1.0	0.8	1.8	3206	27050	30256
2004	236	241	477	1.9	0.2	2.1	4829	19038	23866
2005	227	229	456	2.7	0.2	2.9	10801	18864	29665
2006	243	187	430	1.7	0.1	1.8	5318	15006	20324
2007	211	164	375	0.6	0.1	0.7	15163	12351	27167
2008	..	..	426	..	..	1.6	..	..	17842
2009	..	..	355			0.6			9508

Note : Statistics are collected on a voluntary basis by the State Labour department and Regional Labour Commissioner's Office (Central) and consolidated returns are furnished to the Labour Bureau.

Source : *Indian Labour Journal*, Labour Bureau.

176 : Circulation of Newspapers in India

	Daily Newspapers		Non-Daily Newspapers and Periodicals	
	Number of Publications	Circulation per 1000 Population	Number of Publications	Circulation per 1000 Population
1961	484	12.39	6139	36.68
1971	821	16.81	11397	32.39
1981	1264	22.47	17880	52.79
1991	3229	29.00	26985	35.27
2001	5659	57.74	45974	55.83
2002-03	5966	69.07	49814	64.89
2003-04	6287	68.60	52482	54.45
2004-05	6530	72.26	53883	71.65
2006-07	6800	80.35	55683	83.07

Note : Newspaper means any printed or cyclostyled, periodical work containing public news and comment on public news. Daily newspaper is one that is issued at least four times a week. Circulation is the average number of copies sold or distributed free per publishing day. Periodical is a publication appearing at an interval of a week or more.
Data upto 2001 based on registered numbers with Registrar of Newspapers of India (RNI). Data from 2002-03 based on Annual Statements submitted by publishers.

Source : Office of the Registrar of Newspapers in India.

177 : Life Insurance Business in India

End-March	Number of Insurance Offices			New Life Policies Issued (in million)			Life Insurance Premium Collected, incl. Renewal (Rs. crore)		
	LIC	Private Players	Total	LIC	Private Players	Total	LIC	Private Players	Total
2000-01	2186	13	2199						
2001-02	2190	116	2306				49822	273	50095
2002-03	2191	254	2445	24.55	0.83	25.37	54629	1199	55748
2003-04	2196	416	2612	26.97	1.66	28.63	63534	3120	66654
2004-05	2197	804	3001	23.98	2.23	26.21	75127	7728	82855
2005-06	2220	1645	3865	31.59	3.87	35.46	90792	15084	105876
2006-07	2301	3072	5373	38.23	7.92	46.15	127823	28253	156076
2007-08	2522	6391	8913	37.61	13.26	50.87	149790	51561	201351

Note : LIC - Life Insurance Corporation of India.
Source : Insurance Regulatory and Development Authority (IRDA).

178 : Non-Life Insurance

	New Policies Issued (in million)			Gross Direct Premium (in Rs. crore)		
	Public Sector Players	Private Players	Total	Public Sector Players	Private Players	Total
2001-02				11918	468	12385
2002-03	41.9	1.7	43.6	13520	1350	14870
2003-04	38.4	3.3	41.7	14285	2258	16543
2004-05	44.6	5.1	49.8	14949	3508	18457
2005-06	42.2	8.9	51.1	15976	5363	21339
2006-07	34.0	12.7	44.7	17286	8647	25930
2007-08	38.5	18.7	57.3	17814	10992	28806

Source : Insurance Regulatory and Development Authority (IRDA).

179 : Insurance Density and Insurance Penetration

Calendar Year	Insurance Density			Insurance Penetration		
	Total	Life	Non-Life	Total	Life	Non-Life
2001	11.5	9.1	2.4	2.7	2.2	0.6
2002	14.7	11.7	3	3.3	2.6	0.7
2003	16.4	12.9	3.5	2.9	2.3	0.6
2004	19.7	15.7	4	3.2	2.5	0.6
2005	22.7	18.3	4.4	3.1	2.5	0.6
2006	38.4	33.2	5.2	4.8	4.1	0.6
2007	46.6	40.4	6.2	4.7	4.0	0.6

Note : Insurance density and penetration are measured as ratio (in per cent) of premium to total population and GDP in US $ respectively.

Source : Insurance Regulatory and Development Authority (IRDA).

(numbers in lakh)

180 : Employment in Organised Public Sector by Industry

As on 31-March	Total	Agriculture, Hunting etc.	Mining & Quarrying	Manufacturing	Electricity Gas & Water	Construction	Wholesale and Retail Trade	Transport, Storage & Communications	Finance/ Insurance/ Real Estate etc.	Community/ Social/ Personal Services
1961	70.50	1.80	1.29	3.69	2.24	6.03	0.94	17.24	na	37.27
1971	107.31	2.76	1.82	8.06	4.35	8.80	3.28	22.17	na	56.07
1981	154.84	4.63	8.18	15.02	6.83	10.89	1.17	27.09	7.48	73.55
1991	190.58	5.56	9.99	18.52	9.05	11.49	1.50	30.26	11.94	92.27
2001	191.39	5.02	8.75	14.30	9.35	10.81	1.63	30.42	12.81	98.30
2002	187.74	4.83	8.61	13.50	9.23	10.26	1.57	30.09	12.30	97.35
2003	185.80	5.06	8.47	12.60	9.13	9.48	1.82	29.39	13.77	96.09
2004	181.97	4.93	10.30	11.89	8.74	9.32	1.81	28.15	11.08	92.76
2005	180.07	4.96	10.14	11.30	8.60	9.11	1.84	27.51	14.08	92.52
2006	178.73	4.69	11.46	10.92	8.49	8.94	1.82	26.75	13.90	91.76
2007	176.88	4.75	11.37	10.87	8.49	8.66	1.78	26.37	13.69	90.90

Source : Director General of Employment and Training as published in *Economic Survey*.

181 : Employment in Organised Private Sector by Industry

(numbers in lakh)

As on 31-March	Total	Agriculture, Hunting etc.	Mining & Quarrying	Manufacturing	Electricity Gas & Water	Construction	Wholesale/ Retail Trade	Transport, Storage & Communication	Finance/ Insurance/ Real Estate	Community/ Social/ Personal Service
1961	50.40	6.70	5.50	30.20	0.40	2.40	1.60	0.80	..	2.80
1971	67.70	8.00	4.10	39.70	0.50	1.40	3.00	1.00	..	10.00
1981	73.95	8.58	1.30	45.45	0.35	0.72	2.77	0.60	1.96	12.22
1991	76.77	8.91	1.00	44.81	0.40	0.73	3.00	0.53	2.54	14.85
2001	86.52	9.31	0.79	50.13	0.52	0.57	3.39	0.76	3.70	17.34
2002	84.32	8.55	0.68	48.67	0.42	0.56	3.35	0.76	3.91	17.42
2003	84.21	8.98	0.66	47.44	0.50	0.44	3.60	0.79	4.26	17.56
2004	82.46	9.17	0.65	44.89	0.47	0.45	3.51	0.81	4.58	17.92
2005	84.52	9.83	0.79	44.89	0.49	0.49	3.75	0.85	5.23	18.20
2006	87.71	10.28	0.95	45.49	0.40	0.55	3.87	0.87	6.52	18.78
2007	92.40	9.50	1.00	47.50	0.60	0.70	4.10	1.00	8.60	19.50

Source : Director General of Employment and Training as published in *Economic Survey*.

182 : Census Population, Workers and Non-Workers

Census Year	Population Persons (in million)	Workers (in million)	% to Total Population	Main workers (in million)	% to Total Workers	Non-Workers (in million)	% to Total Population
1951	361.1	139.5	38.6			217.4	60.2
1961	439.2	188.4	42.9			249.9	56.9
1971	548.2	180.7	33.0			367.5	67.0
1981	683.3	244.6	35.8	222.5	91.0	420.7	61.6
1991	846.4	306.0	36.2	278.9	91.1	510.1	60.3
2001	1028.7	402.2	39.1	313.2	77.9	626.4	60.9
Male							
1951	185.6	99.1	53.4			86.5	46.6
1961	226.3	129.0	57.0			96.8	42.8
1971	284.0	144.4	50.8			134.8	47.5
1981	353.3	181.0	51.2	177.5	98.1	162.9	46.1
1991	439.2	218.6	49.8	216.0	98.8	205.0	46.7
2001	532.2	275.0	51.7	240.3	87.4	257.1	48.3

contd...

...contd...

Census Year	Population Persons (in million)	Workers (in million)	% to Total Population	Main workers (in million)	% to Total Workers	Non-Workers (in million)	% to Total Population
Female							
1951	175.5	40.4	23.0			133.1	75.8
1961	212.9	59.4	27.9			153.1	71.9
1971	264.1	36.3	13.7			232.7	88.1
1981	330.0	63.6	19.3	45.0	70.8	257.8	78.1
1991	407.1	87.4	21.5	69.9	80.0	305.2	75.0
2001	496.4	127.2	25.6	72.9	57.3	369.2	74.4

Note : The concept of 'main workers' was used from 1981. Total workers may include main and subsidiary workers. Workers refer to gainfully employed persons.

Source : Census documents.

183 : Labour Force and Labour Force Participation Rate (LFPR) : NSSO Reports

	Labour Force (in million)			Labour Force Participation Rate (%)		
	Rural	Urban	Total	Rural	Urban	Total
			Total			
1972-73	199.6	40.6	240.2	43.9	34.5	42.0
1977-78	228.1	53.5	281.6	45.8	37.5	44.0
1983	247.2	63.2	310.4	45.2	36.2	43.0
1987-88	260.1	74.3	334.4	44.3	35.6	42.1
1993-94	293.0	85.7	378.7	44.9	36.3	42.7
1999-00	305.2	100.7	405.9	42.3	35.4	40.4
2004-05	323.2	94.7	417.7	44.6	38.2	43.0
			Male			
1972-73	128.7	32.9	161.6	55.1	52.1	54.5
1977-78	144.5	41.4	185.9	56.5	54.3	56.0
1983	155.9	50.2	206.1	55.5	54.0	55.1
1987-88	165.0	58.5	223.5	54.9	53.4	54.5
1993-94	189.3	67.3	256.6	56.1	54.3	55.6
1999-00	200.2	80.7	280.8	54.0	54.2	54.1
2004-05	204.9	73.5	278.5	55.1	57.0	55.9
			Female			
1972-73	70.9	7.7	78.6	32.1	14.2	28.6
1977-78	83.6	12.1	95.7	34.5	18.3	31.0
1983.0	91.3	13.0	104.3	34.2	15.9	29.9
1987-88	95.1	15.8	110.9	33.1	16.2	28.8
1993-94	104.7	18.4	123.1	33.0	16.5	28.7
1999-00	105.0	20.0	125.1	30.2	14.7	25.8
2004-05	118.8	21.1	139.4	33.3	17.8	29.4

Note : Data relates to usual status of individuals.
Usual status = principal status + subsidiary status.
Usual activity status relates to the activity status of person during the reference period of 365 days preceeding the date of survey. The activity status on which a person spent relatively longer time (i.e., major time criterion) during 365 days preceding the date of survey is considered as the principal usual activity status of the person. If the same person simultaneously pursue another economic activity for a shorter period that is known as subsidiary activity.
Labour force covers those involved in gainful activity regularly, those involved in gainful activity occasionally and those unemployed.
Labour force participation rate represents size of labour force as per cent of population.

Source : National Sample Survey Organisation (NSSO) - various reports on "Employment and Unemployment".

184 : Educational Composition of Labour Force (%)

	Illiterate	Literate			
		Primary	Middle	Secondary	Graduate & Above
Rural-Male					
1972-73	61.1	29.0	6.3	3.1	0.5
1977-78	55.0	30.8	8.5	4.7	1.0
1983	52.1	29.2	10.8	6.4	1.5
1987-88	48.3	29.6	11.6	8.4	2.1
1993-94	43.7	29.0	13.6	10.9	2.8
1999-00	39.7	27.4	16.0	13.5	3.4
2004-05	33.6	29.4	18.0	9.2	9.8
Rural-Female					
1972-73	91.6	7.1	0.8	0.4	0.1
1977-78	88.1	9.1	1.6	1.0	0.2
1983	86.2	10.2	2.1	1.2	0.3
1987-88	82.3	12.0	3.2	2.0	0.4
1993-94	79.0	13.7	3.9	2.7	0.7
1999-00	73.9	15.7	5.8	3.6	1.0
2004-05	66.2	18.0	8.2	3.7	3.9
Urban-Male					
1972-73	24.8	37.2	15.0	16.6	6.4
1977-78	22.1	33.6	17.2	18.4	8.7
1983	21.7	30.1	18.1	19.9	10.1
1987-88	19.6	30.5	16.4	21.8	11.7
1993-94	17.9	25.4	17.5	24.6	14.6
1999-00	16.0	21.9	18.8	26.4	16.9
2004-05	12.8	22.4	19.5	15.0	30.3
Urban-Female					
1972-73	67.4	16.5	4.0	8.0	4.1
1977-78	58.2	17.9	6.7	10.8	6.4
1983	56.5	17.5	6.3	11.6	8.0
1987-88	51.8	19.0	7.3	12.3	9.6
1993-94	44.5	17.7	8.1	15.1	14.6
1999-00	41.2	17.0	9.7	15.7	16.4
2004-05	34.4	18.8	10.9	7.7	28.2

Note : Percentage falling in each group within a year.
Based on 'usual status' of individuals.
Data for 1972-73,1977-78 and 1999-2000 refers to population age of 5 years and above. For 1983, 1987-88 and 1993-94 it refers to population age 15 years and above.

Source : National Sample Survey Organisation reports on employment and unemployment.

185 : Labour Force Participation Rate for Educated Persons

(%)

	Below Matric	Matric/Higher Secondary	Graduate	Below Matric	Matric/Higher Secondary	Graduate
	Rural-Male			Urban-Male		
1972-73	..	73.67	88.78	..	71.57	86.68
1977-78	..	75.27	89.05	..	72.32	87.97
1983	88.49	74.24	88.78	84.15	71.69	87.37
1987-88	87.56	74.20	90.10	82.90	70.70	86.40
1993-94	88.35	72.08	91.30	83.38	68.33	86.20
1999-00	57.91	74.38	89.97	51.90	67.83	85.21
2004-05	87.79	75.13	90.64	83.68	67.44	84.38
	Rural-Female			Urban-Female		
1972-73	..	34.78	62.05	..	20.91	40.81
1977-78	..	33.66	55.55	..	22.26	43.65
1983	38.16	23.76	37.60	18.89	17.38	35.29
1987-88	39.05	26.30	39.90	18.47	16.20	37.70
1993-94	35.82	20.01	44.80	18.60	14.48	35.50
1999-00	26.99	19.39	40.28	12.58	12.58	30.24
2004-05	50.88	32.70	46.81	25.13	14.67	35.02

Note : Participation rate reflects the number of persons falling within a given educational level as per cent of population of that educational level.

Source : National Sample Survey Organisation - various reports on Employment and Unemployment.

186 : Work Force and Work Force Participation Rate (WFPR)

	Usual Status (PS+SS)					
	Work Force (in million)			Work Force Participation Rate (%)		
	Rural	Urban	Total	Rural	Urban	Total
Total						
1972-73	197.8	38.5	236.3	43.5	32.7	..
1977-78	221.5	49.2	270.7	44.4	34.1	42.3
1983	243.1	59.6	302.7	44.5	34.0	42.0
1987-88	252.5	69.5	322.0	43.4	33.7	41.2
1993-94	290.3	81.8	372.1	44.4	34.7	42.0
1999-00	300.8	96.0	396.8	41.7	33.7	39.7
2004-05	317.8	90.4	408.2	43.9	36.5	42.0
Male						
1972-73	127.2	31.8	159.0	54.5	50.1	..
1977-78	141.4	38.8	180.2	55.2	50.8	54.3
1983	152.7	47.3	200.0	54.7	51.2	53.8
1987-88	160.5	55.0	215.5	53.9	50.6	53.1
1993-94	186.6	64.5	251.1	55.3	52.1	54.5
1999-00	196.8	77.1	273.9	53.1	51.8	52.7
2004-05	201.7	70.7	272.4	54.6	54.9	54.7
Female						
1972-73	70.6	7.2	77.8	31.8	13.4	..
1977-78	80.1	10.4	90.5	73.1	15.6	29.7
1983	90.4	12.3	102.7	34.0	15.1	21.6
1987-88	92.0	14.5	106.5	32.3	15.2	28.5
1993-94	103.7	17.3	121.0	32.8	15.5	28.6
1999-00	104.0	18.9	122.9	29.9	13.9	25.9
2004-05	116.1	19.7	135.8	32.7	16.6	28.7

Note : Usual status = principal status + subsidiary status.
Data based on 'usual status' of individuals.
Work force covers those involved in gainful activity regularly and those involved in gainful activity occasionally. Unemployed excluded.
Work force participation rate represents size of work force as per cent of population.

Source : National Sample Survey Organisation - various reports on Employment and Unemployment.

187 : Percentage Distribution of Employment by Status

	Self-Employed		Regular Employees		Casual Labour	
	Male	Female	Male	Female	Male	Female
			Total			
1972-73	60.6	63.0	19.7	6.3	19.7	30.7
1977-78	58.0	60.7	18.3	5.3	23.7	34.0
1983	55.9	60.0	18.2	5.6	25.9	34.4
1987-88	54.3	58.9	18.6	6.9	27.1	34.2
1993-94	52.9	56.7	17.0	6.3	30.1	37.0
1999-00	52.8	55.6	14.0	7.3	33.2	37.1
2004-05	..	..	..	..	..	..
			Rural			
1972-73	65.9	64.5	12.1	4.1	22.0	31.4
1977-78	62.8	62.1	10.6	2.8	26.6	35.1
1983	60.5	61.9	10.3	2.8	29.2	35.3
1987-88	58.6	60.8	10.0	3.7	31.4	35.5
1993-94	57.9	58.5	8.3	2.8	33.8	38.7
1999-00	55.0	57.3	8.8	3.1	36.2	39.6
2004-05	58.1	63.7	9.0	3.7	32.9	32.6
			Urban			
1972-73	39.2	48.4	50.7	27.9	10.1	23.7
1977-78	40.4	49.5	46.4	24.9	13.2	25.6
1983	40.9	45.8	43.7	25.8	15.4	28.4
1987-88	41.7	47.1	43.7	27.5	14.6	25.4
1993-94	41.7	45.4	42.1	28.6	16.2	26.2
1999-00	41.5	45.3	41.7	33.3	16.8	21.4
2004-05	44.8	47.7	40.6	35.6	14.6	16.7

Source : National Sample Survey Organisation - various reports on Employment and Unemployment.

188 : Employment in Organised and Unorganised Sector

	Numbers (in million)			Share % to Total	
	Organised	Unorganised	Total	Organised	Unorganised
1973-74	18.82	217.48	236.30	7.96	92.04
1977-78	21.24	249.46	270.70	7.85	92.15
1983	24.01	278.69	302.70	7.93	92.07
1987-88	25.71	296.29	322.00	7.98	92.02
1993-94	26.73	315.17	341.90	7.82	92.18
1999-00	27.96	368.84	396.80	7.05	92.95
2004-05	27.79	383.71	411.50	6.75	93.25

Note : Organised sector includes all establishments in the public sector, and non-agricultural establishments employing 10 or more persons in the private sector. Data on employment in public sector and non-agricultural establishments in private sector employing 25 or more persons are collected under provisions of Employment Exchanges (Compulsory Notification of Vacancies) Act,1959. The same from non-agricultural establishments in private sector employing 10-24 persons are being collected on a voluntary basis.

Source : National Sample Survey Organisation - various reports on Employment and Unemployment.

189 : Estimates of Unemployment

	Usual Status (PS+SS)					
	Unemployed (in million)			Unemployment Rate (%)		
	Rural	Urban	Total	Rural	Urban	Total
Total						
1972-73	1.8	2.1	3.9	0.9	5.2	1.6
1977-78	6.6	4.3	10.9	2.9	8.0	3.9
1983	4.1	3.6	7.7	1.7	5.7	2.5
1987-88	7.6	4.8	12.4	2.9	6.5	3.7
1993-94	4.7	4.8	7.5	1.6	5.6	2.5
1999-00	4.2	3.8	8.0	1.4	3.8	2.0
2004-05	5.9	1.8	7.7	1.8	1.9	1.8
Male						
1972-73	1.5	1.6	3.1	1.2	4.8	1.9
1977-78	3.1	2.6	5.7	2.2	6.5	3.1
1983	3.2	2.9	6.1	2.1	5.9	3.0
1987-88	4.5	3.5	8.0	2.8	6.1	3.6
1993-94	3.7	3.6	7.3	2.0	5.4	2.8
1999-00	3.2	2.9	6.1	2.1	4.8	2.2
2004-05	4.0	1.4	5.4	2.1	4.4	1.9
Female						
1972-73	0.3	0.5	0.8	0.5	6.0	1.0
1977-78	3.5	1.7	5.2	5.5	17.8	5.4
1983	0.9	0.7	1.6	1.4	6.9	1.5
1987-88	3.1	1.3	4.4	3.5	8.5	4.0
1993-94	1.0	1.2	2.2	1.4	8.3	1.8
1999-00	1.0	0.9	1.9	1.5	7.1	1.5
2004-05	2.0	0.4	2.4	3.1	9.1	1.7

Note : Unemployment rate is the number of unemployed as a percentage of the labour force. PS - principal status; SS - subsidiary status.

Source : National Sample Survey Organisation - various reports on Employment and Unemployment.

190 : Employment in Different Sectors

	Mines (million)	Plantation (million)	Railways (million)	Insurance (LIC+GIC) (thousand)	Post & Telegraph (thousand)	Telecom-munication (thousand)	Ports (thousand)	Shops/ Establish-ments (thousand)	Restaurants & Theatres (thousand)
1951	549.0	1.25	0.93		193			525	117
1961	671.0	1.18	1.18	55.9	373			1737	332
1971	630.7	..	1.39	76.6	605		107.3	2632	480
1981	749.8	1.34	1.58	96.1	506	229	116.5	4305	689
1991	789.9	1.66	1.66	176.5	596	289	111.3	4518	622
2001	599.3	2.13	1.51	203.4	594	375	88.2	6058	871
2002	581.9	2.11	1.48	201.1	580	423	81.1	6440	923
2003	572.3	2.16	1.45	198.4	566	417	79.1	6168	828
2004	567.9	2.17	1.43	189.1	549	414	74.8	5205	689
2005	559.1	2.19	1.42	186.8		404	68.6		
2006			1.41	186.0					
2007			1.41	184.7					

Note : LIC - Life Insurance Corporation; GIC - General Insurance Corporation.

Source : Directorate of Mines, *Railway Year Book*. LIC & GIC. P&T department, Ministry of Shipping, and as published in Labour Bureau's annual publication and *Statistical Abstracts* of CSO.

III. INFRASTRUCTURE

> Land Use Pattern
> Mineral
> Electricity
> Communication
> Fuel & Energy
> Road
> Railway
> Shipping
> Aviation

191 : Pattern of Land Utilisation

(million hectares)

	Reporting Area	Forest Land	% to Reporting Area	Not Available for Cultivation	Net Area Sown	% to Reporting Area	Others
1950-51	284.3	40.5	14.2	47.5	118.8	41.8	77.5
1960-61	298.5	54.1	18.1	50.8	133.2	44.6	60.4
1970-71	303.8	63.9	21.0	44.6	140.9	46.4	54.4
1980-81	304.2	67.5	22.2	39.6	140.3	46.1	56.8
1990-91	304.9	67.8	22.2	40.5	143.0	46.9	53.6
2000-01	305.2	69.5	22.8	41.5	141.4	46.3	52.8
2001-02	305.1	69.6	22.8	41.8	141.4	46.3	52.3
2002-03	305.3	69.7	22.8	42.1	132.6	43.4	60.9
2003-04	305.6	69.8	22.8	42.3	141.0	46.1	52.5
2004-05	305.6	69.7	22.8	42.5	141.1	46.2	52.3
2005-06	305.4	69.8	22.9	42.6	141.8	46.4	51.2
2006-07	305.5	69.8	22.8	42.6	140.3	45.9	52.8

Note : Total geographical area is 328.73 million hectares.
The decline in net area sown in 2002-03 reflects the impact of severe drought on agricultural operations.
Others ' include pastures, grazing land, land under trees & groves, waste & fallow land.

Source : Ministry of Agriculture.

192 : Cropped and Irrigated Area

(million hectares)

	Gross Cropped Area	Area Sown More than Once	Cropping Intensity (%)	Net Irrigated Area	Gross Irrigated Area	Irrigated Area (%)
1950-51	131.9	13.2	111.1	20.9	22.6	17.1
1960-61	152.8	19.6	114.7	24.7	28.0	18.3
1970-71	165.8	24.9	117.7	31.1	38.2	23.0
1980-81	172.6	34.6	123.1	38.7	49.8	28.9
1990-91	185.7	42.7	129.9	48.0	63.2	34.0
2000-01	185.3	44.0	131.1	55.1	76.2	41.1
2001-02	189.7	48.3	134.1	56.8	79.0	41.6
2002-03	175.5	42.9	132.4	53.7	73.5	41.9
2003-04	190.1	49.1	134.9	56.8	78.3	41.2
2004-05	191.2	50.1	135.5	58.8	81.1	42.4
2005-06	192.6	50.8	135.8	59.9	83.4	43.3
2006-07	193.7	53.4	138.1	60.9	85.8	44.3

Note : Cropping intensity is percentage of gross cropped area to net area sown.
Net irrigated area is the area irrigated through any source once a year for a particular crop.
Gross irrigated area under crops irrigated once and/or more than once in a year. It is counted as many times as the number of times the areas are cropped and irrigated in a year.

Source : Ministry of Agriculture.

193 : Number of Reporting Mines

	All Minerals	Fuels		Metallic Minerals			Non-Metallic Minerals	
		Coal	Lignite	Total	*of which:* Bauxite	*of which:* Iron Ore	Total	*of which:* Lime Stone
1950-51	2703	893		306	11	34	1504	50
1960-61	3174	848	3	693	31	225	1630	175
1970-71	3758	779	2	871	74	393	2106	303
1980-81	3927	460	2	713	93	312	2503	445
1990-91	4075	518	4	714	205	279	2839	619
2000-01	3191	591	5	565	182	208	2030	544
2001-02	3193	564	6	574	181	221	2049	568
2002-03	3145	556	6	591	177	242	1992	556
2003-04	3132	554	8	612	188	266	1958	552
2004-05	3168	554	8	615	191	270	1991	571
2005-06	2970	563	9	589	189	261	1809	549
2006-07	3005	561	9	639	197	290	1796	583
2007-08	2854	558	11	676	209	300	1609	539

Source : Indian Bureau of Mines.

194 : Production of Metallic Minerals

(thousand tonnes)

	Bauxite	Chromite	Gold (Kgs)	Iron Ore	Manganese Ore	Copper Concentrate	Lead Concentrate	Zinc Concentrate
1951	0.67	17	7041	4152	1398	..	2	2
1961	0.48	49	4868	18705	1405	..	6	9
1971	1489	274	3656	34311	1779	..	4	16
1981	1955	343	2495	41618	1632	..	20	53
1990-91	4976	929	2208	54936	1388	..	44	137
2000-01	7993	1972	2615	80587	1595	164	54	366
2001-02	8689	1549	2810	86226	1587	164	52	399
2002-03	9867	3069	3153	99072	1678	152	59	486
2003-04	10924	2905	3457	122838	1776	143	73	590
2004-05	11964	3621	3526	145942	2386	137	82	666
2005-06	12596	3714	3047	165230	1906	125	96	889
2006-07	15733	5296	2488	187696	2116	150	107	947
2007-08	23085	4799	2858	206452	2551	159	126	938

Source : Indian Bureau of Mines.

195 : Production of Non-Metallic Minerals

	Diamond (carats)	Gypsum (million tonnes)	Dolomite (million tonnes)	Kaolin (million tonnes)	Limestone (million tonnes)
1951	1674	0.21	0.01		3
1961	1313	0.87	0.73	0.14	15
1971	19383	1.07	1.32	0.33	25
1981	14834	0.96	2.07	0.50	32
1990-91	18010	1.56	2.56	0.64	68
2000-01	57407	2.67	3.03	0.87	127
2001-02	81436	2.86	3.25	0.82	131
2002-03	84407	2.66	3.63	0.82	156
2003-04	71260	2.77	4.05	0.90	153
2004-05	78316	3.69	4.39	0.93	166
2005-06	44170	3.29	4.75	1.34	170
2006-07	2180	3.01	5.17	1.46	197
2007-08	586	2.61	5.12	1.29	188

Source : Indian Bureau of Mines.

196 : Electricity: Installed Capacity

	Utilities				
	Total Capacity (MW)	Hydro Capacity (MW)	Thermal Capacity (MW)	Thermal % to Total	Nuclear Capacity ('000 MW)
31-12.47	1362	508	854	63	0
31-12-50	1713	560	1153	67	0
31-12.51	1835	575	1260	69	0
31-03-61	4653	1917	2736	59	0
31-03-71	14709	6383	7906	54	420
31-03-81	30214	11791	17562	58	860
31-03-91	66086	18753	45768	69	1565
31-03-01	101626	25153	73612	72	2860
31-03-02	105046	26269	74429	71	2720
31-03-03	107877	26767	76762	71	2720
31-03-04	112684	29507	77969	69	2720
31-03-05	118426	30942	80903	68	2770
31-03-06	124287	32326	82410	66	3360
31-03-07	132329	34654	86015	65	3900
31-03-08	143061	35909	91907	64	4120
31-03-09	147965	36878	93725	63	4120
31-03-10	159399	36863	102454	64	4560

Note : Total includes renewable energy resources in addition to above.
Source : Director General, Central Electricity Authority.

197 : Electricity: Generation

	Utilities				
	Total Generation (GWh)	Hydro Generation (GWh)	Thermal Generation (GWh)	Thermal % to Total	Nuclear Generation (GWh)
1950	5106	2519	2587	51	0
1951	5858	2860	2999	51	0
1960-61	16937	7837	9100	54	0
1970-71	55828	25248	28162	50	2417
1980-81	110844	46541	61301	55	3001
1990-91	264329	71641	186546	71	6141
2000-01	501204	74362	409940	82	16902
2001-02	517439	73579	422300	82	19475
2002-03	532693	64014	446778	84	19390
2003-04	565102	75242	468676	83	17780
2004-05	594456	84610	488329	82	17011
2005-06	623819	101494	498358	80	17324
2006-07	670654	113502	528490	79	18802
2007-08	722625	120387	560071	78	16957
2008-09	723794	113081	590101	82	14713
2009-10	771173	106656	640523	83	18654

Note : Total includes renewable energy resources in addition to above.
Source : Director General, Central Electricity Authority.

198 : Electricity: Net Generation and Consumption Pattern

(billion kWh)

	Net Generation/ Consumption	Per capita Consumption	Pattern of Consumption				
			Domestic	Commercial	Industrial	Agriculture	Tractions
1951	4793	18	595	332	3055	203	330
1960-61	13841	38	1492	848	9584	833	453
1970-71	43724	90	3840	2573	29579	4470	1365
1980-81	82367	132	9246	4682	48069	14489	2266
1990-91	190357	253	31982	11181	84209	50321	4112
2000-01	316600	366	75629	22545	107622	84729	8213
2001-02	374670	559	79694	24139	159507	81673	8106
2002-03	393460	567	83355	25437	168821	84486	8797
2003-04	418334	592	89736	28201	181970	87089	9210
2004-05	447993	613	95659	31381	199448	88555	9495
2005-06	474451	631	100090	35965	214121	90292	9944
2006-07	525672	672	111002	40220	241216	99023	10800
2007-08	577960	717	120918	46685	265406	104182	11108
2008-09	596943	733	124562	48047	274531	107835	11615

Note : Includes both utilities and non-utilities. Pattern of consumption is as on year ended March 31.

Source : Director General, Central Electricity Authority.

199 : Post Offices

As of End-March	Number of Post Offices (thousand)	Letter Boxes (thousand)	Number of Postal Articles Handled (in crore)	Number of Inland Money Orders Issued (in crore)	Postal Revenue (Rs. crore)	Availability of Post Office (per lakh population)
1950-51	36	85	227	5.1		10.0
1960-61	77	143	403	7.6		17.5
1970-71	109	182	646	9.5		19.9
1980-81	139	494	973	11.2		20.3
1990-91	149	520	1468	10.6	841	17.6
2000-01	155	595	1420	11.0	3298	15.1
2001-02	155	589	1103	11.2	3597	14.8
2002-03	156	591	909	10.5	4010	14.6
2003-04	156	597	864	9.9	4257	14.3
2004-05	156	584	736	10.2	4432	14.1
2005-06	155	601	670	9.6	5023	13.8
2006-07	155	590	668	9.9	5322	13.6
2007-08	155	591	639	9.1	5495	13.2

Source : Department of Posts, Ministry of Communication.

200 : Telecommunications

As of End-March	Number of Telephones				
	Fixed Lines DELs (million)	Cellular Mobile Telephones (million)	Total (million)	Tele Density-I (per 100 population)	Tele Density-II (per sq km)
1950-51	0.1	..	0.1	0.0	0.0
1960-61	0.3	..	0.3	0.1	0.1
1970-71	1.0	..	1.0	0.2	0.3
1980-81	2.2	..	2.2	0.3	0.7
1990-91	5.1	..	5.1	0.6	1.5
2000-01	32.7	3.6	36.3	3.5	11.0
2001-02	38.3	6.7	45.0	4.3	13.7
2002-03	41.2	13.3	54.6	5.1	16.6
2003-04	40.9	35.6	76.5	7.8	23.2
2004-05	41.4	57.0	98.4	9.0	30.7
2005-06	40.2	101.9	142.1	12.7	32.2
2006-07	40.8	165.1	205.9	18.2	67.4
2007-08	39.4	261.1	300.5	26.4	..
2008-09	38.0	391.8	429.7	37.0	..
2009-10	37.0	584.3	621.3	52.7	..

Note : DEL: direct exchange line.
Mobile telephony started only from 1997 and private fixed lines from 1999.

Source : Department of Posts, Ministry of Communication.

201 : Production and Consumption of Coal

(million tonne)

	Production of Coal				Consumption of Coal				
	Coking Coal	Non-Coking Coal	Total	Lignite	Total	Power	Steel	Fertiliser	Cement
1950-51	..	..	32.3	..	..	..	..	..	..
1960-61	17.0	38.2	55.2	..	..	..	..	..	..
1970-71	17.8	55.1	72.9	3.5	..	..	..	..	..
1980-81	32.6	81.3	113.9	5.1	95.0	34.5	17.6	..	4.3
1990-91	45.3	166.4	211.7	13.8	205.2	118.6	24.5	..	10.1
2000-01	31.1	278.6	309.6	23.0	315.6	234.6	20.0	3.2	10.3
2001-02	28.7	299.1	327.8	24.8	325.8	242.8	20.3	3.2	11.9
2002-03	30.2	311.1	341.3	26.0	335.7	250.4	18.9	2.5	12.6
2003-04	29.4	331.9	361.3	28.0	353.8	265.5	18.9	5.2	13.7
2004-05	30.2	352.4	382.6	30.3	374.5	303.9	17.5	2.2	14.7
2005-06	31.5	375.5	407.0	30.1	396.7	312.5	18.6	2.3	15.0
2006-07	32.1	398.7	430.8	31.3	..	..	..	..	..
2007-08	34.5	422.6	457.1	34.0					
2008-09	34.8	458.0	492.8	32.4	..	..	..	..	..

Source : Office of Coal Controller, Ministry of Coal.

202 : Crude Oil Statistics

(million tonne)

	Production			Reserves			
	Production	Net Imports	Refinery Throughput	On-Shore	Off-Shore	Total	Field Reserves (in years)
1950-51	0.3	..	0.3	..	..	..	..
1960-61	0.5	6.0	6.6	..	..	..	..
1970-71	6.8	11.7	18.4	..	..	..	..
1980-81	10.5	16.2	25.8	140	328	468	45
1990-91	33.0	20.7	51.8	314	492	806	24
2000-01	32.4	74.1	103.4	320	354	674	..
2001-02	32.0	78.7	107.3	332	409	741	..
2002-03	33.0	82.0	112.6	339	394	733	..
2003-04	33.4	90.4	121.8	357	382	739	..
2004-05	34.0	95.9	127.1	376	410	786	23.0
2005-06	32.2	99.4	130.1	387	369	756	23.0
2006-07	34.0	111.5	146.6	357	369	726	..
2007-08	34.1	121.7	156.1	..	..	..	..
2008-09	33.5	132.8	160.8	..	..	..	..
2009-10	33.7	98.9	160.0	..	..	..	..

Note : Reserves as on January 1 for years 1980-81 to 2000-01, thereafter it is as on April 1.

Source : Ministry of Petroleum and Natural Gas.

203 : Production and Consumption of Petroleum Products

(million tonne)

	Petroleum Products			of which:							
	Production	Net Imports ($)	Consumption	Naphtha		Kerosene		High Speed Diesel		Fuel Oil	
				Production	Consumption	Production	Consumption	Production	Consumption	Production	Consumption
1950-51	0.2	3.1	3.3	na	na	na	0.9	na	0.2	na	0.9
1960-61	5.7	2.5	7.7	na	na	0.9	2.0	1.1	1.2	1.6	1.7
1970-71	17.1	0.8	17.9	1.2	0.9	2.9	3.3	3.8	3.8	4.1	4.7
1980-81	24.1	7.3	30.9	2.1	2.3	2.4	4.2	7.4	10.3	6.1	7.5
1990-91	49.5	6.0	55.0	4.9	3.4	5.5	8.4	17.2	21.1	9.4	9.0
2000-01	95.6	0.9	100.1	9.9	11.7	8.7	11.3	39.1	37.9	11.4	12.7
2001-02	100.0	-3.1	100.4	9.2	11.7	9.7	10.4	39.8	36.5	12.2	13.0
2002-03	104.1	-3.1	104.1	9.7	11.9	10.0	10.4	40.2	36.6	12.2	12.7
2003-04	113.5	-6.6	107.8	11.3	11.9	10.2	10.2	43.3	37.1	13.4	12.9
2004-05	118.6	-9.4	111.6	14.1	14.0	9.3	9.4	45.9	39.7	15.0	13.6
2005-06	119.8	-10.1	113.2	14.5	12.2	9.1	9.5	47.6	40.2	14.3	12.8
2006-07	135.3	-15.9	120.7	16.7	13.9	8.5	9.5	53.5	42.9	15.7	12.6
2007-08	144.9	-18.3	128.9	16.4	13.3	7.8	9.4	58.4	47.7	15.8	12.7
2008-09	150.5	-18.3	133.6	14.8	13.9	8.2	9.3	62.9	51.7	17.7	12.6

Source : Ministry of Petroleum and Natural Gas.

204 : Natural Gas Reserves and Production

(million tonne)

	Reserves			Life (in years)	Gross Production (billion cubic metre)	Net Production (gross flare & waste)
	On-Shore	Off-Shore	Total			
1970-71	..	..	..	..	1.4	0.8
1980-81	82.0	329.0	411.0	174	2.4	1.5
1990-91	246.0	484.0	730.0	41	18.0	12.8
2000-01	294.0	345.0	639.0	22	29.5	27.9
2001-02	315.0	436.0	751.0	24	29.7	28.0
2002-03	327.0	527.0	854.0	27	31.4	30.0
2003-04	339.0	584.0	923.0	29	32.0	30.9
2004-05	340.0	761.0	1101.0	35	31.8	30.8
2005-06	330.0	745.0	1075.0	33	32.2	31.3
2006-07	270.0	785.0	1055.0	..	32.4	30.8
2007-08	..	..	..	..	32.8	31.4
2008-09	..	..	..	..	32.8	
2009-10	..	..	..	..	47.6	

Source : Ministry of Petroleum and Natural Gas.

205 : Total Road Length

(thousand kilometres)

As on 31-March	Total Road Length		Highways		Urban Roads		Project Roads@	
	Total	Surfaced	Total	Surfaced	Total	Surfaced	Total	Surfaced
1951	400	157	222	198	..	..	..	..
1961	525	263	238	210	..	..	..	..
1971	915	398	779	338	72	53	131	61
1981	1485	684	1096	577	123	86	186	21
1991	2331	1091	1931	1006	187	137	210	30
2001	2447	1415	1967	1166	252	192	224	57
2002	2483	1478	2025	1200	250	190	224	61
2003	2601	1518	2045	1209	297	215	259	69
2004	2713	1578	2107	1238	301	218	261	69
2005	..	..	..	..	..	..	..	..

Note : @: Project roads are those specifically constructed for department of forest, navigation, electricity, steel authority, coal mines and sugarcane development authorities.
Total length includes roads under Jawahar Rozgar Yojana (JRY) scheme.

Source : Transport Research Wing, Ministry of Road Transport and Highways.

206 : Number of Motor Vehicles Registered in India

(number in '000s)

As on 31-March	Two-Wheelers	Auto-Rickshaws	Taxis	Jeeps & Cars	Buses	Goods Vehicles	Others	Total
1951	27		12	148	34	82	4	307
1961	88	6	22	288	57	168	36	665
1971	576	37	60	622	94	343	134	1865
1981	2530	142	101	1020	162	554	794	5181
1991	14200	617	244	2711	331	1513	1759	21374
2001	38556	1777	634	6423	634	2948	4018	54991
2002	41581	1878	688	6925	688	2974	4243	58924
2003	47519	2114	825	7774	825	3492	4562	67007
2004	51922	2167	902	8549	902	3749	4661	72718
2005	58800	2441	940	9381	940	4032	5017	81502
2006	64743	2600	1040	10487	1040	4436	5320	89618

Source : Transport Research Wing, Ministry of Road Transport and Highways.

207 : Railway Infrastructure: Route Length and Stations

As on 31-March	Infrastructure		
	Route (kilometres)		Number of Stations
	Total	*of which:* Electrified	
1950-51	53596	388	5976
1960-61	56962	748	6523
1970-71	59997	3706	7066
1980-81	61240	5345	7035
1990-91	62231	9968	7100
2000-01	63028	14856	6853
2001-02	63140	15994	6931
2002-03	63122	16272	6906
2003-04	63221	17503	7031
2004-05	63465	17495	7133
2005-06	63332	17907	7133
2006-07	63327	17800	6909
2007-08	63300	18300	6909
2008-09	64015	18559	7030

Note : Includes steam, diesel and electric.
Source : Railway budget.

208 : Railway Infrastructure : Rolling Stock

As on 31-March	Locomotives*	Coaching Stock & EMU	Seating Capacity (in 1000)	Goods Wagon (in 1000)	Carrying Capacity (Mn tonne)
1950-51	8209	13569	943	213	4.17
1960-61	10624	21024	1432	308	6.3
1970-71	11158	26426	1846	384	9.35
1980-81	10908	30103	2196	401	11.1
1990-91	8408	31843	2473	346	11.5
2000-01	7566	38889	3232	222	10.2
2001-02	7739	39004	3337	217	10.1
2002-03	7681	39592	3413	215	10.0
2003-04	7817	40653	3627	228	10.7
2004-05	7910	42154	3713	222	10.6
2005-06	8025	43515	3807	208	10.0
2006-07	8153	44667	4001	208	10.1
2007-08	8330	46611	4168	204	10.2

Note : Includes steam, diesel and electric; EMU: electric multiple unit.
Source : Railway budget.

209 : Railway Traffic: Passenger

Year	Originating Passenger Traffic (million nos.)	Passenger Kilometres (million)	Passenger Earnings (Rs. crore)	Average lead in Kilo-metres	Average Rate per Passenger kilometre (in paise)
1950-51	1284	66517	98	51.8	1.5
1960-61	1594	77665	132	48.7	1.7
1970-71	2431	118120	296	48.6	2.5
1980-81	3613	208558	828	57.7	4.0
1990-91	3858	295644	3148	76.6	10.6
2000-01	4840	457022	10515	94.6	22.9
2001-02	5093	490912	11196	95.6	22.8
2002-03	5048	515044	12575	102.0	24.4
2003-04	5203	541208	13298	104.0	24.6
2004-05	5378	575702	14114	107.0	24.4
2005-06	5818	614452	15127	107.5	24.5
2006-07	6400	682655	17225	111.7	24.7
2007-08	6524	770000	19844	118.0	25.7
2008-09	7047	839203	21931	121.1	26.1
2009-10	7380	925514	24057	125.4	26.0
2010-11(B)	7773	1005835	26126	129.4	26.0

Note: B - Budget.
Source : Railway budget, Explanatory Memorandum and Railway Year Book.

210 : Railway Traffic : Goods

Year	Revenue Earning Freight Traffic (million tonnes)	Net Tonne Kilometre (billion)	Revenue Earnings (Rs. crore)	Average lead in Revenue Traffic (in km)	Average Rate per Kilometre (in paise)
1950-51	73	38	139	513	3.2
1960-61	120	72	281	604	3.9
1970-71	168	111	601	659	5.4
1980-81	196	148	1551	754	10.5
1990-91	318	236	8247	741	35.0
2000-01	474	312	23045	660	73.8
2001-02	493	333	24845	677	74.6
2002-03	519	353	26505	681	75.0
2003-04	557	381	27618	684	72.5
2004-05	602	407	30489	677	74.8
2005-06	667	440	35535	660	80.8
2006-07	728	481	41073	661	85.4
2007-08	794	521	46426	656	89.0
2008-09	833	551	53433	661	97.0
2009-10	890	584	58716	656	100.5
2010-11(B)	944	623	62489	660	100.3

Note: B - Budget.
Source : Railway budget, Explanatory Memorandum and Railway Year Book.

211 : Strength of Indian Shipping

As on 31-March	Coastal Trade		Overseas Trade	
	Number of Vessels	Gross Registered Tonnage ('000)	Number of Vessels	Gross Registered Tonnage ('000)
1951	71	206	23	167
1961	97	314	75	544
1971	66	231	184	2214
1981	59	250	331	5495
1991	163	524	255	5516
2001	316	697	230	6119
2002	336	734	224	6087
2003	425	805	191	5372
2004	436	807	203	6136
2005	458	811	228	7202
2006	496	817	243	7647
2007	530	842	257	7753
2008	573	893	277	81336

Note : Based on data received from ports and not on entire overseas traffic cargo handled

Source : Ministry of Shipping.

212 : Civil Aviation : Indian Scheduled Operations — Domestic Services

	Aircraft Distance Flown (lakh km)	Passenger			Freight & Mail		
		Numbers Flown (in '000)	Km flown (in million)	Load Factor (%)	Freight Tonne (km million)	Mail Tonne (km million)	Load Factor (%)
1951-52	220	301	205	..	17		..
1961-62	278	745	575	71.5	18	6	75.0
1970-71	334	2123	1559	76.8	14	10	79.6
1980-81	444	4850	3917	68.5	48	15	63.8
1990-91	587	7912	7028	79.4	88	16	75.8
2000-01	1369	13719	12287	61.7	146	24	57.6
2001-02	1471	12840	11551	55.4	145	23	52.1
2002-03	1658	13951	12848	56.3	164	23	51.2
2003-04	1893	15677	14566	58.4	191	19	57.5
2004-05	2136	19445	18031	64.9	229	29	63.9
2005-06	2523	25183	23688	67.7	238	35	67.2
2006-07	3483	35792	33518	68.8	252	23	67.1
2007-08	4394	44355	41717	68.9	272	21	65.7
2008-09	4184	38819	37027	63.7	234	24	59.7

Source : Directorate General of Civil Aviation, Ministry of Civil Aviation.

213 : Civil Aviation : Indian Scheduled Operations — International Services

	Aircraft Distance Flown (lakh km)	Passenger			Freight & Mail		
		Numbers Flown (in '000)	Km Flown (in million)	Load Factor (%)	Freight Tonne (km million)	Mail Tonne (km million)	Load Factor (%)
1950-51	90	148	179				..
1960-61	170	229	698	46.7			44.5
1970-71	259	491	2031	48.7	97	8	50.8
1980-81	427	1944	6763	62.5	330	20	59.4
1990-91	511	2430	8820	66.5	553	11	62.4
2000-01	660	3828	13928	76.0	403	9	72.8
2001-02	745	3669	13237	68.8	360	11	65.5
2002-03	845	4201	15819	73.9	401	10	70.4
2003-04	977	4491	18107	72.5	399	13	66.3
2004-05	1195	5326	22272	71.6	509	115	65.8
2005-06	1534	6071	26657	68.4	560	141	60.7
2006-07	1862	7559	30355	68.0	609	105	59.7
2007-08	2408	9109	36130	66.3	769	209	55.1
2008-09	2755	9640	38905	65.3	927	230	55.2

Source : Directorate General of Civil Aviation, Ministry of Civil Aviation.

IV. PROFILE OF STATES

> Population
> Vital Rates
> Education
> Employment
> Standard of Living
> Agriculture
> Factory Sector
> Establishments
> Banking
> State Finance
> Health Infrastructure
> Housing and Amenities

214 : State-wise Population of India

State/Region	1981		1991		2001	
	Population (million)	Share in All-India (%)	Population (million)	Share in All-India (%)	Population (million)	Share in All-India (%)
All India	683.33	100.00	846.43	100.00	1028.74	100.00
Northern Region	80.91	11.84	103.82	12.27	132.99	12.93
Haryana	12.92	1.89	16.46	1.95	21.15	2.06
Himachal Pradesh	4.28	0.63	5.17	0.61	6.08	0.59
Jammu & Kashmir**	5.99	0.88	7.84	0.93	10.14	0.99
Punjab	16.79	2.46	20.28	2.40	24.36	2.37
Rajasthan	34.26	5.01	44.01	5.20	56.51	5.49
Chandigarh	0.45	0.07	0.64	0.08	0.90	0.09
Delhi	6.22	0.91	9.42	1.11	13.85	1.35
N-Eastern Region	24.75	3.62	31.55	3.73	38.45	3.74
Arunachal Pradesh	0.63	0.09	0.87	0.10	1.10	0.11
Assam*	18.04	2.64	22.41	2.65	26.66	2.59
Manipur***	1.42	0.21	1.84	0.22	2.29	0.22
Meghalaya	1.34	0.20	1.78	0.21	2.32	0.23
Mizoram	0.49	0.07	0.69	0.08	0.89	0.09
Nagaland	0.78	0.11	1.21	0.14	1.99	0.19
Tripura	2.05	0.30	2.76	0.33	3.20	0.31

contd...

...contd...

State/Region	1981		1991		2001	
	Population (million)	Share in All-India (%)	Population (million)	Share in All-India (%)	Population (million)	Share in All-India (%)
Eastern Region	151.37	22.15	186.80	22.07	227.82	22.15
Bihar	52.30	7.65	64.53	7.62	83.00	8.07
Jharkhand	17.61	2.58	21.84	2.58	26.95	2.62
Orissa	26.37	3.86	31.66	3.74	36.81	3.58
Sikkim	0.32	0.05	0.41	0.05	0.54	0.05
West Bengal	54.58	7.99	68.08	8.04	80.18	7.79
A&N Islands	0.19	0.03	0.28	0.03	0.36	0.03
Central Region	163.04	23.86	205.29	24.25	255.87	24.87
Chhattisgarh	14.01	2.05	17.62	2.08	20.83	2.03
Madhya Pradesh	38.17	5.59	48.57	5.74	60.35	5.87
Uttar Pradesh	105.14	15.39	132.06	15.60	166.20	16.16
Uttarakhand	5.73	0.84	7.05	0.83	8.49	0.83
Western Region	98.06	14.35	121.66	14.37	149.28	14.51
Goa	1.01	0.15	1.17	0.14	1.35	0.13
Gujarat	34.09	4.99	41.31	4.88	50.67	4.93
Maharashtra	62.78	9.19	78.94	9.33	96.88	9.42
D&N Haveli	0.10	0.02	0.14	0.02	0.22	0.02
Daman & Diu	0.08	0.01	0.10	0.01	0.16	0.02

contd...

...contd...

State/Region	1981		1991		2001	
	Population (million)	Share in All-India (%)	Population (million)	Share in All-India (%)	Population (million)	Share in All-India (%)
Southern Region	165.19	24.17	197.30	23.31	224.34	21.81
Andhra Pradesh	53.55	7.84	66.51	7.86	76.21	7.41
Karnataka	37.14	5.43	44.98	5.31	52.85	5.14
Kerala	25.45	3.72	29.10	3.44	31.84	3.10
Tamil Nadu	48.41	7.08	55.86	6.60	62.41	6.07
Lakshadweep	0.04	0.01	0.05	0.01	0.06	0.01
Pondicherry	0.60	0.09	0.81	0.10	0.97	0.09

Note : * : The 1981 census not held in Assam. Total population for 1981 has been worked out by interpolation.
** : The 1991 census not held in J & K. Total population for 1991 has been worked out by interpolation.
*** :Manipur data includes estimated population for Mao Maram, Paomata and Puri Senapati districts.

Source : Office of the Registrar General of India, Ministry of Home Affairs.

215 : State-wise Population : By Gender

State/Region	1991		2001			
			Male		Female	
	Male (million)	Female (million)	Total (million)	Male Proportion (%)	Total (in million)	Female Proportion (%)
All India	439.36	407.06	532.22	51.7	496.51	48.3
Northern Region	54.92	48.90	70.33	52.9	62.65	47.1
Haryana	8.83	7.64	11.36	53.7	9.78	46.3
Himachal Pradesh	2.62	2.55	3.09	50.8	2.99	49.2
Jammu & Kashmir**	4.14	3.69	5.36	52.8	4.78	47.2
Punjab	10.78	9.50	12.99	53.3	11.37	46.7
Rajasthan	23.04	20.96	29.42	52.1	27.09	47.9
Chandigarh	0.36	0.28	0.51	56.3	0.39	43.7
Delhi	5.16	4.27	7.61	54.9	6.24	45.1
N-Eastern Region	16.39	15.16	19.84	51.6	18.60	48.4
Arunachal Pradesh	0.47	0.40	0.58	52.8	0.52	47.2
Assam*	11.66	10.76	13.78	51.7	12.88	48.3
Manipur***	0.94	0.90	1.16	50.7	1.13	49.3
Meghalaya	0.91	0.87	1.18	50.7	1.14	49.3
Mizoram	0.36	0.33	0.46	51.7	0.43	48.3
Nagaland	0.64	0.57	1.05	52.6	0.94	47.4
Tripura	1.42	1.34	1.64	51.3	1.56	48.7

contd...

...contd...

State/Region	1991		2001			
	Male (million)	Female (million)	Male		Female	
			Total (million)	Male Proportion (%)	Total (in million)	Female Proportion (%)
Eastern Region	97.15	89.65	117.74	51.7	110.06	48.3
Bihar	33.84	30.69	43.24	52.1	39.75	47.9
Jharkhand	11.36	10.48	13.89	51.5	13.06	48.5
Orissa	16.06	15.60	18.66	50.7	18.11	49.3
Sikkim	0.22	0.19	0.29	53.3	0.25	46.7
West Bengal	35.51	32.57	41.47	51.7	38.71	48.3
A&N Islands	0.15	0.13	0.19	54.2	0.16	45.8
Central Region	108.30	96.99	133.81	52.3	122.06	47.7
Chhattisgarh	8.87	8.74	10.47	50.3	10.36	49.7
Madhya Pradesh	25.39	23.17	31.44	52.1	28.90	47.9
Uttar Pradesh	70.36	61.64	87.57	52.7	78.63	47.3
Uttarakhand	3.67	3.44	4.33	51.0	4.16	49.0
Western Region	62.90	58.76	77.69	52.0	71.62	48.0
Goa	0.59	0.58	0.69	51.0	0.66	49.0
Gujarat	21.36	19.95	26.39	52.1	24.29	47.9
Maharashtra	40.83	38.11	50.40	52.0	46.48	48.0

contd...

...contd...

State/Region	1991		2001			
	Male (million)	Female (million)	Male		Female	
			Total (million)	Male Proportion (%)	Total (in million)	Female Proportion (%)
D&N Haveli	0.07	0.07	0.12	55.2	0.10	44.8
Daman & Diu	0.05	0.05	0.09	49.2	0.10	50.8
Southern Region	99.70	97.60	112.81	50.3	111.53	49.7
Andhra Pradesh	33.72	32.78	38.53	50.6	37.68	49.4
Karnataka	22.95	22.03	26.90	50.9	25.95	49.1
Kerala	14.29	14.81	15.47	48.6	16.37	51.4
Tamil Nadu	28.30	27.56	31.40	50.3	31.00	49.7
Lakshadweep	0.03	0.03	0.03	51.3	0.03	48.7
Pondicherry	0.41	0.40	0.49	50.0	0.49	50.0

Note: * : The 1981 census not held in Assam. Total population for 1981 has been worked out by interpolation.
** : The 1991 census not held in J & K. Total population for 1991 has been worked out by interpolation.
*** : Manipur data includes estimated population for Mao Maram, Paomata and Puri Senapati districts.

Source: Office of the Registrar General of India, Ministry of Home Affairs.

216 : State-wise Population of India : Rural and Urban

State/Region	Rural Population			Urban Population			Urban Population as % of Total	
	1991 (million)	2001 (million)	Decadal Increase (%)	1991 (million)	2001 (million)	Decadal Increase (%)	1991	2001
All India	628.7	742.6	18.12	217.6	286.1	31.48	25.7	27.8
Northern Region	72.2	88.6	22.7	31.5	44.4	41.0	30.3	33.4
Haryana	12.4	15.0	21.2	4.1	6.1	49.2	24.9	28.9
Himachal Pradesh	4.7	5.5	16.6	0.4	0.6	48.9	7.7	9.8
Jammu & Kashmir**	5.9	7.6	29.3	1.8	2.5	39.8	23.0	24.8
Punjab	14.3	16.1	12.6	6.0	8.3	37.7	29.6	33.9
Rajasthan	33.9	43.3	27.7	10.1	13.2	30.8	23.0	23.4
Chandigarh	0.1	0.1	0.0	0.6	0.8	34.8	93.5	89.7
Delhi	0.9	0.9	5.0	8.5	12.9	51.8	90.2	93.2
N-Eastern Region	27.1	32.4	19.6	4.3	6.0	40.2	13.6	15.7
Arunachal Pradesh	0.8	0.9	8.8	0.1	0.2	127.9	11.6	20.8
Assam*	19.9	23.2	16.7	2.5	3.4	37.6	11.2	12.9
Manipur***	1.3	1.7	32.1	0.5	0.6	15.2	27.2	25.1
Meghalaya	1.4	1.9	33.2	0.3	0.5	51.4	16.9	19.6
Mizoram	0.4	0.4	11.9	0.3	0.4	47.0	43.5	49.6
Nagaland	1.0	1.6	64.7	0.2	0.3	71.4	16.5	17.2
Tripura	2.3	2.7	15.4	0.4	0.5	36.4	14.5	17.1

contd...

...contd...

State/Region	Rural Population			Urban Population			Urban Population as % of Total	
	1991 (million)	2001 (million)	Decadal Increase (%)	1991 (million)	2001 (million)	Decadal Increase (%)	1991	2001
Eastern Region	152.4	185.0	21.4	34.4	42.8	24.3	18.4	18.8
Bihar	75.0	74.3	-0.9	11.4	8.7	-23.8	17.7	10.5
Jharkhand	..	21.0	..	..	6.0	..	0.0	22.2
Orissa	27.4	31.3	14.2	4.2	5.5	31.4	13.3	15.0
Sikkim	0.4	0.5	20.2	0.0	0.1	61.8	0.0	11.1
West Bengal	49.4	57.7	16.9	18.7	22.4	19.9	27.5	28.0
A&N Islands	0.2	0.2	20.0	0.1	0.1	16.2	35.6	32.6
Central Region	162.3	199.0	22.6	42.9	56.9	32.4	20.9	22.2
Chhattisgarh	..	16.6	..	..	4.2	..	0.0	20.1
Madhya Pradesh	50.8	44.4	-12.7	15.3	16.0	4.1	31.6	26.5
Uttar Pradesh	111.5	131.7	18.1	27.6	34.5	25.1	20.9	20.8
Uttarakhand	..	6.3	..	..	2.2	..	0.0	25.7
Western Region	76.4	88.5	15.8	45.3	60.8	34.2	37.2	40.7
Goa	0.7	0.7	-3.3	0.5	0.7	34.1	42.7	49.7
Gujarat	27.1	31.7	17.1	14.2	18.9	33.3	34.4	37.4
Maharashtra	48.4	55.8	15.2	30.5	41.1	34.8	38.6	42.4
D&N Haveli	0.1	0.2	70.0	0.0	0.1	330.4	0.0	22.9
Daman & Diu	0.1	0.1	0.9	0.1	0.1	-42.7	98.0	36.3

contd...

...contd...

State/Region	Rural Population			Urban Population			Urban Population as % of Total	
	1991 (million)	2001 (million)	Decadal Increase (%)	1991 (million)	2001 (million)	Decadal Increase (%)	1991	2001
Southern Region	138.2	149.1	7.9	59.1	75.2	27.2	30.0	33.5
Andhra Pradesh	48.6	55.4	13.9	17.9	20.8	16.3	26.9	27.3
Karnataka	31.1	34.9	12.2	13.9	18.0	29.2	30.9	34.0
Kerala	21.4	23.6	10.2	7.7	8.3	7.4	26.5	26.0
Tamil Nadu	36.8	34.9	-5.1	19.1	27.5	43.9	34.2	44.0
Lakshadweep	0.0	0.0	49.1	0.0	0.0	-7.4	56.0	44.2
Pondicherry	0.3	0.3	8.6	0.5	0.6	29.7	61.9	66.6

Source : Office of the Registrar General of India, Ministry of Home Affairs.

217 : State-wise Density (Population per square kilometre)

State/Region	1951	1961	1971	1981	1991	2001
All India	117	142	177	216	267	325
Northern Region						
Haryana	128	172	227	292	372	478
Himachal Pradesh	43	51	62	77	93	109
Jammu & Kashmir	..	..	..	59	77	100
Punjab	182	221	269	333	403	484
Rajasthan	47	59	75	100	129	165
Chandigarh	213	1052	2257	3961	5632	7900
Delhi	1176	1793	2742	4194	6352	9340
N-Eastern Region						
Arunachal Pradesh	..	4	6	8	10	13
Assam	102	138	186	230	286	340
Manipur	26	35	48	64	82	103
Meghalaya	27	34	45	60	79	103
Mizoram	9	13	16	23	33	42
Nagaland	13	22	31	47	73	120
Tripura	61	109	148	196	263	305
Eastern Region						
Bihar	223	267	324	402	685	881
Jharkhand	..	..	..	..	274	338
Orissa	94	113	141	169	203	236
Sikkim	19	23	30	45	57	76
West Bengal	296	394	499	615	767	903
A&N Islands	4	8	14	23	34	43
Central Region						
Chhattisgarh	..	..	..	..	130	154
Madhya Pradesh	59	73	94	118	158	196
Uttar Pradesh	215	251	300	377	548	690
Uttarakhand	..	..	..	..	132	159
Western Region						
Goa	148	159	215	272	316	364
Gujarat	83	105	136	174	211	258
Maharashtra	104	129	164	204	257	315
D&N Haveli	85	118	151	211	282	449
Daman & Diu	434	327	559	705	907	1413
Southern Region						
Andhra Pradesh	113	131	158	195	242	277
Karnataka	101	123	153	194	235	276
Kerala	349	435	549	655	749	819
Tamil Nadu	232	259	317	372	429	480
Lakshadweep	657	753	994	1258	1616	1895
Pondicherry	645	750	959	1229	1683	2030

Source : Office of the Registrar General of India, Ministry of Home Affairs.

218 : State-wise : Sex Ratio (Females per 1000 males)

State/Region	1951	1961	1971	1981	1991	2001
All India	946	941	930	934	926	933
Northern Region	..	..	..	..	890	891
Haryana	871	868	867	870	865	861
Himachal Pradesh	912	938	958	973	976	968
Jammu & Kashmir	873	878	878	892	892	892
Punjab	844	854	865	879	882	876
Rajasthan	921	908	911	919	910	921
Chandigarh	781	652	749	769	790	777
Delhi	768	785	801	808	827	821
N-Eastern Region	..	..	..	..	925	937
Arunachal Pradesh	..	894	861	862	859	893
Assam	868	869	896	910	923	935
Manipur	1036	1015	980	971	958	974
Meghalaya	949	937	942	954	955	972
Mizoram	1041	1009	946	919	921	935
Nagaland	999	933	871	863	886	900
Tripura	904	932	943	946	945	948
Eastern Region	..	..	..	..	923	935
Bihar	990	994	954	946	907	919
Jharkhand	..	..	..	..	922	941
Orissa	1022	1001	988	981	971	971
Sikkim	907	904	863	835	878	875
West Bengal	865	878	891	911	917	934
A&N Islands	625	617	644	760	818	846
Central Region	..	..	..	..	896	912
Chhattisgarh	..	..	..	..	985	989
Madhya Pradesh	967	953	941	941	912	919
Uttar Pradesh	910	909	879	885	876	898
Uttarakhand	..	..	..	..	936	962
Western Region	..	..	..	..	934	922
Goa	1128	1066	981	975	967	961
Gujarat	952	940	934	942	934	920
Maharashtra	941	936	930	937	934	922
D&N Haveli	946	963	1007	974	948	812
Daman & Diu	1125	1169	1099	1062	969	1034
Southern Region	..	..	..	..	979	989
Andhra Pradesh	986	981	977	975	972	978
Karnataka	966	959	957	963	960	965
Kerala	1028	1022	1016	1032	1036	1058
Tamil Nadu	1007	992	978	977	974	987
Lakshadweep	1043	1020	978	975	943	948
Pondicherry	1030	1013	989	985	979	1001

Source : Office of the Registrar General of India, Ministry of Home Affairs.

219 : Slum Population of India

(lakh)

State/Region	Slum Population			Per cent Change		Slum Population as % to Urban Population		
	1981	1991	2001	1981-1991	1991-2001	1981	1991	2001
All India	279.1	462.7	618.3	65.8	33.6	17.5	21.3	28.0
Northern Region	49.8	74.6	103.7	49.8	39.0	na	na	na
Haryana	2.7	6.8	10.1	151.9	48.5	9.7	16.9	16.9
Himachal Pradesh	0.8	1.3	1.6	62.5	23.1	23.3	27.9	28.0
Jammu & Kashmir	6.3	5.9	7.8	-6.3	32.2	49.7	32.2	32.2
Punjab	11.7	14.1	18.9	20.5	34.0	25.1	23.6	23.6
Rajasthan	10.3	24.0	32.7	133.0	36.3	14.2	23.8	23.8
Delhi	18.0	22.5	32.6	25.0	44.9	31.2	26.5	26.5
N-Eastern Region	2.3	8.1	11.2	252.2	38.3	na	na	na
Arunachal Pradesh	0.0	0.2	0.4	na	100.0	0.0	20.0	20.0
Assam	1.2	4.5	5.8	275.0	28.9	7.0	18.0	18.0
Manipur	0.2	0.9	1.1	350.0	22.2	4.5	16.9	16.9
Meghalaya	0.7	0.8	1.2	14.3	50.0	27.4	25.2	25.2
Mizoram	0.0	0.6	1.2	na	100.0	0.0	17.9	18.1
Nagaland	0.0	0.4	0.6	na	50.0	0.0	20.0	20.0
Tripura	0.2	0.7	0.9	250.0	28.6	8.2	17.6	17.6

contd...

...contd...

State/Region	Slum Population			Per cent Change		Slum Population as % to Urban Population		
	1981	1991	2001	1981-1991	1991-2001	1981	1991	2001
Eastern Region	65.8	87.4	112.5	32.8	28.7	na	na	na
Bihar	32.7	26.9	35.4	-17.7	31.6	37.5	23.7	23.7
Jharkhand	na	na	na	na	na	na	na	na
Orissa	2.8	8.4	11.2	200.0	33.3	9.1	19.9	19.9
Sikkim	0.0	0.1	0.1	na	0.0	4.7	25.7	25.7
West Bengal	30.3	52.0	65.8	71.6	26.5	21.0	27.8	27.8
Central Region	36.6	79.4	105.1	116.9	32.4	na	na	na
Chhattisgarh	na	na	na	na	na	na	na	na
Madhya Pradesh	10.8	21.0	28.0	94.4	33.3	10.2	13.7	13.7
Uttar Pradesh	25.8	58.4	77.1	126.4	32.0	13.0	21.2	21.1
Uttarakhand	na	na	na	na	na	na	na	na
Western Region	58.7	105.3	142.9	79.4	35.7	na	na	na
Goa	0.2	0.8	1.1	300.0	37.5	6.9	17.4	17.4
Gujarat	15.3	25.8	34.4	68.6	33.3	14.4	18.1	18.1
Maharashtra	43.2	78.7	107.4	82.2	36.5	19.6	25.8	25.8

contd...

...contd...

State/Region	Slum Population			Per cent Change		Slum Population as % to Urban Population		
	1981	1991	2001	1981-1991	1991-2001	1981	1991	2001
Southern Region	65.3	103.9	138.1	59.1	32.9	na	na	na
Andhra Pradesh	28.6	43.1	60.2	50.7	39.7	22.9	24.1	24.1
Karnataka	5.8	12.9	17.8	122.4	38.0	5.4	9.3	9.3
Kerala	4.1	12.2	16.5	197.6	35.2	8.6	15.9	15.9
Tamil Nadu	26.8	35.7	43.6	33.2	22.1	16.8	18.7	18.7
Union Territories	18.9	26.2	37.6	38.6	43.5	28.8	28.3	26.8

Source : CSO (2002), NSSO survey on slum population.

220 : Crude Birth and Death Rate

State/Region	Crude Birth Rate				Crude Death Rate			
	1981	1991	2001	2008	1981	1991	2001	2008
All India	33.9	29.5	25.4	22.8	12.5	9.8	8.4	7.4
Northern Region								
Haryana	36.6	33.1	26.7	23.0	11.3	8.2	7.6	6.9
Himachal Pradesh#	31.5	28.5	21.0	17.7	11.1	8.9	7.0	7.4
Jammu & Kashmir	31.6	na	20.1	18.8	9.0	na	6.1	5.8
Punjab	30.3	27.7	21.2	17.3	9.4	7.8	7.0	7.2
Rajasthan	37.1	35.0	31.0	27.5	14.3	10.1	7.9	6.8
Chandigarh#	24.6	13.9	16.1	16.4	2.4	4.6	3.5	4.4
Delhi#	26.9	24.7	18.7	18.4	7.1	6.3	5.0	4.8
N-Eastern Region								
Arunachal Pradesh#	na	30.9	22.0	21.8	na	13.5	5.5	5.2
Assam	33.0	30.9	26.8	23.9	12.6	11.5	9.5	8.6
Manipur#	26.6	20.1	18.2	15.8	6.6	5.4	5.1	5.0
Meghalaya#	32.6	32.4	28.3	25.2	8.2	8.8	9.0	7.9

contd...

...contd...

State/Region	Crude Birth Rate				Crude Death Rate			
	1981	1991	2001	2008	1981	1991	2001	2008
Mizoram	na	na	15.7	17.8	na	na	4.4	5.1
Nagaland#	na	18.5	na	17.5	na	3.8	na	4.6
Tripura#	26.4	24.4	16.1	15.4	8.0	7.6	5.6	5.9
Eastern Region								
Bihar	39.1	30.7	31.2	28.9	13.9	9.8	8.2	7.3
Jharkhand	na	na	26.3	25.8	na	na	8.8	7.1
Orissa	33.1	28.8	23.4	21.4	13.1	12.8	10.2	9.0
Sikkim	31.0	22.5	21.6	18.4	8.9	7.5	5.1	5.2
West Bengal	33.2	27.0	20.5	17.5	11.0	8.3	6.8	6.2
A&N Islands#	34.7	20.0	16.8	16.9	8.4	5.8	4.7	4.8
Central Region								
Chhattisgarh	na	na	26.3	26.1	na	na	8.8	8.1
Madhya Pradesh	37.6	35.8	30.8	28.0	16.6	13.8	10.0	8.6
Uttar Pradesh	39.6	35.7	32.1	29.1	16.3	11.3	10.1	8.4
Uttarakhand	na	na	18.5	20.1	na	na	7.8	6.4

contd...

...contd...

State/Region	Crude Birth Rate				Crude Death Rate			
	1981	1991	2001	2008	1981	1991	2001	2008
Western Region								
Goa#	15.5	16.8	13.9	13.6	6.8	7.5	7.5	6.6
Gujarat	34.5	27.5	24.9	22.6	12.0	8.5	7.8	6.9
Maharashtra	28.5	26.2	20.6	17.9	9.6	8.2	7.5	6.6
D&N Haveli#	na	na	29.3	27.0	na	na	6.5	5.4
Daman & Diu#	na	27.9	22.3	17.5	na	9.0	6.7	5.3
Southern Region								
Andhra Pradesh	31.7	26.0	20.8	18.4	11.1	9.7	8.1	7.5
Karnataka	28.3	26.9	22.2	19.8	9.1	9.0	7.6	7.4
Kerala	25.6	18.3	17.2	14.6	6.6	6.0	6.6	6.6
Tamil Nadu	28.0	20.8	19.0	16.0	11.8	8.8	7.6	7.4
Lakshadweep#	na	27.1	20.4	14.3	na	4.7	5.0	7.1
Pondicherry#	21.7	19.2	17.9	16.4	7.3	6.6	7.0	7.5

Note: Crude birth rate is number of live births during the year divided by mid-year population and multiplied by 1000.
Crude death rate is number of deaths during the year divided by mid-year population and multiplied by 1000.
Data for small states and Union Territories are based on three-year moving averages.

Source: Sample Registration System, Office of Registrar General and Census of India *(www.censusindia.gov.in)*.

221 : Fertility Rate and Infant Mortality Rate

State/Region	Total Fertility Rate (15-49 years)			Infant Mortality Rate				
	1992-93	1998-99	2005-06	1971	1981	1991	2001	2008
All India	3.39	2.89	2.68	129	110	80	66	53
Northern Region								
Haryana	3.99	2.88	2.69	72	108	68	66	54
Himachal Pradesh#	2.97	2.14	1.94	..	..	..	54	44
Jammu & Kashmir*	0.00	2.71	2.38	..	..	..	48	49
Punjab	2.92	2.21	1.99	102	81	53	52	41
Rajasthan*	3.63	3.78	3.21	123	108	79	80	63
Chandigarh*#	..	..	..	..	..	35	24	28
Delhi#	3.02	2.40	2.13	..	..	43	29	35
N-Eastern Region								
Arunachal Pradesh#	4.25	2.52	3.03	..	na	65	39	32
Assam	3.53	2.31	2.42	139	106	81	74	56
Manipur#	2.76	3.04	2.83	..	..	22	20	14
Meghalaya#	3.73	4.57	3.80	..	..	57	56	58
Mizoram	2.30	2.89	2.86	..	..	0	19	37
Nagaland#	3.26	3.77	3.74	..	..	7	0	26
Tripura#	2.67	1.87	2.22	..	..	56	39	34
Eastern Region								
Bihar		3.70	4.00	..	118	69	62	57
Jharkhand		2.76	3.31	..	..	..		46

contd...

...contd...

State/Region	Total Fertility Rate (15-49 years)			Infant Mortality Rate				
	1992-93	1998-99	2005-06	1971	1981	1991	2001	2008
Orissa	2.92	2.46	2.37	127	135	124	91	69
Sikkim		2.75	2.02	..	na	51	42	33
West Bengal	2.92	2.29	2.27	..	91	71	51	35
A&N Islands#	..	..	..	..	na	30	18	31
Central Region								
Chhattisgarh		2.79	2.62	..	..	..		35
Madhya Pradesh		3.43	3.12	135	142	117	86	70
Uttar Pradesh		4.06	3.82	167	150	97	83	67
Uttarakhand		2.61	2.55	..	..	..	48	44
Western Region								
Goa#	1.90	1.77	1.79	..	..	21	19	10
Gujarat	2.99	2.72	2.42	144	116	69	60	50
Maharashtra	2.86	2.52	2.11	105	79	60	45	33
D&N Haveli#	..	..	..	..	..	68	58	34
Daman & Diu#	..	..	..	..	..	52	40	31
Southern Region								
Andhra Pradesh	2.59	2.25	1.79	106	86	73	66	64
Karnataka	2.85	2.13	2.07	95	69	77	58	45
Kerala	2.00	1.96	1.93	58	37	16	11	12
Tamil Nadu	2.48	2.19	1.80	113	91	57	49	31
Lakshadweep#	..	..	..	..	..	44	33	31
Pondicherry#	..	..	..	..	..	21	22	25

Note : IMR is the ratio of infant deaths to live births during the year multiplied by 1000; * Data for 1971 pertains to 1972; # Data for small states and Union Territories are based on three-year moving averages.

Source : 1: Sample Registration System, Office of Registrar General and Census of India; 2: NFHS-3, International Institute for Population Sciences, Mumbai.

222 : Life Expectancy at Birth

(years)

State	1981-1985	1991-1995	1997-2001	2001-2005
All India	55.5	60.3	62.2	63.2
Andhra Pradesh	58.4	61.8	63.4	64.1
Assam	51.9	55.7	57.7	58.7
Bihar	52.9	59.3	60.6	61.4
Gujarat	57.6	61.0	63.3	63.9
Haryana	60.3	63.4	65.0	65.9
Karnataka	60.7	62.5	64.3	65.1
Kerala	68.4	72.9	73.6	73.9
Madhya Pradesh	51.6	54.7	56.6	57.7
Maharashtra	60.7	64.8	66.1	66.9
Orissa	53.0	56.5	58.1	59.2
Punjab	63.1	67.2	68.3	69.2
Rajasthan	53.5	59.1	60.9	61.7
Tamil Nadu	56.9	63.3	65.0	66.0
Uttar Pradesh	50.0	56.8	58.8	59.8
West Bengal	57.4	62.1	63.7	64.6

Note : Data for Bihar, MP and UP includes Jharkhand, Chhattisgarh and Uttarakhand respectively.

Data are not available for small states and Union Territories.

Source : Sample Registration System.

223 : Maternal Mortality Ratio

State	1997	1998	1999-2001	2001-2003	2004-2006
All India	408	407	327	301	254
Andhra Pradesh	154	159	220	195	154
Assam	401	409	398	490	480
Bihar	451	452	400	371	312
Gujarat	29	28	202	172	160
Haryana	105	103	176	162	186
Karnataka	195	195	266	228	213
Kerala	195	198	149	110	95
Madhya Pradesh	498	498	407	379	335
Maharashtra	135	135	169	149	130
Orissa	361	367	424	358	303
Punjab	196	199	177	178	192
Rajasthan	677	670	501	445	388
Tamil Nadu	76	79	167	134	111
Uttar Pradesh	707	707	539	517	440
West Bengal	264	266	218	194	141

Note : Maternal mortality ratio is the number of maternal deaths in the age group 15-49 years per one lakh live births.

There is a major data gap in India with regard to these estimates.

Quality of data suffers due to a small sample size and the various difficulties associated with ascertaining the cause of death. This data gives a broad idea of MMR in big states and at the national level. Estimates for small states and Union Territories have not been presented due to small size of the sample.

Source : Sample Registration System.

224 : Literacy Rate

(in percentage)

State/Region	Female Literacy Rate			All Persons		
	1981	1991	2001	1981	1991	2001
All India	30	39	54	43	52	65
Northern Region						
Haryana	27	40	46	44	56	68
Himachal Pradesh	38	52	67	51	64	76
Jammu & Kashmir	20	..	43	33	..	56
Punjab	40	50	63	48	59	70
Rajasthan	14	20	44	30	39	60
Chandigarh	69	72	76	75	78	82
Delhi	63	67	75	72	75	81
N-Eastern Region						
Arunachal Pradesh	24	30	44	36	42	54
Assam	..	43	55	..	53	63
Manipur	35	48	61	50	60	71
Meghalaya	37	45	60	42	49	63
Mizoram	69	79	87	71	82	89
Nagaland	40	55	61	50	62	67
Tripura	38	50	65	50	60	73
Eastern Region						
Bihar	17	22	33	32	37	47
Jharkhand	..	..	39	..	..	54
Orissa	25	35	51	41	49	63
Sikkim	27	47	60	42	57	69
West Bengal	36	47	60	49	58	69
A&N Islands	53	65	75	63	73	81
Central Region						
Chhattisgarh	..	28	52	..	43	65
Madhya Pradesh	19	29	50	34	45	64
Uttar Pradesh	17	24	42	33	41	56
Uttarakhand	..	42	60	..	58	72
Western Region						
Goa	55	67	75	66	76	82
Gujarat	39	49	59	52	61	70
Maharashtra	41	52	67	56	65	77
D & N Haveli	20	27	43	33	41	60
Daman & Diu	47	59	70	60	71	81
Southern Region						
Andhra Pradesh	14	33	50	26	44	60
Karnataka	33	44	57	46	56	67
Kerala	76	86	88	82	90	91
Tamil Nadu	40	51	64	54	63	73
Lakshadweep	55	73	80	68	82	87
Pondicherry	53	66	74	65	75	81

Note : Literacy rates are estimated on the basis of population aged 7 years and above.
Literacy rates for 1981 and 1991 exclude states of Assam and J&K.
Data for Manipur includes estimated population for Mao Maram, Paomata and Puri Senapati districts.

Source : Registrar General of India for relevant years.

225 : Number of Schools

(in numbers)

State/Region	2001-02			2005-06		
	Primary (I-V)	Upper Primary (VI-VIII)	Secondary (IX-XII)	Primary (I-V)	Upper Primary (VI-VIII)	Secondary (IX-XII)
All India	664041	219626	133492	772568	288493	159667
Northern Region	86871	27287	21057	109292	41917	26124
Haryana	11208	1847	4579	12152	2168	5317
Himachal Pradesh	10877	1768	1954	11261	2457	2196
Jammu & Kashmir	10926	3728	1504	13369	5202	1498
Punjab	13074	2512	3901	13291	2481	4043
Rajasthan	38342	16736	7434	56573	28955	11199
Chandigarh	29	16	107	29	9	121
Delhi	2415	680	1578	2617	645	1750
N-Eastern Region	47741	11965	7708	45353	15440	8786
Arunachal Pradesh	1315	347	191	1380	528	223
Assam	33236	8019	4832	30499	9716	5527
Manipur	2573	796	659	2552	831	705
Meghalaya	5646	1041	643	5851	1759	655
Mizoram	1377	851	403	1688	1121	560
Nagaland	1499	479	344	1520	481	449
Tripura	2095	432	636	1863	1004	667
Eastern Region	151181	27956	21710	151649	37066	22588
Bihar	39299	9691	3575	38161	12328	3637
Jharkhand	16643	4187	1157	16186	6232	1162
Orissa	42104	11510	7313	46370	17012	8890
Sikkim	501	129	110	733	205	162
West Bengal	52426	2384	9463	49986	1229	8640
A&N Islands	208	55	92	213	60	97
Central Region	196275	55364	21669	275862	88898	28244
Chhattisgarh	31023	6358	2532	31670	9677	3906
Madhya Pradesh	62530	25090	8471	94890	35133	8504
Uttar Pradesh	88927	20429	9073	134455	40021	13809
Uttarakhand	13795	3487	1593	14847	4067	2025
Western Region	62739	45943	23280	59863	49185	27641
Goa	1033	84	442	1001	72	426
Gujarat	15545	21205	6734	16415	22621	7654
Maharashtra	45971	24574	16059	42267	26377	19503
D&N Haveli	137	58	19	127	91	30
Daman & Diu	53	22	26	53	24	28
Southern Region	119234	51111	38068	130549	55987	46284
Andhra Pradesh	58249	14472	14255	62159	17290	19247
Karnataka	22404	27712	10796	27017	27512	11730
Kerala	6754	2983	4296	6817	3044	5472
Tamil Nadu	31488	5809	8511	34208	8017	9582
Lakshadweep	20	3	13	21	5	12
Pondicherry	319	132	197	327	119	241

Source : Ministry of Higher Education.

226 : Enrolment in Classes

(Number of pupils in thousands)

State/Region	2001-02			2006-07		
	Primary (I-V)	Upper Primary (VI-VIII)	Secondary (IX-XII)	Primary (I-V)	Upper Primary (VI-VIII)	Secondary (IX-XII)
All India	113883	44828	30507	133525	54360	39443
Northern Region	15205	6987	4468	16960	7682	5436
Haryana	1970	989	877	2197	1243	968
Himachal Pradesh	718	402	341	676	406	414
Jammu & Kashmir	1059	476	344	1135	479	363
Punjab	2073	993	856	1923	1074	869
Rajasthan	7932	3307	1434	9327	3565	2037
Chandigarh	58	37	40	51	27	29
Delhi	1394	783	575	1651	888	756
N-Eastern Region	5676	2076	1277	5250	2070	1288
Arunachal Pradesh	162	54	35	201	66	47
Assam	4081	1519	923	3246	1327	826
Manipur	298	127	84	370	147	103
Meghalaya	327	96	57	564	180	89
Mizoram	135	50	36	151	54	40
Nagaland	212	66	39	225	92	55
Tripura	461	166	104	493	204	128
Eastern Region	25701	7452	4630	29039	9668	5436
Bihar	7809	1914	1133	11504	2773	1114
Jharkhand	2854	776	326	4065	1142	413
Orissa	4769	1505	1177	4485	1854	1371
Sikkim	77	25	13	85	31	18
West Bengal	10151	3211	1965	8862	3845	2500
A&N Islands	40	22	17	38	23	20
Central Region	25664	8910	5785	42023	13876	9935
Chhattisgarh	2973	1062	570	3196	1346	670
Madhya Pradesh	8265	2687	1516	11813	4506	2529
Uttar Pradesh	13378	4672	3318	25812	7453	6222
Uttarakhand	1048	489	380	1202	571	514
Western Region	18187	8196	6034	18378	8950	6707
Goa	120	73	62	115	69	63
Gujarat	6495	2381	1712	6561	2533	1852
Maharashtra	11528	5725	4250	11648	6326	4778
D&N Haveli	29	10	5	38	13	7
Daman & Diu	16	8	6	16	9	7
Southern Region	23450	11207	8313	14714	8392	7309
Andhra Pradesh	8626	3090	2445	201	66	47
Karnataka	6517	2756	1871	5725	2997	2420
Kerala	2524	1766	1458	2524	1595	1619
Tamil Nadu	5674	3524	2485	6146	3662	3153
Lakshadweep	8	5	3	7	4	5
Pondicherry	101	66	50	111	68	65

Source : Ministry of Higher Education.

227 : Dropout Rates from Classes

(in per cent)

State/Region	2001-02			2006-07		
	I-V	I-VIII	I-X	I-V	I-VIII	I-X
All India	40.7	53.7	68.6	25.4	46.0	59.9
Northern Region						
Haryana	30.51	12.35	35.94	9.3	0.0	43.3
Himachal Pradesh	16.68	21.90	31.80	6.8	4.5	28.2
Jammu & Kashmir	29.27	30.14	48.94	12.5	41.2	61.8
Punjab	20.34	36.99	38.62	9.9	29.9	46.5
Rajasthan	63.20	53.56	75.36	40.7	62.3	73.6
Chandigarh	12.72	-1.22	11.99	22.5	36.9	54.4
Delhi	27.67	16.29	42.38	-1.0	23.5	35.3
N-Eastern Region						
Arunachal Pradesh	49.77	60.62	76.04	30.4	54.0	66.9
Assam	48.64	69.21	75.61	44.3	73.6	77.7
Manipur	27.06	37.75	53.90	45.7	41.2	43.8
Meghalaya	56.96	76.99	83.44	44.1	60.4	75.9
Mizoram	59.31	59.89	69.73	49.6	62.6	73.2
Nagaland	41.50	53.36	64.94	20.2	38.6	67.4
Tripura	50.53	69.02	76.92	18.2	50.5	74.6
Eastern Region						
Bihar	61.64	74.79	82.87	51.6	76.1	85.1
Jharkhand				41.9		
Orissa	39.38	60.74	73.05	27.8	62.6	66.3
Sikkim	61.76	63.41	88.39	24.3	65.9	85.0
West Bengal	39.86	70.87	78.52	30.1	61.4	72.2
A&N Islands	0.00	26.98	54.87	6.4	9.0	26.2
Central Region						
Chhattisgarh	na	na	na	25.3	na	na
Madhya Pradesh	29.55	50.11	69.88	0.0	48.4	70.5
Uttar Pradesh	49.40	60.11	58.98	31.1	44.2	46.2
Uttarakhand				18.6		
Western Region						
Goa	5.73	4.19	42.21	-5.5	-2.0	39.9
Gujarat	25.05	52.52	70.22	25.7	49.3	57.5
Maharashtra	7.37	37.03	52.28	2.6	21.9	47.5
D&N Haveli	35.41	55.41	71.59	34.3	44.0	70.5
Daman & Diu	0.00	16.68	36.55	5.0	12.8	43.3
Southern Region						
Andhra Pradesh	43.03	63.09	70.12	24.0	56.7	63.6
Karnataka	23.87	50.99	61.65	11.9	38.8	54.1
Kerala	0.00	0.00	16.64	0.0	0.0	1.3
Tamil Nadu	27.24	40.07	57.66	8.0	0.0	41.7
Lakshadweep	17.23	23.42	54.18	-0.2	0.0	36.8
Pondicherry	0.00	2.92	25.26	0.0	0.0	9.7

Source : Ministry of Higher Education.

228 : State-wise Classification and Occupational Distribution of Workers

(numbers in million)

State/Region	1991		2001		2001			
					Occupational Distribution of Workers (%)			
	Total Number of Workers	Share in Total Population (%)	Total Number of Workers	Share in Total Population (%)	Cultivators	Agricultural Labourers	Household Industry Workers	Others
All India	314.12	37.5	402.51	39.1	31.7	26.7	4.1	37.5
Northern Region	33.89	35.3	52.85	39.7	41.5	10.7	3.0	44.8
Haryana	5.10	31.0	8.38	39.6	36.3	15.2	2.5	46.0
Himachal Pradesh	2.21	42.8	2.99	49.2	65.5	3.1	1.7	29.7
Jammu & Kashmir	..	0.0	3.69	36.4	43.4	6.7	6.2	43.7
Punjab	6.26	30.9	9.14	37.5	23.0	16.4	3.4	57.3
Rajasthan	17.10	38.9	23.78	42.1	55.4	10.6	2.7	31.3
Chandigarh	0.22	34.9	0.34	37.7	0.5	0.1	1.0	98.4
Delhi	2.98	31.6	4.53	32.7	0.8	0.3	3.0	95.9
N-Eastern Region	11.73	37.2	14.55	37.8	41.8	13.4	3.5	41.3
Arunachal Pradesh	0.40	46.1	0.48	43.7	58.4	3.9	0.9	36.8
Assam	8.09	36.1	9.56	35.9	39.2	13.5	3.4	43.9
Manipur	0.77	42.1	1.07	46.6	46.1	11.3	9.2	33.5
Meghalaya	0.76	42.6	0.96	41.4	47.8	18.1	1.9	32.2
Mizoram	0.34	48.8	0.47	52.9	53.9	5.9	1.4	38.8
Nagaland	0.52	42.6	0.85	42.7	64.1	4.0	2.1	29.8
Tripura	0.86	31.1	1.16	36.2	26.9	24.0	2.9	46.2

contd...

...contd...

State/Region	1991		2001		2001			
					Occupational Distribution of Workers (%)			
	Total Number of Workers	Share in Total Population (%)	Total Number of Workers	Share in Total Population (%)	Cultivators	Agricultural Labourers	Household Industry Workers	Others
Eastern Region	61.84	33.1	82.38	36.2	26.8	34.9	5.3	33.0
Bihar	27.78	32.2	28.08	33.8	29.2	48.2	3.9	18.8
Jharkhand	..	0.0	10.13	37.6	38.6	28.3	4.1	29.0
Orissa	11.88	37.5	14.27	38.8	29.7	35.0	4.8	30.4
Sikkim	0.17	41.4	0.26	48.6	49.9	6.4	1.2	42.4
West Bengal	21.91	32.2	29.50	36.8	19.0	24.9	7.3	48.8
A&N Islands	0.10	35.2	0.14	38.2	15.5	3.7	5.1	75.6
Central Region	73.14	35.6	92.75	36.3	42.2	26.2	4.5	27.1
Chhattisgarh	..	0.0	9.69	46.5	44.6	31.9	2.1	21.5
Madhya Pradesh	28.34	42.8	25.76	42.7	42.9	28.7	3.9	24.5
Uttar Pradesh	44.80	32.2	54.18	32.6	40.9	25.1	5.3	28.6
Uttarakhand	..	0.0	3.13	36.9	49.8	8.3	2.2	39.7
Western Region	51.06	42.0	63.13	42.3	28.1	25.9	2.3	43.8
Goa	0.41	35.3	0.52	38.8	9.7	6.9	2.7	80.7
Gujarat	16.62	40.2	20.37	40.2	27.6	24.5	1.9	46.1
Maharashtra	33.91	43.0	42.05	43.4	28.6	26.8	2.5	42.1
D&N Haveli	0.07	53.4	0.11	51.8	34.6	12.9	0.7	51.7
Daman & Diu	0.04	37.3	0.07	45.9	5.4	1.8	1.6	91.3

contd...

...contd...

State/Region	1991		2001		2001			
					Occupational Distribution of Workers (%)			
	Total Number of Workers	Share in Total Population (%)	Total Number of Workers	Share in Total Population (%)	Cultivators	Agricultural Labourers	Household Industry Workers	Others
Southern Region	82.47	41.8	96.85	43.2	21.4	31.4	4.5	42.7
Andhra Pradesh	29.96	45.1	34.87	45.7	22.7	39.6	4.5	33.2
Karnataka	18.89	42.0	23.52	44.5	29.5	26.4	4.0	40.1
Kerala	9.15	31.4	10.29	32.3	7.2	16.1	3.5	73.2
Tamil Nadu	24.19	43.3	27.81	44.6	18.4	31.2	5.2	45.2
Lakshadweep	0.01	26.3	0.02	25.2	0.0	0.0	5.9	94.1
Pondicherry	0.27	33.0	0.34	35.1	3.3	21.1	1.8	73.8

Note : * : 1981 census not held in Assam, total population for the year worked out by interpolation.

** 1991 census not held in J&K, total population for the year worked out by interpolation.

*** Data for India and Manipur includes estimated population for Mao Maram, Paomata and Puri Senapati districts of Manipur.

Work is defined as participation in any economically productive activity with or without compensation, wages or profit. Such participation may be physical and/or mental in nature. Work involves not only actual work but also includes effective supervision and direction of work. It even includes part time help or unpaid work on farm, family enterprise or in any other economic activity. All persons engaged in 'work' as defined above are workers. Persons who are engaged in cultivation or milk production even solely for domestic consumption are also treated as workers.

Source : Office of the Registrar General of India, Ministry of Home Affairs, Census data.

229 : Labour Force and Work Force Participation Rate

(in percentage)

State/Region	Labour Force Participation Rate (LFPR)				Work Force Participation Rate (WFPR)			
	Rural		Urban		Rural		Urban	
	1999-2000	2004-05	1999-2000	2004-05	1999-2000	2004-05	1999-2000	2004-05
All India	42.3	44.6	35.4	38.2	41.7	43.9	33.7	36.5
Northern Region								
Haryana	34.9	43.4	32.3	35.3	34.6	42.4	31.4	33.9
Himachal Pradesh	50.9	54.0	34.4	47.4	50.3	53.0	32.2	45.6
Jammu & Kashmir	44.7	42.2	29.6	34.8	44.2	41.6	28.1	33.1
Punjab	41.7	45.8	36.3	38.5	41.0	44.0	35.3	36.5
Rajasthan	44.8	46.3	33.2	35.9	44.6	45.9	32.3	34.9
Chandigarh	63.9	39.9	36.9	35.8	63.5	38.8	35.1	34.3
Delhi	32.4	31.7	34.3	35.1	30.8	31.1	33.2	33.4
N-Eastern Region								
Arunachal Pradesh	37.1	46.2	27.5	32.3	36.9	45.8	26.7	31.9
Assam	36.4	40.1	36.8	36.2	34.9	39.1	33.2	33.6
Manipur	38.7	44.5	35.3	35.8	38.0	44.0	33.0	33.8
Meghalaya	48.8	52.7	31.0	38.7	48.6	52.5	29.6	37.3
Mizoram	50.3	52.3	37.4	39.0	49.9	52.1	36.3	38.3
Nagaland	49.4	53.7	33.5	38.5	48.2	52.7	30.5	36.4
Tripura	30.7	37.3	31.3	41.4	30.3	32.3	29.5	29.8

contd...

...*contd*...

State/Region	Labour Force Participation Rate (LFPR)				Work Force Participation Rate (WFPR)			
	Rural		Urban		Rural		Urban	
	1999-2000	2004-05	1999-2000	2004-05	1999-2000	2004-05	1999-2000	2004-05
Eastern Region								
Bihar	34.4	32.0	28.7	29.0	33.8	31.6	26.6	27.2
Jharkhand	..	43.3	..	33.3	..	42.7	..	31.1
Orissa	43.2	47.6	33.9	38.6	42.3	45.2	31.7	33.4
Sikkim	39.1	45.3	40.7	38.3	38.0	44.3	37.5	36.9
West Bengal	35.9	38.9	37.8	41.0	34.9	37.9	35.0	38.4
A&N Islands	38.4	47.1	45.4	41.6	37.1	44.2	42.2	37.9
Central Region								
Chhattisgarh	..	51.2	..	37.7	..	50.9	..	36.4
Madhya Pradesh	46.4	46.1	33.1	35.7	46.2	45.9	31.9	34.7
Uttar Pradesh	34.8	37.3	31.7	34.2	34.5	37.1	30.4	33.1
Uttarakhand	..	48.0	..	35.1	..	47.4	..	33.2
Western Region								
Goa	39.5	38.5	37.9	39.8	35.9	34.2	30.9	36.3
Gujarat	50.1	51.6	35.2	38.7	49.9	51.3	34.5	37.7
Maharashtra	49.0	52.7	36.7	39.9	48.4	52.1	34.6	38.4
D&N Haveli	47.5	53.3	40.9	46.6	47.0	51.6	40.4	45.2
Daman & Diu	50.9	40.3	38.7	42.8	50.3	40.2	37.6	41.5

contd...

...contd...

State/Region	Labour Force Participation Rate (LFPR)				Work Force Participation Rate (WFPR)			
	Rural		Urban		Rural		Urban	
	1999-2000	2004-05	1999-2000	2004-05	1999-2000	2004-05	1999-2000	2004-05
Southern Region								
Andhra Pradesh	54.6	54.8	36.2	40.6	54.2	54.4	34.8	39.2
Karnataka	49.1	54.6	37.8	39.7	48.7	54.2	36.6	38.6
Kerala	42.2	44.8	41.5	44.0	38.7	40.0	37.3	37.1
Tamil Nadu	52.3	53.4	41.0	43.4	51.3	52.8	39.3	41.8
Lakshadweep	35.6	40.8	34.3	36.3	28.5	37.9	30.8	27.4
Pondicherry	44.3	49.5	36.8	37.3	42.5	46.1	35.2	34.3

Note : Based on 'usual status' of individuals.
Labour force defined as those involved in gainful activity regularly, those involved in gainful activity occasionally and also the unemployed. LFPR represents size of the labour force as a per cent of the population.
Work force defined as those involved in gainful activity regularly and those involved in gainful activity occasionally. WFPR represents the size of the workforce as a per cent of population.

Source : NSSO Reports No. 455, 458 and 515 on *Employment and Unemployment Situation in India.*

230 : Unemployment Rates According to Usual Status (PS+SS) (or Usual Status Adjusted)

State/Region	Rural (%) 1999-2000	Rural (%) 2004-05	Urban (%) 1999-2000	Urban (%) 2004-05
All India	1.5	1.7	4.8	4.5
Northern Region				
Haryana	0.8	2.2	2.7	4.0
Himachal Pradesh	1.2	1.8	6.6	3.8
Jammu & Kashmir	1.1	1.5	5.0	4.9
Punjab	1.8	3.8	2.7	5.0
Rajasthan	0.4	0.7	2.5	2.9
Chandigarh	0.7	2.6	4.8	4.0
Delhi	4.7	1.9	3.3	4.8
N-Eastern Region				
Arunachal Pradesh	0.5	0.9	2.9	1.2
Assam	3.9	2.6	9.7	7.2
Manipur	1.9	1.1	6.7	5.5
Meghalaya	0.4	0.3	4.6	3.5
Mizoram	0.9	0.3	3.0	1.9
Nagaland	2.4	1.8	9.1	5.5
Tripura	1.2	13.3	5.8	28.0
Eastern Region				
Bihar	1.8	1.5	7.4	6.4
Jharkhand	..	1.4	..	6.5
Orissa	1.9	5.0	6.7	13.4
Sikkim	2.8	2.4	7.5	3.7
West Bengal	2.8	2.5	7.6	6.2
A&N Islands	3.4	6.2	6.9	8.8
Central Region				
Chhattisgarh	..	0.6	..	3.5
Madhya Pradesh	0.5	0.5	3.5	2.8
Uttar Pradesh	0.8	0.6	4.1	3.3
Uttarakhand	..	1.3	..	5.4
Western Region				
Goa	9.3	11.1	18.5	8.7
Gujarat	0.4	0.5	2.0	2.4
Maharashtra	1.4	1.0	5.8	3.6
D&N Haveli	1.0	3.3	1.4	3.0
Daman & Diu	1.0	0.3	3.0	3.0
Southern Region				
Andhra Pradesh	0.8	0.7	3.9	3.6
Karnataka	0.7	0.7	3.3	2.8
Kerala	8.2	10.7	10.2	15.6
Tamil Nadu	2.0	1.2	4.0	3.5
Lakshadweep	19.4	7.5	10.0	25.0
Pondicherry	4.0	7.0	4.1	8.1

Note: Unemployment rate is the percentage of unemployed persons to total number of persons in the labour force.

Source: NSSO Report No. 458 and 515 on *Employment and Unemployment Situation in India.*

231 : Employment in Organised Sector

(numbers in lakh)

State/Region	Public Sector 1997	Public Sector 2006	Public Sector CAGR (%)	Private Sector 1997	Private Sector 2006	Private Sector CAGR (%)
All India	195.66	181.89	(0.80)	87.55	87.15	(0.05)
Northern Region	31.76	30.04	(0.62)	10.39	11.27	0.91
Haryana	4.24	3.88	(0.98)	2.33	2.61	1.27
Himachal Pradesh	2.46	2.50	0.18	0.43	0.65	4.70
Jammu & Kashmir	2.00	2.00	0.00	0.11	0.11	0.00
Punjab	5.93	5.54	(0.75)	2.48	2.83	1.48
Rajasthan	10.24	9.47	(0.86)	2.64	2.58	(0.26)
Chandigarh	0.63	0.60	(0.54)	0.19	0.28	4.40
Delhi	6.26	6.05	(0.38)	2.21	2.21	0.00
N-Eastern Region	9.05	9.19	0.17	5.82	6.56	1.34
Assam	5.49	5.24	(0.52)	5.57	6.27	1.32
Manipur	0.78	0.76	(0.29)	0.02	0.03	4.61
Meghalaya	0.69	0.73	0.63	0.08	0.09	1.32
Mizoram	0.40	0.40	0.00	0.01	0.01	0.00
Nagaland	0.69	0.72	0.47	0.03	0.04	3.25
Tripura	1.00	1.34	3.31	0.11	0.12	0.97
Eastern Region	36.76	35.42	(0.41)	11.51	11.73	0.21
Bihar	14.42	4.06	(13.14)	2.55	0.25	(22.74)
Jharkhand	..	12.01	..	..	2.76	..
Orissa	7.09	6.48	(0.99)	0.94	0.90	(0.48)
West Bengal	14.93	12.51	(1.95)	7.98	7.79	(0.27)
A&N Islands	0.32	0.36	1.32	0.04	0.03	(3.15)
Central Region	35.31	30.77	(1.52)	7.84	6.75	(1.65)
Chhattisgarh	..	3.09	..	..	0.32	..
Madhya Pradesh	14.19	9.06	(4.86)	2.48	1.51	(5.36)
Uttar Pradesh	21.12	16.36	(2.80)	5.36	4.55	(1.80)
Uttarakhand	..	2.26	..	..	0.37	..
Western Region	33.73	30.47	(1.12)	23.99	24.62	0.29
Goa	0.70	0.81	1.63	0.39	0.46	1.85
Gujarat	9.55	8.25	(1.61)	8.34	9.35	1.28
Maharashtra	23.46	21.39	(1.02)	15.17	14.68	(0.36)
Daman & Diu	0.02	0.02	0.00	0.09	0.13	4.17
Southern Region	49.05	46.00	(0.71)	28.00	26.22	(0.73)
Andhra Pradesh	15.11	13.88	(0.94)	5.42	5.96	1.06
Karnataka	10.84	10.52	(0.33)	7.57	8.64	1.48
Kerala	6.25	6.15	(0.18)	5.60	4.06	(3.51)
Tamil Nadu	16.45	15.04	(0.99)	9.32	7.34	(2.62)
Pondicherry	0.40	0.41	0.27	0.09	0.22	10.44

Note : Data for Arunachal pradesh, Dadra and Nagar Haveli and Lakshadweep are not covered under employment market information (EMI) programme. CAGR refers to compounded annual growth rate between the two years.

Source : Directorate General of Employment and Training, Ministry of Labour & Employment.

232 : Human Development Index

State	1981	Rank	1991	Rank	2001	Rank
All India	0.302		0.381		0.472	
Northern Region						
Haryana	0.360	15	0.443	16	0.509	5
Himachal Pradesh	0.398	10	0.469	13		
Jammu & Kashmir	0.337	19	0.402	21		
Punjab	0.411	9	0.475	12	0.537	2
Rajasthan	0.256	28	0.347	27	0.424	9
Chandigarh	0.550	1	0.674	1		
Delhi	0.495	3	0.624	2		
N-Eastern Region						
Arunachal Pradesh	0.242	31	0.328	29		
Assam	0.272	26	0.348	26	0.386	14
Manipur	0.461	4	0.536	9		
Meghalaya	0.317	21	0.365	24		
Mizoram	0.411	9	0.548	7		
Nagaland	0.328	20	0.486	11		
Tripura	0.287	24	0.389	22		
Eastern Region						
Bihar	0.237	32	0.308	32	0.367	15
Orissa	0.267	27	0.345	28	0.404	11
Sikkim	0.342	18	0.425	18		
West Bengal	0.305	22	0.404	20	0.472	8
A&N Islands	0.394	11	0.574	5		
Central Region						
Madhya Pradesh	0.245	30	0.328	30	0.394	12
Uttar Pradesh	0.255	29	0.314	31	0.388	13
Western Region						
Goa	0.445	5	0.575	4		
Gujarat	0.360	14	0.431	17	0.479	6
Maharashtra	0.363	13	0.452	15	0.523	4
D&N Haveli	0.276	25	0.361	25		
Daman & Diu	0.438	6	0.544	8		
Southern Region						
Andhra Pradesh	0.298	23	0.377	23	0.416	10
Karnataka	0.346	16	0.412	19	0.478	7
Kerala	0.500	2	0.591	3	0.638	1
Tamil Nadu	0.343	17	0.466	14	0.531	3
Lakshadweep	0.434	7	0.532	10		
Pondicherry	0.386	12	0.571	6		

Note : Human dedevlopment index is a composite of variables capturing attainments in three dimensions of human development *viz.*, economic situation, education and health. These have been captured by per capita monthly expenditure adjusted for inequality, a combination of literacy rate and intensity of formal education and a combination of life expectancy at age 1 and infant mortality rate. 2001 data are for major states only.

Source : Planning Commission.

233 : State-wise Poverty Line

State	State Specific Poverty Lines in Terms of Per capita Consumption Expenditure per Month (in Rs.)							
	Rural				Urban			
	1973-74	1983-84	1993-94	2004-05	1973-74	1983-84	1993-94	2004-05
All India	49.63	89.50	205.84	356.30	56.64	115.65	281.35	538.60
Northern Region								
Haryana	49.95	88.57	233.79	414.76	52.42	103.48	258.23	504.49
Himachal Pradesh	49.95	88.57	233.79	394.28	51.93	102.26	253.61	504.49
Jammu & Kashmir	46.59	91.87	233.79	391.26	37.17	99.62	253.61	553.77
Punjab	49.95	88.57	233.79	410.38	51.93	101.03	253.61	466.16
Rajasthan	50.96	80.24	215.89	374.57	59.99	113.55	280.85	559.63
Chandigarh	49.95	88.57	233.79	410.38	51.93	101.03	253.61	466.16
Delhi	49.95	88.57	233.79	410.38	67.95	123.29	309.48	612.91
N-Eastern Region								
Arunachal Pradesh	49.82	98.32	232.05	387.64	50.26	97.51	212.42	378.84
Assam	49.82	98.32	232.05	387.64	50.26	97.51	212.42	378.84
Manipur	49.82	98.32	232.05	387.64	50.26	97.51	212.42	378.84
Meghalaya	49.82	98.32	232.05	387.64	50.26	97.51	212.42	378.84
Mizoram	49.82	98.32	232.05	387.64	50.26	97.51	212.42	378.84
Nagaland	49.82	98.32	232.05	387.64	50.26	97.51	212.42	378.84
Tripura	49.82	98.32	232.05	387.64	50.26	97.51	212.42	378.84

contd...

...contd...

State	State Specific Poverty Lines in Terms of Per capita Consumption Expenditure per Month (in Rs.)							
	Rural				Urban			
	1973-74	1983-84	1993-94	2004-05	1973-74	1983-84	1993-94	2004-05
Eastern Region								
Bihar	57.68	97.48	212.16	354.36	61.27	111.80	238.49	435.00
Jharkhand	..	..	..	366.56	..	..	..	451.24
Orissa	46.87	106.28	194.03	325.79	59.34	124.81	298.22	528.49
Sikkim	49.82	98.32	232.05	387.64	50.26	97.51	212.42	378.84
West Bengal	54.49	105.55	220.74	382.82	54.81	105.91	247.53	449.32
A&N Islands	54.49	96.15	196.53	351.86	..	120.30	296.63	547.42
Central Region								
Chhattisgarh	..	..	..	322.41	..	..	..	560.00
Madhya Pradesh	50.2	83.59	193.10	327.78	63.02	122.82	317.16	570.15
Uttar Pradesh	48.92	83.85	213.01	365.84	57.37	110.23	258.65	483.26
Uttarakhand	..	..	..	478.02	..	..	..	637.67
Western Region								
Goa	50.47	88.24	194.94	362.25	59.48	126.47	328.56	665.90
Gujarat	47.4	83.29	202.11	353.93	62.17	123.22	297.22	541.16
Maharashtra	50.47	88.24	194.94	362.25	59.48	126.47	328.56	665.90
D&N Haveli	50.47	88.24	194.94	362.25	59.48	126.47	328.56	665.90
Daman & Diu	50.47	88.24	194.94	362.25	59.48	126.47	328.56	665.90

contd...

...contd...

State	Rural 1973-74	Rural 1983-84	Rural 1993-94	Rural 2004-05	Urban 1973-74	Urban 1983-84	Urban 1993-94	Urban 2004-05
Southern Region								
Andhra Pradesh	41.71	72.66	163.02	292.95	53.96	106.43	278.14	542.89
Karnataka	47.24	83.31	186.63	324.17	58.22	120.19	302.89	599.66
Kerala	51.68	99.35	243.84	430.12	62.78	122.64	280.54	559.39
Tamil Nadu	45.09	96.15	196.53	351.86	51.54	120.30	296.63	547.42
Lakshadweep	51.68	99.35	243.84	430.12	62.78	122.64	280.54	559.39
Pondicherry	45.09	96.15	196.53	351.86	51.54	120.30	296.63	547.42

Table heading: State Specific Poverty Lines in Terms of Per capita Consumption Expenditure per Month (in Rs.)

Note: Currently, a minimum consumption expenditure, anchored in an average (food) energy adequacy norm of 2400 and 2100 calories per capita per day, is used to define state-specific poverty lines, seperately for rural and urban areas. These poverty lines are then applied on the NSSO's household consumer expenditure distributions to estimate the proportions and number of poor at the state level. Poverty lines at All-India are implicitily derived from All-India Poverty Ratio and NSS consumption expenditure distribution for the year.

Source: Planning Commission, GoI.

234 : State-wise Population Below Poverty Line

(number in lakh)

State	Rural				Urban			
	1973-74	1983-84	1993-94	2004-05	1973-74	1983-84	1993-94	2004-05
NSSO Round	28th	38th	50th	61st	28th	38th	50th	61st
All India	2612.9	2519.6	2440.3	2209.2	600.5	709.4	763.4	808.0
Northern Region								
Haryana	30.1	22.0	36.6	21.5	8.2	7.6	7.3	10.6
Himachal Pradesh	9.4	7.1	15.4	6.1	0.4	0.3	0.5	0.2
Jammu & Kashmir	18.4	13.1	19.1	3.7	2.1	2.5	1.9	2.2
Punjab	30.5	16.8	17.8	15.1	10.0	11.9	7.4	6.5
Rajasthan	101.4	96.8	94.7	87.4	27.1	30.1	33.8	47.5
Chandigarh	0.1	0.1	0.1	0.1	0.8	1.1	0.7	0.7
Delhi	1.1	0.4	0.2	0.6	21.8	18.0	15.3	22.3
N-Eastern Region								
Arunachal Pradesh	2.6	2.7	3.6	1.9	0.1	0.1	0.1	0.1
Assam	76.4	73.4	94.3	54.5	5.5	4.3	2.0	1.3
Manipur	5.1	4.8	6.3	3.8	0.8	0.9	0.5	0.2
Meghalaya	4.9	5.0	7.1	4.4	0.6	0.6	0.3	0.2
Mizoram	1.6	1.6	1.6	1.0	0.2	0.4	0.3	0.2
Nagaland	2.7	3.2	4.9	3.9	0.3	0.3	0.2	0.1
Tripura	7.9	8.4	11.4	6.2	0.7	0.6	0.4	0.2

contd...

...contd...

State	Rural				Urban			
	1973-74	1983-84	1993-94	2004-05	1973-74	1983-84	1993-94	2004-05
NSSO Round	28th	38th	50th	61st	28th	38th	50th	61st
Eastern Region								
Bihar	336.5	417.7	450.9	336.7	34.1	44.4	42.5	32.4
Jharkhand	..	..	..	103.2	..	..	..	13.2
Orissa	142.2	164.7	140.9	151.8	12.2	16.7	19.7	26.7
Sikkim	1.1	1.2	1.8	1.1	0.1	0.1	0.0	0.0
West Bengal	258.0	268.6	209.9	173.2	41.3	50.1	44.7	35.1
A&N Islands	0.6	0.8	0.7	0.6	0.2	0.3	0.3	0.3
Central Region								
Chhattisgarh	..	..	..	71.5	..	..	..	19.5
Madhya Pradesh	231.2	215.5	216.2	175.7	45.1	62.5	82.3	74.0
Uttar Pradesh	450.0	448.0	496.2	473.0	85.7	108.7	108.3	117.0
Uttarakhand	..	..	..	27.1	..	..	..	8.9
Western Region								
Goa	3.2	1.2	0.4	0.4	1.0	1.1	1.5	1.6
Gujarat	94.6	72.9	62.2	63.5	43.8	45.0	43.0	27.2
Maharashtra	210.8	193.8	193.3	171.1	76.6	97.1	111.9	146.3
D&N Haveli	0.4	0.2	0.7	0.7	0.0	0.0	0.1	0.2
Daman & Diu	..	..	0.0	0.1	..	..	0.2	0.1

contd...

...contd...

State	Rural				Urban			
	1973-74	1983-84	1993-94	2004-05	1973-74	1983-84	1993-94	2004-05
NSSO Round	28th	38th	50th	61st	28th	38th	50th	61st
Southern Region								
Andhra Pradesh	178.2	114.3	79.5	64.7	47.5	50.2	74.5	61.4
Karnataka	128.4	100.5	96.0	75.1	42.3	49.3	60.5	63.8
Kerala	111.4	81.6	56.0	32.4	24.2	25.2	20.5	17.2
Tamil Nadu	172.6	181.6	121.7	76.5	66.9	78.5	80.4	69.1
Lakshadweep	0.2	0.1	0.1	0.1	0.0	0.1	0.1	0.1
Pondicherry	1.6	1.6	0.9	0.8	1.1	1.7	2.4	1.6

Note: The following approximations have been made
Poverty ratio of Assam is used for all north-eastern states.
Poverty ratio of Punjab is used for Chandigarh.
Poverty ratio of Maharashtra is used for Goa, Daman & Diu and D&N Haveli.
Poverty Ratio of Kerala is used for Lakshadweep.
Poverty ratio of Tamil Nadu is used for Pondicherry and A&N Islands.

Source: Planning Commission.

235 : State-wise Poverty Ratio

(in percentage)

State	Rural				Urban			
	1973-74	1983	1993-94	2004-05	1973-74	1983-84	1993-94	2004-05
NSSO Round	28th	38th	50th	61st	28th	38th	50th	61st
All India	56.4	45.7	37.3	28.3	49.0	40.8	32.4	25.7
Northern Region								
Haryana	34.2	20.6	28.0	13.6	40.2	24.2	16.4	15.1
Himachal Pradesh	27.4	17.0	30.3	10.7	13.2	9.4	9.2	3.4
Jammu & Kashmir	45.5	26.0	30.3	4.6	21.3	17.8	9.2	7.9
Punjab	28.2	13.2	12.0	9.1	28.0	23.8	11.4	7.1
Rajasthan	44.8	33.5	26.5	18.7	52.1	37.9	30.5	32.9
Chandigarh	28.0	23.8	12.0	7.1	28.0	23.8	11.4	7.1
Delhi	24.4	7.7	1.9	6.9	52.2	27.9	16.0	15.2
N-Eastern Region								
Arunachal Pradesh	52.7	42.6	45.0	22.3	36.9	21.7	7.7	3.3
Assam	52.7	42.6	45.0	22.3	36.9	21.7	7.7	3.3
Manipur	52.7	42.6	45.0	22.3	36.9	21.7	7.7	3.3
Meghalaya	52.7	42.6	45.0	22.3	36.9	21.7	7.7	3.3
Mizoram	52.7	42.6	45.0	22.3	36.9	21.7	7.7	3.3
Nagaland	52.7	42.6	45.0	22.3	36.9	21.7	7.7	3.3
Tripura	52.7	42.6	45.0	22.3	36.9	21.7	7.7	3.3

contd...

...contd...

State	Rural				Urban			
	1973-74	1983	1993-94	2004-05	1973-74	1983-84	1993-94	2004-05
NSSO Round	28th	38th	50th	61st	28th	38th	50th	61st
Eastern Region								
Bihar	63.0	64.4	58.2	42.1	53.0	47.3	34.5	34.6
Jharkhand	..	..	..	46.3	..	..	..	20.2
Orissa	67.3	67.5	49.7	46.8	55.6	49.2	41.6	44.3
Sikkim	52.7	42.6	45.0	22.3	36.9	21.7	7.7	3.3
West Bengal	73.2	63.1	40.8	28.6	34.7	32.3	22.4	15.8
A&N Islands	57.4	54.0	32.5	22.9	49.4	47.0	39.8	22.2
Central Region								
Chhattisgarh	..	..	..	40.8	..	..	..	41.2
Madhya Pradesh	62.7	48.9	40.6	36.9	57.7	53.1	48.4	42.1
Uttar Pradesh	56.5	46.5	42.3	33.4	60.1	49.8	35.4	30.6
Uttarakhand	..	..	..	40.8	..	..	..	36.5

contd...

...contd...

State	Rural				Urban			
	1973-74	1983	1993-94	2004-05	1973-74	1983-84	1993-94	2004-05
NSSO Round	28th	38th	50th	61st	28th	38th	50th	61st
Western Region								
Goa	46.9	14.8	5.3	5.4	37.7	27.0	27.0	21.3
Gujarat	46.4	29.8	22.2	19.1	52.6	39.1	27.9	13.0
Maharashtra	57.7	45.2	37.9	29.6	43.9	40.3	35.2	32.2
D&N Haveli	46.9	14.8	52.0	39.8	37.7	27.0	39.9	19.1
Daman & Diu	..	..	5.3	5.4	..	..	27.0	21.2
Southern Region								
Andhra Pradesh	48.4	26.5	15.9	11.2	50.6	36.3	38.3	28.0
Karnataka	55.1	36.3	29.9	20.8	52.5	42.8	40.1	32.6
Kerala	59.2	39.0	25.8	13.2	62.7	45.7	24.6	20.2
Tamil Nadu	57.4	54.0	32.5	22.8	49.4	47.0	39.8	22.2
Lakshadweep	59.2	39.0	25.8	13.3	62.7	45.7	24.6	20.2
Pondicherry	57.4	54.0	32.5	22.8	49.4	47.0	39.8	22.2

Source : Planning Commission.

236 : Gross State Domestic Product

State/Region	Constant (1999-2000) Prices				Current Prices	
	1999-2000		2009-10		2009-10	
	GSDP (Rs. crore)	Per capita (Rs.)	GSDP (Rs. crore)	Per capita (Rs.)	GSDP (Rs. crore)	Per capita (Rs.)
All India	1786526	17847	3049992	26342	4543772	39244
Northern Region	290390		548982	35227	850702	54587
Haryana	51375	25160	120407	48455	209510	84313
Himachal Pradesh***	14112	23551	26646	38378	36924	53182
Jammu & Kashmir**	15660	15905	23060	20604	31793	28407
Punjab	67162	28161	110775	38859	192364	67480
Rajasthan	82720	15188	148200	22350	219769	33143
Chandigarh***	4141	44336	10693	83409	16431	128167
Delhi**	55220	41956	109201	65156	143911	85866
N-Eastern Region	52502		86783	19889	128976	29558
Arunachal Pradesh***	1612	15122	3028	25108	4536	37612
Assam	34833	13365	56702	18877	88023	29305
Manipur***	3260	14633	4899	18348	6344	23760
Meghalaya***	3578	15995	6459	25349	9611	37720
Mizoram***	1550	1808	2495	23173	3663	34021
Nagaland*	2802	15137	4850	18490	5978	22791
Tripura**	4867	15286	8350	24036	10821	31149

contd...

...contd...

State/Region	Constant(1999-2000) Prices				Current Prices	
	1999-2000		2009-10		2009-10	
	GSDP (Rs. crore)	Per capita (Rs.)	GSDP (Rs. crore)	Per capita (Rs.)	GSDP (Rs. crore)	Per capita (Rs.)
Eastern Region	264694		494425	19365	740462	29002
Bihar	50174	6304	109420	11416	155051	16177
Jharkhand***	34323	13113	54655	17956	75711	24874
Orissa	42986	11870	90229	22287	150946	37285
Sikkim***	896	17432	1756	29513	2612	43899
West Bengal***	135376	17142	236806	27062	353967	40451
A&N Islands**	939	26905	1559	35271	2175	49208
Central Region	295181		461949	15676	689239	23389
Chhattisgarh	27249	13292	60080	24522	107848	44020
Madhya Pradesh**	80132	13658	103503	15162	142500	20874
Uttar Pradesh***	175179	10890	270850	14083	398732	20732
Uttarakhand***	12621	15248	27516	28671	40159	41845

contd...

...*contd*...

State/Region	Constant(1999-2000) Prices				Current Prices	
	1999-2000		2009-10		2009-10	
	GSDP (Rs. crore)	Per capita (Rs.)	GSDP (Rs. crore)	Per capita (Rs.)	GSDP (Rs. crore)	Per capita (Rs.)
Western Region	364021		640950	38801	915023	55393
Goa**	6330	48064	11028	70332	17215	109790
Gujarat**	109861	22395	213674	37954	306813	54498
Maharashtra**	247830	26257	416248	38785	590995	55068
Southern Region	436632		816903	33596	1219370	50148
Andhra Pradesh	128797	17156	263773	31533	406641	48613
Karnataka***	101247	18811	181338	31305	271902	46939
Kerala***	69168	21830	135203	39815	189841	55905
Tamil Nadu***	134185	21784	228479	34417	339212	51097
Pondicherry***	3235	34089	8110	65615	11774	95259

Note : * Data for 2009-10 pertains to 2006-07.
** Data for 2009-10 pertains to 2007-08.
** *Data for 2009-10 pertains to 2008-09.

Source : Directorate of Economics & Statistics of respective state governments, Central Statistical Organisation.

237 : Per Capita Consumption Expenditure

State	2000-01				2006-07			
	Rural		Urban		Rural		Urban	
	Total (Rs.)	Share of Food (%)	Total (Rs.)	Share of Food (%)	Total (Rs.)	Share of Food (%)	Total (Rs.)	Share of Food (%)
All India	494.9	56.3	914.6	43.8	695.2	52.3	1312.5	39.4
Northern Region								
Haryana	682.3	52.8	897.9	45.3	1012.7	47.4	1336.1	39.4
Himachal Pradesh	700.8	56.8	1178.5	45.9	1117.5	48.4	1732.9	39.1
Jammu & Kashmir	679.8	60.5	1047.6	50.4	972.8	54.7	1284.5	47.9
Punjab	771.2	48.7	973.2	43.0	1198.1	42.7	1609.2	37.1
Rajasthan	538.3	56.7	793.4	46.8	767.4	52.8	1184.7	42.9
Delhi			1308.7	36.5			1803.9	37.3
N-Eastern Region								
Arunachal Pradesh	569.3	59.0			916.6	46.7		
Assam	457.3	65.6	789.4	52.8	721.4	56.8	1368.9	46.2
Tripura	634.5	60.3	988.6	52.9	577.3	59.8	1170.3	46.6
Eastern Region								
Bihar	396.3	61.6	595.4	51.4	541.3	57.8	865.0	50.4
Jharkhand	385.1	0.0	690.6	52.8	553.0	58.2	1119.2	46.4
Orissa	392.5	62.8	772.7	48.2	458.6	57.9	1072.1	42.1
West Bengal	473.1	61.6	902.2	47.3	629.9	58.9	1371.3	40.2

contd...

...contd...

State	2000-01				2006-07			
	Rural		Urban		Rural		Urban	
	Total (Rs.)	Share of Food (%)	Total (Rs.)	Share of Food (%)	Total (Rs.)	Share of Food (%)	Total (Rs.)	Share of Food (%)
Central Region								
Chhattisgarh	394.8	58.3	740.0	46.2	528.3	51.5	1048.3	39.6
Madhya Pradesh	390.0	53.1	727.4	42.9	514.9	51.2	1001.7	40.8
Uttar Pradesh	452.7	54.1	737.8	44.8	653.2	52.2	996.4	43.9
Uttarakhand							1154.8	
Western Region								
Gujarat	591.2	58.6	953.2	45.4	796.6	54.3	1422.0	39.6
Maharashtra	506.8	53.5	1033.9	42.3	776.1	47.9	1673.5	35.1
Southern Region								
Andhra Pradesh	490.2	55.7	928.4	41.3	727.1	52.3	1360.7	37.3
Karnataka	531.0	54.3	900.5	43.3	624.3	52.4	1180.2	39.7
Kerala	841.3	49.6	1203.7	43.2	1250.4	40.4	1681.5	34.4
Tamil Nadu	525.7	55.3	969.5	42.9	728.8	50.5	1227.2	39.6
Union Territories	791.1	54.7	1054.6	46.4	1117.9	47.2	1974.9	33.9
N-Eastern States	619.9	59.2	988.4	49.3	790.0	53.3	1323.3	43.2

Notes : Data for all states/UTs taken for All-India estimates. Separate estimates have been presented for rural/urban consumers of major states (20 million or more population as per Census 2001). Combines estimates for northeastern states and UTs are given. Northeastern states includes Arunachal pradesh, Manipur, Meghalaya,Mizoram, Nagaland,Sikkim and Tripura. UTs include A&N Islands, Chandigarh, D&N Haveli, Daman and Diu, Lakshadweep and Pondicherry.

Source : NSSO Report No. 476 and 527.

238 : Agricultural Productivity (Yield)

(Kg/hectare)

State/Region	Foodgrains		Pulses		Oilseeds	
	1999-2000	2008-09	1999-2000	2008-09	1999-2000	2008-09
All-India	1704	1898	635	655	853	1026
Northern Region						
Haryana	3047	3323	571	1032	1311	1731
Himachal Pradesh	1754	1828	470	1096	526	523
Jammu & Kashmir	1508	1780	490	461	704	615
Punjab	4028	4216	688	829	1067	1267
Rajasthan	975	1225	360	467	760	1165
Chandigarh	..	..	..	..	..	..
Delhi	802	..	250	..	2600	..
N-Eastern Region						
Arunachal Pradesh	1125	..	1000	..	1008	..
Assam	1409	1620	552	543	459	503
Manipur	2328	..	na	..	462	..
Meghalaya	1531	..	742	..	667	..
Mizoram	1781	..	1780	..	1000	..
Nagaland	977	..	794	..	1007	..
Tripura	2119	..	587	..	677	..
Eastern Region						
Bihar	1617	1755	863	804	725	974
Jharkhand	..	1678	..	754	..	559
Orissa	1025	1354	387	473	469	593
Sikkim	1317	..	910	..	760	..
West Bengal	2178	2588	768	816	808	1009
A&N Islands	2496	..	333	..		
Central Region						
Chhattisgarh	..	1029	..	546	..	562
Madhya Pradesh	1208	1170	766	810	982	1075
Uttar Pradesh	2188	2374	968	908	870	883
Uttarakhand	..	1773	..	609	..	1000
Western Region						
Goa	3228	..	882	..	1769	..
Gujarat	1186	1583	579	757	619	1311
Maharashtra	931	997	613	555	974	865
D&N Haveli	1394	..	763	..	1000	..
Daman & Diu	2464	..	1000	..		..
Southern Region						
Andhra Pradesh	1919	2711	486	821	536	860
Karnataka	1286	1491	442	465	602	573
Kerala	2094	2465	796	979	611	696
Tamil Nadu	2343	2049	431	309	1483	1663
Lakshadweep	..	..	..	..	..	..
Pondicherry	2041	..	672	..	222	..

Source : Agricultural Statistics at a Glance, 2008.

239 : Agriculture Inputs

Region/State	Irrigated Area under All Crops (%) (% to Cropped Area)		Fertiliser Use per hectare (kg/hectare of Cropped Area)	
	2000-01	2006-07	2000-01	2007-08
All India	40.2	44.3	86.7	117.1
Northern Region				
Haryana	85.4	85.4	147.2	187.6
Himachal Pradesh	19.1	19.3	36.7	53.2
Jammu & Kashmir	40.3	40.7	60.1	71.8
Punjab	96.0	97.2	161.8	210.0
Rajasthan	31.9	37.0	31.1	45.5
Chandigarh			25.5	0.0
Delhi			85.5	8.9
N-Eastern Region				
Arunachal Pradesh	16.4	19.0	2.4	2.7
Assam	5.6	5.3	35.7	57.3
Manipur	36.0	22.9	102.0	85.3
Meghalaya	22.6	27.1	14.5	15.8
Mizoram	14.0	19.2	12.4	39.9
Nagaland	24.9	26.2	1.4	2.2
Tripura	13.9	36.5	20.7	41.2
Eastern Region				
Bihar	47.8	58.4	98.2	162.8
Jharkhand		9.9		68.5
Orissa	27.0	30.9	37.9	51.9
Sikkim	14.3	9.4	8.5	0.0
West Bengal	37.0	56.4	116.8	144.2
A&N Islands			9.1	18.9
Central Region				
Chhattisgarh	19.6	25.9		76.9
Madhya Pradesh	24.0	32.5	36.9	66.4
Uttar Pradesh	67.3	74.1	115.3	149.6
Uttaranchal		45.7		118.9
Western Region				
Goa	20.9	21.9	34.2	41.9
Gujarat	33.9	39.5	70.1	143.6
Maharashtra	17.4	19.7	74.3	103.1
D&N Haveli			34.2	36.4
Daman & Diu			52.0	158.7
Southern Region				
Andhra Pradesh	43.7	47.4	159.6	199.6
Karnataka	26.6	29.0	109.5	115.7
Kerala	15.2	16.8	59.4	69.8
Tamil Nadu	55.1	56.6	145.3	178.3
Lakshadweep			0.0	0.0
Pondicherry			550.6	1032.5

contd...

...contd...

Region/State	Consumption of Electricity for Agricultural Purposes (GWh)			
	2000-01		2007-08	
	GWh	(% Share)	GWh	(% Share)
All India	84729	26.8	104182	20.8
Northern Region	17405	28.3	22042	25.3
Haryana	4535	45.1	7335	40.2
Himachal Pradesh	19	0.9	27	0.5
Jammu & Kashmir	142	5.0	271	6.7
Punjab	5534	28.5	10022	33.5
Rajasthan	7046	42.0	8145	34.4
Chandigarh	2	0.3	1	0.1
Delhi	127	1.3	37	0.2
N-Eastern Region	99	3.1	44	1.0
Arunachal Pradesh	0	0.0	0	0.0
Assam	41	2.1	20	0.8
Manipur	0	0.0	0	0.1
Meghalaya	0	0.0	1	0.1
Mizoram	0	0.0	0	0.0
Nagaland	0	0.0	0	0.0
Tripura	58	19.1	24	6.0
Eastern Region	2744	8.4	1941	4.1
Bihar	1549	13.5	659	15.0
Jharkhand	0	0.0	67	0.6
Orissa	196	3.2	172	1.5
Sikkim	0	0.0	0	0.0
West Bengal	999	6.7	1110	4.2
A&N Islands	0	0.0	0	0.0
Central Region	10158	23.0	18906	24.7
Chhattisgarh	0	0.0	1459	13.8
Madhya Pradesh	4898	26.5	7536	31.9
Uttar Pradesh	5260	20.4	6200	16.5
Uttaranchal	0	0.0	300	6.3
Western Region	25381	30.5	23672	19.9
Goa	13	1.2	39	1.5
Gujarat	15489	46.1	10946	24.8
Maharashtra	9876	20.9	12676	18.7
D&N Haveli	1	0.1	2	0.2
Daman & Diu	2	0.3	9	0.3
Southern Region	28942	31.6	37124	24.8
Andhra Pradesh	11748	43.4	15241	35.6
Karnataka	7435	40.1	10844	36.5
Kerala	350	3.4	241	2.0
Tamil Nadu	9312	27.2	10717	20.7
Lakshadweep	0	0.0	82	5.0
Pondicherry	97	6.9	0	0.0

Note : % share - Share of agricultural consumption to total consumption.
Source : Agricultural Statistics at A Glance, 2009, Ministry of Agriculture.

240 : Production of Foodgrains

(thousand tonnes)

State/Region	1980-81	1990-91	Growth (%)	2000-01	Growth (%)	2006-07	Growth (%)
All India	129302	176128	3.1	196572	1.1	217027	1.7
Northern Region	26935	42522	4.7	50886	1.8	57240	2.0
Haryana	6045	9561	4.7	13294	3.4	14763	1.8
Himachal Pradesh	1184	1434	1.9	1112	(2.5)	1382	3.7
Jammu & Kashmir	1307	1344	0.3	1115	(1.9)	1573	5.9
Punjab	11903	19249	4.9	25325	2.8	25313	(0.0)
Rajasthan	6497	10935	5.3	10041	(0.8)	14209	6.0
N-Eastern Region	3826	4892	2.5	5963	2.0	5058	(2.7)
Arunachal Pradesh	131	219	5.2	215	(0.1)	246	2.2
Assam	2706	3442	2.4	4167	1.9	3060	(5.0)
Manipur	292	286	(0.2)	396	3.3	399	0.1
Meghalaya	155	154	(0.0)	216	3.4	232	1.2
Mizoram	35	82	8.9	124	4.3	56	(12.3)
Nagaland	105	194	6.3	323	5.2	436	5.2
Tripura	403	516	2.5	523	0.1	630	3.1
Eastern Region	24169	30601	2.4	32970	0.7	38205	2.5
Bihar	9911	12259	2.1	12056	(0.2)	11099	(1.4)
Jharkhand	..	..		2011		3687	10.6
Orissa	5977	6942	1.5	4984	(3.3)	7345	6.7
Sikkim	..	130		103	(2.3)	100	(0.5)
West Bengal	8281	11270	3.1	13815	2.1	15975	2.5

contd...

...contd...

(thousand tonnes)

State/Region	1980-81	1990-91	Growth (%)	2000-01	Growth (%)	2006-07	Growth (%)
Central Region	37357	53669	3.7	57528	0.7	62502	1.4
Chhattisgarh	..	..		2901		5805	12.3
Madhya Pradesh	12412	17998	3.8	10185	(5.5)	13747	5.1
Uttar Pradesh	24945	35671	3.6	42715	1.8	41215	(0.6)
Uttarakhand	..	..		1726		1735	0.1
Western Region	14359	17166	1.8	12827	(2.9)	19292	7.0
Goa	126	138	0.9	153	1.0	147	(0.6)
Gujarat	4475	4844	0.8	2539	(6.3)	6499	17.0
Maharashtra	9758	12184	2.2	10135	(1.8)	12645	3.8
Southern Region	22656	27278	1.9	36397	2.9	34732	(0.8)
Andhra Pradesh	9992	12330	2.1	16029	2.7	16229	0.2
Karnataka	5880	6399	0.9	10986	5.6	9599	(2.2)
Kerala	1298	1111	(1.5)	765	(3.7)	641	(2.9)
Tamil Nadu	5487	7438	3.1	8617	1.5	8263	(0.7)
Union Territories	287	263	(0.9)	243	(0.8)	255	0.8

Note : Growth per cent refers to compounded annual growth rates between the two preceding years cited here; Negative values in brackets.
Source : Ministry of Agriculture.

241 : Gross State Domestic Product from Agriculture

(Rs. crore)

State/Region	Gross State Domestic Product (at constant 1999-2000 prices)					
	1999-00			2006-07		
	Agriculture	% Share to GSDP	Total GSDP	Agriculture	% Share to GSDP	Total GSDP
All India						
Northern Region						
Haryana	15857	30.92	51278	19392	21.07	92053
Himachal Pradesh	2681	19.00	14112	4183	18.30	22854
Jammu & Kashmir	4376	27.94	15660	5519	25.44	21698
Punjab	24822	36.95	67176	28536	31.31	91148
Rajasthan	23281	28.14	82720	30217	25.84	116946
Chandigarh*	51	1.30	3937	54	0.70	7743
Delhi*	846	1.53	55165	693	0.82	84078
N-Eastern Region						
Arunachal Pradesh*	440	27.27	1615	512	20.41	2510
Assam	11229	32.24	34833	12734	25.54	49850
Manipur	753	23.09	3260	1007	23.32	4318
Meghalaya	755	21.10	3578	1041	19.46	5350
Mizoram	318	20.51	1550	321	14.43	2221
Nagaland*	666	23.79	2800	1456	29.84	4880
Tripura*	1327	27.26	4867	1622	20.91	7757
Eastern Region						
Bihar	15202	30.28	50200	21729	26.81	81054
Jharkhand	5036	14.75	34147	6908	13.06	52884
Orissa	11364	26.48	42910	13493	19.94	67676
Sikkim	183	20.44	896	284	18.74	1516
West Bengal*	35009	25.90	135182	39310	20.61	190728
A&N Islands*	193	20.75	930	199	16.29	1223
Central Region						
Chhattisgarh	5852	21.30	27475	7389	16.63	44429
Madhya Pradesh	22439	28.00	80132	22984	23.88	96254
Uttar Pradesh	58131	33.19	175160	64142	27.18	236001
Uttarakhand	3300	26.15	12621	4034	17.22	23434
Western Region						
Goa	637	10.07	6330	518	5.21	9940
Gujarat*	15975	14.54	109861	29140	17.20	169454
Maharashtra*	36162	14.61	247457	40666	11.98	339425
D&N Haveli						
Daman & Diu						
Southern Region						
Andhra Pradesh	32530	25.14	129403	45149	21.72	207904
Karnataka	25138	25.84	97302	24441	17.20	142097
Kerala	12422	18.10	68617	15539	14.54	106833
Tamil Nadu	20170	15.03	134187	22161	11.46	193404
Lakshadweep						
Pondicherry	154	4.75	3235	145	3.14	4614

Note : * Data pertains to 1999-2000 and 2005-06.
Source : EPWRF(2009), *Domestic Product of States in India 1960-61 to 2006-07.*

242 : Production of Rice

(in thousand tonnes)

State/Region	1981	1991	Growth (%)	2001	Growth (%)	2007	Growth (%)
All India	53508	74173	3.3	84837	1.4	93206	1.6
Northern Region	5272	9173	5.7	12545	3.2	14356	2.3
Haryana	1228	1834	4.1	2695	3.9	3371	3.8
Himachal Pradesh	125	107	(1.6)	125	1.6	124	(0.2)
Jammu & Kashmir	546	555	0.2	415	(2.9)	554	4.9
Punjab	3223	6535	7.3	9154	3.4	10138	1.7
Rajasthan	150	142	(0.5)	156	0.9	170	1.5
N-Eastern Region	3526	4524	2.5	5539	2.0	4562	(3.2)
Arunachal Pradesh	88	143	4.9	133	(0.7)	146	1.6
Assam	2523	3270	2.6	3999	2.0	2916	(5.1)
Manipur	273	274	0.0	382	3.4	386	0.2
Meghalaya	133	120	(1.0)	179	4.1	200	1.9
Mizoram	28	64	8.5	104	5.0	30	(18.9)
Nagaland	91	152	5.3	230	4.2	264	2.3
Tripura	390	501	2.5	513	0.2	621	3.2
Eastern Region	17402	22301	2.5	24151	0.8	29549	3.4
Bihar	5635	6564	1.5	5443	(1.9)	4989	(1.4)
Jharkhand	..	..		1645		2968	10.3
Orissa	4301	5275	2.1	4614	(1.3)	6825	6.7
Sikkim	..	25		21	(1.7)	22	0.1
West Bengal	7466	10437	3.4	12428	1.8	14746	2.9
Central Region	9623	15998	5.2	15652	(0.2)	18090	2.4
Chhattisgarh	..	..		2369		5041	13.4
Madhya Pradesh	4053	5738	3.5	982	(16.2)	1368	5.7
Uttar Pradesh	5570	10260	6.3	11679	1.3	11124	(0.8)
Uttarakhand	..	..		622		556	(1.8)
Western Region	3035	3239	0.7	2528	(2.4)	4089	8.3
Goa	117	134	1.4	127	(0.6)	130	0.5
Gujarat	557	791	3.6	472	(5.0)	1390	19.7
Maharashtra	2361	2314	(0.2)	1929	(1.8)	2569	4.9
Southern Region	14651	18938	2.6	24422	2.6	22560	(1.3)
Andhra Pradesh	7011	9654	3.3	12458	2.6	11872	(0.8)
Karnataka	2208	2415	0.9	3847	4.8	3446	(1.8)
Kerala	1272	1087	(1.6)	751	(3.6)	631	(2.9)
Tamil Nadu	4159	5782	3.4	7366	2.5	6611	(1.8)
Union Territories	124	118	(0.5)	128	0.8	149	2.6

Note : Growth per cent refers to compounded annual growth rates between the two preceding years cited here; Negative values in brackets.

Source : *Agricultural Statistics at a Glance*, 2008.

243 : Production of Wheat

(in thousand tonnes)

State/Region	1981	1991	Growth (%)	2001	Growth (%)	2007	Growth (%)
All India	36192	55023	4.3	69582	2.4	75728	1.4
Northern Region	14210	23803	5.3	31167	2.7	32701	0.8
Haryana	3492	6440	6.3	9669	4.1	10055	0.7
Himachal Pradesh	443	602	3.1	251	(8.4)	502	12.2
Jammu & Kashmir	204	297	3.8	149	(6.7)	492	22.1
Punjab	7677	12155	4.7	15551	2.5	14596	(1.1)
Rajasthan	2394	4309	6.1	5547	2.6	7056	4.1
N-Eastern Region	137	126	(0.8)	111	(1.2)	78	(5.8)
Arunachal Pradesh	4	7	5.8	6	(0.8)	6	0.3
Assam	118	105	(1.2)	86	(2.0)	67	(4.0)
Manipur	..	..		..		..	
Meghalaya	4	6	3.7	7	1.6	1	(25.3)
Mizoram	..	..		..		..	
Nagaland	.	1		10	22.6	1	(28.8)
Tripura	10	7	(3.9)	2	(10.8)	2	(3.3)
Eastern Region	2901	4166	3.7	5623	3.0	4855	(2.4)
Bihar	2306	3560	4.4	4438	2.2	3911	(2.1)
Jharkhand	.	.		104		129	3.7
Orissa	122	56	(7.6)	13	(13.6)	6	(12.5)
Sikkim	.	20		10	(6.4)	9	(1.9)
West Bengal	473	530	1.1	1059	7.2	800	(4.6)
Central Region	16529	24433	4.0	30832	2.4	33250	1.3
Chhattisgarh	.	.		80		92	2.4
Madhya Pradesh	3144	5833	6.4	4869	(1.8)	7326	7.0
Uttar Pradesh	13385	18600	3.3	25168	3.1	25031	(0.1)
Uttarakhand	.	.		715		801	1.9
Western Region	2230	2362	0.6	1597	(3.8)	4631	19.4
Goa	.	.		.		.	
Gujarat	1298	1444	1.1	649	(7.7)	3000	29.1
Maharashtra	931	919	(0.1)	948	0.3	1631	9.5
Southern Region	187	134	(3.3)	252	6.5	214	(2.7)
Andhra Pradesh	6	9	4.3	8	(1.2)	9	2.0
Karnataka	180	125	(3.6)	244	6.9	205	(2.9)
Kerala	..	..		..		..	
Tamil Nadu	1	0		0		.	
Union Territories	120	111	(0.8)	99	(1.2)	79	(3.7)

Note : Growth per cent refers to compounded annual growth rates between the two preceding years cited here; Negative values in brackets.

Source : *Agricultural Statistics at a Glance*, 2008.

244 : Production of Pulses (in thousand tonnes)

State/Region	1981	1991	Growth (%)	2001	Growth (%)	2007	Growth (%)
All India	10619	14256	3.0	11065	(2.5)	14189	4.2
Northern Region	1929	2405	2.2	908	(9.3)	1692	10.9
Haryana	505	540	0.7	99	(15.6)	140	5.9
Himachal Pradesh	20	14	(3.9)	20	3.9	29	6.6
Jammu & Kashmir	35	25	(3.5)	13	(6.2)	14	1.6
Punjab	200	108	(5.9)	44	(8.5)	27	(7.9)
Rajasthan	1170	1719	3.9	732	(8.2)	1481	12.5
N-Eastern Region	54	80	3.9	107	2.9	131	3.5
Arunachal Pradesh		4		7	4.9	8	3.4
Assam	47	49	0.3	62	2.5	59	(0.9)
Manipur	1	.		3		5	5.8
Meghalaya	2	2	4.8	4	3.8	3	(3.1)
Mizoram	0	7		4	(5.1)	6	6.8
Nagaland	2	12	18.0	21	5.8	45	13.5
Tripura	2	6	10.4	6	(0.5)	5	(1.8)
Eastern Region	1957	2211	1.2	1154	(6.3)	1208	0.8
Bihar	833	916	1.0	621	(3.8)	438	(5.6)
Jharkhand				96		258	17.9
Orissa	886	1086	2.1	213	(15.0)	352	8.7
Sikkim	.	16		5	(10.9)	6	2.7
West Bengal	238	193	(2.1)	219	1.3	154	(5.7)
Central Region	4534	5876	2.6	4725	(2.2)	5706	3.2
Chhattisgarh				268		494	10.7
Madhya Pradesh	2011	3104	4.4	2275	(3.1)	3203	5.9
Uttar Pradesh	2524	2772	0.9	2160	(2.5)	1975	(1.5)
Uttarakhand				22		34	7.7
Western Region	1098	2071	6.6	1838	(1.2)	2913	8.0
Goa				10		16	9.2
Gujarat	267	627	8.9	191	(11.2)	593	20.8
Maharashtra	831	1444	5.7	1637	1.3	2304	5.9
Southern Region	1046	1614	4.4	2334	3.8	2539	1.4
Andhra Pradesh	415	696	5.3	1054	4.2	1347	4.2
Karnataka	463	552	1.8	956	5.7	893	(1.1)
Kerala	22	18	(2.0)	11	(5.3)	8	(3.8)
Tamil Nadu	147	348	9.0	313	(1.1)	291	(1.2)
Union Territories	8	9	1.1	11	1.7	9	(2.8)

Note : Growth per cent refers to compounded annual growth rates between the two preceding years cited here; Negative values in brackets.

Source : Ministry of Agriculture.

245 : Production of Oilseeds

(thousand tonnes)

State/Region	1991	2001	2007	Growth (CAGR%) 1991-01	Growth (CAGR%) 2001-07
All India	18603	18434	24286	(0.1)	4.7
Northern Region	3154	2729	6129	(1.4)	14.4
Haryana	646	571	835	(1.2)	6.5
Himachal Pradesh	5	10	7	7.3	(5.7)
Jammu & Kashmir	36	28	42	(2.6)	7.1
Punjab	111	87	78	(2.3)	(1.8)
Rajasthan	2356	2033	5167	(1.5)	16.8
N-Eastern Region	224	249	234	1.1	(1.1)
Arunachal Pradesh	20	26	23	2.6	(2.0)
Assam	169	160	134	(0.6)	(2.9)
Manipur	1	1	1	0.0	(9.8)
Meghalaya	5	6	7	1.6	0.8
Mizoram	6	5	4	(1.0)	(5.7)
Nagaland	12	46	63	14.8	5.2
Tripura	10	5	3	(7.5)	(6.7)
Eastern Region	1559	855	1025	(5.8)	3.1
Bihar	150	131	147	(1.3)	2.0
Jharkhand	..	28	50		10.1
Orissa	941	118	175	(18.8)	6.8
Sikkim	14	7	7	(7.1)	0.7
West Bengal	454	571	645	2.3	2.1
Central Region	4534	5344	7030	1.7	4.7
Chhattisgarh	..	89	161		10.5
Madhya Pradesh	3191	4096	5814	2.5	6.0
Uttar Pradesh	1343	1145	1033	(1.6)	(1.7)
Uttarakhand	..	15	21		6.4
Western Region	4000	3764	6295	(0.6)	8.9
Goa	1	3	5	12.3	6.2
Gujarat	2106	1662	2569	(2.3)	7.5
Maharashtra	1893	2099	3721	1.0	10.0
Southern Region	5133	5493	3574	0.7	(6.9)
Andhra Pradesh	2542	2511	1362	(0.1)	(9.7)
Karnataka	1338	1538	1125	1.4	(5.1)
Kerala	11	4	3	(10.8)	(1.5)
Tamil Nadu	1242	1440	1084	1.5	(4.6)
Union Territories	5	3	4	(5.4)	2.5

Source : Ministry of Agriculture.

246 : Production of Cotton

(in 1000 bales of 170 kg each)

State/Region	Raw Cotton 1991	2001	2007	Growth % (CAGR) 1991-2001	2001-2007
All India	9840	9527	22832	(0.3)	15.7
Northern Region	3983	3388	5439	(1.6)	8.2
Haryana	1155	1383	1814	1.8	4.6
Himachal Pradesh	0	0	0		
Jammu & Kashmir	1	0	0		
Punjab	1909	1199	2878	(4.5)	15.7
Rajasthan	918	805	747	(1.3)	(1.3)
N-Eastern Region	10	17	16	5.2	(1.1)
Arunachal Pradesh	.	.	.		
Assam	1	1	1	(2.2)	0.0
Manipur	0	0	0		
Meghalaya	5	8	8	3.6	0.0
Mizoram	2	6	5	10.3	(3.4)
Nagaland	0	0	0		(10.9)
Tripura	1	1	2		3.5
Eastern Region	9	68	123	21.9	10.3
Bihar	1	0	.		
Jharkhand		.	.		
Orissa	9	65	108	22.3	8.7
Sikkim	.	.	.		
West Bengal	0	3	15		32.6
Central Region	413	250	836	(4.9)	22.3
Chhattisgarh		0	0		
Madhya Pradesh	397	245	829	(4.7)	22.5
Uttar Pradesh	16	5	7	(11.6)	6.5
Uttarakhand		.	.		
Western Region	3203	2964	13405	(0.8)	28.6
Goa	.	.	.		
Gujarat	1323	1161	8787	(1.3)	40.1
Maharashtra	1880	1803	4618	(0.4)	17.0
Southern Region	2222	2841	3014	2.5	1.0
Andhra Pradesh	1110	1663	2181	4.1	4.6
Karnataka	690	855	610	2.2	(5.5)
Kerala	13	6	2	(7.3)	(17.2)
Tamil Nadu	409	317	221	(2.5)	(5.8)
Union Territories	2	2	0	1.0	(28.3)

Source : Ministry of Agriculture.

247 : Production of Sugarcane

(in thousand tonnes)

State/Region	1991	2001	2007	Growth % (CAGR) 1991-01	2001-07
All India	240784	295751	355359	2.1	3.1
Northern Region	15053	16562	16290	1.0	(0.3)
Haryana	7800	8170	9580	0.5	2.7
Himachal Pradesh	32	61	59		
Jammu & Kashmir	18	0	1		
Punjab	6000	7770	6020	2.6	(4.2)
Rajasthan	1203	561	630	(7.3)	1.9
N-Eastern Region	1810	1108	1376	(4.8)	3.7
Arunachal Pradesh	.	.	17		
Assam	1522	988	1055	(4.2)	1.1
Manipur	63	24	23		
Meghalaya	2	0	0	(20.6)	0.0
Mizoram	2	6	5	13.5	(5.4)
Nagaland	130	35	234		37.2
Tripura	91	54	42		(4.0)
Eastern Region	12214	6562	8639	(6.0)	4.7
Bihar	7805	3988	5956		
Jharkhand		145	142		
Orissa	3549	964	1274	(12.2)	4.8
Sikkim	.	.	.		
West Bengal	859	1466	1267		(2.4)
Central Region	104954	115086	142873	0.9	3.7
Chhattisgarh		9	19		
Madhya Pradesh	1392	1660	2806	1.8	9.1
Uttar Pradesh	103562	106068	133948	0.2	4.0
Uttarakhand		7349	6100		
Western Region	49100	62357	94256	2.4	7.1
Goa	84	73	58		
Gujarat	10600	12695	15630	1.8	3.5
Maharashtra	38416	49589	78568	2.6	8.0
Southern Region	57654	94077	91926	5.0	(0.4)
Andhra Pradesh	12667	17690	21692	3.4	3.5
Karnataka	20964	42924	28670	7.4	(6.5)
Kerala	543	276	440	(6.6)	8.1
Tamil Nadu	23480	33188	41124	3.5	3.6
Union Territories	261	205	161	(2.4)	(4.0)

Source : Ministry of Agriculture.

248 : Number of Factories

(number)

State/Region	Number of Factories					
	1990-91	Share in %	2000-01	Share in %	2005-06	Share in %
All India	110179	100.0	131270	100.0	140160	100.0
Northern Region	16948	15.4	21353	16.3	23576	16.8
Haryana	3070	2.8	4448	3.4	4304	3.1
Himachal Pradesh	282	0.3	507	0.4	808	0.6
Jammu & Kashmir	235	0.2	356	0.3	519	0.4
Punjab	6255	5.7	7137	5.4	8332	5.9
Rajasthan	3358	3.0	5112	3.9	6005	4.3
Chandigarh	295	0.3	295	0.2	296	0.2
Delhi	3453	3.1	3498	2.7	3312	2.4
N-Eastern Region	1932	1.8	1892	1.4	2405	1.7
Arunachal Pradesh						
Assam	1548	1.4	1435	1.1	1864	1.3
Manipur	60	0.1	59	0.0	59	0.0
Meghalaya	32	0.0	30	0.0	66	0.0
Mizoram						
Nagaland	50	0.0	129	0.1	109	0.1
Tripura	242	0.2	239	0.2	307	0.2
Eastern Region	10532	9.6	10814	8.2	11210	8.0
Bihar	3409	3.1	1535	1.2	1669	1.2
Jharkhand			1500	1.1	1590	1.1
Orissa	1465	1.3	1665	1.3	1862	1.3
Sikkim						
West Bengal	5606	5.1	6091	4.6	6077	4.3
A&N Islands	52	0.0	23	0.0	12	0.0
Central Region	14379	13.1	14875	11.3	15832	11.3
Chattisgarh			1275	1.0	1478	1.1
Madhya Pradesh	3962	3.6	3221	2.5	2951	2.1
Uttar Pradesh	10417	9.5	9635	7.3	10503	7.5
Uttarakhand			744	0.6	900	0.6
Western Region	26938	24.4	35319	26.9	35967	25.7
Goa	220	0.2	524	0.4	543	0.4
Gujarat	10943	9.9	14090	10.7	14055	10.0
Maharashtra	15595	14.2	18528	14.1	18711	13.3
D&N Haveli	127	0.1	902	0.7	1124	0.8
Daman & Diu	53	0.0	1275	1.0	1534	1.1
Southern Region	39450	35.8	47017	35.8	51170	36.5
Andhra Pradesh	15205	13.8	14029	10.7	15790	11.3
Karnataka	5911	5.4	7010	5.3	7835	5.6
Kerala	3484	3.2	4853	3.7	5643	4.0
Tamil Nadu	14617	13.3	20601	15.7	21265	15.2
Lakshadweep						
Pondicherry	233	0.2	524	0.4	637	0.5

Note : Share in per cent represents the percentage share from each individual state in the total.

Source : *Annual Survey of Industries* (Factory Sector).

249 : Factories : Invested Capital

(Rs. crore)

State/Region	1990-91	Share in %	2000-01	Share in %	2005-06	Share in %
All India	194913	100.0	571799	100.0	901579	100.0
Northern Region	24465	12.6	65268	11.4	96921	10.8
Haryana	6106	3.1	21874	3.8	29872	3.3
Himachal Pradesh	1308	0.7	4577	0.8	10845	1.2
Jammu & Kashmir	146	0.1	564	0.1	1925	0.2
Punjab	8133	4.2	15008	2.6	23732	2.6
Rajasthan	6898	3.5	18553	3.2	23910	2.7
Chandigarh	118	0.1	404	0.1	667	0.1
Delhi	1757	0.9	4289	0.8	5970	0.7
N-Eastern Region	1919	1.0	7491	1.3	11699	1.3
Arunachal Pradesh						
Assam	1523	0.8	7309	1.3	10910	1.2
Manipur	15	0.0	7	0.0	14	0.0
Meghalaya	263	0.1	49	0.0	424	0.0
Mizoram						
Nagaland	34	0.0	50	0.0	73	0.0
Tripura	84	0.0	76	0.0	278	0.0
Eastern Region	28999	14.9	63311	11.1	98906	11.0
Bihar	10228	5.2	2920	0.5	5297	0.6
Jharkhand		0.0	20325	3.6	24828	2.8
Orissa	6209	3.2	14809	2.6	28676	3.2
Sikkim						
West Bengal	12518	6.4	25221	4.4	40024	4.4
A&N Islands	44	0.0	36	0.0	79	0.0
Central Region	34605	17.8	81342	14.2	114139	12.7
Chhattisgarh		0.0	9053	1.6	20670	2.3
Madhya Pradesh	13652	7.0	19733	3.5	26769	3.0
Uttar Pradesh	20953	10.7	49010	8.6	59412	6.6
Uttarakhand		0.0	3546	0.6	7287	0.8
Western Region	54833	28.1	210982	36.9	345708	38.3
Goa	453	0.2	4076	0.7	6154	0.7
Gujarat	18696	9.6	93001	16.3	163972	18.2
Maharashtra	35399	18.2	103631	18.1	157704	17.5
D&N Haveli	243	0.1	7332	1.3	9852	1.1
Daman & Diu	42	0.0	2941	0.5	8026	0.9
Southern Region	50092	25.7	143405	25.1	234207	26.0
Andhra Pradesh	20362	10.4	39121	6.8	59858	6.6
Karnataka	7863	4.0	35685	6.2	62007	6.9
Kerala	3809	2.0	10378	1.8	14651	1.6
Tamil Nadu	17700	9.1	55785	9.8	93767	10.4
Lakshadweep						
Pondicherry	358	0.2	2436	0.4	3923	0.4

Note : Share in per cent represents the percentage share from each individual state in the total.

Source : *Annual Survey of Industries* (Factory Sector).

250 : Number of Factory Workers

(number)

State/Region	1990-91	Share in %	2000-01	Share in %	2005-06	Share in %
All India	6307143	100.0	6135235	100.0	7136098	100.0
Northern Region	840621	13.3	808237	13.2	1053141	14.8
Haryana	189469	3.0	217532	3.5	305740	4.3
Himachal Pradesh	36202	0.6	29788	0.5	42614	0.6
Jammu & Kashmir	10632	0.2	18371	0.3	32287	0.5
Punjab	311670	4.9	278303	4.5	350747	4.9
Rajasthan	181076	2.9	175566	2.9	227081	3.2
Chandigarh	8871	0.1	6503	0.1	6814	0.1
Delhi	102701	1.6	82174	1.3	87858	1.2
N-Eastern Region	106904	1.7	104318	1.7	135196	1.9
Arunachal Pradesh						
Assam	90878	1.4	92474	1.5	110036	1.5
Manipur	815	0.0	695	0.0	1734	0.0
Meghalaya	3434	0.1	870	0.0	3602	0.1
Mizoram						
Nagaland	1908	0.0	2440	0.0	2455	0.0
Tripura	9869	0.2	7839	0.1	17369	0.2
Eastern Region	980578	15.5	740605	12.1	701683	9.8
Bihar	280420	4.4	49190	0.8	56901	0.8
Jharkhand		0.0	134317	2.2	113591	1.6
Orissa	116918	1.9	99127	1.6	110246	1.5
Sikkim						
West Bengal	578651	9.2	455812	7.4	420663	5.9
A&N Islands	4589	0.1	2159	0.0	282	0.0
Central Region	907763	14.4	687403	11.2	804526	11.3
Chhattisgarh		0.0	65894	1.1	84678	1.2
Madhya Pradesh	287899	4.6	191131	3.1	165807	2.3
Uttar Pradesh	619864	9.8	401674	6.5	500540	7.0
Uttarakhand		0.0	28704	0.5	53601	0.8
Western Region	1451408	23.0	1452796	23.7	1685868	23.6
Goa	12520	0.2	21255	0.3	29968	0.4
Gujarat	523929	8.3	553704	9.0	669324	9.4
Maharashtra	908457	14.4	817305	13.3	879248	12.3
D&N Haveli	4297	0.1	29545	0.5	49318	0.7
Daman & Diu	2205	0.0	30987	0.5	58010	0.8
Southern Region	2019869	32.0	2341876	38.2	2755684	38.6
Andhra Pradesh	699885	11.1	763892	12.5	819703	11.5
Karnataka	307929	4.9	359199	5.9	498526	7.0
Kerala	228353	3.6	262981	4.3	289480	4.1
Tamil Nadu	766377	12.2	925389	15.1	1114421	15.6
Lakshadweep						
Pondicherry	17325	0.3	30415	0.5	33554	0.5

Note : Share in per cent represents the percentage share from each individual state in the all-India total.

Source : *Annual Survey of Industries* (Factory Sector).

251 : Wages to Workers

(Rs. crore)

State/Region	1990-91	Share in %	2000-01	Share in %	2005-06	Share in %
All India	6307143	100.0	6135235	100.0	7136098	100.0
Northern Region	840621	13.3	808237	13.2	1053141	14.8
Haryana	189469	3.0	217532	3.5	305740	4.3
Himachal Pradesh	36202	0.6	29788	0.5	42614	0.6
Jammu & Kashmir	10632	0.2	18371	0.3	32287	0.5
Punjab	311670	4.9	278303	4.5	350747	4.9
Rajasthan	181076	2.9	175566	2.9	227081	3.2
Chandigarh	8871	0.1	6503	0.1	6814	0.1
Delhi	102701	1.6	82174	1.3	87858	1.2
N-Eastern Region	106904	1.7	104318	1.7	135196	1.9
Arunachal Pradesh						
Assam	90878	1.4	92474	1.5	110036	1.5
Manipur	815	0.0	695	0.0	1734	0.0
Meghalaya	3434	0.1	870	0.0	3602	0.1
Mizoram						
Nagaland	1908	0.0	2440	0.0	2455	0.0
Tripura	9869	0.2	7839	0.1	17369	0.2
Eastern Region	980578	15.5	740605	12.1	701683	9.8
Bihar	280420	4.4	49190	0.8	56901	0.8
Jharkhand		0.0	134317	2.2	113591	1.6
Orissa	116918	1.9	99127	1.6	110246	1.5
Sikkim						
West Bengal	578651	9.2	455812	7.4	420663	5.9
A&N Islands	4589	0.1	2159	0.0	282	0.0
Central Region	907763	14.4	687403	11.2	804526	11.3
Chhattisgarh		0.0	65894	1.1	84578	1.2
Madhya Pradesh	287899	4.6	191131	3.1	165807	2.3
Uttar Pradesh	619864	9.8	401674	6.5	500540	7.0
Uttarakhand		0.0	28704	0.5	53601	0.8
Western Region	1451408	23.0	1452796	23.7	1685868	23.6
Goa	12520	0.2	21255	0.3	29968	0.4
Gujarat	523929	8.3	553704	9.0	669324	9.4
Maharashtra	908457	14.4	817305	13.3	879248	12.3
D&N Haveli	4297	0.1	29545	0.5	49318	0.7
Daman & Diu	2205	0.0	30987	0.5	58010	0.8
Southern Region	2019869	32.0	2341876	38.2	2755684	38.6
Andhra Pradesh	699885	11.1	763892	12.5	819703	11.5
Karnataka	307929	4.9	359199	5.9	498526	7.0
Kerala	228353	3.6	262981	4.3	289480	4.1
Tamil Nadu	766377	12.2	925389	15.1	1114421	15.6
Lakshadweep						
Pondicherry	17325	0.3	30415	0.5	33554	0.5

Note : Share in per cent represents the percentage share from each individual state in the all-India total.

Source: *Annual Survey of Industries* (Factory Sector).

252 : Factories : Value of Output

(in Rs. crore)

State/Region	1993-94	Share in %	2000-01	Share in %	2005-06	Share in %
All India	252757	100.0	926902	100.0	1908356	100.0
Northern Region	36177	14.3	133581	14.4	247712	13.0
Haryana	9438	3.7	44675	4.8	85799	4.5
Himachal Pradesh	1079	0.4	6482	0.7	17908	0.9
Jammu & Kashmir	439	0.2	1343	0.1	6995	0.4
Punjab	11953	4.7	35019	3.8	59439	3.1
Rajasthan	7929	3.1	30784	3.3	54221	2.8
Chandigarh	414	0.2	980	0.1	2669	0.1
Delhi	4925	1.9	14298	1.5	20682	1.1
N-Eastern Region	2950	1.2	9263	1.0	27190	1.4
Arunachal Pradesh	..					
Assam	2839	1.1	8741	0.9	25609	1.3
Manipur	9	0.0	18	0.0	44	0.0
Meghalaya	38	0.0	101	0.0	884	0.0
Mizoram	..					
Nagaland	24	0.0	92	0.0	116	0.0
Tripura	41	0.0	311	0.0	536	0.0
Eastern Region	31407	12.4	78995	8.5	167863	8.8
Bihar	11437	4.5	7255	0.8	16785	0.9
Jharkhand	..		19278	2.1	41634	2.2
Orissa	4630	1.8	13243	1.4	27977	1.5
Sikkim	..					
West Bengal	15291	6.0	39183	4.2	81373	4.3
A&N Islands	48	0.0	36	0.0	94	0.0
Central Region	38124	15.1	119193	12.9	214084	11.2
Chhattisgarh	..		12743	1.4	30099	1.6
Madhya Pradesh	13614	5.4	36712	4.0	49543	2.6
Uttar Pradesh	24510	9.7	64854	7.0	118861	6.2
Uttarakhand	..		4884	0.5	15580	0.8
Western Region	84876	33.6	342007	36.9	756721	39.7
Goa	880	0.3	8089	0.9	15421	0.8
Gujarat	25379	10.0	127977	13.8	307955	16.1
Maharashtra	57649	22.8	184971	20.0	373589	19.6
D&N Haveli	874	0.3	13665	1.5	33401	1.8
Daman & Diu	93	0.0	7305	0.8	26355	1.4
Southern Region	59224	23.4	243865	26.3	494786	25.9
Andhra Pradesh	15654	6.2	61347	6.6	118016	6.2
Karnataka	11543	4.6	46259	5.0	131178	6.9
Kerala	5823	2.3	26711	2.9	43268	2.3
Tamil Nadu	25667	10.2	103540	11.2	189982	10.0
Lakshadweep	..					
Pondicherry	538	0.2	6008	(0.6)	12342	(0.6)

Note : Share in per cent represents the percentage share from each individual state in the all-India total.

Source : *Annual Survey of Industries* (Factory Sector).

253 : Factories : Net Value Added

(in Rs. crore)

State/Region	1990-91	Share in %	2000-01	Share in %	2005-06	Share in %
All India	51515	100.0	143621	100.0	311864	100.0
Northern Region	6590	12.8	18751	13.1	37903	12.2
Haryana	1636	3.2	5571	3.9	13589	4.4
Himachal Pradesh	378	0.7	1308	0.9	5693	1.8
Jammu & Kashmir	76	0.1	159	0.1	1011	0.3
Punjab	1857	3.6	4301	3.0	6617	2.1
Rajasthan	1556	3.0	5258	3.7	8027	2.6
Chandigarh	70	0.1	145	0.1	227	0.1
Delhi	1016	2.0	2009	1.4	2738	0.9
N-Eastern Region	751	1.5	1431	1.0	3961	1.3
Arunachal Pradesh						
Assam	734	1.4	1284	0.9	3576	1.1
Manipur	0	0.0	2	0.0	10	0.0
Meghalaya	11	0.0	8	0.0	231	0.1
Mizoram						
Nagaland	-1	0.0	7	0.0	35	0.0
Tripura	8	0.0	130	0.1	109	0.0
Eastern Region	6964	13.5	12830	8.9	28705	9.2
Bihar	2598	5.0	729	0.5	422	0.1
Jharkhand			4044	2.8	12518	4.0
Orissa	1153	2.2	2352	1.6	6287	2.0
Sikkim						
West Bengal	3198	6.2	5699	4.0	9471	3.0
A&N Islands	14	0.0	6	0.0	6	0.0
Central Region	7632	14.8	19239	13.4	34000	10.9
Chhattisgarh			2493	1.7	6976	2.2
Madhya Pradesh	3007	5.8	6208	4.3	7142	2.3
Uttar Pradesh	4625	9.0	9577	6.7	16426	5.3
Uttarakhand			961	0.7	3457	1.1
Western Region	16716	32.4	52818	36.8	133241	42.7
Goa	158	0.3	1470	1.0	3295	1.1
Gujarat	4468	8.7	16856	11.7	47872	15.4
Maharashtra	12004	23.3	31261	21.8	74354	23.8
D&N Haveli	73	0.1	1861	1.3	3246	1.0
Daman & Diu	14	0.0	1370	1.0	4474	1.4
Southern Region	12862	25.0	38552	26.8	74054	23.7
Andhra Pradesh	2981	5.8	8879	6.2	17661	5.7
Karnataka	2769	5.4	8302	5.8	20895	6.7
Kerala	1222	2.4	3554	2.5	4468	1.4
Tamil Nadu	5793	11.2	16536	11.5	27981	9.0
Lakshadweep						
Pondicherry	97	0.2	1281	0.9	3050	1.0

Note : Share in per cent represents the percentage share from each individual state in the all-India total.

Source : *Annual Survey of Industries* (Factory Sector).

254 : Factories : Gross Capital Formation

(in Rs. crore)

State/Region	1990-91	Share in %	2000-01	Share in %	2005-06	Share in %
All India	24292	100.0	61415	100.0	171567	100.0
Northern Region	2483	10.2	6770	11.0	17567	10.2
Haryana	410	1.7	2655	4.3	5748	3.4
Himachal Pradesh	113	0.5	566	0.9	2338	1.4
Jammu & Kashmir	17	0.1	92	0.2	535	0.3
Punjab	897	3.7	1360	2.2	4308	2.5
Rajasthan	833	3.4	1556	2.5	3699	2.2
Chandigarh	16	0.1	58	0.1	139	0.1
Delhi	195	0.8	483	0.8	800	0.5
N-Eastern Region	261	1.1	2412	3.9	1440	0.8
Arunachal Pradesh						
Assam	198	0.8	2380	3.9	1234	0.7
Manipur	8	0.0	0	0.0	1	0.0
Meghalaya	42	0.2	12	0.0	68	0.0
Mizoram						
Nagaland		0.0	4	0.0	10	0.0
Tripura	13	0.1	16	0.0	128	0.1
Eastern Region	3809	15.7	7270	11.8	17003	9.9
Bihar	1180	4.9	526	0.9	-580	-0.3
Jharkhand		0.0	3486	5.7	5199	3.0
Orissa	767	3.2	904	1.5	7931	4.6
Sikkim						
West Bengal	1843	7.6	2374	3.9	4447	2.6
A&N Islands	19	0.1	-19	0.0	5	0.0
Central Region	4038	16.6	7848	12.8	22355	13.0
Chhattisgarh		0.0	824	1.3	5625	3.3
Madhya Pradesh	1796	7.4	1919	3.1	3918	2.3
Uttar Pradesh	2242	9.2	4849	7.9	10678	6.2
Uttarakhand		0.0	255	0.4	2134	1.2
Western Region	7474	30.8	21695	35.3	66101	38.5
Goa	33	0.1	608	1.0	1084	0.6
Gujarat	2703	11.1	7302	11.9	33064	19.3
Maharashtra	4700	19.3	12320	20.1	28805	16.8
D&N Haveli	25	0.1	814	1.3	2025	1.2
Daman & Diu	13	0.1	651	1.1	1123	0.7
Southern Region	6227	25.6	15420	25.1	47101	27.5
Andhra Pradesh	2235	9.2	3451	5.6	10751	6.3
Karnataka	867	3.6	4343	7.1	14155	8.3
Kerala	429	1.8	309	0.5	2305	1.3
Tamil Nadu	2661	11.0	7112	11.6	19175	11.2
Lakshadweep						
Pondicherry	35	0.1	204	0.3	714	0.4

Note : Share in per cent represents the percentage share from each individual state in the all-India total.

Source : *Annual Survey of Industries* (Factory Sector).

255 : Number of Enterprises Engaged in all (Agricultural & Non-Agricultural) Activities

Region/State/UTs	Rural + Urban Enterprises (OAE+Estt.) (Nos.)			
	1980	Share in %	1990	Share in %
All India	18361551	100.0	25002162	100.0
Northern Region	2388037	13.0	2896636	11.6
Haryana	319679	1.7	457120	1.8
Himachal Pradesh	139342	0.8	182981	0.7
Jammu & Kashmir	196525	1.1	0	0.0
Punjab	463132	2.5	599309	2.4
Rajasthan	963623	5.2	1169168	4.7
Chandigarh	15843	0.1	33329	0.1
Delhi	289893	1.6	454729	1.8
N-Eastern Region	160917	0.9	759611	3.0
Arunachal Pradesh	10974	0.1	20812	0.1
Assam	0	0.0	495195	2.0
Manipur	34745	0.2	61263	0.2
Meghalaya	32370	0.2	49971	0.2
Mizoram	13498	0.1	23122	0.1
Nagaland	15689	0.1	23772	0.1
Tripura	53641	0.3	85476	0.3
Eastern Region	3567766	19.4	5094031	20.4
Bihar	1044757	5.7	1228451	4.9
Jharkhand	0	0.0	0	0.0
Orissa	803662	4.4	1093528	4.4
Sikkim	8254	0.0	10686	0.0
West Bengal	1703901	9.3	2749865	11.0
A&N Islands	7192	0.0	11501	0.0
Central Region	3506750	19.1	4506529	18.0
Chhattisgarh	0	0.0	0	0.0
Madhya Pradesh	1340830	7.3	1873497	7.5
Uttar Pradesh	2165920	11.8	2633032	10.5
Uttarakhand	0	0.0	0	0.0
Western Region	3082088	16.8	4190072	16.8
Goa	47869	0.3	60715	0.2
Gujarat	1188409	6.5	1497652	6.0
Maharashtra	1839393	10.0	2623593	10.5
D&N Haveli	1876	0.0	2701	0.0
Daman & Diu	4541	0.0	5411	0.0
Southern Region	5655993	30.8	7555283	30.2
Andhra Pradesh	1614160	8.8	2486661	9.9
Karnataka	1374971	7.5	1693898	6.8
Kerala	871897	4.7	1228643	4.9
Tamil Nadu	1767481	9.6	2111030	8.4
Lakshadweep	4647	0.0	4531	0.0
Puducherry	22837	0.1	30520	0.1

contd...

...contd...

	Rural + Urban Enterprises (OAE+Estt.) (Nos.)			
Region/State/UTs	1998	Share in %	2005	Share in %
All India	30348888	100.0	41826989	100.0
Northern Region	3947282	13.0	5282258	12.6
Haryana	532817	1.8	833898	2.0
Himachal Pradesh	225478	0.7	267773	0.6
Jammu & Kashmir	215600	0.7	324908	0.8
Punjab	717114	2.4	1071666	2.6
Rajasthan	1530585	5.0	1961465	4.7
Chandigarh	39836	0.1	64805	0.2
Delhi	685852	2.3	757743	1.8
N-Eastern Region	909753	3.0	1473097	3.5
Arunachal Pradesh	20694	0.1	28734	0.1
Assam	593169	2.0	983693	2.4
Manipur	80489	0.3	104732	0.3
Meghalaya	56497	0.2	83207	0.2
Mizoram	24943	0.1	47730	0.1
Nagaland	29534	0.1	35578	0.1
Tripura	104427	0.3	189423	0.5
Eastern Region	6153619	20.3	7783912	18.6
Bihar	1442774	4.8	1224652	2.9
Jharkhand	0	0.0	491372	1.2
Orissa	1449665	4.8	1830298	4.4
Sikkim	13059	0.0	19362	0.0
West Bengal	3234396	10.7	4204740	10.1
A&N Islands	13725	0.0	13488	0.0
Central Region	5167451	17.0	6718334	16.1
Chhattisgarh	0	0.0	637305	1.5
Madhya Pradesh	2124440	7.0	1735262	4.1
Uttar Pradesh	3043011	10.0	4020610	9.6
Uttarakhand	0	0.0	325157	0.8
Western Region	5230466	17.2	6743557	16.1
Goa	71658	0.2	73515	0.2
Gujarat	1914576	6.3	2426022	5.8
Maharashtra	3234022	10.7	4225312	10.1
D&N Haveli	3977	0.0	8530	0.0
Daman & Diu	6233	0.0	10178	0.0
Southern Region	8940317	29.5	13825831	33.1
Andhra Pradesh	2902542	9.6	3996982	9.6
Karnataka	1911631	6.3	2538874	6.1
Kerala	1564671	5.2	2803828	6.7
Tamil Nadu	2514124	8.3	4433391	10.6
Lakshadweep	4542	0.0	3182	0.0
Puducherry	42807	0.1	49574	0.1

Note : OAE: own account enterprises: Enterprise owned and operated with the help of household labour only.
Estt.: establishment is an enterprise engaged in economic activities with the assistance of at least one hired worker on a regular basis.
Share in per cent represents percentage of individual states to total.

Source : CSO (2007), *Economic Census*, 2005 and earlier issues.

256 : Economic Census : Total Employment

(numbers)

State/Region	1980	1990	CAGR (%)	1998	CAGR (%)	2005	CAGR (%)
All India	53667727	72072698	3.0	83299471	1.8	100904121	2.8
Northern Region	7052308	8717068	2.1	11969899	4.0	14466144	2.7
Haryana	973966	1353234	3.3	1559007	1.8	2244817	5.3
Himachal Pradesh	344333	468650	3.1	576898	2.6	659479	1.9
Jammu & Kashmir	489054	0		473640		751532	6.8
Punjab	1335909	1769757	2.9	2099656	2.2	2702069	3.7
Rajasthan	2317048	2837880	2.1	3541910	2.8	4301288	2.8
Chandigarh	121022	203005	5.3	217916	0.9	250572	2.0
Delhi	1470976	2084542	3.6	3500872	6.7	3556387	0.2
N-Eastern Region	512396	2532738	17.3	3180655	2.9	3464555	1.2
Arunachal Pradesh	44025	93274	7.8	80536	(1.8)	110385	4.6
Assam	0	1689494	0.0	2194589	3.3	2208169	0.1
Manipur	104959	157364	4.1	200726	3.1	236076	2.3
Meghalaya	108578	169976	4.6	184453	1.0	242342	4.0
Mizoram	45835	72354	4.7	77457	0.9	106706	4.7
Nagaland	74602	129829	5.7	174637	3.8	175169	0.0
Tripura	134397	220447	5.1	268257	2.5	385708	5.3
Eastern Region	10136969	13612898	3.0	15405252	1.6	17281569	1.7
Bihar	2777224	3453506	2.2	3429211	(0.1)	2269556	(5.7)
Jharkhand	0	0		0		1152486	

contd...

...contd...

State/Region	1980	1990	CAGR (%)	1998	CAGR (%)	2005	CAGR (%)
Orissa	1948574	2612163	3.0	3094753	2.1	3705574	2.6
Sikkim	30509	47296	4.5	47603	0.1	68489	5.3
West Bengal	5342873	7447514	3.4	8771042	2.1	10032250	1.9
A&N Islands	37789	52419	3.3	62643	2.3	53214	(2.3)
Central Region	9032863	11794429	2.7	12735760	1.0	14376691	1.7
Chhattisgarh	0	0		0		1515167	
Madhya Pradesh	3290016	4885617	4.0	5255830	0.9	3978566	(3.9)
Uttar Pradesh	5742847	6908812	1.9	7479930	1.0	8145089	1.2
Uttarakhand	0	0		0		737869	
Western Region	10662283	13940058	2.7	16004917	1.7	17765527	1.5
Goa	239479	218679	(0.9)	215794	(0.2)	228133	0.8
Gujarat	3652367	4725996	2.6	5279910	1.4	6099523	2.1
Maharashtra	6750368	8960318	2.9	10444718	1.9	11308510	1.1
D&N Haveli	7201	14475	7.2	32906	10.8	66941	10.7
Daman & Diu	12868	20590	4.8	31589	5.5	62420	10.2
Southern Region	16270908	21475507	2.8	24002988	1.4	33549635	4.9
Andhra Pradesh	4712163	6734280	3.6	7511795	1.4	11201513	5.9
Karnataka	3866119	5080269	2.8	5253439	0.4	6345586	2.7
Kerala	2451533	3289030	3.0	3849109	2.0	5732936	5.9
Tamil Nadu	5145843	6235698	1.9	7191025	1.8	10062970	4.9
Lakshadweep	13966	16051	1.4	15794	(0.2)	11968	(3.9)
Pondicherry	81284	120179	4.0	181826	5.3	194662	1.0

Source : *Economic Census* (2005); All India Report and previous issues.

257 : Number of Scheduled Commercial Bank Offices

Region/State/ Union Territories	End-Dec.		End-Mar.		End-Mar.		C-D Ratio (%)
	1969	Share %	2001	Share %	2009	Share %	2009
All India	9007	100.0	35724	100.0	82408	100.0	72.6
Northern Region	1416	15.7	5080	14.2	17794	21.6	68.5
Haryana	191	2.1	749	2.1	2201	2.7	61.5
Himachal Pradesh	48	0.5	619	1.7	961	1.2	38.5
Jammu & Kashmir	48	0.5	502	1.4	1007	1.2	46.3
Punjab	415	4.6	1135	3.2	3357	4.1	65.5
Rajasthan	393	4.4	1994	5.6	4041	4.9	80.2
Chandigarh	25	0.3	12	0.0	3916	4.8	114.1
Delhi	296	3.3	69	0.2	2311	2.8	68.5
N-Eastern Region	99	1.1	1303	3.6	2192	2.7	35.8
Arunachal Pradesh	..	0.0	59	0.2	77	0.1	24.8
Assam	89	1.0	831	2.3	1429	1.7	38.3
Manipur	..	0.0	53	0.1	81	0.1	38.7
Meghalaya	..	0.0	130	0.4	205	0.2	27.6
Mizoram	..	0.0	66	0.2	95	0.1	58.7
Nagaland	4	0.0	42	0.1	86	0.1	30.7
Tripura	6	0.1	122	0.3	219	0.3	29.8
Eastern Region	953	10.6	7830	21.9	13726	16.7	48.9
Bihar	309	3.4	2678	7.5	3916	4.8	27.3
Jharkhand	0	0.0	998	2.8	1750	2.1	32.0
Orissa	111	1.2	1634	4.6	2756	3.3	50.8
Sikkim	..	0.0	33	0.1	71	0.1	42.4
West Bengal	533	5.9	2470	6.9	5196	6.3	60.8
A&N Islands	..	0.0	17	0.0	37	0.0	32.2
Central Region	1179	13.1	8258	23.1	16330	19.8	44.8
Chhattisgarh	0	0.0	710	2.0	1254	1.5	53.3
Madhya Pradesh	361	4.0	1951	5.5	4089	5.0	57.4
Uttar Pradesh	818	9.1	5059	14.2	9881	12.0	42.1
Uttaranchal	0	0.0	538	1.5	1106	1.3	25.6
Western Region	2128	23.6	4508	12.6	12823	15.6	85.2
Goa	96	1.1	153	0.4	424	0.5	26.5
Gujarat	833	9.2	1727	4.8	4481	5.4	63.2
Maharashtra	1199	13.3	2619	7.3	7876	9.6	90.8
D&N Haveli	..	0.0	6	0.0	24	0.0	20.8
Daman & Diu	..	0.0	3	0.0	18	0.0	18.9
Southern Region	3227	35.8	8745	24.5	23147	28.1	88.4
Andhra Pradesh	618	6.9	2794	7.8	6698	8.1	97.6
Karnataka	851	9.4	2364	6.6	5991	7.3	76.6
Kerala	642	7.1	1351	3.8	4186	5.1	60.4
Tamil Nadu	1104	12.3	2199	6.2	6133	7.4	108.9
Lakshadweep	..	0.0	9	0.0	11	0.0	5.4
Pondicherry	12	0.1	28	0.1	128	0.2	51.9

Note: C-D Ratio: credit deposit ratio.
Total Includes A&N Islands, D&N Haveli and Manipur for 1969.
1969 data is for commercial banks
The data is based on the Master Office Files of bank branches, which are regularly updated. The information presented in this table is the latest available and may not match with the data published earlier.

Source: RBI Statistical Table.

258 : Scheduled Commercial Bank : Deposits (Rs. crore)

Region/State/ Union Territories	End-Dec.		End-Mar.		End-Mar.	
	1969	Share (%)	2001	Share (%)	2009	Share (%)
All India	5172	100.0	949434	100.0	3937337	100.0
Northern Region	976	18.9	223032	23.5	897754	22.8
Haryana	64	1.2	19887	2.1	87204	2.2
Himachal Pradesh	18	0.3	7413	0.8	23607	0.6
Jammu & Kashmir	35	0.7	9892	1.0	29355	0.7
Punjab	231	4.5	44298	4.7	120667	3.1
Rajasthan	94	1.8	27539	2.9	91914	2.3
Chandigarh	41	0.8	7565	0.8	27857	0.7
Delhi	493	9.5	106438	11.2	517150	13.1
N-Eastern Region	54	1.0	15409	1.6	63247	1.6
Arunachal Pradesh	0	0.0	614	0.1	3682	0.1
Assam	48	0.9	9858	1.0	39427	1.0
Manipur	0	0.0	432	0.0	2368	0.1
Meghalaya	0	0.0	1646	0.2	6157	0.2
Mizoram	0	0.0	396	0.0	1746	0.0
Nagaland	1	0.0	897	0.1	3473	0.1
Tripura	5	0.1	1565	0.2	6394	0.2
Eastern Region	934	18.1	126263	13.3	445352	11.3
Bihar	186	3.6	26801	2.8	86653	2.2
Jharkhand	0	0.0	15464	1.6	55513	1.4
Orissa	36	0.7	15072	1.6	70626	1.8
Sikkim	0	0.0	609	0.1	2517	0.1
West Bengal	712	13.8	67931	7.2	228649	5.8
A&N Islands	0	0.0	386	0.0	1394	0.0
Central Region	553	10.7	131331	13.8	449939	11.4
Chhattisgarh	0	0.0	7518	0.8	39437	1.0
Madhya Pradesh	126	2.4	29084	3.1	100971	2.6
Uttar Pradesh	427	8.3	85373	9.0	264369	6.7
Uttaranchal	0	0.0	9356	1.0	45162	1.1
Western Region	1742	33.7	235306	24.8	1218766	31.0
Goa	52	1.0	7142	0.8	23910	0.6
Gujarat	460	8.9	55049	5.8	187906	4.8
Maharashtra	1230	23.8	172489	18.2	1004898	25.5
D&N Haveli	0	0.0	222	0.0	771	0.0
Daman & Diu	0	0.0	404	0.0	1281	0.0
Southern Region	913	17.7	218093	23.0	862279	21.9
Andhra Pradesh	173	3.3	54446	5.7	217453	5.5
Karnataka	255	4.9	54743	5.8	256709	6.5
Kerala	166	3.2	44178	4.7	135173	3.4
Tamil Nadu	313	6.1	63065	6.6	246992	6.3
Lakshadweep	0	0.0	55	0.0	480	0.0
Pondicherry	6	0.1	1607	0.2	5472	0.1

Note : Share per cent indicates share of each individual state in the total
Total Includes A&N Islands, D&N Haveli and Manipur for 1969
1969 data is for commercial banks
The data is based on the Master Office Files of bank branches, which are regularly updated. The information presented in this table is the latest available and may not match with the data published earlier.

Source : RBI Basic Statistical Return and RBI Statistical Table 1969.

259 : Scheduled Commercial Bank : Credit

(Rs. crore)

Region/State/Uts	End-Dec.		End-Mar.		End-Mar.	
	1969	Share (%)	2001	Share (%)	2009	Share (%)
All India	3729	100.0	538434	100.0	2857526	100.0
Northern Region	388	10.4	122036	22.7	615261	21.5
Haryana	30	0.8	8155	1.5	53617	1.9
Himachal Pradesh	4	0.1	1576	0.3	9100	0.3
Jammu & Kashmir	4	0.1	3410	0.6	13587	0.5
Punjab	77	2.1	18186	3.4	79064	2.8
Rajasthan	47	1.3	12841	2.4	73680	2.6
Chandigarh	26	0.7	7520	1.4	31788	1.1
Delhi	200	5.4	70349	13.1	354425	12.4
N-Eastern Region	21	0.6	4250	0.8	22642	0.8
Arunachal Pradesh	0	0.0	89	0.0	914	0.0
Assam	21	0.6	3160	0.6	15115	0.5
Manipur	0	0.0	173	0.0	916	0.0
Meghalaya	0	0.0	281	0.1	1702	0.1
Mizoram	0	0.0	95	0.0	1025	0.0
Nagaland	0	0.0	112	0.0	1065	0.0
Tripura	0	0.0	340	0.1	1905	0.1
Eastern Region	786	21.1	46351	8.6	217753	7.6
Bihar	51	1.4	5542	1.0	23624	0.8
Jharkhand	0	0.0	4335	0.8	17789	0.6
Orissa	18	0.5	6065	1.1	35856	1.3
Sikkim	0	0.0	88	0.0	1066	0.0
West Bengal	717	19.2	30257	5.6	138969	4.9
A&N Islands	0	0.0	63	0.0	449	0.0
Central Region	262	7.0	42888	8.0	201735	7.1
Chhattisgarh	0	0.0	2895	0.5	21018	0.7
Madhya Pradesh	71	1.9	13847	2.6	57957	2.0
Uttar Pradesh	191	5.1	24121	4.5	111185	3.9
Uttaranchal	0	0.0	2026	0.4	11575	0.4
Western Region	1389	37.2	177641	33.0	1037797	36.3
Goa	24	0.6	1865	0.3	6343	0.2
Gujarat	232	6.2	26702	5.0	118684	4.2
Maharashtra	1133	30.4	148989	27.7	912368	31.9
D&N Haveli	0	0.0	32	0.0	160	0.0
Daman & Diu	0	0.0	54	0.0	242	0.0
Southern Region	886	23.8	145268	27.0	762338	26.7
Andhra Pradesh	163	4.4	35128	6.5	212178	7.4
Karnataka	186	5.0	33369	6.2	196719	6.9
Kerala	114	3.1	19108	3.5	81612	2.9
Tamil Nadu	418	11.2	57120	10.6	268963	9.4
Lakshadweep	0	0.0	6	0.0	26	0.0
Pondicherry	5	0.1	538	0.1	2840	0.1

Note : Share per cent indicates share of each individual state in the total
Total Includes A&N Islands, D&N Haveli and Manipur for 1969.
1969 data is for commercial banks.
The data is based on the Master Office Files of bank branches, which are regularly updated. The information presented in this table is the latest available and may not match with the data published earlier.

Source : RBI Statistical Table 1969 and 2008-09.

260 : Gross Fiscal Deficit

(Rs. crore)

State/Region	1990-91	% to GSDP	2000-01*	% to GSDP	2009-10 (BE)**
All States	18787	3.3#	89533	4.3#	199510
Northern Region	3113		16103		33324
Haryana	386	2.8	2265	3.9	8557
Himachal Pradesh	279	9.9	1845	11.8	1592
Jammu & Kashmir	661	18.3	2166	13.0	2205
Punjab	1242	6.6	3904	5.2	9660
Rajasthan	545	2.6	4313	5.2	8420
Delhi			1610	2.7	2890
N-Eastern Region	767		3413		15083
Arunachal Pradesh	26	5.1	210	11.8	1118
Assam	568	5.3	1540	4.2	10864
Manipur	40	4.8	234	7.5	407
Meghalaya	41	4.6	250	6.3	614
Mizoram	(94)	(27.7)	375	21.6	212
Nagaland	102	15.6	359	10.1	591
Tripura	86	8.3	445	8.1	1277
Eastern Region	3865		19180		37373
Bihar	1595	6.0	4884	8.5	3696
Jharkhand					4232
Orissa	616	5.7	3325	7.6	6004
Sikkim	20	8.6	51	5.0	457
West Bengal	1634	4.7	10920	7.6	22984
Central Region	4087		12981		34370
Chhattisgarh	0		(48)	(0.2)	2564
Madhya Pradesh	1019	3.3	2712	3.4	6436
Uttar Pradesh	3068	5.5	10180	5.6	23299
Uttarakhand			136	0.9	2071
Western Region	3505		17376		40099
Goa	96	7.6	413	6.1	1389
Gujarat	1798	6.4	7988	7.2	12148
Maharashtra	1611	2.5	8976	3.6	26562
Southern Region	3450	3.4	20479	4.3	43050
Andhra Pradesh	967	2.9	7306	5.0	16152
Karnataka	559	2.4	4219	4.1	8493
Kerala	799	5.7	3878	5.4	5681
Tamil Nadu	1126	3.6	5076	3.5	11823
Puducherry					901

Note : Negative values in brackets and it indicates surplus in deficit indicator.
* Includes NCT Delhi.
** Includes NCT Delhi and Puducherry.
# Data calculated as % to GDP at current market prices (1989-2000 Series).

Source : RBI (2010), *Handbook of Statistics on State Government Finances 2010.*

261 : Outstanding Liabilities of State Governments

(Rs. crore)

State/Region	As at End-March				
	1991	% to GSDP	2001	% to GSDP	2010
All States	132504	23.3	602074	28.6	1666028
Northern Region	21414		106684		272461
Haryana	3076	20.9	14650	25.2	40324
Himachal Pradesh	1329	41.7	8705	55.6	22619
Jammu & Kashmir	3358	81.0	9101	54.5	26179
Punjab	7071	38.4	30763	41.2	67721
Rajasthan	6580	27.5	35541	43.1	90972
Delhi			7924	12.9	24646
N-Eastern Region	6486		19587		51513
Arunachal Pradesh	280	55.9	739	45.5	3363
Assam	4341	39.7	10227	24.9	25053
Manipur	392	47.5	1870	49.5	4967
Meghalaya	218	21.4	1388	34.3	3853
Mizoram	330	84.8	1375	79.2	4583
Nagaland	409	53.4	1604	45.1	4625
Tripura	516	39.8	2384	43.4	5069
Eastern Region	24788		118391		305999
Bihar	10633	38.1	29942	52.3	60617
Jharkhand			8448	26.3	25741
Orissa	5156	45.2	24220	56.7	48619
Sikkim	142	58.0	852	84.0	2338
West Bengal	8857	23.6	54929	38.3	168684
Central Region	27537		116298		324132
Chhattisgarh			6967	26.4	17620
Madhya Pradesh	7777	24.7	22127	27.9	67190
Uttar Pradesh	19760	32.8	83098	45.8	221106
Uttarakhand			4106	27.9	18216
Western Region	21859		113204		336608
Goa	903	67.3	2822	41.8	8039
Gujarat	8078	26.5	42781	38.5	120759
Maharashtra	12878	19.4	67601	27.0	207810
Southern Region	30424		127910		375315
Andhra Pradesh	8150	23.0	41809	28.8	127581
Karnataka	5898	23.6	25301	24.6	76762
Kerala	4983	30.2	26259	36.4	70761
Tamil Nadu	7043	20.3	34541	23.5	95232
Puducherry	4350	56.3			4979

Note: All states includes Puducherry and Delhi also.

Source : RBI (2010), *State Finances-A Study of Budgets of 2009-10.*

262 : Development Expenditures of State-Governments

(Rs. crore)

	1990-01		2000-01		2009-10BE	
	Devt. Exp.	% to Total Exp.	Devt. Exp.	% to Total Exp.	Devt. Exp.	% to Total Exp.
All States	63370	69.6	210543	64.3	659075	62.4
Northern Region	9244	67.7	35803	61.3	109679	62.2
Haryana	1669	69.6	5701	17.6	23046	71.0
Himachal Pradesh	802	71.7	3263	25.0	7723	59.1
Jammu & Kashmir	1341	66.3	5031	22.5	14354	64.1
Punjab	2365	69.6	6723	18.8	15992	44.8
Rajasthan	3068	64.9	10213	20.5	32018	64.4
Delhi	..		4873	21.1	16546	71.8
N-Eastern Region	3771	70.5	10546	16.7	36414	57.8
Arunachal Pradesh	301	75.9	824	18.0	3461	75.7
Assam	1741	71.4	4627	13.2	18847	53.9
Manipur	333	74.9	762	16.8	2554	56.4
Meghalaya	303	74.7	981	21.4	3310	72.2
Mizoram	280	55.8	873	25.0	2228	63.9
Nagaland	367	66.4	1070	22.4	2658	55.6
Tripura	446	72.8	1409	23.2	3356	55.2
Eastern Region	10501	72.2	32210	18.1	106503	59.9
Bihar	4173	79.1	10089	21.3	32386	68.3
Jharkhand	..		0	0.0	14934	65.0
Orissa	2095	68.7	6062	18.5	20708	63.1
Sikkim	148	80.6	504	14.3	1847	52.3
West Bengal	4086	67.8	15555	21.9	36628	51.6
Central Region	12499	68.9	31470	15.2	128817	62.2
Chhattisgarh	..		1284	5.6	17214	75.4
Madhya Pradesh	4189	71.0	10515	21.6	30162	61.9
Uttar Pradesh	8310	67.9	18865	15.5	72732	59.8
Uttarakhand	..		806	5.7	8709	62.0
Western Region	12111	72.8	47836	26.2	120016	65.6
Goa	311	78.6	1121	19.6	3655	63.9
Gujarat	4067	74.4	19643	34.2	36904	64.3
Maharashtra	7733	71.8	27071	22.6	79457	66.3
Southern Region	15244	70.7	52678	19.1	177382	64.3
Andhra Pradesh	4784	72.7	18381	18.2	72199	71.5
Karnataka	3534	71.0	12922	21.2	41006	67.2
Kerala	2188	64.8	7157	19.9	17412	48.3
Tamil Nadu	4738	71.6	14218	19.3	43577	59.2
Puducherry	..		..		3188	77.6

Note : Includes both revenue expenditure and capital outlay on education, including sports and culture. BE - budget estimates.

Source : RBI (2009), *State Finances-A Study of Budgets of 2009-10.*

263 : Social Sector Expenditure

(Rs. crore)

State/Region	1990-2001	% to Total Exp.	2000-01	% to Total Exp.	2009-10BE	% to Total Exp.
All States	35132	38.6	124919	36.8	416395	39.4
Northern Region						
Haryana	776	32.4	3387	37.0	12154	37.5
Himachal Pradesh	444	39.7	1963	36.9	4571	35.0
Jammu & Kashmir	600	29.7	2044	26.1	6631	29.6
Punjab	957	28.1	3887	27.6	9051	25.4
Rajasthan	1866	39.5	7224	41.3	22735	45.7
Delhi	–	–	3000	40.8	10290	44.7
N-Eastern Region						
Arunachal Pradesh	128	32.1	325	26.9	1107	24.2
Assam	932	34.7	3077	40.3	11428	32.7
Manipur	151	33.4	449	32.5	1205	26.6
Meghalaya	160	39.3	578	40.6	1801	39.3
Mizoram	153	30.6	505	39.2	1336	38.3
Nagaland	182	33.0	585	31.9	1306	27.3
Tripura	264	43.1	896	42.0	1940	35.0
Eastern Region						
Bihar	2381	38.3	7408	43.7	21136	44.5
Jharkhand	–	–	–	–	10322	44.9
Orissa	1113	36.5	4065	36.8	14037	42.8
Sikkim	61	33.3	259	27.3	1067	30.2
West Bengal	2824	46.9	9623	36.0	28472	40.1
Central Region						
Chhattisgarh	–	–	968	50.5	12255	53.7
Madhya Pradesh	2439	41.3	7153	42.3	18735	38.4
Uttar Pradesh	4711	38.5	12135	33.1	45473	37.4
Uttarakhand	–	–	355	32.0	5542	39.5
Western Region						
Goa	162	40.9	518	26.4	1784	31.2
Gujarat	1993	36.4	9681	35.6	21316	37.1
Maharashtra	3792	35.2	15429	36.6	59821	49.9
Southern Region						
Andhra Pradesh	2741	41.7	10006	35.6	35668	35.3
Karnataka	1842	37.0	7541	38.3	24526	40.2
Kerala	1477	43.7	5242	39.9	12734	35.3
Tamil Nadu	2985	45.1	9618	39.4	28052	38.1
Puducherry	–	–	–	–	1724	42.0

Note: Includes expenditure on social services, rural development, food storage and warehousing under revenue expenditure and capital outlays including education and loans and advances by state governments.

Source: RBI (2009), *State Finances-A Study of Budgets of 2009-10.*

264 : Number of Government Hospitals and Beds

State/Region As on 1.1.2008	Number of		Population Served per Government	
	Hospitals	Beds	Hospitals	Beds
All India	11289	494510	101403	2315
Northern Region	1232	88930		
Haryana	149	7719	162221	3131
Himachal Pradesh	149	8109	44262	813
Jammu & Kashmir	92	3945	120641	2813
Punjab	231	10620	114247	2485
Rajasthan	475	32067	133491	1977
Chandigarh	6	2612	193500	444
Delhi	130	23858	130423	711
N-Eastern Region	451	15093		
Arunachal Pradesh	200	2218	5920	533
Assam	100	3000	278780	9293
Manipur	28	1920	83429	1067
Meghalaya	34	2619	72647	943
Mizoram	20	1224	47900	783
Nagaland	38	1850	57132	1174
Tripura	31	2262	111258	1525
Eastern Region	4365	94205		
Bihar	1717	22494	54533	4163
Jharkhand	500	5414	59490	5494
Orissa	1707	14551	23231	2725
Sikkim	31	1020	1906	579
West Bengal	383	49681	224869	1734
A&N Islands	27	1045	16630	430
Central Region	2215	69771		
Chhattisgarh	218	9428	105202	2433
Madhya Pradesh	377	19918	179228	3392
Uttar Pradesh	925	32460	198143	5646
Uttarakhand	695	7965	13685	1194
Western Region	919	63468		
Goa	33	2841	48364	562
Gujarat	388	29868	145943	1896
Maharashtra	492	30306	219455	3563
D&N Haveli	2	261	149500	1146
Daman & Diu	4	192	45500	948
Southern Region	2107	163043		
Andhra Pradesh	359	34333	224825	2351
Karnataka	892	49492	64518	1163
Kerala	250	28395	134140	1217
Tamil Nadu	581	47198	112959	1391
Lakshadweep	9	200	8111	365
Pondicherry	16	3425	1204	75250

Note : Government Hospitals includes those run by Central, state and local bodies.
Source : National Health Profile, 2008.

265 : Number of Doctors Registered with State Medical Councils

State/Region	1991	2001	2008	Population/ Doctor
All India	393640	577095	725190	1579
Northern Region				
Haryana	644	1146	3347	7221
Himachal Pradesh			442	14915
Jammu & Kashmir	4407	6875	10096	1099
Punjab	26636	32558	37925	696
Rajasthan	14041	20438	26592	2384
Delhi	10042	23523	37696	450
N-Eastern Region				
Arunachal Pradesh			181	6531
Assam	10499	14586	17587	1585
Eastern Region				
Bihar	26376	33070	37753	2480
Jharkhand			1420	20947
Orissa	11087	14315	16068	2468
Sikkim			442	1336
West Bengal	41722	49941	56488	1525
Central Region				
Chhattisgarh			1924	11922
Madhya Pradesh	11187	19021	32154	2101
Uttar Pradesh	33178	43492	52181	3512
Uttarakhand				
Western Region				
Goa		2030	2773	576
Gujarat	22392	33653	42985	
Maharashtra	49365	80764	96560	1118
Southern Region				
Andhra Pradesh	33367	44575	54382	1484
Karnataka	32813	61163	78531	733
Travancore-Cochin	19465	30173	37440	923
Tamil Nadu	46419	65771	80223	818

Note: Figures in last column denote population served by doctors.
Source: Medical Council of India.

266 : Number of Health Centres (Mainly in Rural Areas)

State/Region	Public Health Centres (PHCs)		Sub-centres		Community Health Centres (CHCs)	
	1996	2007	1996	2007	1996	2007
All India	21855	22370	132778	145272	2420	4045
Northern Region	3041	3219	17551	19916	517	702
Haryana	397	411	2299	2433	63	86
Himachal Pradesh	245	443	1954	2071	47	71
Jammu & Kashmir	335	374	1700	1888	45	80
Punjab	484	484	2852	2858	105	126
Rajasthan	1572	1499	8692	10612	256	337
Chandigarh	0	0	12	13	1	2
Delhi	8	8	42	41	0	0
N-Eastern Region	960	1086	7301	7648	161	213
Arunachal Pradesh	47	85	223	379	9	31
Assam	619	610	5280	5109	105	100
Manipur	72	72	420	420	16	16
Meghalaya	88	103	337	398	9	26
Mizoram	38	57	261	366	6	9
Nagaland	33	84	244	397	5	21
Tripura	63	75	536	579	11	10
Eastern Region	4864	4223	28842	29405	400	849
Bihar	2209	1648	14799	8909	148	70
Jharkhand		330		3958		194
Orissa	1056	1279	5927	5927	157	231
Sikkim	24	24	147	147	2	4
West Bengal	1558	922	7873	10356	89	346
A&N Islands	17	20	96	108	4	4
Central Region	5137	5559	32090	35812	452	823
Chhattisgarh		518		4692		118
Madhya Pradesh	1376	1149	11937	8834	190	270
Uttar Pradesh	3761	3660	20153	20521	262	386
Uttarakhand		232		1765		49
Western Region	2683	2901	17239	17958	487	687
Goa	21	19	175	172	5	5
Gujarat	957	1073	7284	7274	185	273
Maharashtra	1695	1800	9725	10453	295	407
D&N Haveli	6	6	34	38	0	1
Daman & Diu	4	3	21	21	2	1
Southern Region	5170	5382	29555	34533	403	771
Andhra Pradesh	1283	1570	7894	12522	46	167
Karnataka	1459	1679	7793	8143	224	254
Kerala	959	909	5094	5094	54	107
Tamil Nadu	1436	1181	8681	8683	72	236
Lakshadweep	7	4	14	14	3	3
Pondicherry	26	39	79	77	4	4

Source : National Health Profile, 2008.

267 : Expenditure on Public Health and Family Welfare

(Rs. crore)

	1990-91	% to Total	2000-01	% to Total	2008-09	% to Total
All States	482240	5.3	1613992	4.6	3857394	4.2
Northern Region	69172	5.1	305118	5.0	651974	4.5
Haryana	8711	3.6	29827	3.3	68403	2.7
Himachal Pradesh	7689	6.9	29970	5.6	58638	4.7
Jammu & Kashmir	10016	5.0	38261	4.9	95959	5.3
Punjab	16968	5.0	64014	4.5	96849	3.2
Rajasthan	25788	5.5	90299	5.2	187349	4.6
Delhi	0	0.0	52747	7.2	144776	7.2
N-Eastern Region	26408	4.7	80164	4.7	242261	5.1
Arunachal Pradesh	1793	4.5	5988	5.0	9302	2.7
Assam	12824	4.8	35551	4.7	139768	5.6
Manipur	1950	4.3	6662	4.8	16517	4.0
Meghalaya	2412	5.9	8043	5.6	17587	4.4
Mizoram	1551	3.1	6394	5.0	15726	6.3
Nagaland	2846	5.2	8898	4.8	17355	4.6
Tripura	3032	4.9	8628	4.0	26006	5.0
Eastern Region	93551	6.0	299609	5.4	605672	4.3
Bihar	32483	5.2	99643	5.9	163464	4.2
Jharkhand	0	0.0	0	0.0	99708	5.3
Orissa	14058	4.6	45894	4.2	104885	3.8
Sikkim	1010	5.5	3472	3.7	8605	2.7
West Bengal	46000	7.6	150600	5.6	229010	4.4
Central Region	95758	5.3	243405	4.3	874684	5.0
Chhattisgarh	0	0.0	7917	4.1	88698	4.7
Madhya Pradesh	28160	4.8	86159	5.1	162892	3.9
Uttar Pradesh	67598	5.5	145907	4.0	562587	5.6
Uttarakhand	0	0.0	3422	3.1	60507	4.9
Western Region	78262	4.7	263955	3.7	475803	3.2
Goa	3260	8.2	8635	4.4	18715	4.2
Gujarat	25240	4.6	91892	3.4	154463	3.1
Maharashtra	49762	4.6	163428	3.9	302625	3.1
Southern Region	119089	5.5	421741	4.9	1007000	3.9
Andhra Pradesh	32979	5.0	133403	4.7	321720	3.3
Karnataka	24959	5.0	100533	5.1	242403	4.1
Kerala	22199	6.6	69067	5.3	154213	4.7
Tamil Nadu	38952	5.9	118738	4.9	272146	4.2
Pondicherry	0	0	0	0.0	16518	5.0

Note: Per cent to total denotes percentage to total disbursements.
Source : RBI (2008), *State Finances-A Study of Budgets of 2008-09.*

268 : Percentage Distribution of Type of Households

State/Region	1991			2001		
	Pucca	Semi-*Pucca*	*Kutcha*	*Pucca*	Semi-*Pucca*	*Kutcha*
All India	41.61	30.95	27.44	51.62	30.13	18.24
Northern Region						
Haryana	50.14	35.73	14.13	65.75	28.29	5.96
Himachal Pradesh	53.03	40.99	5.99	64.55	32.57	2.87
Jammu & Kashmir				54.14	32.84	13.01
Punjab	76.97	11.07	11.96	86.11	8.86	5.02
Rajasthan	56.13	22.94	20.93	64.86	21.03	14.11
Chandigarh	82.49	8.42	9.10	89.87	6.94	3.18
Delhi	85.60	4.61	9.79	91.67	4.87	3.50
N-Eastern Region						
Arunachal Pradesh	14.94	11.72	73.34	20.68	18.16	61.16
Assam	14.62	15.16	70.22	19.47	31.23	49.12
Manipur	5.40	40.65	53.95	8.39	55.13	36.47
Meghalaya	13.30	33.72	52.98	22.14	37.49	40.37
Mizoram	19.10	42.52	38.38	52.84	25.69	21.47
Nagaland	12.62	36.47	50.91	16.19	50.50	33.30
Tripura	5.50	20.71	73.79	9.81	45.99	44.19
Eastern Region						
Bihar	30.18	36.00	33.82	40.21	25.51	34.28
Jharkhand				31.46	57.57	10.97
Orissa	18.71	22.06	59.23	27.78	25.02	47.20
Sikkim	26.95	39.11	33.94	37.87	46.26	16.07
West Bengal	32.61	29.38	38.01	40.44	37.27	22.30
A&N Islands	10.40	47.25	42.35	28.40	38.56	33.05
Central Region						
Chhattisgarh				25.43	72.00	2.57
Madhya Pradesh	30.47	64.87	4.66	41.54	55.78	2.68
Uttar Pradesh	41.03	30.34	28.63	53.38	25.56	21.06
Uttarakhand				86.32	6.60	7.08
Western Region						
Goa	50.70	44.47	4.82	70.15	27.84	2.01
Gujarat	56.93	39.01	4.06	63.37	31.83	5.45
Maharashtra	52.20	36.14	11.67	57.85	34.33	7.82
D&N Haveli	20.80	22.54	56.66	45.74	51.65	2.60
Daman & Diu	79.80	17.33	2.87	92.50	6.34	1.63
Southern Region						
Andhra Pradesh	38.41	22.58	39.01	54.69	21.31	24.00
Karnataka	42.55	40.90	16.55	54.94	35.52	9.54
Kerala	55.97	19.13	24.90	68.16	21.60	10.24
Tamil Nadu	45.54	18.03	36.44	58.41	18.19	23.41
Lakshadweep	88.84	9.04	2.12	95.29	2.93	1.78
Pondicherry	44.48	12.16	42.96	60.43	13.89	25.68

Note : All India figures for 1991 exclude Jammu and Kashmir.
Source : *Statistical Abstract of India*, CSO.

269 : Percentage Distribution of Households Having Electricity

State/Region	1991			2001		
	Rural	Urban	Total	Rural	Urban	Total
All India	30.54	75.78	42.37	43.53	87.58	55.85
Northern Region						
Haryana	63.20	89.31	70.35	78.50	92.94	82.89
Himachal Pradesh	85.86	96.24	87.01	94.48	97.38	94.81
Jammu & Kashmir				74.77	97.94	80.66
Punjab	76.98	94.60	82.31	89.49	96.48	91.91
Rajasthan	32.44	76.67	35.03	44.02	89.61	54.69
Chandigarh	65.25	85.48	83.12	97.41	96.68	96.77
Delhi	59.85	81.38	79.48	85.50	93.38	92.86
N-Eastern Region						
Arunachal Pradesh	33.88	80.96	40.85	44.53	89.42	54.69
Assam	12.44	63.21	18.74	16.54	74.29	24.90
Manipur	41.73	75.45	50.92	52.53	81.99	60.04
Meghalaya	16.34	83.04	29.16	30.66	88.14	42.74
Mizoram	35.47	85.50	59.20	90.33	94.42	69.63
Nagaland	47.16	75.58	53.42	56.88	90.33	63.60
Tripura	28.50	80.43	36.93	31.75	86.36	41.81
Eastern Region						
Bihar	5.57	58.77	12.57	5.13	59.28	10.25
Jharkhand				9.99	75.61	24.30
Orissa	17.45	62.11	23.54	19.35	74.98	26.91
Sikkim	57.12	92.37	60.66	75.02	97.09	77.76
West Bengal	17.75	70.19	32.90	20.27	79.56	37.45
A&N Islands	53.62	90.55	63.52	68.09	95.22	76.78
Central Region						
Chhattisgarh				46.11	82.85	53.10
Madhya Pradesh	34.49	72.52	43.30	92.76	62.32	69.98
Uttar Pradesh	10.96	67.76	21.91	19.84	79.92	31.90
Uttarakhand				50.35	90.92	60.32
Western Region						
Goa	81.82	88.77	84.69	92.43	94.73	93.57
Gujarat	58.43	82.96	65.93	72.17	93.39	80.40
Maharashtra	53.45	86.07	69.40	65.17	94.28	77.49
D&N Haveli	51.20	87.57	54.42	82.63	95.84	85.99
Daman & Diu	92.87	95.46	94.13	97.46	98.31	97.76
Southern Region						
Andhra Pradesh	37.50	73.31	46.30	43.53	87.58	55.85
Karnataka	43.75	76.27	52.47	72.16	90.53	78.55
Kerala	41.95	67.65	48.43	65.53	84.32	70.24
Tamil Nadu	44.49	76.80	54.74	71.18	86.00	78.18
Lakshadweep	97.65	99.11	98.46	99.37	99.67	99.70
Pondicherry	51.20	71.71	63.58	81.00	91.40	87.81

Note : All India figures for 1991 exclude Jammu and Kashmir.

Source : *Housing and Amenities*, Paper 2 Of 1993;Census India and Central Electricity Authority.

270 : Percentage Distribution of Households Having Safe Drinking Water Facilities

State/Region	1991			2001		
	Rural	Urban	Total	Rural	Urban	Total
All India	55.54	81.38	62.30	73.20	90.00	77.90
Northern Region						
Haryana	67.14	93.18	74.32	81.10	97.30	86.10
Himachal Pradesh	75.51	91.93	77.34	87.50	97.30	88.60
Jammu & Kashmir				54.90	95.70	65.20
Punjab	92.09	94.24	92.74	96.90	98.90	97.60
Rajasthan	50.62	86.51	58.96	60.40	93.50	68.20
Chandigarh	98.11	97.68	97.73	99.90	99.80	99.80
Delhi	91.01	96.24	95.78	90.10	97.70	97.20
N-Eastern Region						
Arunachal Pradesh	66.87	88.20	70.02	73.70	90.70	77.50
Assam	43.28	64.07	45.86	56.80	70.40	58.80
Manipur	33.72	52.10	38.72	29.30	59.40	37.00
Meghalaya	26.82	75.42	36.16	29.50	73.50	39.00
Mizoram	12.89	19.88	16.21	23.80	47.80	36.00
Nagaland	55.60	45.47	53.37	47.50	42.30	46.50
Tripura	30.60	71.12	37.18	45.00	85.80	52.50
Eastern Region						
Bihar	56.55	73.39	58.76	86.10	91.20	86.60
Jharkhand				35.50	68.20	42.60
Orissa	35.32	62.83	39.07	62.90	72.30	64.20
Sikkim	70.98	92.95	73.19	67.00	97.10	70.70
West Bengal	80.26	86.23	81.98	87.00	92.30	88.50
A&N Islands	59.43	90.91	67.87	66.80	97.80	76.70
Central Region						
Chhattisgarh				66.20	88.80	70.50
Madhya Pradesh	45.56	79.45	53.41	61.50	88.60	68.40
Uttar Pradesh	56.62	85.78	62.24	85.50	97.20	87.80
Uttarakhand				83.00	97.80	86.70
Western Region						
Goa	30.54	61.71	43.41	58.30	82.10	70.10
Gujarat	60.04	87.23	69.78	76.90	95.40	84.10
Maharashtra	54.02	90.50	68.49	68.40	95.40	79.80
D&N Haveli	41.17	90.97	45.57	70.50	96.10	77.00
Daman & Diu	56.90	86.76	71.42	94.90	98.90	96.30
Southern Region						
Andhra Pradesh	48.98	73.82	55.08	76.90	90.20	80.10
Karnataka	67.31	81.38	71.68	80.50	92.10	84.60
Kerala	12.22	38.68	18.89	16.90	42.80	23.40
Tamil Nadu	64.28	74.17	67.42	85.30	85.90	85.60
Lakshadweep	3.41	18.79	11.90	4.60	4.60	4.60
Pondicherry	92.86	86.05	88.75	96.60	95.50	95.90

Note: All India figures for 1991 exclude Jammu and Kashmir.
Source: *Statistical Abstract of India*, CSO.

V. INTERNATIONAL COMPARISONS

> People

> Environment

> Economy

> External Sector

271 : Total Population

(in million)

Countries	1990	2008	2020* *Projected?	CAGR (%) 1990-2008	2008-2020	1990-2020
World	5291	6692	7674	1.3	1.1	1.2
Russia	148	142	135	(0.2)	(0.4)	(0.3)
Japan	123	128	124	0.2	(0.3)	0.0
Germany	79	82	80	0.2	(0.2)	0.0
Italy	57	61	60	0.4	(0.1)	0.2
France	57	62	62	0.5	(0.0)	0.3
UK	57	61	65	0.4	0.5	0.4
Korea, Rep.of	43	49	50	0.7	0.1	0.5
USA	255	304	309	1.0	0.1	0.6
Spain	39	46	49	1.0	0.5	0.8
China	1142	1326	1431	0.8	0.6	0.8
Sri Lanka	17	20	22	0.8	0.7	0.8
Thailand	57	67	71	0.9	0.5	0.8
Canada	28	33	37	1.0	1.0	1.0
Argentina	33	40	44	1.2	0.9	1.0
Australia	17	21	24	1.1	1.0	1.1
Brazil	150	192	209	1.4	0.7	1.1
Chile	13	17	19	1.4	0.8	1.1
Indonesia	177	228	254	1.4	0.9	1.2
Mexico	83	106	120	1.3	1.0	1.2
South Africa	37	49	53	1.6	0.6	1.2
Turkey	56	74	84	1.6	1.1	1.4
Peru	22	29	33	1.6	1.1	1.4
India	862	1140	1367	1.6	1.5	1.5
Bangladesh	116	160	186	1.8	1.2	1.6
Egypt	58	82	99	2.0	1.6	1.8
Philippines	62	90	110	2.1	1.7	1.9
Malaysia	18	27	32	2.2	1.4	1.9
Nepal	19	29	35	2.3	1.7	2.1
Saudi Arabia	16	25	32	2.4	2.0	2.2
Pakistan	116	166	226	2.0	2.6	2.3

Note : Countries arranged according to ascending CAGR for 1990-2020.
Negative values in brackets.
CAGR : Compounded annual growth rate.

Source : *World Development Report* (2007 and 2010).

272 : Density of Population and Urban Share

Countries	Density of Population People per sq km		Urban Population as % to Total Population	
	2005	2008	1990	2010
World	50	52	2.6	2.6
Australia	3	3	85.4	89.1
Canada	4	4	76.6	80.6
Russia	9	9	73.4	72.8
Saudi Arabia	12	11	76.6	82.1
Argentina	14	15	87.0	92.4
Chile	22	22	83.3	89.0
Brazil	22	23	74.8	86.5
Peru		23	68.9	71.6
USA	32	33	75.3	82.3
South Africa	39	40	52.0	61.7
Mexico	54	55	71.4	77.8
Egypt	74	82	43.5	42.8
Malaysia	77	82	49.8	72.2
Spain	87	91	75.4	77.4
Turkey	94	96	59.2	69.6
France	111	113	74.1	77.8
Indonesia	122	126	30.6	53.7
Thailand	126	132	29.4	34.0
China	140	142	27.4	44.9
Nepal		200	8.9	18.2
Italy	199	204	66.7	68.4
Pakistan	202	215	30.6	37.0
Germany	236	236	73.1	73.8
UK	249	254	88.7	90.1
Philippines	279	303	48.8	66.4
Sri Lanka	304	310	17.2	15.1
Japan	351	350	63.1	66.8
India	368	383	25.5	30.1
Korea, Rep. of	489	492	73.8	81.9
Bangladesh	1090	1229	19.8	28.1

Note : Countries arranged in ascending order of density in 2008.
Source : *World Development Report* (2007 and 2010).

273 : Dependency Ratio

Countries	Child Dependency Ratio			Old Age Dependency Ratio		
	1990	2005	2010	1990	2005	2010
World	53.8	43.6	41.2	10.0	11.5	11.6
Saudi Arabia	75.1	62.4	49.1	4.1	4.8	4.6
Bangladesh	79.8	58.3	47.4	5.6	5.9	6.1
Nepal	78.1	68.0	59.8	5.9	6.5	6.8
Pakistan	82.1	66.1	61.7	7.0	6.6	6.9
Philippines	72.6	57.5	53.8	5.8	6.4	6.9
South Africa	67.2	51.7	46.6	5.5	6.7	7.1
Egypt	78.4	54.5	50.8	6.9	7.8	7.3
Malaysia	63.5	51.4	44.0	6.2	7.3	7.3
India	**64.9**	51.2	**47.9**	**5.6**	8.5	**7.7**
Turkey	60.5	43.2	39.0	6.8	9.0	8.8
Indonesia	59.3	42.7	39.7	6.3	8.3	9.0
Peru	66.3	50.8	46.7	6.9	8.9	9.3
Mexico	67.4	48.7	42.7	7.6	8.3	10.0
Brazil	58.5	42.3	37.7	7.4	9.2	10.2
Thailand	45.9	34.4	30.3	7.1	10.3	10.9
China	42.9	30.1	27.7	8.3	10.7	11.4
Sri Lanka	51.1	35.1	35.7	8.9	10.6	11.4
Chile	46.7	37.2	32.5	9.6	12.1	13.5
UK	36.9	27.1	22.3	7.2	24.2	15.2
Korea, Rep. of	36.9	25.8	22.3	7.2	13.1	15.2
Argentina	50.2	41.6	38.6	15.3	11.5	16.6
Russia	34.3	21.6	20.8	15.1	19.5	17.9
USA	33.0	31.1	30.3	18.7	18.4	19.4
Canada	30.4	25.4	23.5	16.6	18.9	20.3
Australia	32.9	29.0	28.1	16.8	18.8	20.7
Spain	29.8	20.7	22.0	20.5	23.8	25.3
France	30.5	27.9	28.4	21.6	25.5	26.2
Italy	27.0	21.2	25.4	22.3	30.3	26.4
Germany	23.3	21.4	20.2	21.7	28.1	30.9
Japan	26.3	21.1	20.5	17.2	29.7	35.1

Note : Countries are arranged in an ascending order of old age dependency ratio in 2010. Child dependency ratio : population aged under 15 years expressed as percentage of the proportion of working age (15-64 years of age). Old age dependency ratio : population aged 65 years and above expressed as percentage of the population of working age (15-64 years of age).

Source : *World Development Report* (2007 and 2010).

274 : Crude Death and Birth Rate and Life Expectancy at Birth

Countries	Crude Death Rate (CDR)		Crude Birth Rate (CBR)		Life Expectancy at Birth (Years)	
	1991	2005	1991	2005	1990	2006
World	9	9	26	20	65	68
South Africa	9	21	31	24	62	51
Bangladesh	13	8	34	26	55	64
India	10	8	38	24	59	64
Pakistan	11	7	41	26	59	65
Russia	11	16	12	10	69	66
Nepal						66
Indonesia	9	7	25	20	62	68
Thailand	6	7	21	16	67	70
Egypt	9	6	32	26	63	71
Philippines	7	5	28	24	66	71
Turkey	7	6	28	19	66	71
Brazil	7	7	24	20	66	72
China	7	6	22	12	69	72
Peru						73
Saudi Arabia	5	4	37	27	68	73
Malaysia	5	5	29	21	70	74
Mexico	5	4	28	18	71	74
Argentina	9	8	21	18	72	75
Sri Lanka	6	6	21	18	71	75
Chilo	6	5	23	16	74	78
Korea, Rep. of	6	5	16	9	71	78
USA	9	8	16	14	75	78
Germany	11	10	10	8	75	79
UK	11	10	14	12	76	79
Canada	7	7	15	11	77	80
Australia	7	6	15	13	77	81
France	9	9	13	13	77	81
Italy	9	10	10	10	77	81
Spain	9	9	10	11	77	81
Japan	7	9	10	8	79	82

Note : Countries are arranged in an ascending order of life expectancy in 2006.
Crude death rate and birth rate indicate the number of deaths and live births occuring per thousand population in a year.
Life expectancy at birth is the number of years a newborn infant could expect to live if patterns of age-specific mortality rates at the time of birth were to stay the same throughout the child's life.

Source : *World Development Report* (2007 and 2010).

275 : Infant and Child Mortality and Fertility Rate

Countries	Infant Mortality Rate (IMR)		Child Mortality Rate (CMR)		Total Fertility Rate (TFR)	
	1990	2005	1990	2006	1990-1995	2005-2010
World	64	51	92	73	3.1	2.6
Italy	8	4	9	4	1.3	1.3
Japan	5	3	6	4	1.5	1.3
Russia	21	14	27	16	1.9	1.3
Spain	8	4	9	4	1.3	1.3
Germany	7	4	9	4	1.5	1.4
Canada	7	5	8	6	1.9	1.5
Australia	8	5	10	6	1.9	1.8
China	38	23	45	24	2.1	1.8
UK	8	5	10	6	1.8	1.8
France	7	4	9	4	1.8	1.9
Sri Lanka	26	12	32	13	2.5	1.9
Thailand	31	18	31	8	2.2	1.9
Chile	18	8	21	9	2.6	2.0
Mexico	37	22	53	35	3.3	2.1
USA	9	6	11	8	2.1	2.1
Turkey	67	26	82	26	3.0	2.2
Argentina	26	15	29	16	3.0	2.3
Brazil	50	31	57	20	2.8	2.3
Indonesia	60	28	91	34	3.1	2.3
Korea, Rep. of	8	5	9	5	3.7	2.4
Malaysia	16	10	22	12	3.8	2.7
India	80	56	115	76	3.8	2.8
South Africa	45	55	60	69	3.3	2.8
Bangladesh	100	54	149	69	4.4	3.0
Egypt	76	28	91	35	4.3	3.1
Philippines	41	25	62	32	4.3	3.2
Saudi Arabia	35	21	44	25	5.9	3.8
Pakistan	100	79	130	97	5.8	4.1
Nepal						
Peru						

Note : Countries are arranged in ascending order of fertility rate in 2005-2010. IMR is number of infants per 1000 live births in a year, who die before reaching the age of 1. TFR is number of children that would be born to a woman if she were to live to the end of her childbearing years and bear children in accordance with current age-specific rates.

Child Mortality Rate (CMR) is the probability of a child born in a specific year or a period dying before reaching the age of five, if subject to age specific mortality rates of that period. Hence CMR is not a rate but a probability of death derived from life table and expressed as rate per 1000 live birth.

Source : *World Development Report* (2007 and 2003).

276 : Adult Literacy Rate and Gross Enrolment Ratio

Countries	Adult Literacy Rate (% of Adults Aged 15 and Above)—2007			Gross Enrolment Ratio in Education (%)—2007		
	Total	Female	Male	Total	Female	Male
World	83.9	..	..	67.5	..	..
Pakistan	54.2	39.6	67.7	39.3	34.4	43.9
Bangladesh	53.5	48.0	58.7	52.1	52.5	51.8
Nepal	56.5	43.6	70.3	60.8	58.1	63.4
India	66.0	54.5	76.9	61.0	57.4	64.3
Indonesia	92.0	88.8	95.2	68.2	66.8	69.5
China	93.3	90.0	96.5	68.7	68.5	68.9
Sri Lanka	90.8	89.1	92.7	68.7	69.9	67.5
Turkey	88.7	81.3	96.2	71.1	66.3	75.7
Malaysia	91.9	89.6	94.2	71.5	73.1	69.8
Egypt	66.4	57.8	74.6	76.4	..	..
South Africa	88.0	87.2	88.9	76.8	77.3	76.3
Thailand	94.1	92.6	95.9	78.0	79.6	76.6
Saudi Arabia	85.0	79.4	89.1	78.5	78.0	79.1
Philippines	93.4	93.7	93.1	79.6	81.6	77.8
Mexico	92.8	91.4	94.4	80.2	79.0	81.5
Russia	99.5	99.4	99.7	81.9	86.1	78.0
Chile	96.5	96.5	96.6	82.5	82.0	83.0
France	99.0	99.0	99.0	82.7	97.4	93.5
Japan	99.0	99.0	99.0	86.6	85.4	87.7
Brazil	90.0	90.2	89.8	87.2	89.4	85.1
Germany	99.0	99.0	99.0	88.1	87.5	88.6
Peru	89.6	84.6	94.9	88.1	89.9	86.4
Argentina	97.6	97.7	97.6	88.6	93.3	84.0
UK	99.0	99.0	99.0	89.2	92.8	85.9
Italy	98.9	98.6	99.1	91.8	94.7	89.1
USA	99.0	99.0	99.0	92.4	96.9	88.1
Spain	97.9	97.3	98.6	96.5	99.9	93.3
Korea, Rep. of	99.0	99.0	99.0	98.5	90.6	105.8
Canada	99.0	99.0	99.0	99.3	101.0	97.6
Australia	99.0	99.0	99.0	114.2	115.7	112.8

Note : Countries arranged as per ascending gross enrolment ratio.
Source : *Human Development Report*, 2009.

277 : Education Inputs

Countries	Public Expenditure on Education				Pupils per Teacher (Primary)	
	% of GDP		% of Government Expenditure			
	1991	2005	1991	2005	1991	2005
World	..	4.7	..	..	33	29
Argentina	3.3	3.5	..	12.0	18	17
Australia	4.9	4.8	14.8	13.3	17	..
Bangladesh	1.5	2.5	10.3	14.2	63	51
Brazil	..	4.1	..	10.9	23	22
Canada	6.5	5.2	14.2	12.5	15	..
Chile	2.4	3.7	10.0	18.5	25	27
China	..	..	..	..	22	21
Egypt	3.9	..	..		..	22
France	5.5	5.9	..	11.0	12	19
Germany	..	4.7	..	9.7	17	14
India	3.7	3.7	12.2	10.7	60	40
Indonesia	1.0	0.9	..	9.0	23	20
Italy	3.0	4.9	..	9.8	12	11
Jamaica	4.5	4.5	12.8	9.5	37	28
Japan	..	3.7	..	10.7	21	19
Korea, Rep. of	3.8	4.6	25.6	15.0	34	29
Malaysia	5.1	8.0	18.0	28.0	20	18
Mexico	3.8	5.8	15.3	23.8	30	28
New Zealand	6.1	6.8	..	20.9	19	16
Pakistan	2.6	2.3	7.4	10.9	41	38
Philippines	3.0	3.2	10.5	17.2	33	35
Russia	3.6	3.7	..	12.3	..	17
Saudi Arabia	5.8	6.8	17.8	27.8	16	..
South Africa	5.9	5.4	..	17.9	..	36
Spain	4.1	4.3	..	11.2	21	14
Sri Lanka	3.2	..	8.4	..	12	22
Thailand	3.1	4.2	20.0	27.5	18	21
Turkey	2.4	4.0	..	13.6	29	..
UK	4.8	5.5	..	11.9	20	18
USA	5.1	5.9	12.3	15.2	..	14

Note : .. - Not available.

Source : *World Development Report* (2007 and 1994); *Human Development Report* (2007/08).

278 : Health Expenditure and Infrastructure

Countries	Public Expenditure on Health		Physicians per 1000 People		Hospital Beds per 1000 People	
	per capita PPP US$ (2006)	% to Govt. Expenditure (2006)	1990	2000-2005	1990	2000-2005
World	..	..	1.4	..	3.7	..
Pakistan	8	1	1.9	2.2	8.5	6.1
India	21	3	0.5	0.6	0.8	0.9
Nepal	24	9				
Bangladesh	26	7	0.2	0.3	0.3	..
Indonesia	44	5	0.1	0.1	0.7	..
Philippines	88	6	0.1	1.2	1.4	1.0
Sri Lanka	105	8	..	0.2	1.1	0.7
Egypt	129	7	0.8	0.5	2.1	2.2
China	144	10	1.5	1.5	2.6	2.5
Peru	171	13				
Thailand	223	11	0.2	0.4	1.6	..
Malaysia	226	7	0.4	0.7	2.1	1.9
Mexico	327	11	1.0	1.5	1.0	1.0
South Africa	364	10	0.6	0.8	..	..
Brazil	367	7	1.4	2.1	3.3	2.7
Chile	367	14	1.1	1.1	3.2	2.6
Russia	404	11	4.1	4.3	13.1	10.5
Turkey	461	17	0.9	1.3	2.4	2.6
Saudi Arabia	468	9	1.4	1.4	2.5	2.2
Argentina	758	14	2.7	..	4.6	4.1
Korea, Rep. of	819	12	0.8	1.6	3.1	7.1
Spain	1732	15	..	3.2	4.6	3.8
Italy	2022	14	..	4.2	7.2	4.4
Japan	2067	18	1.7	2.0	..	14.3
Australia	2097	17	2.2	2.5	9.2	7.4
UK	2434	17	1.6	2.2	5.9	4.2
Germany	2548	18	2.8	3.4	10.4	8.9
Canada	2585	18	2.1	2.1	6.0	3.7
France	2833	17	3.1	3.4	9.7	7.7
USA	3074	19	1.8	2.3	4.9	3.3

Note : Countries arranged according to per capita PPP (purchasing power parity) US$.

Source : *World Development Report* and *Human Development Report*, 2008.

279 : Labour Force and Labour Force Participation Rate

Countries	Labour Force				Labour Force Participation Rate(%)			
	Total (milllion)		Female (% of Total)		Male		Female	
	1990	2005	1990	2005	1990	2005	1990	2005
World	2390.7	3027.5	39.9	40.1	83.8	85.5	57.9	58.9
Argentina	13.0	18.4	34.4	42.9	82.4	84.7	61.1	43.5
Australia	8.4	10.3	41.3	45.5	80.8	84.4	67.4	61.5
Bangladesh	46.9	63.9	40.2	36.9	88.1	89.8	55.2	64.5
Brazil	62.4	91.3	35.0	42.9	83.6	88.8	61.0	47.6
Canada	14.7	17.6	44.0	46.4	82.6	84.9	72.8	68.3
Chile	5.0	6.5	30.5	35.1	76.0	80.9	40.9	35.2
China	650.1	776.0	44.8	44.6	87.8	88.9	75.8	79.1
Egypt	16.6	22.9	26.3	21.7	76.9	76.7	21.6	27.6
France	24.8	27.1	43.3	45.9	73.5	75.0	62.4	57.0
Germany	38.3	41.0	40.4	45.2	79.3	81.4	67.4	56.8
India	335.1	435.0	29.9	28.4	84.3	86.6	36.0	40.3
Indonesia	75.3	107.2	38.4	37.9	87.1	82.9	53.0	52.1
Italy	23.9	24.4	37.1	40.1	74.3	76.7	50.1	44.6
Jamaica	1.1	1.2	46.8	43.6	78.0	83.0	59.3	71.3
Japan	63.9	66.6	40.6	41.1	84.8	83.1	60.5	57.1
Korea, Rep. of	19.1	24.4	39.3	40.8	77.3	75.3	54.2	49.7
Malaysia	7.1	11.0	34.8	35.8	83.7	82.7	48.1	45.3
Mexico	29.5	42.3	30.6	35.2	83.0	85.4	42.6	36.2
New Zealand	1.7	2.2	43.1	46.6	83.3	83.0	71.2	63.2
Pakistan	35.2	56.5	23.3	27.0	85.7	88.1	33.7	28.8
Philippines	23.4	37.1	36.6	39.8	84.7	83.7	23.4	56.5
Russia	77.2	73.2	48.3	49.0	75.3	81.6	67.1	71.7
Saudi Arabia	5.1	7.5	11.4	15.2	80.4	81.3	18.5	15.6
South Africa	14.4	19.6	41.6	38.2	81.9	81.6	49.3	57.4
Spain	16.0	20.9	34.3	41.0	80.7	80.3	57.2	41.9
Sri Lanka	7.3	8.4	34.8	30.4	81.9	82.9	38.5	48.2
Thailand	30.4	35.7	46.6	46.2	84.5	90.6	71.0	79.2
Turkey	21.0	26.6	29.4	26.4	76.0	84.5	27.2	36.2
UK	29.4	30.6	44.0	46.0	81.9	87.9	69.3	67.2
USA	129.3	155.5	44.4	46.2	81.5	85.1	70.1	67.5

Note : Labour force participation rate is the proportion of the population between ages 15 and 64 that is economically active.Total labour force comprises people of ages 15 years and above who meet the ILO definition of economically active population and includes both employed and unemployed.

Source : *World Development Report* (2007 and 2003).

280 : Unemployment in 2006

Countries	Number of Unemployed (in '000) 1996-2005	Unemployment Rate 1996-2005	
		% of Labour Force	Female (% of Male Rate)
Thailand	496	1.4	80
Nepal	178	1.8	85
Mexico	1367	3.2	118
Korea, Rep. of	824	3.5	76
Malaysia	370	3.6	100
Japan	2730	4.1	91
China	8390	4.2	
Bangladesh	2002	4.3	117
India	16634	4.3	100
USA	7002	4.6	100
Australia	527	4.9	104
Saudi Arabia	327	5.2	274
UK	1602	5.3	86
Canada	1106	6.3	94
Italy	1674	6.8	165
Chile	440	6.9	139
Philippines	2619	7.4	99
Pakistan	3566	7.7	194
Sri Lanka	623	7.7	216
Russia	5775	7.8	105
Germany	4250	8.4	119
Spain	1837	8.5	18
Brazil	8264	8.9	172
Indonesia	10854	9.1	155
France	2729	9.4	121
Turkey	2445	9.9	106
Argentina	1141	10.6	135
Egypt	2241	11.0	311
Peru	437	11.4	143
South Africa	4385	26.6	100

Note : Countries arranged in the ascending order of unemployment rate.
Source : *Human Development Report.*

281 : Human Development Index (HDI)

Countries	1980	1990	2000	2006	Rank	2007	Rank
Argentina	0.793	0.804	..	0.861	47	0.866	49
Australia	0.871	0.902	0.954	0.968	2	0.970	2
Bangladesh	0.328	0.389	0.493	0.535	148	0.543	146
Brazil	0.685	0.710	0.790	0.808	75	0.813	75
Canada	0.890	0.933	0.948	0.965	4	0.966	4
Chile	0.748	0.795	0.849	0.874	43	0.878	44
China	0.533	0.608	0.719	0.763	99	0.772	92
Egypt	0.496	0.580	0.665	0.700	122	0.703	123
France	0.876	0.909	0.941	0.958	11	0.961	8
Germany	0.869	0.896	..	0.945	22	0.947	22
India	0.427	0.489	0.556	0.604	134	0.612	134
Indonesia	0.522	0.624	0.673	0.729	111	0.734	111
Italy	0.857	0.889	0.927	0.950	19	0.951	18
Japan	0.887	0.918	0.943	0.958	10	0.960	10
Korea, Rep. of	0.722	0.802	0.869	0.933	26	0.937	26
Malaysia	0.666	0.737	0.797	0.825	66	0.829	66
Mexico	0.756	0.782	0.825	0.849	54	0.854	53
Nepal	0.309	0.407	0.500	0.547	144	0.553	144
Pakistan	0.402	0.449	..	0.568	142	0.572	141
Peru	0.687	0.708	0.771	0.799	83	0.806	78
Philippines	0.652	0.697	0.726	0.747	105	0.751	105
Russia	..	0.821	..	0.811	73	0.817	71
Saudi Arabia	..	0.744	..	0.840	58	0.843	59
South Africa	0.658	0.698	0.688	0.680	128	0.683	129
Spain	0.855	0.896	0.931	0.952	15	0.955	14
Sri Lanka	0.649	0.683	0.729	0.755	102	0.759	102
Thailand	0.658	0.706	0.753	0.780	86	0.783	87
Turkey	0.628	0.705	0.758	0.802	78	0.806	79
UK	0.861	0.891	0.932	0.945	21	0.947	21
USA	0.894	0.923	0.949	0.955	12	0.956	13

Note : HDI is an index which measures the country's attainment in longevity, knowledge and income. Ranking is for 188 countries in year 2006 and 2007, with a lower number signifying a better HDI.

Source : *Human Development Report*, 2009.

282 : Human Poverty Index (HPI)

Countries	HPI (2007)	Rank (2007)	Population Below Poverty Line (%)		
			< $ 1.25 a day (2000-2007)	< $ 2.00 a day (2000-2007)	National Poverty Line
Argentina	3.7	13	4.5	11.3	..
Australia	12.0	14	..	..	..
Bangladesh	36.1	112	49.6	81.3	40.0
Brazil	8.6	43	5.2	12.7	21.5
Canada	11.2	12	..	..	..
Chile	3.2	10	< 2	< 2.4	17.0
China	7.7	36	15.9	36.3	2.8
Egypt	23.4	82	< 2	18.4	16.7
France	11.0	8	..	..	..
Germany	10.1	6	..	..	..
India	28.0	88	41.6	75.6	28.6
Indonesia	17.0	69	..	..	16.7
Italy	29.8	25	..	..	..
Japan	11.6	13	..	..	..
Korea, Rep. of	..	..	< 2	< 2	..
Malaysia	6.1	25	< 2	7.8	..
Mexico	5.9	23	< 2	4.8	17.6
Nepal	32.1	99	55.1	77.6	30.9
Pakistan	33.4	101	22.6	60.3	32.6
Peru	10.2	47	7.9	18.5	53.1
Philippines	12.4	54	22.6	45.0	25.1
Russia	7.4	32	< 2	< 2	19.6
Saudi Arabia	12.1	53	3.5	10.2	..
South Africa	25.4	85	26.2	42.9	..
Spain	12.4	17	..	..	..
Sri Lanka	16.8	67	14.0	39.7	22.7
Thailand	8.5	41	< 2	11.5	13.6
Turkey	8.3	40	2.7	9.0	27.0
UK	14.6	21	..	..	..
USA	15.2	22	..	..	..

Source : *Human Development Report*, 2010.

283 : Indices of Gender Development and Empowerment

Countries	Gender Development Index			Gender Empowerment Measure		
	1970	2007	Rank	1993	2007	Rank
Argentina	0.580	0.862	46	0.415	0.699	24
Australia	0.725	0.966	1	0.590	0.870	7
Bangladesh	0.174	0.536	123	0.291	0.264	108
Brazil	0.418	0.810	63	0.383	0.504	82
Canada	0.766	0.959	4	0.685	0.830	12
Chile	..	0.871	41	..	0.526	75
China	..	0.770	75	0.478	0.533	72
Egypt	0.261	..		0.280	0.287	107
France	..	0.956	6	..	0.779	17
Germany	..	0.939	20	..	0.852	9
India	0.250	0.594	114	0.235	..	
Indonesia	0.307	0.726	82	0.367	0.408	96
Italy	0.651	0.945	15	0.593	0.741	21
Japan	0.702	0.945	14	0.445	0.567	57
Korea, Rep. of	..	0.926	25	0.282	0.554	61
Malaysia	..	0.823	58	..	0.542	68
Mexico	0.476	0.847	48	0.471	0.629	39
Nepal	..	0.545	119	..	0.486	83
Pakistan	0.196	0.532	124	0.165	0.386	99
Peru		0.804	65		0.640	36
Philippines	0.455	0.748	86	0.438	0.560	59
Russia	..	0.816	59	..	0.556	60
Saudi Arabia	..	0.816	60	..	0.299	106
South Africa	..	0.680	109	0.523	0.687	26
Spain	..	0.949	9	..	0.835	11
Sri Lanka	0.468	0.756	83	0.306	0.389	98
Thailand	..	0.782	72	..	0.514	76
Turkey	..	0.788	70	..	0.379	101
UK	0.690	0.943	17	0.530	0.790	15
USA	0.810	0.942	19	0.645	0.767	18

Note : Gender development index measures the country's achievement in capabilities such as longevity, knowledge and income and captures inequality between women and men. Gender empowerment measure captures participation of women *vis-à-vis* men in economic, political and professional areas.

Source : *Human Development Report*, 2009.

284 : Legatum Prosperity Index (LPI) : 2009

Countries	Overall Rank	Economic Fundamentals	Entrepre-neurship	Democratic Institutions	Education	Health	Safety & Security	Governance	Personal Freedom	Social Capital
Argentina	38	53	48	45	38	39	45	69	27	56
Australia	6	7	15	5	6	21	14	10	4	4
Bangladesh	87	80	86	75	89	90	80	60	56	72
Brazil	41	54	37	38	58	64	79	53	16	62
Canada	7	6	4	6	16	22	9	9	3	9
Chile	36	36	47	27	49	48	27	22	31	85
China	75	29	38	100	64	53	65	93	91	70
Egypt	88	72	65	90	55	50	64	91	95	100
France	17	17	14	14	15	14	23	18	15	48
Germany	14	23	8	21	19	6	21	17	17	19
India	45	43	55	36	86	88	87	41	47	5
Indonesia	61	68	63	58	75	78	63	61	100	14
Italy	21	25	26	23	17	11	31	35	40	37
Jamaica	49	71	51	56	71	55	57	73	24	61
Japan	16	8	7	20	20	9	12	20	22	40
Korea, Rep. of	26	21	16	32	30	31	36	27	70	31
Malaysia	39	24	28	69	52	40	48	37	83	52

contd...

...contd...

Countries	Overall Rank	Economic Fundamentals	Entrepre-neurship	Democratic Institutions	Education	Health	Safety & Security	Governance	Personal Freedom	Social Capital
Mexico	43	34	29	61	60	51	72	51	73	45
New Zealand	10	27	18	4	10	19	13	11	6	1
Pakistan	99	70	79	79	101	87	101	81	104	36
Philippines	55	63	41	67	70	75	78	66	20	81
Russia	69	39	42	85	28	46	99	85	88	84
Saudi Arabia	81	44	81	101	56	42	56	67	98	43
South Africa	51	58	46	47	69	82	96	47	50	30
Spain	19	11	25	15	12	17	28	21	13	71
Sri Lanka	58	81	82	71	77	72	97	59	39	17
Thailand	44	37	39	81	54	66	58	40	74	22
Turkey	69	50	56	49	68	56	83	48	94	103
UK	12	13	2	11	21	23	22	13	19	11
USA	9	14	1	2	7	27	19	16	8	7

Note : Legatum prosperity index identifies 9 key factors that drive economic growth and personal well-being, which are foundations of prosperity. Each of these factors is represented in a sub-index and a country's final prosperity index ranking is generated by averaging its scores across all 9 sub-indices, equally weighted.The 2009 index is based on statistical analysis of more than 40 years of data for more than 100 countries accounting for 90 per cent of population. Data comprises 70 different variables which has been grouped into 9 sub-indices.: Lower the number better is the country's standing.

Source : *www.Legatum.com*

285 : Carbon Dioxide Emissions : Top 30 Countries

Rank	Country	Carbon Dioxide Emissions 1990 (million metric tonnes)	2005 (million metric tonnes)	Growth (%) 1990-2005	Share in World Total (%) 1990	Share in World Total (%) 2005	Per Capita Emissions 1990 (metric tonnes)	Per Capita Emissions 2005 (metric tonnes)
	World	**20693**	26544	**28.3**	**100.0**	**100.0**	**4.3**	**4.3**
1	USA	4874	5841	19.8	23.6	22.0	19.5	19.7
2	China	2211	5060	128.9	10.7	19.1	1.9	3.9
3	Russia	2194	1544	(29.6)	10.6	5.8	14.8	10.8
4	Japan	1058	1214	14.7	5.1	4.6	8.6	9.5
5	**India**	**597**	1149	92.5	2.9	4.3	**0.7**	**1.1**
6	Germany	968	814	(15.9)	4.7	3.1	12.2	9.9
7	Canada	433	552	27.5	2.1	2.1	15.6	17.1
8	UK	558	533	(4.5)	2.7	2.0	9.7	8.8
9	Korea, Rep. of	227	449	97.8	1.1	1.7	5.3	9.3
10	Iran	178	431	142.1	0.9	1.6	3.3	6.2
11	Italy	390	398	454.0	1.9	1.5	7.0	7.7
12	France	355	388	9.3	1.7	1.5	6.3	6.4
13	Australia	260	377	45.0	1.3	1.4	15.2	18.5
14	Indonesia	151	349	131.1	0.7	1.3	0.8	1.6
15	Spain	208	342	64.4	1.0	1.3	5.3	7.9
16	Brazil	195	334	71.3	0.9	1.3	1.3	1.8
17	South Africa	255	331	29.8	1.2	1.2	7.2	7.1
18	Saudi Arabia	169	320	89.3	0.8	1.2	10.3	13.8
19	Ukraine	681	297	(56.4)	3.3	1.1	13.1	6.3
20	Poland	349	296	(15.2)	1.7	1.1	9.2	7.8
21	Mexico	413	293	393.0	2.0	1.1	3.5	3.8
22	Turkey	129	219	69.8	0.6	0.8	2.3	3.0
23	Thailand	79	214	170.9	0.4	0.8	1.4	3.4
24	Netherlands	158	183	15.8	0.8	0.7	10.6	11.2
25	Kazakhstan	233	155	(33.5)	1.1	0.6	14.3	10.2
26	Venezuela	112	150	33.9	0.5	0.6	5.7	5.6
27	Egypt	81	149	84.0	0.4	0.6	1.5	2.0
28	Malaysia	52	138	165.4	0.3	0.5	2.9	5.4
29	United Urab Rep.	52	112	115.4	0.3	0.4	28.0	27.3
30	Algeria	68	91	33.8	0.3	0.3	2.7	2.8

Source : *Human Development Report*, 2010.

286 : Energy Production and Use

Countries	Production (million metric tonnes of oil equivalent		Energy Use (kWh per Capita)		Electric Power Consumption (kWh per capita)	
	1990	2006	1990	2006	2001	2008
World	**8637.3**	**11525.2**	**1685**	**2750**	2389	2846
Nepal	5.8	9.4		80	58	80
Bangladesh	12.8	25.0	123	146	95	144
Sri Lanka	5.5	9.4	324	400	296	417
Pakistan	43.4	79.3	402	480	374	474
India	**319.9**	**565.8**	**426**	**503**	402	542
Indonesia	102.8	179.1	548	530	402	566
Philippines	26.2	43.0	428	578	501	586
Peru	10.0	13.6		899	678	961
Egypt	32.0	62.5	573	1382	958	1384
Mexico	123.0	177.4	1494	1993	1794	2036
China	863.2	1878.7	763	2040	993	2332
Turkey	52.9	94.0	943	2053	1573	2238
Brazil	140.0	224.1	897	2060	1894	2171
Thailand	43.9	103.4	803	2080	1462	2055
Argentina	46.1	69.1	1415	2620	2085	2659
Chile	14.1	29.8	1067	3207	2487	3318
Malaysia	23.3	68.3	1269	3388	2743	3667
South Africa	91.2	129.8	2592	4810	4417	4986
Italy	148.1	184.2	261	5762	5299	5713
Russia	878.9	876.2	5211	6122	5209	6317
UK	212.3	231.1	3686	6192	6115	6120
Spain	91.2	144.6	2345	6213	5207	6296
Saudi Arabia	61.3	146.1	4114	7079	5670	7247
Germany	355.6	348.6	4485	7175	6636	7184
France	227.6	272.7	4006	7585	7485	7772
Korea, Rep. of	93.4	216.5	2161	8063	5907	8502
Japan	443.9	527.6	3610	8220	7971	8474
Australia	87.7	122.5	5130	11309	10055	11249
USA	1926.3	2320.7	7722	13515	13670	13652
Canada	209.5	269.7	7534	16766	16991	16995

Note : Countries arranged in ascending order of per capita use in 2006.
Energy production refers to forms of primary energy—crude oil, natural gas oi!, oil from non-conventional sources—natural gas, solid fuel (coal, lignite and other derived fuels) and combustible renewable and waste and primary electricity, all converted to oil equivalènt.
Energy use refers to use of primary energy before transformation to other end use fuels. It is computed as indigeneous production plus imports and stock changes minus exports and fuels supplied to ships and aircrafts engaged in international transport.
Combustible renewable and waste comprises solid and liquid biomass, biogas and industrial and muncipal waste measured as percentage of total energy use.

Source : *World Development Report*, 2007/2010.

287 : Environmental Sustainability

Countries	Carbon dioxide Emissions per capita in metric tonnes (Energy Related)		Access to Improved Water Supply (% of Population)		Access to Improved Sanitation Facilities (% of population)	
	1990	2004	1990	2004	1990	2004
World	4.0	4.2	77	83	45	57
Argentina	3.2	3.7	94	96	81	91
Australia	15.2	18.5	100	100	100	100
Bangladesh			72	74	20	39
Brazil	1.3	1.8	83	90	71	75
Canada	15.6	17.1	100	100	100	100
Chile	2.5	3.6	90	95	84	91
China	1.9	3.9	70	77	23	44
Egypt	1.5	2.0	94	98	54	70
France	6.3	6.4	100	100	..	..
Germany	12.2	9.9	100	100	100	100
India	0.7	1.1	70	86	14	33
Indonesia	0.8	1.6	72	77	46	55
Italy	7.0	7.7	..	..	..	..
Japan	8.6	9.5	100	100	100	100
Korea, Rep. of	5.3	9.3	..	92	..	..
Malaysia	2.9	5.4	98	99	..	94
Mexico	3.5	3.8	82	97	58	79
Pakistan	0.6	0.8	83	91	37	59
Philippines	0.6	0.9	87	85	57	72
Russia	14.8	10.8	94	97	87	87
Saudi Arabia	10.3	13.8	90	..	..	..
South Africa	7.2	7.1	83	88	69	65
Spain	5.3	7.9	100	100	100	100
Thailand	1.4	3.4	95	99	80	99
Turkey	2.3	3.0	85	96	85	88
UK	9.7	8.8	100	100	..	..
USA	19.5	19.7	100	100	100	100

Source : *World Development Indicators*, 2010.

288 : Statistics on Traffic and Congestion

Countries	Motor Vehicles				Road Density 2004
	per 1000 people		per km of roads		
	1990	2004	1990	2004	
Argentina	181	181	27	37	15
Australia	530	na	11	na	11
Bangladesh	1	1	0	1	184
Brazil	88	170	8	18	21
Canada	605	577	20	34	15
Chile	81	136	13	26	11
China	5	15	4	11	20
Egypt	29	na	33	na	9
France	494	597	32	38	173
Germany	405	580	53	207	..
India	4	9	2	3	114
Indonesia	16	na	7	na	20
Italy	529	610	99	73	165
Jamaica	52	na	7	na	194
Japan	469	586	52	63	323
Korea, Rep. of	79	302	60	145	102
Malaysia	124	254	26	75	30
Mexico	119	211	41	93	18
New Zealand	524	701	19	31	35
Pakistan	6	14	4	8	34
Philippines	10	34	4	13	67
Russia	87	174	14	48	3
Saudi Arabia	165	na	19	na	8
South Africa	139	144	26	24	30
Spain	360	558	43	34	133
Sri Lanka	21	34	4	na	151
Thailand	50	108	8	18	55
Turkey	48	na	38	na	11
UK	400	510	64	79	160
USA	758	808	30	37	70

Note : na: not available.
Road density refers to km of road per 100 sq km of land.

Source : *World Development Indicators*, 2007.

289 : Per Capita GDP (at Current Prices)

(US $)

Country	1980	1990	2000	2006	2007	2008
Argentina	7478	4345	7726	5458	6617	8171
Australia	10900	18591	20234	36180	42864	46824
Bangladesh	220	270	334	418	464	521
Brazil	1372	3464	3762	5870	7107	8295
Canada	10988	21084	23653	39270	43404	45085
Chile	2493	2409	4944	8942	9881	10117
China	313	341	946	2022	2560	3259
Egypt	552	1779	1566	1506	1771	2162
France	12865	22017	22576	36865	41940	46037
Germany	10750	19593	23168	35468	40480	44729
India	254	362	441	760	942	1017
Indonesia	644	699	807	1636	1915	2239
Italy	8169	20029	19293	31918	35963	38996
Japan	9172	24774	36800	34150	34287	38457
Korea, Rep. of	1745	6414	11347	19707	21653	19136
Malaysia	1812	2432	3992	5951	6934	8118
Mexico	3044	3157	6419	9082	9693	10200
Pakistan	347	447	539	821	905	1022
Philippines	672	718	987	1351	1624	1845
Russia	..	..	1768	6929	9103	11807
Saudi Arabia	17629	7689	9216	15050	15825	18855
South Africa	2764	3039	2986	5442	5922	5685
Spain	6005	13408	14464	28030	32153	35117
Sri Lanka	301	511	915	1430	1623	1972
Thailand	696	1518	1967	3171	3743	4116
Turkey	2235	3860	4245	7767	9422	10479
UK	9630	17782	25142	40321	45922	43734
USA	12249	23198	35252	44857	46674	47440

Note : Values are based on GDP in national currency converted into US $, divided by population.

Source : International Monetary Fund.

290 : Real GDP : Per cent Growth

Country	Decadal Averages		Annual Growth			
	1999-2000	2001-2009	2006	2007	2008	2009
World	3.1	3.4	5.1	5.2	3.0	-0.6
Italy	1.6	0.2	2.0	1.5	-1.3	-5.0
Japan	1.2	0.5	2.0	2.4	-1.2	-5.2
Germany	2.1	0.6	3.2	2.5	1.2	-5.0
France	2.0	1.2	2.4	2.3	0.3	-2.2
Mexico	3.5	1.4	4.9	3.3	1.5	-6.5
UK	2.5	1.4	2.9	2.6	0.5	-4.9
USA	3.4	1.6	2.7	2.1	0.4	-2.4
Canada	2.9	1.8	2.9	2.5	0.4	-2.6
Spain	2.9	2.3	4.0	3.6	0.9	-3.6
Australia	3.4	3.0	2.6	4.7	2.4	1.3
Brazil	2.5	3.2	4.0	5.7	5.1	5.4
Saudi Arabia	2.7	3.2	3.2	2.0	4.3	0.1
Turkey	3.7	3.4	6.9	4.7	0.7	-4.7
South Africa	1.8	3.6	5.6	5.5	3.7	-1.8
Chile	6.5	3.6	4.6	4.6	3.7	-1.5
Korea, Rep. of	6.1	3.9	5.2	5.1	2.3	0.2
Nepal	5.0	4.0	3.4	3.3	5.3	4.7
Thailand	4.4	4.0	5.1	4.9	2.5	-2.3
Argentina	4.2	4.1	8.5	8.7	6.8	0.9
Malaysia	7.1	4.3	5.8	6.2	4.6	-1.7
Philippines	3.0	4.4	5.3	7.1	3.8	0.9
Pakistan	3.9	4.6	6.1	5.6	2.0	2.0
Sri Lanka	5.2	4.9	7.7	6.8	6.0	3.5
Egypt	4.4	4.9	6.8	7.1	7.2	4.7
Russia	..	5.0	7.7	8.1	5.6	-8.9
Indonesia	4.0	5.1	5.5	6.3	6.0	4.5
Bangladesh	4.9	5.8	6.5	6.3	6.0	6.0
India	5.6	7.1	9.8	9.4	7.3	5.7
China	10.4	10.5	11.6	13.0	9.6	8.7

Note : Countries arranged in ascending order of GDP growth during 2001-2009.
Source : *World Economic Outlook*- October 2009 and 2010, International Monetary Fund.

291 : Gross Domestic Product

Countries	GDP (US$ million)		Average Annual Growth (%)		Value Added as % of GDP		
	1990	2008	1990-2000	2000-2008	Agriculture	Industry	Services
					2008		
World	21784509	60587016	2.9	2.8	3	28	69
Bangladesh	30129	78992	4.8	18.1	8	71	23
China	354644	4326187	10.0	10.4	11	49	40
India	316937	1217490	6.0	7.9	18	29	53
Russia	516814	1607806	(4.7)	6.8	5	38	57
Turkey	150642	794228	3.8	5.9	10	28	52
Pakistan	40010	168276	3.8	5.8	20	27	53
Malaysia	44024	194927	7.0	5.5	10	48	42
Sri Lanka	8032	40714	5.3	5.5	13	29	57
Argentina	141352	328385	4.3	5.3	9	34	57
Indonesia	114426	514389	4.2	5.2	14	48	37
Thailand	85345	260693	4.2	5.2	12	46	43
Philippines	44312	166909	3.3	5.1	15	32	53
Egypt	43130	152818	4.4	4.7	14	36	50
Korea, Rep. of	263777	929121	5.8	4.5	3	37	60

contd...

...*contd*...

Countries	GDP (US$ million)		Average Annual Growth (%)		Value Added as % of GDP		
	1990	2008	1990-2000	2000-2008	Agriculture	Industry	Services
					2008		
Chile	31559	169458	6.6	4.4	4	47	49
South Africa	112014	276764	2.1	4.3	3	31	66
Saudi Arabia	116778	467601	2.1	4.1	2	70	27
Brazil	461952	1612539	2.0	3.6	7	28	65
Nepal		12615		3.5	34	17	50
Australia	319265	1015217	4.0	3.3			
Spain	520969	1604174	2.7	3.3	3	30	67
Mexico	262710	1085951	3.1	2.7	4	37	59
Canada	574192	1400091	3.1	2.5			
UK	989524	2645593	2.7	2.5	1	23	76
USA	5757500	14204322	3.5	2.5	1	22	77
France	1239256	2853062	1.9	1.7	2	21	77
Japan	3018112	4909272	1.1	1.6	1	30	68
Germany	1707383	3652824	1.8	1.2	1	30	69
Italy	1133407	2293008	1.5	0.9	2	27	71

Note : Countries arranged in descending order of GDP growth in 2000-2008.

Source : *World Development Report* (2003 and 2010).

292 : GDP based on Purchasing Power Parity (PPP) : Valuation of Country

Country	Gross Domestic Product(PPP) (current international $ in billion)			Per Capita GDP (PPP) (current international $ in billion)			% Share of GDP in World GDP		
	1990	2000	2008	1990	2000	2008	1990	2000	2008
Argentina	182	339	573	5610	9210	14408	0.71	0.81	0.82
Australia	300	516	799	17550	26764	36918	1.17	1.23	1.15
Bangladesh	59	117	226	524	834	1399	0.23	0.28	0.33
Brazil	782	1234	1984	5335	7204	10466	3.05	2.94	2.85
Canada	542	888	1300	19627	28979	39098	2.12	2.12	1.88
Chile	63	145	243	4809	9501	14529	0.25	0.35	0.35
China	910	3013	7927	796	2377	5970	3.55	7.19	11.35
Egypt	132	248	443	2561	3910	5897	0.51	0.59	0.64
France	1028	1535	2130	18129	25998	34205	4.01	3.66	3.07
Germany	1438	2167	2918	18213	26343	35539	5.61	5.17	4.21
India	722	1523	3298	833	1455	2780	2.82	3.63	4.75
Indonesia	277	501	910	1539	2441	3980	1.08	1.19	1.31
Italy	972	1397	1818	17147	24489	30631	3.79	3.33	2.63
Jamaica	14	17	24	5654	6735	8967	0.05	0.04	0.03
Japan	2327	3213	4356	18851	25334	34116	9.02	7.66	6.35
Korea, Rep. of	350	775	1345	8164	16495	27692	1.29	1.75	1.84
Malaysia	88	213	384	4841	9083	14081	0.34	0.51	0.56

contd...

...contd...

Country	Gross Domestic Product(PPP) (current international $ in billion)			Per Capita GDP (PPP) (current international $ in billion)			% Share of GDP in World GDP		
	1990	2000	2008	1990	2000	2008	1990	2000	2008
Mexico	605	1046	1551	7272	10673	14534	2.36	2.49	2.23
New Zealand	46	75	116	13496	19380	27083	0.18	0.18	0.17
Pakistan	135	244	422	1248	1777	2624	0.53	0.58	0.63
Philippines	108	179	318	1752	2320	3515	0.42	0.43	0.46
Russia	..	1123	2265	..	7646	15948	..	2.68	3.28
Saudi Arabia	220	353	593	14488	17253	23814	0.86	0.84	0.86
South Africa	199	292	493	5396	6567	10136	0.78	0.70	0.71
Spain	551	900	1395	14193	22349	30589	2.15	2.15	2.02
Sri Lanka	25	51	92	1543	2770	4589	0.10	0.12	0.13
Thailand	164	310	547	2903	4962	8239	0.64	0.74	0.80
Turkey	291	513	915	5555	8169	13139	1.14	1.22	1.34
UK	961	1516	2228	16789	25737	36358	3.75	3.61	3.22
USA	5801	9951	14441	23198	35252	47440	22.66	23.47	20.61

Note : These data form the basis for the country weights used to generate the *World Economic Outlook* country group composites for the domestic economies. However, the IMF is not a primary source for purchasing power parity (PPP) data. WEO weights have been created from primary sources and are used solely for the purpose of generating country group composites. For primary source information, refer to one of the following sources—Organisation for Economic Co-operation and Development, World Bank or the Penn World Tables.

Source : International Monetary Fund.

293 : Structure of Demand

Countries	% of GDP							
	Final Consumption Expenditure				Gross Capital Formation		Gross Domestic Savings	
	Household		Government					
	1990	2005	1990	2005	1990	2005	1990	2005
World	60	61	17	17	23	22	22	21
Argentina	77	61	3	12	14	22	13	24
Australia	59	59	19	18	23	26	19	20
Bangladesh	86	76	4	6	17	25	14	30
Brazil	59	56	19	20	20	21	19	22
Canada	56	55	23	20	21	21	18	23
Chile	61	57	10	12	25	23	24	17
China	46	37	14	14	36	44	40	51
Egypt	73	71	11	13	29	18	21	21
France	57	57	22	24	22	20	21	18
Germany	57	59	20	19	24	17	24	21
India	66	59	12	11	24	33	22	32
Indonesia	59	65	9	8	31	22	28	24
Italy	57	59	20	20	22	21	21	20
Jamaica	65	73	13	15	26	32	19	20
Japan	53	57	13	18	33	23	34	26
Korea, Rep. of	52	53	12	14	38	30	37	32
Malaysia	52	44	14	13	32	20	30	36
Mexico	70	68	8	12	23	22	20	21
New Zealand	61	59	19	18	20	25	17	17
Pakistan	74	80	15	8	19	17	23	18
Philippines	72	80	10	10	24	15	20	31
Russia	49	49	21	17	30	21	36	32
Saudi Arabia	47	26	29	23	15	16	18	
South Africa	57	63	20	20	18	18	20	14
Spain	60	58	17	18	26	30	23	22
Sri Lanka	77	77	10	9	23	26	17	20
Thailand	57	58	9	12	41	32	33	29
Turkey	69	69	11	13	24	25	24	18
UK	63	65	20	22	20	17	16	14
USA	67	70	17	16	18	19	15	13

Source : *World Development Report*, 2007.

294 : Agricultural Input : Land

	Land Area (sq km)		Arable Land (hectares per person)		Agricultural Land (% of land area)	
	2008	Share in %	1995-1997	2005-2007	1995-1997	2005-2007
World	129611322	100.0	0.24	0.22	38.0	38.1
Russian Federation	16377740	12.6	0.86	0.85	na	na
China	9327489	7.2	0.10	0.11	57.4	59.0
United States	9161920	7.1	0.67	0.57	45.5	44.9
Canada	9093510	7.0	1.54	1.38	7.5	7.4
Brazil	8459420	6.5	0.35	0.32	30.6	31.2
Australia	7682300	5.9	2.12	2.27	60.3	56.6
India	2973190	2.3	0.17	0.14	60.8	60.5
Argentina	2736690	2.1	0.00	0.81	46.9	48.4
Saudi Arabia	2000000	1.5	0.19	0.15	0.0	0.0
Mexico	1943950	1.5	0.27	0.24	55.1	55.0
Indonesia	1811570	1.4	0.09	0.10	23.3	26.8
Peru	1280000	1.0	0.15	0.13	16.5	16.8
South Africa	1214470	0.9	0.37	0.31	82.0	81.9
Egypt, Arab Rep.	995450	0.8	0.04	0.04	3.3	3.5
Pakistan	770880	0.6	0.17	0.13	34.7	35.2
Turkey	769630	0.6	0.39	0.32	51.1	52.5
Chile	743800	0.6	0.14	0.08	20.5	21.3
France	547660	0.4	0.32	0.30	54.8	53.8
Thailand	510890	0.4	0.27	0.23	40.8	38.5
Spain	498980	0.4	0.36	0.29	60.0	57.7
Japan	364500	0.3	0.04	0.03	14.8	12.8
Germany	348770	0.3	0.14	0.14	49.7	48.7
Malaysia	328550	0.3	0.09	0.07	24.0	24.0
Philippines	298170	0.2	0.07	0.06	37.4	38.4
Italy	294140	0.2	0.15	0.13	52.2	48.5
United Kingdom	241930	0.2	0.11	0.10	72.3	72.3
Nepal	143350	0.1	0.10	0.08	29.1	29.4
Bangladesh	130170	0.1	0.06	0.05	67.6	69.5
Korea, Rep. of	96920	0.1	0.04	0.03	20.4	19.2
Sri Lanka	64630	0.0	0.05	0.05	36.0	36.9

Note : na : not available.
Countries arranged according to their share in world land area in descending order.

Source : *World Development Indicators.*

295 : Agricultural Inputs and Mechanisation

	Fertiliser Consumption (kg/hectare of Arable Land)		Land under Cereal Production (million hectare)		Tractors (per 100 sq km of Arable Land)	
	1990-1992	2005-2007	1996-1998	2007-2008	1995-1997	2005-2007
World	..	124	683.6	697.8	173	199
India	758	1355	101.1	99.8	93	187
China	2321	3387	92.3	86.1	56	124
United States	1015	1614	61.3	58.6	243	259
Russian Federation	139	128	40.5	41.8	76	36
Brazil	656	1583	17.0	19.6	138	132
Australia	275	430	16.5	19.2	81	67
Canada	476	822	18.3	16.2	157	162
Indonesia	1330	1712	15.2	15.7	3	2
Pakistan	962	1735	12.5	13.1	151	208
Turkey	0	0	14.0	12.2	335	447
Bangladesh	1136	1929	11.3	11.6	2	3
Thailand	598	1160	11.2	11.5	111	530
Mexico	686	644	10.5	10.2	117	99
Argentina	73	468	10.5	9.6	93	80
France	2918	1959	9.1	9.3	707	625
Philippines	935	1394	6.2	6.9	97	124
Germany	2616	2062	6.9	6.8	992	673
Spain	1186	1459	6.8	6.4	578	782
Italy	2195	1662	4.2	3.9	1860	2539
South Africa	549	456	5.0	3.4	77	43
Nepal	340	191	3.3	3.4	73	123
United Kingdom	3323	2670	3.4	3.0	784	744
Egypt, Arab Rep.	3977	5705	2.7	3.0	311	333
Japan	3779	3536	2.1	2.0	0	0
Peru	246	949	1.0	1.2	37	36
Korea, Rep. of	4932	4384	1.2	1.0	658	1458
Sri Lanka	2016	2953	0.8	1.0	190	213
Malaysia	0	8497	0.7	0.7		
Saudi Arabia	1446	1044	0.7	0.6		
Chile	1215	4801	0.6	0.5	233	397

Note : Countries arranged in descending order of share in land under cereal production in descending order.

Source : *World Development Indicators.*

296 : Top 10 Rice/Paddy Producing Countries

(million tonnes)

Countries	2001			2007		
	Production	Share (%)	Rank	Production	Share (%)	Rank
World	598.2	100.0		659.6	100.0	
China	179.3	30.0	1	187.4	28.4	1
India	139.9	23.4	2	144.6	21.9	2
Indonesia	50.5	8.4	3	57.2	8.7	3
Bangladesh	36.3	6.1	4	43.1	6.5	4
Vietnam	32.1	5.4	5	35.9	5.4	5
Thailand	26.5	4.4	6	32.1	4.9	6
Myanmar	21.9	3.7	7	32.6	4.9	7
Philippines	13.0	2.2	8	16.2	2.5	8
Brazil	10.2	1.7	10	11.1	1.7	9
Japan	11.3	1.9	9	10.9	1.7	10

Source : Food and Agriculture Organization.

297 : Top 10 Wheat Producing Countries

(million tonnes)

Countries	2001			2007		
	Production	Share (%)	Rank	Production	Share (%)	Rank
World	589.8	100.0		611.1	100.0	
China	93.9	15.9	1	109.3	17.9	1
India	69.7	11.8	2	75.8	12.4	2
USA	53.0	9.0	3	55.8	9.1	3
Russia	47.0	8.0	5	49.4	8.1	4
France	31.5	5.3	4	32.8	5.4	5
Pakistan	19.0	3.2	10	23.3	3.8	8
Germany	22.8	3.9	7	20.8	3.4	7
Canada	20.6	3.5	9	20.1	3.3	6
Turkey	19.0	3.2	11	17.2	2.8	9
Argentina	15.4	2.6	12	16.5	2.7	10

Source : Food and Agriculture Organization.

298 : Top Five Cotton Producing Countries

(million tonnes)

Countries	2001		2007	
	Production	Rank	Production	Rank
China	5.3	1	7.6	1
India	1.7	4	4.4	2
USA	4.4	2	4.2	3
Pakistan	1.8	3	2.0	4
Brazil	0.9	7	1.4	5

Source : Food and Agriculture Organization.

299 : Top Five Groundnut Producing Countries

(million tonnes)

Countries	2001		2007	
	Production	Rank	Production	Rank
China	14.5	1	13.1	1
India	7.0	2	9.2	2
Nigeria	2.7	3	3.8	3
USA	1.9	4	1.7	4
Indonesia	1.2	5	1.4	5

Source : Food and Agriculture Organization.

300 : Top Five Sugarcane Producing Countries

(million tonnes)

Countries	2001		2007	
	Production	Rank	Production	Rank
Brazil	345.9	1	549.7	1
India	296.0	2	355.5	2
China	78.0	3	113.7	3
Thailand	49.6	4	64.4	4
Pakistan	43.6	6	54.7	5

Source : Food and Agriculture Organization.

301 : Revenue, Expenditure and Fiscal Balance

% of GDP

Countries	Revenue		Expenditure		Fiscal Balance	
	1995	2005	1995	2005	1995	2005
World	na	26.6	na	28.2	na	(1.7)
Argentina	na	18.1	na	18.3	na	(0.5)
Australia	na	26.0	na	24.8	na	1.1
Bangladesh	na	10.0	na	8.8	na	(0.7)
Brazil	26.9	..	32.9		na	(2.7)
Canada	20.6	20.0	24.6	18.1	(4.4)	1.7
Chile	na	24.4	na	18.7	na	4.7
China	5.4	9.5	na	11.1	na	(2.1)
Egypt	25.9	19.5	23.8	22.6	(1.1)	(5.7)
France	43.3	43.1	47.3	46.1	(4.1)	(2.8)
Germany	29.9	28.7	38.6	31.2	(8.3)	(2.3)
India	12.3	12.5	14.5	15.8	(2.2)	(3.6)
Indonesia	17.7	18.5	9.7	17.0	3.0	(1.1)
Italy	40.3	35.7	48.0	39.4	(7.5)	(3.5)
Jamaica	na	35.1	33.3	33.8	na	(1.2)
Japan	20.7	na	na	na	na	na
Korea, Rep. of	17.8	23.4	14.3	21.4	2.4	0.8
Malaysia	24.4	23.7	17.2	20.1	2.4	(4.3)
Mexico	15.3	na	15.0	na	(0.6)	na
New Zealand	na	38.0	na	32.5	na	4.6
Pakistan	17.2	12.9	19.1	14.5	(5.3)	(3.2)
Philippines	17.7	15.1	15.9	18.0	(0.8)	(3.0)
Russia	na	30.7	na	20.0	na	9.9
Saudi Arabia	na	na	na	..	na	..
South Africa	na	30.2	na	29.6	na	0.2
Spain	32.0	26.9	37.1	24.9	(5.8)	1.5
Sri Lanka	20.4	16.1	26.0	21.0	(7.6)	(7.3)
Thailand	na	21.0	na	16.3	na	2.5
Turkey	17.7	na	19.1	na	(1.8)	na
UK	37.2	38.0	37.1	41.1	0.3	(2.9)
USA	27.6	27.2	27.1	27.5	(1.2)	(1.6)

Note : na : not available.
Source : *World Development Report*, 2007.

302 : Consumer Price Inflation

Countries	Average Annual Price Increase (%)			Annual Increase (%)				
	1981-1990	1991-2000	2001-2009	2005	2006	2007	2008	2009
World	16.0	12.2	2.2	3.8	3.6	3.9	5.9	na
Japan	2.1	0.8	0.0	(0.3)	0.3	0.0	1.4	(1.4)
Germany	2.6	2.3	1.0	1.9	1.8	2.3	2.8	0.1
France	6.3	1.8	1.0	1.9	1.9	1.6	3.2	0.1
UK	6.1	2.7	1.4	2.0	2.3	2.3	3.6	2.2
Canada	5.9	2.0	1.0	2.2	2.0	2.1	2.4	0.3
China	6.9	7.2	1.5	1.8	1.5	4.8	5.9	(0.7)
Malaysia	3.2	3.5	1.6	3.0	3.6	2.0	5.4	0.6
Italy	9.8	3.7	1.2	2.2	2.2	2.0	3.5	0.8
Saudi Arabia	(0.2)	0.8	2.4	0.6	2.3	4.1	9.9	5.1
USA	4.7	2.8	1.4	3.4	3.2	2.9	3.8	(0.3)
Thailand	4.4	4.5	1.8	4.5	4.6	2.2	5.5	(0.8)
Spain	9.3	4.0	1.5	3.4	3.6	2.8	4.1	(0.3)
Australia	7.5	2.2	1.6	2.7	3.5	2.3	4.4	1.8
Korea, Rep. of	7.0	5.1	1.7	2.8	2.2	2.5	4.7	2.8
Chile	20.3	9.4	2.4	3.1	3.4	4.4	8.7	1.7
Mexico	65.1	18.3	2.4	4.0	3.6	4.0	5.1	5.3
Philippines	(9.2)	8.7	3.2	7.6	6.2	2.8	9.3	3.2
India	8.9	9.0	4.0	4.2	6.2	6.4	8.3	10.9
Bangladesh	10.3	5.6	4.1	7.0	7.1	9.1	7.7	6.1
South Africa	14.7	9.0	3.8	3.4	4.7	7.1	11.5	7.1
Brazil	339.9	204.4	2.8	6.9	4.2	3.6	5.7	4.9
Egypt	17.4	8.9	5.8	8.8	4.2	11.0	11.7	16.2
Pakistan	6.9	9.1	6.4	9.3	7.9	7.8	12.0	20.8
Indonesia	8.6	13.2	4.9	10.5	13.1	6.0	9.8	4.8
Argentina	437.2	15.7	4.9	9.6	10.9	8.8	8.6	6.3
Sri Lanka	12.2	9.7	7.0	11.0	10.0	15.8	22.6	3.4
Russia	..	..	6.4	12.7	9.7	9.0	14.1	11.7
Turkey	45.6	75.9	4.8	8.2	9.6	8.8	10.4	6.3
Nepal				4.5	8.0	6.4	7.7	13.2
Peru				1.6	2.0	1.8	5.8	2.9

Note : na : not available.

Source : *World Economic Outlook*, April 2010.

303 : Priorities in Government Spending

Countries	% of GDP Health 1990	Health 2004	Education 1991	Education 2002-2005	Military 1990	Military 2005	Expenditure 1990	Expenditure 2005
Argentina	..	4.3	3.3	3.8	1.2	1.0	4.4	5.8
Australia	8.2	6.5	4.9	4.7	2.0	1.8	..	..
Bangladesh	0.9	0.9	1.5	2.5	1.0	1.0	2.5	1.3
Brazil	3.9	4.8	..	4.4	2.4	1.6	1.8	7.9
Canada	9.3	6.9	6.5	5.2	3.0	1.1	..	..
Chile	..	2.9	2.4	3.5	4.3	3.8	8.8	6.7
China	3.1	1.8	2.2	1.9	2.7	2.0	2.0	1.2
Egypt	5.0	2.2	3.9	..	4.7	2.8	7.1	2.8
France	8.8	8.2	5.5	5.9	3.4	2.5	..	..
Germany	8.6	8.2	..	4.6	2.8	1.4	..	..
India	3.2	0.9	3.7	3.6	3.2	2.8	2.6	3.6
Indonesia	2.5	1.0	1.0	0.9	1.8	1.2	8.7	6.3
Italy	7.7	6.5	3.0	4.7	2.1	1.9	..	..
Jamaica	2.9	2.8	4.5	5.3	0.6	0.6	14.4	10.1
Japan	6.7	6.3	..	3.6	0.9	1.0	..	..
Korea, Rep. of	6.4	2.9	3.8	4.6	3.7	2.6	..	..
Malaysia	1.6	2.2	5.1	6.2	2.6	2.4	9.8	7.2
Mexico	2.9	3.0	3.8	5.4	0.4	0.4	4.3	5.7
New Zealand	7.3	6.5	6.1	6.5	1.9	1.0	..	..
Pakistan	4.5	0.4	2.6	2.3	5.8	3.5	4.8	2.2
Philippines	5.3	1.4	3.0	2.7	1.4	0.9	8.1	10.0
Russia	..	3.7	3.6	3.6	12.3	4.1	..	5.5
Saudi Arabia	2.1	2.5	5.8	6.8	14.0	8.2	..	..
South Africa	..	3.5	5.9	5.4	3.8	1.5	..	2.0
Spain	6.4	5.7	4.1	4.3	1.8	1.1	..	..
Sri Lanka	2.3	2.0	3.2	..	2.1	2.6	4.8	1.9
Thailand	5.6	2.3	3.1	4.2	2.6	1.1	6.2	11.0
Turkey	2.8	5.6	2.4	3.7	3.5	2.8	4.9	11.6
UK	6.1	7.0	4.8	5.4	3.9	2.7	..	..
USA	12.2	6.9	5.1	5.9	5.3	4.1	..	..

Source : *Human Development Report*, 2007/2008.

304 : Financial Development Index : 2008

Countries	Overall Index		Factors, Policies and Institutions					
	Score	Rank among 52 Countries	Institutional Environment		Business Environment		Financial Stability	
			Score	Rank	Score	Rank	Score	Rank
Argentina	3.04	47	3.35	45	3.92	39	2.92	50
Australia	4.98	11	5.94	13	5.24	14	5.13	21
Brazil	3.28	40	3.69	40	4.00	37	3.60	44
Canada	5.26	5	6.06	7	5.43	8	5.26	14
Chile	3.79	30	5.38	21	4.89	22	4.47	31
China	4.09	24	3.33	46	4.07	35	5.17	19
Egypt	3.32	37	4.07	35	3.91	40	3.41	47
France	5.25	6	5.83	16	5.20	15	5.17	20
Germany	5.28	3	6.08	6	5.41	10	5.77	6
India	3.63	31	3.42	43	3.61	45	4.67	28
Indonesia	3.31	38	4.46	29	3.46	49	3.65	43
Italy	4.38	22	4.66	26	4.63	29	4.82	24
Japan	5.28	4	5.88	14	5.17	16	5.71	8
Korea, Rep. of	4.55	19	5.08	23	5.42	9	4.42	32
Malaysia	4.48	20	5.14	22	4.80	23	5.18	18

contd...

...contd...

Countries	Overall Index		Factors, Policies and Institutions					
			Institutional Environment		Business Environment		Financial Stability	
	Score	Rank among 52 Countries	Score	Rank	Score	Rank	Score	Rank
Mexico	3.21	43	4.31	31	3.81	44	4.69	27
Pakistan	3.46	34	3.09	49	3.46	50	4.11	37
Philippines	3.03	48	3.60	41	3.50	48	3.32	48
Russia	3.40	36	3.10	48	4.08	34	4.41	33
Saudi Arabia	3.90	27	4.18	33	4.54	31	5.97	3
South Africa	4.00	25	4.58	27	4.03	36	4.72	26
Spain	4.90	12	5.62	19	4.80	24	5.00	22
Thailand	3.82	29	4.46	29	4.24	33	4.54	29
Turkey	3.30	39	3.36	44	4.38	32	2.73	52
UK	5.83	2	6.09	5	5.34	11	4.97	23
USA	5.85	1	5.98	12	5.32	12	5.51	10

Note: Financial development index captures the factors, policies and institutions that lead to effective financial intermediation and markets, and deep and broad access to capital and financial services.
Source: *The Financial Development Report*, 2008; World Economic Forum.

305 : Financial Development Index : 2008

Countries	Financial Intermediation						Capital Availability (size, depth and access)	
	Banks		Non-Banks		Financial Markets			
	Score	Rank	Score	Rank	Score	Rank	Score	Rank
Argentina	2.85	46	2.48	22	2.18	37	3.54	46
Australia	4.12	21	4.26	6	4.58	8	5.60	14
Brazil	2.47	52	2.82	21	2.28	34	4.10	37
Canada	5.15	6	4.37	5	4.07	13	6.47	5
Chile	3.72	30	1.68	44	2.10	40	4.27	35
China	4.97	7	3.30	15	2.66	30	5.14	24
Egypt	3.40	34	1.75	41	2.15	38	4.58	31
France	4.55	14	5.29	3	5.07	4	5.66	11
Germany	4.85	9	4.12	7	4.87	7	5.84	9
India	2.61	50	3.24	16	2.99	22	4.90	28
Indonesia	4.60	13	1.58	46	1.70	46	3.72	42
Italy	4.41	16	3.35	14	3.83	15	4.97	25
Japan	4.92	8	4.50	4	5.03	5	5.72	10
Korea, Rep. of	4.81	11	3.62	11	3.15	20	5.33	20
Malaysia	5.72	2	1.93	35	2.93	23	5.65	12
Mexico	2.65	49	1.88	38	1.77	45	3.37	48
Pakistan	3.91	25	1.73	42	3.58	17	4.33	33
Philippines	2.96	42	1.78	40	1.97	42	4.07	38
Russia	2.87	45	3.71	10	2.08	41	3.56	45
Saudi Arabia	4.07	23	1.40	49	2.73	29	4.43	32
South Africa	4.09	22	2.42	23	2.83	28	5.30	21
Spain	4.84	10	3.77	9	3.86	14	6.38	6
Thailand	4.45	15	1.89	37	2.25	36	4.95	26
Turkey	3.32	37	2.19	28	3.07	21	4.04	39
UK	5.51	3	6.55	1	5.87	2	6.48	4
USA	5.80	1	6.05	2	6.15	1	6.15	8

Note: Financial development index captures the factors, policies and institutions that lead to effective financial intermediation and markets, and deep and broad access to capital and financial services.

Source: *The Financial Development Report*, 2008; World Economic Forum.

306 : Wealth of Nations

($ per capita)

Countries	Total Wealth	Produced Capital and Urban Land	Intangible Capital	Natural Capital	of which:	
					Crop Land	Sub-soil Assets
World	95860	16850	74998	4011	1496	1302
Nepal	3802	609	1964	1229	767	0
Bangladesh	6000	817	4221	961	810	83
India	6820	1154	3738	1928	1340	201
Pakistan	7871	975	5529	1368	549	265
China	9387	2956	4208	2223	1404	511
Indonesia	13869	2382	8015	3472	1245	1549
Sri Lanka	14731	2710	11204	817	485	0
Philippines	19351	2673	15129	1549	1308	30
Egypt	21879	3897	14734	3249	1705	1544
Thailand	35854	7624	24294	3936	2370	469
Russia	38709	15593	5900	17217	1262	11777
Malaysia	46687	13065	24520	9103	1369	6922
Turkey	47859	8580	35774	3504	2270	180
South Africa	59629	7270	48959	3400	1238	1118
Mexico	61872	18959	34420	8493	1195	6075
Chile	77726	10688	56094	10944	2443	5188
Brazil	86972	9643	70528	6752	1998	1708
Argentina	139232	19111	109809	10312	3632	3253
Korea, Rep. of	141282	31399	107864	2020	1241	33
Spain	261205	38531	217300	4374	2806	50
Canada	324979	54276	235982	34771	2829	18566
Australia	371031	58179	288686	24167	4365	11491
Italy	372666	51943	316045	4678	2639	361
UK	408753	55239	346347	7167	583	4739
France	468024	57814	403874	6335	2747	87
Japan	493241	150258	341470	1513	710	28
Germany	496447	68678	423323	4445	1176	269
USA	512612	79851	418009	14752	2752	7106

Note : Countries are arranged in ascending order by wealth.
Source : *World Development Report* 2010.

307 : Exports: Decadal Growth

(billion US $)

Countries	Decadal Averages								
	1981-1990			1991-2000			2001-2008		
	Export (US $ billion)	Growth (%)	Share (%)	Export (US $ billion)	Growth (%)	Share (%)	Export (US $ billion)	Growth (%)	Share (%)
World	2289.1	6.1	100.00	4878.9	6.5	100.00	11578.2	14.9	100.00
Argentina	8.5	5.9	0.37	20.0	8.5	0.41	47.0	16.2	0.41
Australia	26.8	6.6	1.17	52.7	5.1	1.08	120.0	17.2	1.04
Bangladesh	1.0	9.1	0.05	3.1	11.5	0.06	8.4	16.7	0.07
Brazil	26.6	5.5	1.16	45.1	6.0	0.92	125.4	20.3	1.08
Canada	95.7	6.8	4.18	191.0	8.2	3.91	396.9	9.6	3.43
Chile	5.2	6.9	0.23	14.2	9.5	0.29	44.8	21.0	0.39
China	35.3	13.5	1.54	148.0	15.4	3.03	799.8	30.1	6.91
Egypt	4.1	7.2	0.18	3.5	2.4	0.07	12.2	29.9	0.11
France	133.4	7.0	5.83	266.9	3.7	5.47	507.2	9.7	4.38
Germany	249.0	8.5	10.88	483.4	3.3	9.91	1096.1	13.8	9.47
India	11.3	8.1	0.49	29.4	9.3	0.60	105.5	23.4	0.91
Indonesia	20.8	2.5	0.91	45.9	10.2	0.94	102.5	16.0	0.89
Italy	102.8	8.6	4.49	215.5	3.8	4.42	718.0	116.3	6.20
Jamaica	0.8	3.0	0.04	1.2	1.5	0.03	1.9	9.9	0.02

contd...

...contd...

Countries	Decadal Averages								
	1981-1990			1991-2000			2001-2008		
	Export (US $ billion)	Growth (%)	Share (%)	Export (US $ billion)	Growth (%)	Share (%)	Export (US $ billion)	Growth (%)	Share (%)
Japan	205.2	8.5	8.96	397.5	5.5	8.15	683.3	9.4	5.90
Korea, Rep. of	39.7	14.5	1.74	116.6	10.6	2.39	306.6	16.3	2.65
Malaysia	17.7	9.5	0.77	66.8	13.3	1.37	157.3	14.1	1.36
Mexico	28.5	9.4	1.25	90.8	15.4	1.86	244.9	12.2	2.12
New Zealand	6.8	6.0	0.30	12.2	3.9	0.25	24.0	12.5	0.21
Pakistan	3.6	9.0	0.16	8.0	5.2	0.16	16.6	12.5	0.14
Philippines	5.9	4.1	0.26	21.2	17.4	0.43	49.1	6.5	0.42
Russia	0.0	0.0	0.00	74.8	14.1	1.53	260.3	6.7	2.25
Saudi Arabia	45.0	(4.5)	1.97	52.2	8.4	1.07	174.1	29.5	1.50
South Africa	19.8	(0.2)	0.86	26.7	2.7	0.55	57.8	16.1	0.50
Spain	30.9	10.9	1.35	88.7	7.7	1.82	213.7	13.4	1.85
Sri Lanka	1.4	6.9	0.06	3.8	11.3	0.08	7.4	9.6	0.06
Thailand	11.5	14.5	0.50	49.5	12.1	1.01	124.4	16.3	1.07
Turkey	8.5	17.6	0.37	21.4	8.1	0.44	78.2	23.3	0.68
UK	120.9	5.8	5.28	236.8	4.5	4.85	425.2	7.7	3.67
USA	266.5	6.2	11.64	590.6	7.2	12.11	1093.5	9.3	9.44

Source : *International Financial Statistics Year Book* (2009), IMF.

308 : Exports: Annual Growth

(billion US $)

Countries	Annual								
	2006			2007			2008		
	Export (US $ billion)	Growth (%)	Share (%)	Export (US $ billion)	Growth (%)	Share (%)	Export (US $ billion)	Growth (%)	Share (%)
World	12066.0	15.8	100.00	13765.6	14.1	100.00	15991.4	16.2	100.00
Argentina	46.6	15.3	0.39	55.8	19.7	0.41	70.6	26.5	0.44
Australia	123.3	16.5	1.02	141.1	14.4	1.03	187.0	32.5	1.17
Bangladesh	9.1	26.4	0.08	10.2	12.1	0.07	11.8	15.7	0.07
Brazil	137.8	16.3	1.14	160.6	16.5	1.17	197.9	23.2	1.24
Canada	389.5	8.4	3.23	416.7	7.0	3.03	452.2	8.5	2.83
Chile	58.7	42.1	0.49	67.7	15.3	0.49	66.5	(1.8)	0.42
China	969.4	27.2	8.03	1217.8	25.6	8.85	1428.7	17.3	8.93
Egypt	13.7	28.0	0.11	16.2	18.2	0.12	26.2	61.7	0.16
France	488.4	10.0	4.05	550.8	12.8	4.00	606.0	10.0	3.79
Germany	1122.1	14.7	9.30	1323.8	18.0	9.62	1463.9	10.6	9.15
India	120.9	21.4	1.00	145.4	20.3	1.06	176.9	21.7	1.11
Indonesia	103.5	19.4	0.86	118.7	14.7	0.86	147.6	24.3	0.92
Italy	416.2	11.6	3.45	499.9	20.1	3.63	548.8	9.8	3.43
Jamaica	1.9	26.7	0.02	2.1	10.5	0.02	2.5	19.0	0.02

contd...

...contd...

Countries	Annual								
	2006			2007			2008		
	Export (US $ billion)	Growth (%)	Share (%)	Export (US $ billion)	Growth (%)	Share (%)	Export (US $ billion)	Growth (%)	Share (%)
Japan	649.9	9.2	5.39	700.5	7.8	5.09	786.4	12.3	4.92
Korea, Rep. of	325.5	14.5	2.70	371.5	14.1	2.70	422.0	13.6	2.64
Malaysia	160.6	14.0	1.33	176.0	9.6	1.28	209.7	19.1	1.31
Mexico	250.4	17.1	2.08	272.1	8.7	1.98	291.8	7.2	1.82
New Zealand	22.4	3.2	0.19	27.0	20.5	0.20	30.6	13.3	0.19
Pakistan	16.9	5.0	0.14	17.8	5.3	0.13	20.4	14.6	0.13
Philippines	47.4	18.8	0.39	50.3	6.1	0.37	49.0	(2.6)	0.31
Russia	303.9	0.0	2.52	354.4	0.0	2.57	471.8	0.0	2.95
Saudi Arabia	188.5	4.3	1.56	205.5	9.0	1.49	328.9	60.0	2.06
South Africa	58.2	12.8	0.48	69.8	19.9	0.51	84.6	21.2	0.53
Spain	213.3	11.7	1.77	248.9	16.7	1.81	277.7	11.6	1.74
Sri Lanka	6.9	9.5	0.06	7.7	11.6	0.06	8.4	9.1	0.05
Thailand	130.8	18.7	1.08	153.1	17.0	1.11	172.9	12.9	1.08
Turkey	85.5	16.3	0.71	107.1	25.3	0.78	132.0	23.2	0.83
UK	427.7	15.2	3.54	435.0	1.7	3.16	459.9	5.7	2.88
USA	1038.3	14.5	8.61	1163.0	12.0	8.45	1301.1	11.9	8.14

Source : *International Financial Statistics Year Book* (2009),IMF.

309 : Imports : Decadal and Annual

(billion US $)

	Decadal Averages						Annual					
	1981-1990	Growth(%)	1991-2000	Growth(%)	2001-2008	Growth(%)	2006	Growth(%)	2007	Growth(%)	2008	Growth(%)
World	2377.3	6.0	4996.5	6.6	10384.2	12.2	12212.0	14.8	14052.1	15.1	16195.7	15.3
Argentina	5.2	(7.0)	21.8	24.7	28.8	18.4	34.2	19.2	44.7	30.7	57.4	28.4
Australia	30.5	7.4	58.2	5.6	120.7	14.2	139.3	11.2	165.3	18.7	200.2	21.1
Bangladesh	2.8	4.1	5.9	9.4	13.3	13.9	15.0	16.3	17.3	15.3	22.5	30.1
Brazil	18.2	(0.2)	45.7	11.4	88.5	16.8	95.8	23.5	126.6	32.2	182.4	44.1
Canada	88.5	7.5	176.3	7.2	309.5	7.2	357.6	7.8	389.3	8.9	417.4	7.2
Chile	4.9	6.2	15.2	10.1	32.4	17.1	38.4	17.4	47.2	22.9	61.9	31.1
China	38.6	11.9	130.8	16.1	631.5	22.7	791.6	19.9	956.3	20.8	1131.6	18.3
Egypt	13.7	16.3	11.9	1.1	20.7	20.5	20.7	4.5	27.1	30.9	48.8	80.1
France	145.1	6.3	264.1	3.3	473.1	11.0	539.5	10.9	623.4	15.6	706.0	13.2
Germany	206.9	7.0	433.3	4.0	781.8	12.0	922.3	18.2	1056.0	14.5	1199.0	13.5
India	17.1	4.9	34.9	8.7	138.2	25.1	175.2	22.7	215.2	22.8	292.7	36.0
Indonesia	14.5	8.9	35.0	7.9	68.8	16.1	78.8	4.2	93.1	18.1	129.8	39.4
Italy	113.4	6.7	199.0	3.3	378.6	11.5	440.8	14.6	509.9	15.7	558.5	9.5
Jamaica	1.405	6.5	2.6	6.2	4.8	11.5	5.3	17.8	6.4	20.8	7.7	20.3
Japan	157.9	5.7	298.2	5.5	500.1	9.6	579.6	12.6	619.8	6.9	762.6	23.0

contd...

India
Indonesia
Italy
Jamaica
Japan
2.1
271.7

				Averages			Annual					
[illegible]	[illegible]	[illegible]	[illegible]	Growth(%)	2001-2008	Growth(%)	2006	Growth(%)	2007	Growth(%)	2008	Growth(%)
[illegible]	[illegible]	[illegible]	[illegible]	10.8	257.4	13.9	309.4	18.5	356.8	15.3	435.3	22.0
[illegible]	[illegible]	[illegible]	[illegible]	12.3	112.2	9.6	131.1	14.6	146.8	12.0	164.4	12.0
[illegible]	[illegible]	[illegible]	101.5	15.9	232.5	7.7	268.2	15.7	296.6	10.6	325.2	9.6
[illegible]	[illegible]	[illegible]	12.3	4.5	23.5	12.4	26.4	0.8	30.9	17.0	34.4	11.3
[illegible]	[illegible]	[illegible]	10.2	4.7	22.8	19.4	29.8	17.3	32.6	9.4	42.3	29.8
[illegible]	[illegible]	[illegible]	27.2	11.8	46.6	6.4	54.1	15.1	57.7	6.7	60.3	4.5
[illegible]	[illegible]	[illegible]	51.2	5.3	150.4	0.0	181.2	0.0	245.8	0.0	321.2	0.0
[illegible]	[illegible]	(1.0)	28.7	3.1	60.0	18.7	69.8	17.3	90.2	29.2	115.1	27.6
[illegible]	[illegible]	0.8	26.1	5.5	60.1	17.1	78.7	26.3	88.4	12.3	99.5	12.6
Spain	[illegible]	10.9	115.3	6.3	274.9	13.7	326.0	13.4	385.0	18.1	417.0	8.3
Sri Lanka	[illegible]	3.0	5.0	9.1	8.9	10.8	10.3	17.0	11.3	9.7	14.0	23.9
Thailand	15.0	15.6	54.0	8.1	107.9	14.6	128.7	8.9	140.8	9.4	178.8	27.0
Turkey	12.7	11.6	36.5	11.5	111.0	19.4	139.6	19.5	169.8	21.6	201.8	18.8
UK	141.1	7.4	268.9	4.3	471.5	8.5	546.6	13.2	620.8	13.6	632.9	1.9
USA	377.3	7.6	811.0	9.4	1630.3	7.2	1919.4	10.8	2017.0	5.1	2165.2	7.3

Source : *International Financial Statistics Year Book* (2009), IMF.

310 : Indicators of Trade Openness

Country	Trade (Export+Import) (US $ billion)						Trade Openness (Trade as % to GDP)					
	1980	1990	2000	2006	2007	2008	1980	1990	2000	2006	2007	2008
Argentina	18.6	16.4	51.5	80.8	100.5	128.0	8.88	11.62	18.12	37.99	38.59	39.41
Australia	44.3	81.7	135.4	262.6	306.4	387.2	27.63	25.73	34.72	34.77	33.66	38.21
Bangladesh	3.4	5.3	13.2	24.1	27.5	34.3	17.21	17.34	28.06	36.96	37.32	40.74
Brazil	45.1	53.9	113.7	233.6	287.2	380.3	27.73	10.62	17.65	21.44	21.54	24.18
Canada	130.3	250.9	521.4	747.1	806.0	869.6	48.45	43.05	71.93	58.48	56.47	57.99
Chile	10.5	16.1	37.7	97.1	114.9	128.4	38.09	51.06	50.13	66.16	70.11	75.77
China	38.0	115.4	474.3	1761.0	2174.1	2560.3	12.30	29.58	39.58	66.26	64.28	59.16
Egypt	7.9	21.7	18.7	34.4	43.3	75.0	35.34	23.79	18.86	32.04	33.22	46.12
France	250.9	451.0	612.5	1027.9	1174.2	1312.0	36.30	36.12	45.94	45.27	45.20	45.76
[illegible]many	380.9	756.3	1045.5	2044.4	2379.8	2662.9	46.10	48.88	54.86	70.03	71.50	72.50
[illegible]	23.5	41.5	93.9	296.1	360.6	469.6	13.24	13.24	20.32	33.82	32.75	38.92
[illegible]	32.7	47.5	108.5	182.3	211.8	277.4	34.33	37.79	65.55	50.03	49.02	54.20
[illegible]	[illegible]	352.5	477.9	857.0	1009.8	1107.3	38.83	31.04	43.42	45.95	47.69	47.85
[illegible]	[illegible]	3.1	4.6	7.2	8.5	10.2	76.62	60.95	51.05	60.14	65.43	72.71
[illegible]	[illegible]	[illegible]	858.7	1229.5	1320.3	1549.0	25.37	17.10	18.40	28.18	30.14	31.54

contd...

...contd...

Country	Trade (Export+Import) (US $ billion)						Trade Openness (Trade as % to GDP)					
	1980	1990	2000	2006	2007	2008	1980	1990	2000	2006	2007	2008
Korea, Rep. of	39.8	134.9	332.8	634.9	728.3	857.3	59.82	49.04	62.39	66.71	69.41	92.27
Malaysia	23.7	58.7	180.2	291.7	322.8	374.1	95.13	133.35	192.16	185.74	173.45	168.81
Mexico	40.2	84.3	349.1	518.6	568.7	617.0	19.53	32.07	55.51	54.46	55.46	56.70
New Zealand	10.9	18.9	27.2	48.8	57.9	65.0	48.67	42.78	51.94	45.99	44.89	50.62
Pakistan	8.0	13.0	19.9	46.7	50.4	62.7	27.97	26.88	26.86	36.63	35.19	38.10
Philippines	14.0	21.1	76.8	101.5	108.0	109.3	43.24	47.82	101.17	86.36	74.98	65.48
Russia	0.0	0.0	154.7	485.1	600.2	793.0	..	..	59.55	49.03	46.37	47.30
Saudi Arabia	139.3	68.5	107.8	258.3	295.7	444.0	84.78	58.65	57.12	72.43	76.93	94.58
South Africa	45.2	42.0	59.7	136.9	158.2	184.1	56.16	37.47	44.90	53.08	55.83	66.52
Spain	54.8	143.1	266.2	539.3	633.9	694.7	24.41	27.48	45.71	43.64	43.93	43.37
Sri Lanka	3.1	4.6	11.7	17.2	19.0	22.4	71.05	55.37	69.45	60.82	58.73	56.56
Thailand	15.7	56.1	131.0	259.5	293.9	351.7	48.59	65.52	106.71	125.37	119.45	128.68
Turkey	10.8	35.3	82.3	225.1	276.9	333.8	11.48	17.42	30.88	42.54	42.66	45.73
UK	225.7	409.7	616.0	974.3	1055.8	1092.8	41.60	40.25	41.60	39.88	37.71	40.78
USA	482.6	910.6	2041.2	2957.7	3180.0	3466.3	17.31	15.70	20.51	22.07	22.59	24.00

Note : Trade openness worked out by EPWRF.
Source : International Monetary Fund.

311 : Foreign Direct Investment

(million US $)

Countries	Inflow			Outflow		
	1991	2001	2007	1991	2001	2007
World	155751 (6385.9)	824445 (38063.0)	1833324 (32051.1)	200464 (100.0)	751297 (100.0)	1996514 (100.0)
Argentina	2439 (100.0)	2166 (100.0)	5720 (100.0)	49 (0.0)	161 (0.0)	1196 (0.1)
Australia	4303 (176.4)	8305 (383.4)	22266 (389.3)	1200 (0.6)	11974 (1.6)	24209 (1.2)
Bangladesh	1 (0.0)	355 (16.4)	666 (11.6)	0 (0.0)	21 (0.0)	21 (0.0)
Brazil	1102 (45.2)	22457 (1036.8)	34585 (604.6)	1015 (0.5)	-2258 -(0.3)	7067 (0.4)
Canada	2881 (118.1)	27663 (1277.1)	108655 (1899.6)	5834 (2.9)	36029 (4.8)	53818 (2.7)
Chile	822 (33.7)	4200 (193.9)	14457 (252.7)	125 (0.1)	1610 (0.2)	3830 (0.2)
China	4366 (179.0)	46878 (2164.3)	83521 (1460.2)	913 (0.5)	6885 (0.9)	22469 (1.1)
Egypt	253 (10.4)	510 (23.5)	11578 (202.4)	62 (0.0)	12 (0.0)	665 (0.0)
France	15167 (621.9)	50476 (2330.4)	157970 (2761.7)	25132 (12.5)	86767 (11.5)	224650 (11.3)
Germany	4727 (193.8)	26414 (1219.5)	50925 (890.3)	22938 (11.4)	39684 (5.3)	167431 (8.4)
India	75 (3.1)	5472 (252.6)	22950 (401.2)	-11 (0.0)	1397 (0.2)	13649 (0.7)
Indonesia	1482 (60.8)	-2926 -(135.1)	6928 (121.1)	13 (0.0)	125 (0.0)	4790 (0.2)
Italy	2482 (101.8)	14871 (686.6)	40199 (702.8)	7326 (3.7)	21472 (2.9)	90781 (4.5)
Jamaica	171 (7.0)	614 (28.3)	779 (13.6)	38 (0.0)	89 (0.0)	-45 (0.0)

contd...

...contd...

Countries	Inflow						Outflow					
	1991		2001		2007		1991		2001		2007	
Japan	1284	(52.6)	6241	(288.1)	22549	(394.2)	31638	(15.8)	38333	(5.1)	73549	(3.7)
Malaysia	4043	(165.8)	554	(25.6)	8403	(146.9)	175	(0.1)	267	(0.0)	10989	(0.6)
Mexico	4761	(195.2)	29483	(1361.2)	24686	(431.6)	177	(0.1)	4404	(0.6)	8256	(0.4)
New Zealand	1691	(69.3)	-110	-(5.1)	2768	(48.4)	1469	(0.7)	-1084	-(0.1)	2840	(0.1)
Pakistan	272	(11.2)	383	(17.7)	5333	(93.2)	-4	(0.0)	31	(0.0)	98	(0.0)
Philippines	556	(22.8)	195	(9.0)	2928	(51.2)	27	(0.0)	-140	(0.0)	3442	(0.2)
Russia		(0.0)	2748	(126.9)	52475	(917.4)		(0.0)	2533	(0.3)	45652	(2.3)
Saudi Arabia	165	(6.8)	504	(23.3)	24318	(425.1)	-128	-(0.1)	39	(0.0)	13139	(0.7)
South Africa	248	(10.2)	6789	(313.4)	5692	(99.5)	4	(0.0)	-3180	-(0.4)	3727	(0.2)
Spain	11624	(476.6)	28342	(1308.5)	53385	(933.3)	4133	(2.1)	33106	(4.4)	119605	(6.0)
Sri Lanka	67	(2.7)	172	(7.9)	529	(9.2)	5	(0.0)	0	(0.0)	95	(0.0)
Thailand	2049	(84.0)	5061	(233.7)	9575	(167.4)	183	(0.1)	430	(0.1)	1756	(0.1)
UK	14846	(608.7)	52623	(2429.5)	223966	(3915.5)	16409	(8.2)	58855	(7.8)	265791	(13.3)
USA	22799	(934.8)	159461	(7362.0)	232839	(4070.6)	32696	(16.3)	124873	(16.6)	313787	(15.7)

Note : Figures in brackets are percentages to total.
Source : *World Development Report* (2007 and 2003).

312 : External Sector Sustainability (Current Account Balance as Per cent to GDP)

Country	Decadal Average (%)			Annual (%)			
	1981-1990	1991-2000	2000-2008	2005	2006	2007	2008
Argentina	(1.6)	(3.2)	2.1	1.7	2.3	1.6	1.4
Australia	(4.7)	(4.1)	(5.9)	(5.8)	(5.3)	(6.3)	(4.6)
Bangladesh	(3.3)	(1.2)	0.1	0.0	1.2	1.1	1.9
Brazil	(2.1)	(2.0)	(1.0)	1.6	1.3	0.1	(1.8)
Canada	(2.3)	(1.3)	1.7	1.9	1.4	1.0	0.5
Chile	(6.4)	(2.7)	0.4	1.2	4.9	4.4	(2.0)
China	(0.0)	1.5	6.4	7.2	9.5	11.0	9.8
Egypt	(4.1)	1.2	1.8	3.2	1.6	1.9	0.5
France	(0.6)	1.4	0.4	(0.4)	(0.5)	(1.0)	(2.3)
Germany	2.4	(1.1)	3.9	5.1	6.1	7.5	6.4
India	(1.9)	(1.1)	(0.5)	(1.3)	(1.1)	(1.0)	(2.2)
Indonesia	(3.0)	(0.3)	2.8	0.1	3.0	2.4	0.1
Italy	(1.3)	0.7	(1.6)	(1.7)	(2.6)	(2.4)	(3.4)
Jamaica	(9.1)	(3.3)	(12.4)	(9.9)	(9.6)	(15.7)	(19.8)
Japan	2.3	2.5	4.1	3.6	3.9	4.8	3.2
Korea	0.7	0.7	1.7	1.8	0.6	0.6	(0.7)
Malaysia	(3.0)	(0.6)	14.1	15.0	16.0	15.4	17.9
Mexico	(0.8)	(3.5)	(2.0)	(0.5)	(0.5)	(0.8)	(1.4)
New Zealand	(5.2)	(4.7)	(7.7)	(8.5)	(8.7)	(8.2)	(8.9)
Pakistan	(2.5)	(3.1)	(1.4)	(1.4)	(3.9)	(4.8)	(8.3)
Philippines	(1.7)	(3.1)	0.9	2.0	4.5	4.9	2.5
Russia	0.0	4.3	11.6	11.0	9.5	6.0	6.1
Saudi Arabia	(6.1)	(5.9)	19.5	28.5	27.8	24.3	28.6
South Africa	0.6	(0.2)	(3.6)	(4.0)	(6.3)	(7.3)	(7.4)
Spain	(1.0)	(1.8)	(7.2)	(7.4)	(9.0)	(10.0)	(9.6)
Sri Lanka	(8.5)	(4.8)	(4.8)	(2.5)	(5.3)	(4.3)	(9.4)
Thailand	(4.1)	(1.1)	2.8	(4.3)	1.1	5.7	(0.1)
Turkey	(1.0)	(1.1)	(3.9)	(4.6)	(6.0)	(5.8)	(5.7)
UK	(1.3)	(1.4)	(2.7)	(2.6)	(3.3)	(2.7)	(1.7)
USA	(1.9)	(1.8)	(5.8)	(5.9)	(6.0)	(5.2)	(4.9)

Note : Current account balance is the balance on current transactions excluding exceptional financing. It includes all transactions other than those in capital and financial items. Major classifications are goods and services, income and current transfers.

Negative values in brackets

Source : International Monetary Fund.

313 : Reserves (excluding Gold) Import Ratio : Number of Weeks

	2001	2002	2003	2004	2005	2006	2007	2008
World	17.6	19.9	21.3	21.5	20.8	21.7	23.9	21.8
Argentina	37.2	60.7	53.2	43.8	49.3	47.0	52.0	40.6
Australia	14.6	14.8	18.8	17.0	17.4	20.0	7.8	8.0
Bangladesh	7.9	11.1	14.1	13.1	11.2	13.2	15.6	13.2
Brazil	31.7	39.2	49.9	41.1	35.7	46.2	73.7	55.0
Canada	7.8	8.5	7.7	6.4	5.2	5.1	5.5	5.5
Chile	42.9	46.7	42.6	33.5	26.9	26.3	18.6	19.4
China	46.0	51.3	51.4	56.9	64.7	70.2	83.2	na
Egypt	52.7	55.1	65.0	57.8	54.1	61.4	58.0	34.3
France	5.5	4.7	4.2	4.1	3.0	4.1	3.8	2.5
Germany	5.5	5.4	4.4	3.5	3.0	2.4	2.2	1.9
India	47.3	62.3	70.9	66.0	48.0	50.7	64.5	44.0
Indonesia	36.9	42.7	43.7	33.0	22.8	27.1	30.7	19.9
Italy	5.4	6.0	5.3	4.1	3.4	3.0	2.9	3.5
Jamaica	29.4	24.2	17.1	25.5	25.3	22.7	15.2	11.9
Japan	58.9	71.1	90.1	95.4	84.3	78.9	79.9	68.8
Korea, Rep. of	37.9	41.5	45.2	46.1	41.9	40.2	38.2	24.0
Malaysia	20.8	21.7	27.8	32.5	31.8	32.6	35.8	28.8
Mexico	13.2	14.9	17.2	16.1	16.6	14.8	15.3	15.2
New Zealand	13.9	17.2	17.1	15.6	17.6	27.7	29.0	16.9
Pakistan	18.6	37.4	43.6	28.4	20.6	20.1	22.4	8.8
Philippines	20.1	18.6	18.0	16.1	17.6	19.3	27.2	28.6
Russia	28.6	34.2	45.5	58.6	66.3	84.8	98.7	66.8
Saudi Arabia	29.3	33.2	31.9	31.7	23.2	20.5	19.5	13.7
South Africa	11.1	10.5	8.2	12.8	15.5	15.2	17.4	16.0
Spain	10.0	11.0	4.9	2.5	1.7	1.7	1.6	1.5
Sri Lanka	11.2	13.9	17.7	13.9	15.6	14.4	16.2	9.5
Thailand	27.2	30.6	28.2	26.8	22.3	26.4	31.5	31.6
Turkey	23.7	27.3	25.5	19.0	22.5	22.7	22.5	18.1
UK	5.5	5.8	4.8	4.6	4.1	3.9	4.1	3.6
USA	2.5	2.9	3.0	2.6	1.6	1.5	1.5	1.6

Note : na : not available.
Source : *International Financial Statistics Year Book* (2009), IMF.

314 : External Debt and Sustainability Indicator

	Stock of External Debt (US$ bn)			External Debt to National Income (%)		
	1990	2000	2007	1990	2000	2007
All Developing Countries	1283.1	2177.8	3466.0	na	na	na
Argentina	62.2	140.9	127.8	46.0	50.9	49.7
Brazil	119.7	241.6	237.5	26.6	38.5	18.7
China	55.3	145.7	373.6	15.4	12.3	11.6
Chile	19.2	37.3	58.6	64.5	51.6	40.3
Colombia	17.2	33.9	45.0	45.1	37.0	22.5
Croatia	na	12.4	48.6	na	69.3	97.7
India	83.8	101.3	223.3	26.7	22.0	18.9
Indonesia	69.9	144.3	140.8	64.0	93.6	33.9
Kazakhstan	na	12.4	96.1	na	72.5	103.7
Malaysia	15.3	41.9	53.7	36.4	48.6	29.4
Mexico	104.4	150.9	178.1	41.1	26.6	17.7
Poland	49.4	64.8	195.4	88.8	38.2	47.7
Philippines	30.6	58.3	65.8	69.4	72.3	41.9
Russia	na	160.0	370.2	na	63.2	29.4
Romania	1.1	11.2	85.4	3.0	30.4	51.5
South Africa	na	24.9	43.4	na	19.2	15.8
Thailand	28.1	79.7	63.1	33.3	66.0	26.5
Turkey	49.4	116.8	251.5	23.5	44.4	38.8
Ukraine	na	12.2	73.6	na	40.2	52.9
Venezuela	33.2	42.0	43.1	71.7	30.2	18.7

Note : na : not available. Data for India pertains to financial year and not calender year.

Source : *Global Development Finance*, World Bank.

315 : Solvency Indicators

	Debt Service Ratio			Interest Service Ratio		
	1990	2000	2007	1990	2000	2007
Argentina	37.0	69.3	13.0	16.3	28.8	6.1
Brazil	22.1	93.5	27.8	6.1	24.7	7.5
China	11.7	9.3	2.2	5.4	2.4	0.8
Chile	25.9	24.8	14.2	16.7	9.0	2.9
Colombia	40.9	27.7	22.0	17.9	12.0	7.6
Croatia	na	31.9	33.0	na	6.3	5.8
India	31.9	14.5	4.8	18.7	5.6	2.1
Indonesia	33.3	22.4	10.5	13.3	9.9	3.6
Kazakhstan	na	32.0	49.6	na	7.4	7.1
Malaysia	12.6	5.6	4.6	3.4	2.0	1.0
Mexico	20.7	30.4	12.5	13.4	7.3	3.7
Poland	4.9	20.4	25.6	1.7	5.0	3.5
Philippines	27.0	14.3	13.7	13.3	6.1	5.4
Russia	na	9.9	9.1	na	4.7	3.6
Romania	0.3	20.1	19.1	0.2	5.6	5.4
South Africa	na	9.8	5.9	na	3.2	2.0
Thailand	16.9	16.3	8.1	6.5	5.6	0.9
Turkey	29.4	35.9	32.1	13.5	11.9	7.9
Ukraine	na	18.6	16.9	na	3.6	4.3
Venezuela	23.3	16.7	7.4	15.1	7.7	3.7

Note : na : not available. Data for India pertains to financial year and not calender year.

Source : *Global Development Finance*, World Bank.

316 : Short-Term Debt Indicators

(%)

	Short-Term Debt to Total Debt (%)			Short-Term Debt to Reserves (%)			Short-term Debt to GNP (%)		
	1990	2000	2007	1990	2000	2007	1990	2000	2007
Argentina	10.8	20.1	29.8	168.3	112.6	82.5	7.7	10.2	14.8
Brazil	19.8	12.8	16.5	257.8	93.8	21.8	5.3	4.9	3.1
China	16.8	9.0	54.5	27.0	7.6	13.2	2.6	1.1	6.3
Chile	17.6	16.6	22.7	49.9	41.0	79.0	11.3	8.5	9.1
Colombia	8.4	8.5	11.9	29.5	31.9	25.5	3.8	3.1	2.7
Croatia	na	7.6	10.5	na	26.7	37.3	na	5.3	10.3
India	10.2	3.6	20.5	146.5	8.6	14.8	2.9	0.8	3.9
Indonesia	15.9	15.7	24.8	128.6	77.1	61.4	10.2	14.7	8.4
Kazakhstan	na	7.7	12.2	0.0	45.8	66.6	na	5.6	12.7
Malaysia	12.4	10.9	28.4	17.9	16.0	15.0	4.5	5.3	8.3
Mexico	15.4	12.5	5.1	157.4	53.2	10.3	6.3	3.3	0.9
Poland	14.5	9.4	10.8	217.4	36.5	21.0	10	6.8	4.5
Philippines	19.4	14.9	30.9	205.3	35.2	91.8	17.3	5.7	14.7
Russia	na	9.8	21.4	na	56.5	16.6	na	6.2	6.3
Romania	79.8	6.8	35.7	66.2	22.5	76.3	2.4	2.1	18.4
South Africa	na	38.4	38.2	na	124.0	50.3	na	7.4	6.0
Thailand	29.6	18.7	34.3	58.4	45.6	24.7	9.9	12.3	9.1
Turkey	19.2	24.8	16.6	124.6	123.0	54.6	4.5	11.0	6.4
Ukraine	na	3.7	31.1	na	30.3	70.5	na	1.5	16.5
Venezuela	6.0	19.5	27.1	15.7	51.5	34.7	4.3	7.1	5.1

Note: na : not available. GNP: gross national product.
Data for India pertains to financial year and not calander year.

Source: *Global Development Finance*, World Bank.

317 : Real Effective Exchange Rates (Base Year 2000 = 100)

	2001	2002	2003	2004	2005	2006	2007
Argentina	105.9	44.3	49.2	47.0	47.0	46.0	45.1
Australia	97.8	103.8	116.7	126.8	130.7	129.9	138.9
Bangladesh	95.6	91.4	85.7	83.0	80.2	77.1	74.5
Brazil	83.0	74.0	76.0	80.8	99.3	110.9	118.9
Canada	96.3	95.7	106.7	113.1	119.8	125.9	131.2
Chile	89.8	84.4	80.2	85.6	91.8	95.4	93.5
China	103.9	101.7	96.3	94.2	92.7	92.8	96.1
Egypt	90.4	78.6	56.5	55.0	59.9	61.4	61.4
France	99.9	101.9	107.8	108.6	107.5	105.5	107.3
Germany	98.7	100.2	105.3	106.4	104.1	102.5	103.8
India	100.2	98.8	99.6	100.1	102.6	100.6	109.7
Indonesia	95.7	116.4	125.8	120.8	118.5	137.3	137.6
Italy	100.4	103.6	110.9	112.2	109.7	108.3	109.6
Jamaica	99.5	97.4	83.1	82.8	88.0	89.8	85.1
Japan	89.2	83.9	85.7	87.0	81.3	73.7	68.3
Korea, Rep. of	93.1	97.2	99.9	101.5	111.8	118.0	116.1
Malaysia	104.9	104.9	99.9	95.3	95.0	97.0	99.2
Mexico	105.2	105.4	95.6	92.9	96.1	96.2	96.2
New Zealand	98.9	108.4	125.3	134.7	140.8	129.9	140.2
Pakistan	90.2	92.5	90.7	89.2	90.2	91.7	89.9
Philippines	95.2	95.8	89.6	87.1	92.7	102.9	111.8
Russia	117.2	121.0	123.3	130.4	139.4	151.7	156.3
Saudi Arabia	103.4	101.3	94.6	89.2	86.6	86.3	84.2
South Africa	87.7	75.8	100.2	109.8	110.9	105.0	114.7
Spain	100.9	104.3	109.9	111.8	112.1	113.0	114.6
Sri Lanka	98.6	98.1	96.8	90.8	98.5	104.0	97.1
Thailand	94.5	96.9	96.0	96.0	97.5	104.3	110.0
Turkey	78.9	89.2	98.5	102.9	115.1	113.4	116.4
UK	96.9	97.3	93.6	101.5	100.0	99.8	96.0
USA	104.9	104.9	98.9	94.5	91.7	90.2	86.2

Note : Real effective exchange rate is the index of the trade weighted average nominal exchange rate, adjusted for changes in the consumer price index. A rise in the index indicates a loss of competitiveness.

Source : UNCTAD based on IMF direction of trade and IFS database.